INTRAMURAL SPORTS

PAT MUELLER
DIRECTOR OF INTRAMURAL SPORTS
UNIVERSITY OF MINNESOTA

and

ELMER D. MITCHELL
PROFESSOR EMERITUS OF PHYSICAL EDUCATION
UNIVERSITY OF MICHIGAN

THIRD EDITION

THE RONALD PRESS COMPANY · NEW YORK

Library of Congress Catalog Card Number: 60-7765

PRINTED IN THE UNITED STATES OF AMERICA

Preface

A well-balanced intramural sports program includes team games, individual and dual sports, and corecreational activities conducted both formally and informally for all students and faculty, in high school or college. In most schools the intramural department is a segment of the department of physical education or athletics. The number of activities and special events the intramural department sponsors depends, to a great extent, upon local facilities and equipment, financial appropriations, and personnel. And the success of the program rests upon the interest of the personnel and participants.

This book endeavors to face squarely the problems involved in setting up an efficient intramural department and to provide practical information and workable ideas to carry out an attractive program of activities. It can be used in professional courses in physical education, as a guide for school and college supervisors, and for community recreation and playground leaders.

The book first discusses the organization and administration of an intramural department. It presents various departmental organizational plans, and it comments upon the staff and student personnel essential to administering the plans. It then covers the entire scope of administrative duties: finances, facilities and equipment, units of competition, kinds of activities, eligibility rules and other regulations, evaluation and adaptation of the program, and publicity and awards.

Next, the book treats methods of running competitions. It explains how to direct various kinds of meets, how to adapt tournaments to the sport and entrants involved, how to organize leagues, and how to work out an appropriate system of awards for groups or individuals. To expedite the director's or program leader's work in planning the sports competitions, innumerable tournament forms and tables worked out by the authors and the tests and scoring tables compiled by Sigma Delta Psi, national honorary athletic fraternity, are included. These ready references can be used for figuring numbers of rounds, byes, and games for single and double elimination and round robin tournaments; placing byes or seeded players on tournament draw sheets; constructing draw sheets for different numbers of entrants; working out handicaps and percentages; and determining points for group and individual winners.

One chapter describes how to make such devices as flash cards, assignment and reservation boards, rules containers, officials' platforms, and shot and discus markers to facilitate scoring and supervision. These aids, which add to the success of the intramural activity, can be made quickly and inexpensively.

Since those in charge of intramural sports programs may also conduct extramural activities, corecreation programs, and special events such as clinics, festivals, and carnivals, the book covers these areas and their relationship to the over-all intramural program. And, although the majority of the principles, procedures, and problems described in this book apply alike to programs administered for men or for women, certain aspects and practices specific to the women's sports and recreation program are presented.

This book, the first published work in this area, originally appeared in 1924 under the title *Intramural Athletics.* Because of increasing interest in intramural sports, especially on the college level, and the resulting variety in the programs, the book was brought up to date in 1939 and the title was changed to *Intramural Sports.* Since then the intramural sports program on both the high-school and college levels has grown and developed by leaps and bounds. At present no physical education department is considered adequate unless it includes intramural activities. To keep abreast of the changing times in the intramural field, it was imperative to publish a third edition of this pioneer work. This book now includes the intramural sports program on the university, college, high-school, and elementary-school levels.

The authors wish to express their appreciation to the following groups for their permission to use materials from their publications: American Bowling Congress; American Association for Health, Physical Education, and Recreation; Athletic and Recreation Federation of College Women; The Athletic Institute; Division for Girls and Women's Sports of the American Association for Health, Physical Education, and Recreation; National Association of Secondary School Principals of the National Education Association; and Sigma Delta Psi. They are deeply indebted to Robert Upton (Bob) Reid of Minneapolis for his untiring assistance in preparing and editing the material for this edition; to Earl N. Riskey of the University of Michigan for his help with the materials on mechanical aids in Chapter 15; to Beverly Bye, Kathy Warrington, and Marjorie J. Wilson for typing the manuscript; and to many others, particularly friends and families, for their patience and understanding during the preparation of the book.

PAT MUELLER
ELMER D. MITCHELL

February, 1960

Contents

INTRAMURAL SPORTS

1

Nature and Objectives of Intramural Sports

Intramural sports are a phase of the larger recreation movement that has a prominent place in American culture. This movement includes all forms of active play and sports, as well as social recreation, art, music, dramatics, dance, nature lore, hobbies, camping, social service activities, and the quieter forms of recreation such as reading, listening to the radio, and watching television. This larger recreation movement has grown in the present century to the extent that it is an accepted institution of our American way of life, and it promises to grow even more with increasing automation and the accompanying increasing leisure time. The intramural sports movement, however, is primarily concerned with active recreation, embodying team play and individual competition.

NATURE OF INTRAMURAL SPORTS

The word "intramural" is derived from the Latin words *intra,* meaning within, and *muralis,* meaning wall. It has been paired off with other words such as sports, athletics, and activities, and when so combined, implies a program of sports and other activities conducted within the walls or imaginary boundaries of a school or other institution. The term *intramural sports* is generally accepted as the best title for recreational sports and activities promoted within the confines of an educational institution and under its jurisdiction. This term is also commonly used to designate similar programs in military and industrial organizations.

In the past, when the intramural program was composed mostly of those sports which were also played on a varsity athletic level, the term *intramural athletics* was used to title the program. However, "sports" has a more inclusive connotation than "athletics," and intramural directors and supervisors favor the title intramural sports for the present-day program. It conveys the idea of more informal student participation in various kinds of physical recreation and nonstrenuous activities involving special interests and skills. Some directors of intramural programs use the expression *intramural activities,* especially if the program encompasses not only sports but also card games, music, dramatics, crafts, and other activities of a nonphysical nature. In some schools, the Student Union sponsors the latter or social-type recreation activities, and the intramural department conducts physical recreation activities.

The word "intramurals" is an abbreviation for programs offered by the various intramural sports, athletic, and activities departments. This shortened title appeals to participants because it is concise and all-inclusive. The symbol I-M is often used to signify the intramural sports department or program.

The term *extramural (intermural) activities* is generally used when reference is made to programs or sports in which teams represent two or more schools or organizations. As opposed to intramurals, extramurals theoretically consist of activities which take place outside the confines of a school. Broadly defined, extramural activities include interscholastic and intercollegiate athletics. However, not all extramurals can be classified as interschool or intercollege; a team representing a school or institution might play against a local industrial or other amateur team, which does not represent an educational institution. Extramural contests also can be arranged between intramural champions, all star teams, fraternity chapters, or other organized student groups of two or more schools. In contrast to the varsity athletic program, extramural activities usually include all students regardless of ability or skill and require fewer practice sessions to prepare for competition.

Scope of the Intramural Program

Small and large schools and colleges alike should sponsor an intramural program open to both student and faculty participation. The program should be free to all and participation elective or voluntary. A well-organized and administered program provides opportunities for students and staff members, including their families, to enjoy scheduled competitive and informal "free play" sports activities. In many places, members of the faculty are not included in programs sponsored by intramural departments because facilities are inadequate to handle both students and staff. However, if at all possible, intramural departments should make provision for recreation for all. The more progressive departments offer recreational activities for staff members and thus gain additional support for their over-all intramural program. Some schools provide special locker facilities for staff members and schedule faculty-student competition and faculty-family recreation sessions.

Although the intramural program is basically designed for the student of moderate ability, activities of all kinds should be offered so that every student, regardless of ability, can participate in some phase of the program. "Every" student means both boys and girls, and also means the strong and weak, the tall and short, the physically handicapped and those with below average, average, and above average ability. For the intramural program, all the student needs is the desire to participate—the degree of skill is the least important prerequisite.

A well-balanced intramural program sponsors team games, individual and dual sports, corecreational activities, co-operative clubs and informal groups. The impromptu free-play aspect of the program is as important as scheduled competitive games and contests; thus, facilities and equipment should be available for informal play. Class schedules and work might prevent a student from participating in scheduled activities, but facilities should be available when he has time to go to the gymnasium to shoot baskets, play handball, or go to the pool for a swim.

In addition to actually playing in the intramural program, students can share in the planning and supervision of the program. Athletic councils composed of faculty members and students offer many helpful suggestions to the intramural director. Some programs under faculty supervision are almost completely conducted by students through well-organized managerial systems. Athletic contests are usually officiated by students. Through I-M special interest clubs, students share their experiences and techniques in activities such as judo, fencing, and soccer with other members. Some even serve as club instructors for the novice or beginner.

Place in the Total Program

Modern education is concerned with the total growth and development of each child. Every phase of the school program affects this development to varying degrees. Physical education—education through physical activities—is an integral part of education and has aims and objectives similar to those of education. The intramural program, as a part of physical education and education in general, is curricular rather than extracurricular and has aims and objectives similar to those of physical education.

The broad physical education program consists of three phases: the instructional program (class activities), the varsity program, and the intramural program. All three educate the individual through physical activities. If one of the three is missing, physical education is operating at a 33⅓ per cent deficit. It is also possible to have all three programs and still have mediocre education, depending on the quality of leadership and administration.

There is room for all three programs in any department of

physical education; in actuality, they complement each other. A wide variety of sports skills are learned in the physical education classes. Intramural directors are well aware of the importance of instruction to participants. They realize that students might not enter the I-M program unless they perform the activity reasonably well. A good example on the college level is squash, a sport which requires considerable skill and practice. If instruction is not provided through the required physical education program or through clinics and clubs, the intramural squash tournament may fail to draw many entrants. The only entrants may be those who learned the sport at other schools or from friends. Team sports such as touch football, basketball, softball, and baseball usually do not present as much of a problem. Students have more opportunities to learn the skills of these popular sports—on the sandlot, in the municipal recreation program, or in physical education classes. Yet there are many students who do not enter these sports because they believe they lack the skills to perform with satisfactory success. No one likes to fail, and intramural participants are no exception. The intramural program is easier to promote if the school has required physical education or a well-organized and developed elective physical education program. If adequate instruction is not available to the student through physical education activity classes, it might be necessary for the intramural department to organize clubs or clinics in order to provide instruction.

The intramural program serves as a "laboratory" offering students the opportunity to develop further and enjoy the skills they previously learned in physical education activity classes. Most of these activities have "carry-over" value, which means the student continues to utilize his skills in after-school life. The physical education class instruction and intramural laboratory program provide pleasant experiences which help shape the individual's recreational attitudes. These attitudes and habits benefit the student during and after his school career.

The intercollegiate and interscholastic varsity programs

are organized for highly skilled specialists. Thus, only a few reap the benefits of this phase of the physical education program. The majority of students need other athletic outlets. A broad and properly administered I-M program fills this need. Some students who participate in intramural activities develop sufficient skills to permit their joining a varsity squad. However, the intramural program should not be considered or organized as a training center for the varsity program. Development of varsity material is incidental, yet some of the larger schools have numerous intramural participants with the ability to make varsity teams. These athletes often fail to participate on the varsity squads because of lack of confidence in themselves, lack of desire to pay the price in practice and conditioning, a heavy class schedule, or the need to work. In intramurals, this individual plays but one or twice a week and is able to maintain his athletic interest.

The I-M program also serves athletes who quit or are dropped from the varsity. When squads are cut, intramural directors should work closely with varsity coaches to assist athletes in making the transition to some I-M activity. Often, athletes have an opportunity to return to the varsity team after participating on intramural teams. Because some individuals develop late and all develop at different rates, coaches should encourage broad programs of intramurals and physical education, particularly at the elementary, junior, and senior high-school levels.

An ideal over-all physical education system for all levels is the answer to improving student participation in sports programs, especially in intramurals. The "ideal" means well-organized and administered physical education programs in the elementary schools, high schools, and colleges. At the elementary level, pupils should learn in their required classes physical skills such as running, throwing, climbing, and rhythms. Through elementary and junior high-school grades, there should be definite progression through games, contests, relays, and rhythms in order to develop beginning, intermediate, and advanced skills. This sequential progression should also include competition in team sports with the emphasis on participation rather than winning. The desire to win takes care of itself. The elementary and junior high-school period is the most opportune time to develop not only activity skills but also desirable attitudes of the need for participation in recreational activities.

In an ideal physical education system, it is at the senior high-school level where students should be permitted to elect their physical education class activities and take part in voluntary intramural and varsity athletic programs. At this stage, they should be shown the values and contributions of physical education and spend class time learning new skills and perfecting previously learned skills. At the college level, there should be a wider range of activities offered in the physical education activity classes, the intramural program, and the intercollegiate program, and students should be permitted to elect from these. With this type of ideal physical education system prevailing throughout all school levels, the goal of "sports for all" could be realized.

Intramural handbooks and other I-M written material proclaim the "sports for all" or "a sport for everyone and everyone in a sport" theory. These slogans should be the goal of every intramural department, but it is doubtful if many programs achieve or even approach this ultimate result. Certainly, every I-M program should have a wide variety of activities to offer the opportunity of a sport for everyone or all who are interested; however, the idea that everyone will participate in sports is unrealistic. People working in intramurals often mistakenly assume that everyone is interested in sports. Even if interest in sports is inherent, the competition of interest in other school activities reduces sports participation. Some students prefer to participate in dramatics, music, student government, or some other campus activity. They may not have the time to take part in the I-M program, too. In some schools and colleges where the majority of the students commute, there is a low percentage of participation because the students will not remain after classes until late afternoon or early evening to play on a team or participate in an activity. These students get their "intramural recreation" from the local YMCA, settlement house, church league, or municipal recreation program. From a school loyalty standpoint, it would be better if commuter students could take part in their own school intramural program.

Perhaps the only schools to attain the goal of "sports for all" are the smaller ones which have well-balanced programs and required physical education classes. Every student is then exposed to sports through class instruction and is encouraged to participate either in the intramural program or varsity program, or both. Thus, under this system everyone participates in a sport. It is unlikely that every student would take part in a sport through the intramural program alone. But a few schools with a balanced program—required physical education classes, varsity sports, and intramural activities—could claim to have everyone in a sport.

There is considerable difference of opinion among the "play for all" advocates and the "make the best better" adherents. Some I-M directors—the play-for-all sponsors—believe it better to provide for a large number of students regardless of what is provided or how it is provided. Others—the make-the-best-better directors—advocate fewer and better activities. In attempting to reach the goal of "sports for all," consideration must be accorded to program quality as well as quantity. A large measure of the "unlimited potential" for an intramural sports program can be reached if there is co-operation among everyone concerned in the varsity, the physical education instructional, and the intramural programs.

OBJECTIVES OF INTRAMURAL SPORTS

Intramural objectives should point toward the development of the total individual—physically, socially, emotionally, spiritually, and intellectually. As general education strives to develop the total individual, so, then, do physical education and intramural sports. There are two types of objectives—immediate and remote. The immediate objectives deal with the habits, knowledges, and attitudes from the participant's point of view. The remote objectives deal with the ideals toward which intramural personnel are striving, and in so doing, place the emphasis on educational values.

Recreation

Through intramural sports, a student's leisure time is employed in a wholesome way. Relaxation through physical recreation activities is just as important during school life as after-school life.

The recreative concept of intramural sports should always be kept in mind. While certain rugged sports that require tedious training are beneficial to the program, there should be greater emphasis on sports that are enjoyed spontaneously without a great amount of preparation. Sports should never be organized to the point where the fun is organized out of them. Participation should be an enjoyable experience apart from the success in earning intramural recognition.

The student learns to make wise use of his leisure time. A variety of activities is offered which enables the student to develop a repertoire of leisure-time pursuits which not only enrich his present life, but add to the wholesome enjoyment of his later life. Intramural activities are truly one of the concrete ways by which students prepare for wise and joyful use of leisure time; and this is an important contribution in a day when all eyes are on educational institutions to see that they provide for leisure education in a world where there is enforced leisure because of the decreasing number of working hours each day and week.

Physical Fitness

Participation in intramural sports develops strength and endurance, also the neuromuscular co-ordination that makes for agility and confident control of one's movements. Participation develops the ability to handle the body gracefully and efficiently. The qualities of strength, endurance, and agility are useful in a direct way in meeting the emergencies of life; and, indirectly, they comprise a great asset to any individual through the inner confidence and self-assurance they bring and through the outward addition they give to his carriage and presence. The importance of bodily co-ordination and training in motor skills is therefore stressed in the physical education programs of our schools and the national physical fitness program of our country.

Constitutional soundness is an important feature for success in life. Yet physical exercise, which is so important in securing this soundness, is seldom practiced under present living conditions. Many of the student's occupations of today, both in connection with his studies and his leisure time, are of the passive type. This is unfortunate, for moderate exercise, in which the large fundamental muscles of the body are employed, makes an important contribution to physical fitness. Exercise develops the muscles of the body and aids in healthful posture. The increased activity of the heart and lungs serves to eliminate waste products of the body and to hasten the bringing of food to the tissues.

Intramural departments requiring yearly health examinations are contributing to the development of an attitude toward having periodic health examinations throughout life —an important objective of preventive medicine.

Mental and Emotional Health

The mental hygiene aspects of intramural sports programs have received a great deal of consideration during the past few years. The development of an alert mind is essential. Properly conducted intramural activities develop wholesome mental attitudes. Mental hygienists everywhere are advocating the need for enjoyable, recreative activities. Participation in such activities gives objective interests and outlooks—it takes the individual's mind off himself and focuses it on outside, interesting objects, and thereby combats tendencies to become moody, too introspective, and too introverted. The individual also learns to adapt himself to group standards. From the standpoint of mental hygiene, intramural activities prove valuable in providing relaxation from work and study. Change of activity is important in relaxation, as is congenial companionship.

Emotionally, an individual participating in intramurals can attain personal satisfactions and meet personal needs. These needs include the need for accomplishment, need for self-expression and creativity, need for recognition, need for new experiences, and need for belonging. A further emotional objective is development of self-reliance and self-esteem. Students have an ideal opportunity to develop their individuality and emotional maturity through intramural sports.

Social Contacts

The chance to meet other individuals of one's own age is one of the most valuable experiences that a person gains in his school life. On the athletic field, these associations are carried on under conditions that simulate adult social and competitive life in many respects. Such an experience in group relations gives a person a broad viewpoint; makes him a better judge of the character of his associates; gives him more self-assurance when in the company of other individuals; teaches him the meaning of loyalty and co-operation; and teaches him lessons in sportsmanlike conduct. It gives the student actual experience in group living which is of inestimable value in "getting along" in the numerous social groups in which he finds himself. Friendships established in the classroom are often increased on the playing field.

Group Loyalty

The feeling of unity that a school team develops among all the individuals belonging to the school is always considered as a praiseworthy feature of varsity competition. This same loyalty is exemplified in miniature by the various class, homeroom, fraternity, and other intramural teams.

The feeling engendered is that of belonging to a cause that is larger than one's individual self and of willingness, if necessary, to sacrifice one's own interest for the welfare of the group. This devotion is symbolic of the patriotism of a citizen to the state and nation and therefore is a worthwhile attitude to cultivate in youth.

This group loyalty should not develop into a narrow partisanship which expresses an attitude of hostility or discourtesy toward opponents. Fortunately, such occasions are rare in intramural competition; in fact, two organizations frequently gain mutual respect and good will as an outcome of their meeting together in friendly rivalry. The rivalry one sees in intramural competition is natural and wholesome. There is no need for an artificial "build-up" once the program is under way; rivalry and desire for competition develop by themselves—in fact, they are often spontaneous.

Permanent Interest in Sports

One of the main criticisms against present varsity athletic systems is that they do not create a lasting interest in participation—that the athlete drops his interest in exercise and play immediately after graduation. He was trained in competitive sports which require a number of players and adequate facilities and equipment. These are factors which often preclude the possibility of engaging in team sports after he graduates. The intramural type of game does not promote a high type of specialization. The intramural athlete is apt to engage in a number of activities, with the result that he gains a knowledge of many varieties of exercise and an average ability in all of them. While high-school intramural activities are usually limited to five or six sports of a seasonal nature, a concurrent offering throughout the year of individualistic activities is also encouraged.

The intramural program has greater carry-over value for those students who are either unable to participate in the "standard" sports for physical reasons or are just not interested in them. Rarely does an adult become interested in any form of sport unless he learned the rudiments of it in his childhood and youth. Therein lies the importance of school promotion of a wide variety of athletic activities that can be continued after one's school days are over. The spirit of play once acquired continues to demand expression.

SUMMARY

1. Intramural sports are a phase of the larger recreation movement that embodies all forms of active play and sport, as well as social recreation, art, music, dramatics, dance, nature lore, hobbies, camping, social service activities, and quieter forms of recreation such as reading, listening to the radio, and watching television.
2. *Intramural sports* is generally accepted as the proper designation for recreational sports and activities promoted within the confines of an educational institution and under its jurisdiction.
3. *Extramurals* (intermurals) refers to competitive sports which take place outside the walls or boundaries of a school, organization, or institution between or among teams representing two or more schools, organizations, or institutions.
4. The well-organized and administered intramural program provides opportunities for every student and staff member to participate in scheduled competitive and informal, "free play" sports activities.
5. Intramurals must be on an elective or voluntary basis and are for both boys and girls.
6. The impromptu "free play" aspect of intramurals is just as important as the scheduled competitive games and contests phase.
7. The intramural program is an integral part of physical education and both have aims and objectives similar to those of general education.
8. The intramural program serves as a "laboratory" providing students with the opportunity to develop further and enjoy the skills learned in physical education activity classes.
9. Intramural experiences help shape the individual's recreational attitudes, many of which should benefit the student during his after-school life.

10. The "ideal over-all physical education system" is the answer to improving student participation in athletic programs and consists of well-organized and -administered physical education programs in the elementary schools, high schools, and colleges.
11. Although "sports for all" is desirable, realistically, it is an almost impossible attainment on a voluntary basis.
12. Much of the "unlimited potential" for an intramural sports program can be reached if there is co-operation among everyone concerned in the varsity, the physical education, and the intramural programs.
13. All objectives of intramural sports must point toward the development of the total individual—physically, socially, emotionally, spiritually, and intellectually.
14. Relaxation through physical recreation activities is just as important in school life as after-school life.
15. Participation in intramural sports develops strength and endurance, also the neuromuscular co-ordination that helps agility and confident control of one's movements.
16. Students have an ideal opportunity to develop their individuality and emotional maturity through intramural sports.
17. Intramural sports give the student actual experience in group living which is of inestimable value to him in "getting along" in the numerous social groups in which he finds himself.
18. The feeling engendered in intramural sports is that of belonging to a cause that is larger than one's individual self and of willingness, if necessary, to sacrifice one's own interest for the welfare of the group.
19. Intramurals develop a permanent interest in sports which make students better spectators and participants after graduation.

2

Growth of the Intramural Program

The growth of intramural sports has been haphazard. Until the 1920's, the programs were of a hit-or-miss nature, owing in general to the fact that the two more prominent departments of physical exercise—physical education and varsity athletics—were so involved with their own programs that the *athletic* needs of the great mass of students were almost entirely neglected.

Early physical education departments fostered strictly formal gymnastic programs. As a result, the early athletic programs developed independently under student and alumni control. Later, these programs narrowed considerably, until they resulted in varsity training for the few, where winning was paramount, and all available revenues, facilities, and leadership were centered on the specialized teams. Intramural sports grew up, consequently, as a neglected orphan, uncared for by either the physical education or varsity athletic departments, and with little system or plan. Certain definite stages or trends stand out, however, which provide the background for the present-day movement.

BEGINNINGS OF THE PROGRAM

The beginnings of athletics in colleges were intramural in nature. Students interested in a particular sport or activity banned together in activity clubs, somewhat in the manner of the sport clubs in English universities. (Indeed, the English influence upon American sports in the early 1860's was so strong that almost all the sports participated in were of English origin. Only gradually were rules of some of the games or sports adapted or changed, or new sports invented such that they took on peculiarly American characteristics.) Later on these student groups began to expend time and energy in developing specialized teams to represent their college in outside competition with other athletic groups, in colleges, schools, or municipalities, as the case happened to be. This, then, was the beginning of a varsity-like program.

Gradually, in a somewhat similar manner the natural desire for sports and competition, which is strong in the normal youth, sought expression in impromptu challenge games on the part of students who were not skilled enough to make the varsity teams. Students, of their own accord, began to rally around a unit. This unit at first was loosely organized, generally involving intramural competition between freshman and sophomore classes. An example of such "organization" is cited below:

> In the fall of 1857 at Princeton University, a few members of the freshman class met and organized, "The Nassau Baseball Club," to play baseball, although few members had seen the game and fewer had played it. But it became popular among members of the class, and a diamond was laid out in the "pasture" lot by the present casino . . . The object of the standing committee was to remove all bricks, stones and other obstructions on the ground which were liable to impede the operations of the energetic club.
>
> After a few weeks' practicing, with an audacity unusual for freshmen, they challenged the sophomore class to a match game. The "Sophs" were as innocent of all knowledge regarding the game as new born babes but they were not to be downed by a lot of freshmen. One faction favored the contest, but another fearing it would go hard with them, declared it was beyond the dignity of their class to submit to such impertinence. However, after much consideration, the challenge was accepted, and the presidents of the classes were chosen as umpires. A referee was elected whose duty it was to decide between the umpires whenever they should disagree. Each side consisted of fifteen players, and the whole game was conducted with laudable and good feeling. After each side had played five innings the "Sophs" had beaten their antagonists by twenty-one rounds and were declared victorious. The announcement was received with deafening hurrahs.

The freshmen throwing their caps into the air and showing other indications of a spirit unbroken by defeat replied by giving them three lusty cheers for their immortal class." [1]

In the process of time, students organized class committees to plan for competitions among all four classes. This more premeditated procedure led to league championships, an advance over the earlier custom wherein the challenge between two teams was the limit of competition. Classes elected managers to take care of the details of organizing teams for class leagues. In some colleges, fraternity associations formed committees to conduct interfraternity athletics. Later, these fraternity associations were not too friendly to the idea of relinquishing their own authority to faculty supervision and to newly organized intramural departments, but gradually they realized the value of merging their interests with the larger program. During the student-organization stage the beginning of a movement for centralization began to appear but did not progress beyond the point of centralization for one unit taken by itself.

DEVELOPMENT OF CENTRAL CONTROL

Between the years of 1905 and 1912, the number of student-controlled activities increased to the point that authorities recognized the necessity for some stronger and more permanent centralized authority. The various athletic associations, forerunners of present-day athletic departments, which permitted use of their fields and facilities for intramural activities, began to step in and exert a form of control. In 1913, Michigan and Ohio State Universities each inaugurated a Department of Intramural Athletics headed by one man who was expected to handle the demands for intramural competition in the various leading sports. In 1917, the Committee on Intramural Sports of the Athletic Research Society, an early group of scientific-minded physical educators,

[1] Frank Presbrey, *Athletics at Princeton* (New York: Frank Presbrey Co., 1901), p. 69.

recommended a comprehensive classification of playing-units in its annual report.

This move toward a unified system in place of permitting the students to conduct leagues which had no relation to one another was important to the athletic associations. It permitted the associations to exercise direct control over their own fields, equipment, and showers, which, under the student-control system, were loaned temporarily to the various organizations wishing to use them. This control meant that fields and courts were assigned impartially and without confusion; that games were better supervised; and, furthermore, that responsibility for loss of, or damage to, equipment could be easily traced. The athletic associations also found that the promotion of intramural activities—the "athletics for all" concept—stifled much criticism on the part of people who opposed varsity athletics on the ground it favored only a few skilled performers.

In these early phases of intramural growth, the athletic associations had the rather natural idea that the intramural athletic program would furnish a recruiting ground for future varsity material. This idea is still prevalent among some institutions, but longer experience established the more comprehensive ideal of athletic fun and benefit for all.

The success of playground leaders in handling teams on a large scale; the increased interest of the public in all forms of athletic sports; the importance ascribed to athletics in the training camps during the First World War and the correspondingly great strides that were made in developing mass athletic programs—all contributed to the great boom in college intramural sports which began in 1918. Not until about 1925, however, were intramural activities appearing in high schools, and not until 1930, was the high-school program well under way. Prior to 1930, the development of standards in interscholastic athletics engaged the major attention of physical education teachers and coaches in high schools; but, following the establishment of standards, schoolmen turned their attention to the recreational needs of the student body. The intramural directors of Western Conference Colleges (now numbering ten) gave special attention to high-school intramural problems at their annual meeting in 1930.

Women were quick to realize the values of an intramural program. Interscholastic and intercollegiate athletic competition for girls and women had been on the wane for some time, as a result of opposition from women leaders in athletics. The informal characteristics of intramural sports appealed to women physical education directors. The very nature of the intramural program readily adapted itself as an augmenting factor to the more informal physical education program for girls.

The Women's Division of the National Amateur Athletic Federation, organized in 1923, at once became influential in women's physical education circles in attempts to avoid the intensified specialization and pressures to win of men's interschool athletics. In 1932, the National Section on Women's Athletics (now the Division for Girls and Women's Sports) in The American Physical Education Association (now the American Association for Health, Physical Education, and Recreation) also focused attention on proper promotion of women's programs. The Division of Girls and Women's Sports is today a potent factor in developing standards for sports and athletics and in advocating a wide range of intramural activities.

EMPHASIS UPON PARTICIPANT WELFARE

Leaders of intramural programs at first judged the success of programs by the numbers that participated in intramural competition. This emphasis upon quantity gradually became secondary to a new emphasis upon the quality of the participation and the benefits obtained by each individual. Some intramural departments will not permit students to participate in certain types of activities without a proper physical examination and some training. Even though they recognize that certain sports, boxing and wrestling, for example, have a strong popular appeal, the intramural departments carry the responsibility for denying these forms of exercise whenever they believe participation might be harmful to the average student. Therefore, many intramural departments do not include the more vigorous sports in the program; those that do place them under rigid supervision. In the latter case, an excellent policy is to require a student to present a health card indicating he has recently been examined by a physician, before he can participate in the vigorous sports.

Many intramural departments have attempted to provide instruction in sports techniques for all intramural candidates even though handicapped by limited staffs and facilities. In 1933, under the Federal Emergency Relief Administration and later under the National Youth Administration programs which afforded financial aid to youth, many college students secured part-time assignments in the intramural departments, services paid for by the federal government. Those departments which benefited from such student assistance were able to expand their types of programs. Federal aid in the construction of facilities was also a boon to intramural directors. Newly acquired buildings, athletic fields, tennis courts, golf courses, and swimming pools extended the scope of the intramural programs everywhere.

More recently, college intramural departments have utilized the services of graduate students in physical education departments, augmenting both the caliber of the program and the number of intramural teachers. The contributions these graduate students make to the program are not necessarily limited to sports supervision; they can introduce new techniques and perhaps new sports. Their previous experience in teaching and coaching makes them especially valuable as intramural instructors. Through such part-time graduate assistants, departments secure expert talent in some sports in which the full-time physical education staff members may not have experience.

FORMATION OF AN INTRAMURAL ASSOCIATION

As the intramural movement grows, there is increasing effort to set standards for its improvement through an over-all intramural organization. The individual directors realize they have many peculiar problems of their own to solve and consequently appreciate the advantages of meeting as a group to pool their experiences and exchange successful ideas.

The intramural directors of colleges in the Western Conference have held annual meetings to exchange ideas since 1920. In 1933, the College Physical Education Association provided a section for the discussion of intramural sports at its annual meeting. In 1938, under the Division of Men's Athletics, the American Association for Health, Physical Education, and Recreation also established a section for Intramural Athletics, although reports on intramural programs were given in the Division of Men's Athletics prior to that time.

Further progress was achieved in 1950, when the National Intramural Association was formed. This was the first national group devoted strictly to intramurals. In 1955, the College Physical Education Association, the American Association for Health, Physical Education, and Recreation, and the National Association for Physical Education of College Women jointly sponsored an intramural conference in Washington, D.C., at which 100 delegates from 79 institutions in the United States and Canada were in attendance. Discussions centered about the role of intramurals in the education of college students, organization and administration of intramurals, facilities, and types of programs.

BROADENING OF THE SCOPE OF THE PROGRAM

Whereas the traditional intramural program fostered the organized competitive type of sport solely, the present trend is toward expansion of the program to include sports with carry-over value and to provide for impromptu play. Sports such as golf, badminton, archery, bowling, tennis, swimming, handball, squash, skating, skiing, and horseshoes are prominent in many intramural departments. Some schools have widened the scope of their services to include outing activities such as camping, hiking, sailing, picnicking, and nature trips. This broadening of the intramural concept accounts for the shift in department titles, from the old Intramural Athletics to the newer Intramural Sports or Intramural Activities.

Sports that are unorganized and merely enjoyed for themselves (impromptu play activities) and individual sports that are organized into competitive leagues or tournaments are the ones that have the best carry-over possibilities. The older practice stressed group and team activities at the sacrifice of individual and dual games and sports. The criticism of this practice is that the members of the groups are helpless when the team disbands, for their own specialty is largely dependent upon the team as a whole. Therefore, it is necessary to include in a program both types of activity in proper proportion, for while team games carry certain educational values, still it is the individual game that stands the participant in good stead when his school days are over. As an adult, the group spirit he acquired with the team is continued in his relations with his business or professional associates; and the joy of activity for itself that he gains from his individual play seeks expression in active recreations apart from his occupation.

During and after the Second World War, as was also the case after the First World War, there was added incentive for the development of intramural sports programs. Returning veterans who swelled student enrollments were interested in continuing the sports competition they enjoyed while in military service. The GI's participated in sports through the mass athletic and physical training programs of the military services.

Currently, intramural directors are doing all in their power to encourage students to participate in some form of organized or informal sports competition. There is more emphasis on including recreational activities which extend beyond sports and athletics. The widespread movement of today includes not only colleges and universities but also high-school and elementary programs as well. Whereas, previously, intramural programs were confined to participation by men, women are now participating in sports programs through the girls' and women's athletic or recreation associations. Considerable emphasis is also given to individual and dual sports, corecreational activities, and sport clubs. A great increase in corecreational programs developed with opportunities for girls to participate in tennis, golf, bowling, badminton, swimming, archery, and others, and the consequent high level of skill that girls are able to attain in them. The equalizing of playing ability makes it enjoyable for boys and girls to play together, and as a result, many mixed doubles tournaments are successfully conducted.

Some of the large universities are constructing recreational gymnasiums and intramural buildings to take care of the increased emphasis on recreational programs. With the predicted increased enrollments of the future, there will be increased emphasis placed on the development of intramural sports programs. Staffs, facilities, and equipment must be constantly expanded and improved. It is conceivable that in the distant future the importance of intramural programs will increase to the extent that there will be "a sport for everyone and everyone in a sport."

SUMMARY

1. Intramural sports grew in a haphazard manner with the athletic needs of the masses almost entirely neglected.
2. The beginnings of athletics in colleges were of intramural nature.
3. Intramurals were the outgrowth of students' natural desires for sports and competition.
4. Early intramurals were organized by student committees and fraternity associations with little or no faculty supervision.

5. A subsequent stage unified intramurals under a more permanent centralized authority such as faculty-student committees and later intramural departments.
6. After the First World War, high schools, colleges, and universities expanded their intramural programs to include large numbers of boys and girls and men and women.
7. Later emphasis was placed on the welfare of participants —quality programs as well as quantity.
8. National and regional intramural associations developed because of the need to pool experiences and interchange successful ideas.
9. In addition to stressing competitive team sports, increased attention is also given to recreational activities which have a "carry-over" value.
10. Since the Second World War, there is continued expansion of intramural programs at all school levels.
11. Increased enrollments in the future will provide an even greater challenge to those responsible for developing and administering intramural programs.

3

Departmental Organization and Personnel

The intramural department, while maintaining a separate identity, seldom exists as a separate administrative unit. If it does, it is usually responsible to some larger governing board which also administers the service program in physical education, the varsity athletic program, and sometimes the health program.

In high schools, whether junior or senior and almost without exception, the intramural program is administered by the physical education department and receives its budget from that source. Sometimes a separate budget is set up for an intramural program but more often the money for the program is expended from physical education funds without making any attempt at differentiation.

In colleges and universities, the intramural program is usually administered from one of four sources: (1) the physical education department, (2) the intercollegiate athletic department, (3) a separate unit primarily controlled by students, or (4) an administrative unit which governs all activities relative to physical education, varsity athletics, and sometimes health. Centralization of administration of physical education, varsity athletics, intramural sports, and recreation in an enlarged physical education department creates a unified program.

One of the first plans of control was to run the intramural program as part of the varsity athletic program. This was "natural" in the earlier days because then the varsity departments usually sponsored the intramural programs. Such a tie-up has certain advantages. In general, the varsity department has more funds than physical education, and, if sympathetic to the intramural program, it can expend more money for facilities, equipment, and staff. From the varsity standpoint, there is an advantage in the existence of a comprehensive intramural program because it offsets the criticism that the stadiums, field houses, and athletic fields exist only for the benefit of a few highly trained athletes.

While the alliance of intramurals with the physical education department can give the intramural program less financial security, it usually gives it more educational standing. The welfare of the participating students receives more careful attention. Again, the intramural department is assured of a settled budget, one not dependent upon the success of the varsity teams and gate receipts.

In some state universities, provision for salaries of the intramural staff members, secretarial assistance, and current expenses (office supplies, playing equipment, and part-time help) is made in the budget allotted from legislative appropriations. At the same time, the maintenance of outdoor and indoor facilities is provided through gate receipts; this assistance includes lighting, heating, and janitorial service.

TYPES OF ADMINISTRATIVE PLANS

Although intramural sports are successfully conducted under different schemes of administration, it is undeniable that the big advances in this field occurred under the one-man plan, in which an intramural director is responsible for promoting and co-ordinating the various phases of the work, on either a full-time or part-time basis.

Many of the larger universities have a full-time specialist responsible for conducting an intramural program, and some of the smaller schools have one man from the physical education or athletic staff responsible for administration of this work, though he may only devote part of his time to it. Some of the high schools in the larger cities lighten the class work of one of the members of the physical education staff and assign him to organize the intramural activities. It is customary, however, for each member of the physical education staff to share supervision of intramural activities, although the direct responsibility for the administration of intramurals is designated to one person. Some smaller schools use an assistant coach or the varsity coach as intramural director. By thus combining the duties, a school or college secures a good man whose services they could not otherwise afford.

Not all schools follow the one-man plan of administration and, therefore, it is necessary to show the relative merits and defects of other plans that have been used over a period of years. These include the student control plan, physical education director plan, varsity coach plan, and one-man plan. While most of these types of administration are considered experimental or traditional, some are still in operation in different parts of the country.

Student Control Plan

A number of schools approve of students controlling their athletic sports. The idea sounds democratic. With an institution of any size, however, the difficulties become insurmountable. Student management is good only to a certain point. After that point is reached, it is bound to break down. If the work is centralized in the hands of a few students, it becomes too much for them to handle in addition to their school work; and on the other hand, if it is spread out among a large number of students, there is constant endeavor to dodge work and shift responsibility when things go wrong. Furthermore, the large system brings impersonal relationships among the students and this leads to a chance for politics to enter into the selections. The fact that the student body forms a transient group makes for a constant change of policies with resulting confusion. Again, students usually do not take proper measures to safeguard their welfare when competing; nor are they often interested in promoting activities for other than the more eager players. Students rarely possess the mature judgment often required in settling controversial issues which inevitably arise during the school year.

These arguments do not imply that student help is not successfully enlisted in intramural administration; but they do insist that student self-government is most successful, and most appreciated by the students themselves, when it is carried on under an experienced director or faculty adviser—and one who makes decisions without bias.

Physical Education Director Plan

Physical education directors often assume the responsibility for intramural work as an extra load. This procedure fails to make a clear-cut distinction between the physical education program and intramural activities and leaves the intramural program without an identity of its own. This is an obvious weakness. It makes intramural work stand secondary in the estimation of the physical education director, who, when pressed with other duties, may neglect those things that do not stand foremost in his mind. On the other hand, the physical education director can become so interested in the intramural phase of the program that he overly stresses it. This is quite natural because the students exert their influence for more intramural activities and less formalized teaching procedures.

The strong point of the physical education director plan, when it is working well, is that it is convenient to reach everyone who takes required work. There are many difficulties to contend with, however, in actual practice. The units for competition are frequently evolved from groups selected more or less artificially from physical education classes. Moreover, it is very difficult to secure satisfactory competition, since both good and poor players are put together on the same basis. This latter fault is remedied by selecting the teams according to some rating plan which equalizes the players' abilities, but this creates a great amount of detailed work, not only in classifying, but also in arranging schedules apart from the class periods. The time necessary for equalizing competition for wider participation, however, is surely worth it in interest, welfare to the students, and increased enthusiasm for the intramural program.

Varsity Coach Plan

Some authorities adhere to the varsity coach plan in spite of its obvious failings. Under this plan, the varsity coach of each sport is responsible for an intramural program in the same sport. This idea sounds plausible because the coach is a specialist in his particular sport and is naturally interested in building a strong following of players from which he can seek varsity talent. The primary difficulty results from the fact that the varsity coach, in the midst of his season of competition, is manacled to the present system which demands, in many cases, a winning team above all else, and, therefore, the intramural work is not only slighted but frequently neglected entirely. The only practical way to enlist the varsity coach's interest in this enterprise is to conduct intramural leagues in his sport before or after the varsity season. Then he has the time and is more interested in helping because of the opportunity to find possible varsity material. The varsity coach plan has another weakness in its lack of unity and over-all administrative control. With each coach conducting a certain amount of intramural work independently of his colleagues, there is great confusion in opinions, methods, schedules, and awards, with the result that any co-ordinating method of arousing a steady year-round interest is impossible. The centralization of important detail work is also difficult.

Where the varsity coaches are utilized in the intramural program, it is usually during the seasons when they are not responsible for coaching. In some of the larger universities, the coaches of the recreative sports can lend some intramural assistance even when their varsity season is under way.

Intramural Director Plan

The plan of centralizing the work in one person does away with many of the difficulties of the previous plans. The fact that this person is primarily responsible for the success of the work makes him much more enthusiastic about it—much more so than in the two previous plans where intramural work is a secondary job. Once an efficient system is established, the interest is cumulative and the program continues to thrive on the work of the past.

As a department grows, there is more and more office work. In the beginning, the intramural director often supervises field work and even officiates. As the number of teams and participants increases, he finds it necessary to have others officiate the games and he acts as field supervisor. Then comes the time when the duties become so multitudinous that the director's work is largely confined to the office. In this case, he needs an efficient field man to conduct the games; to see that teams are assigned to special playing areas, equipment is ready, and officials—including timekeepers, scorers, and referees—are on the job.

Five plans for departmental organizations are presented in diagrammatic form. They cover a large university program, a plan for organization of campus recreation, a college program, a plan for a women's program, and a high-school intramural program. (See Figs. 1–5.) These plans are suggestive in nature and serve as guides in setting up departmental organizations. In many cases, the main features of the plans are applicable to local situations even though variations in minor details may be more suitable. The intramural director should be the final judge of the plan for organization which seems best suited to his school's situation.

Nearly all the large university intramural departments started on a very modest basis as regards a paid staff. The directors increased their staff by enlisting student assistants through a graded managerial scheme in which certain campus honors made up for lack of financial remuneration.

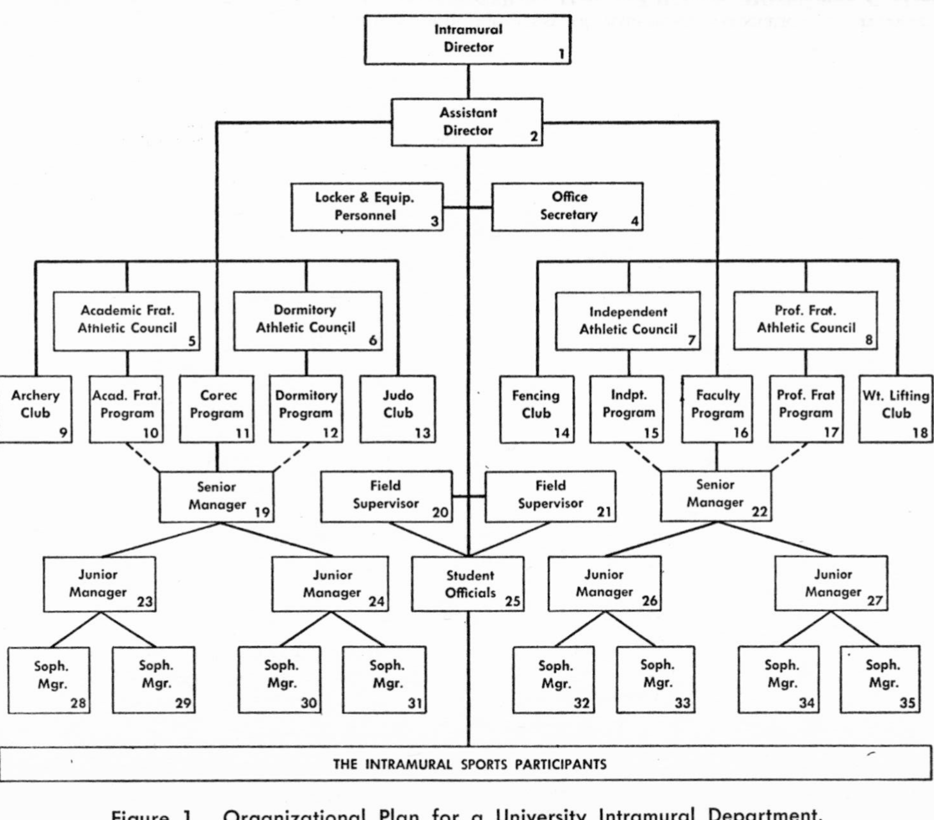

Figure 1. Organizational Plan for a University Intramural Department.

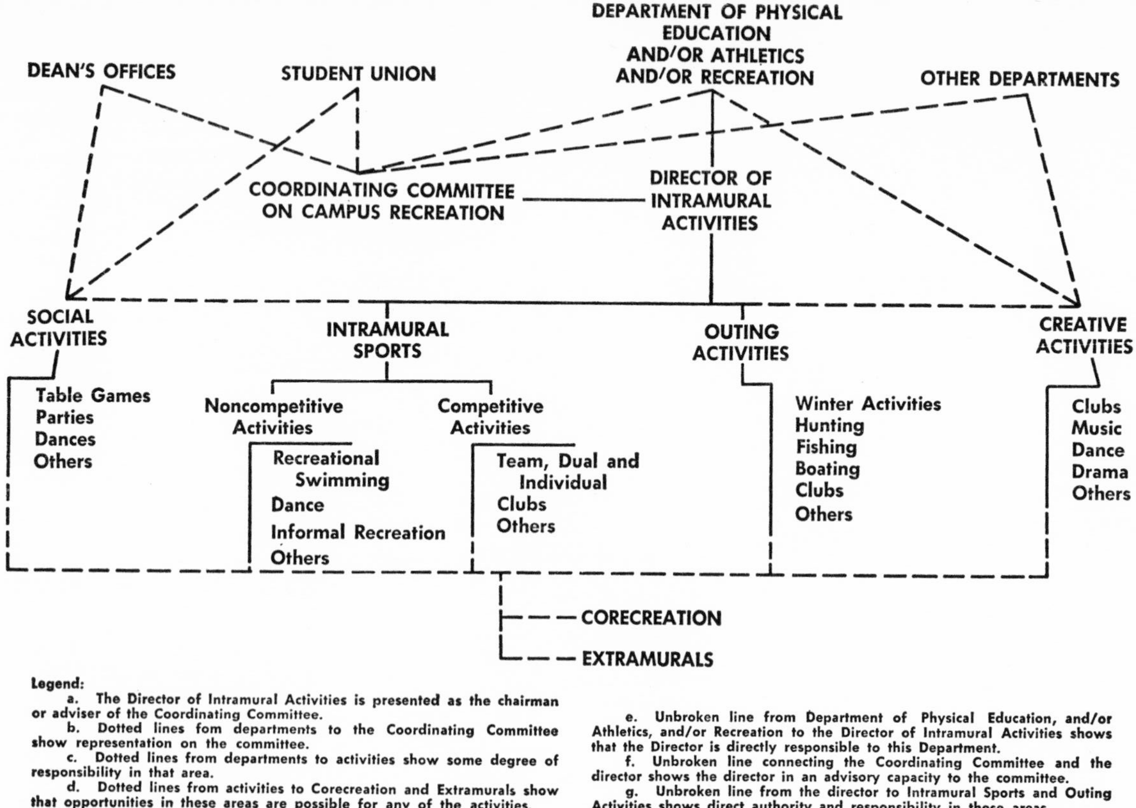

Figure 2. Suggested Organization of Campus Recreation. Courtesy of American Association for Health, Physical Education, and Recreation. From *Intramural Sports for College Men and Women*, Washington Conference Report, p. 10. Published by the Association, 1956.

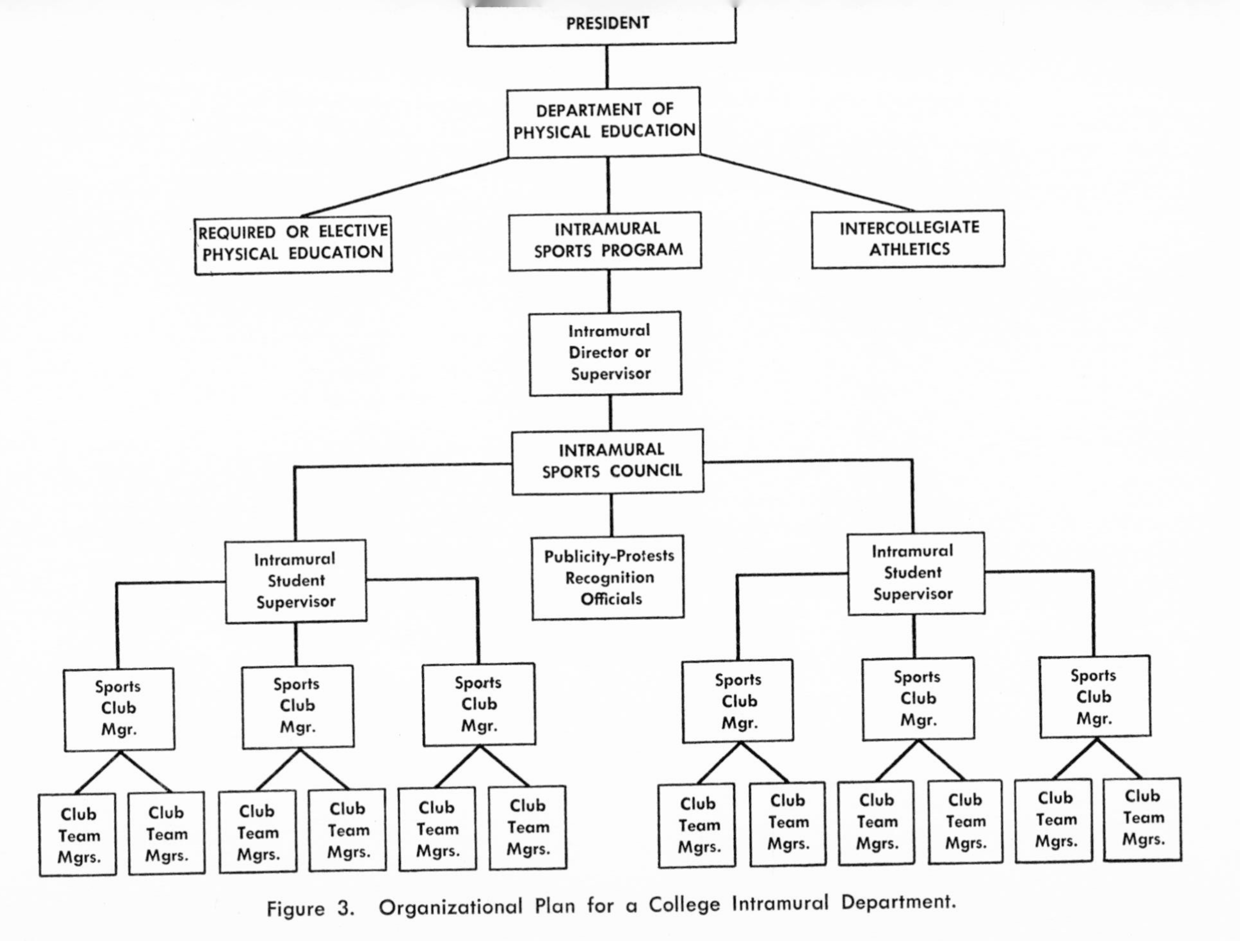

Figure 3. Organizational Plan for a College Intramural Department.

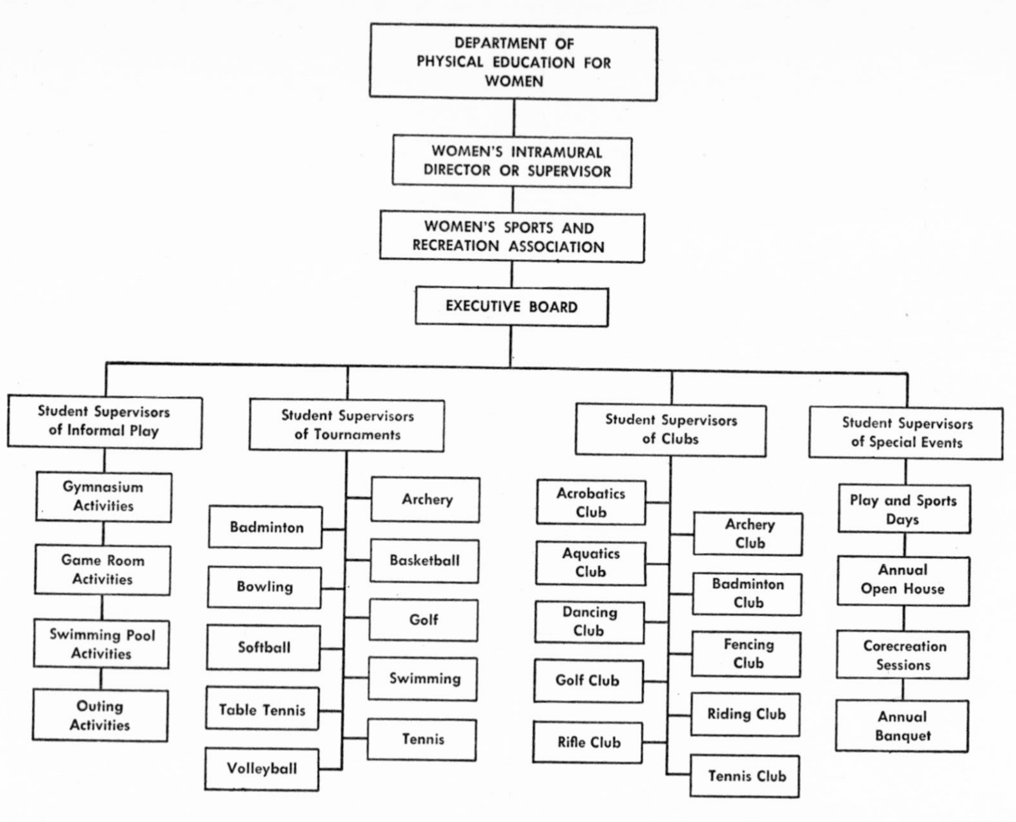

Figure 4. Organizational Plan for an Intramural Sports Program for Women.

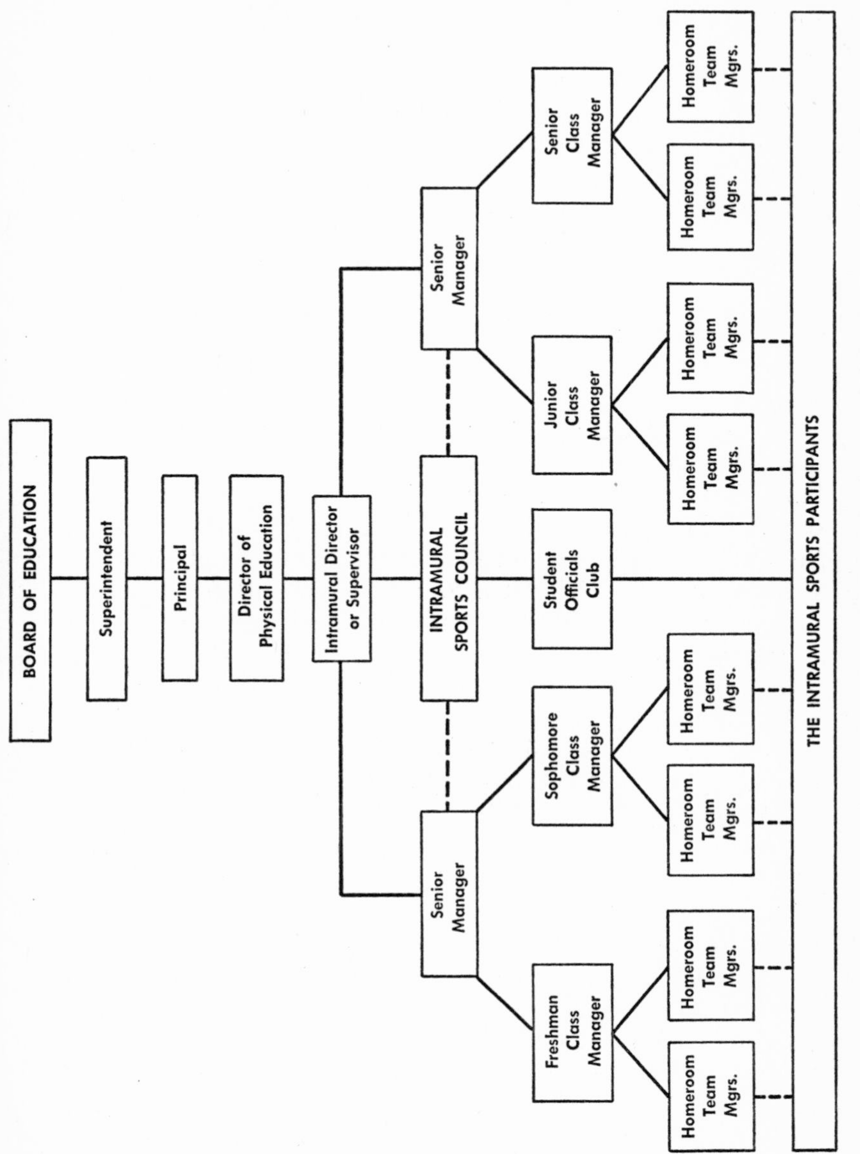

Figure 5. Organizational Plan for a High-School Intramural Sports Program.

As the departments grow, the work increases. There is specialization within the department and additional assistants are necessary to handle the increased program. The duties of these various officials, both paid and voluntary, are discussed later.

In the high school or small college, the beginning of a system can be made by securing a part-time man acting in somewhat the same capacity as the faculty manager in varsity athletics. If such a man is secured from the faculty, he should either receive some compensation for this extra work or be relieved of some of his classroom duties. The constant guidance and co-operation with the physical education department is absolutely essential, however, in this scheme.

The work of an intramural director, while it involves a general knowledge of all sports, does not require a thorough knowledge of coaching techniques. It does require a thorough background in physical education. The director must be a good organizer who has a close regard for details and is strictly impartial. The director must constantly evaluate his program to satisfy the students' needs and interests. Service to the students is the director's primary obligation.

The work of conducting a large intramural program involves innumerable details which must be attended to if the schedules are to be followed without conflict, if maximum use is to be obtained from the available facilities, and if teams and officials are to be notified as to the proper time to be present. In schedules where many games are played, disputes arise over the work of the officials and the eligibility of the players. The intramural director is usually the final source of appeal for all complaints and the more impersonally he sizes up a situation and tactfully handles it, the more successful he is in obtaining the confidence and good will of the student body. Sometimes, the director organizes a student committee or athletic council to assist him; usually, the final responsibility rests with him. Above all, the intramural director must be an educator as well as an administrator.

PERSONNEL FOR CENTRALIZED PLAN

The preferred plan of organization is that of a separate department in charge of a director especially trained in intramural work. A department organized on this plan is simple or complex according to the size of the institution and the amount of aid given by school authorities. The following paragraphs indicate general duties of personnel necessary to carry out an intramural program for a large university. This general plan can serve as a model for a school of any size; smaller schools can dispense with certain officials by doubling up on the duties or by employing part-time instead of full-time help. Numbers in parentheses below correspond to those on the organizational plan shown in Figure 1.

Intramural Director (1)

The intramural director is responsible for the entire program. He selects and promotes the activities and administers the program efficiently. He integrates the work of his department with that of the entire school. He is an executive in the sense that he delegates many of the duties, and his success depends upon the wise selection of subordinates. The director is then free to direct policies, co-ordinate the work with other related departments, and serve on various school committees.

Assistant Director (2)

The assistant director relieves the director of organizational details. The assistant director deals directly with the student managers and is responsible for maintaining this phase of the organization. His main function is that of supervision—supervision of both the paid and voluntary workers and of the program of activities. It is often advantageous, depending on the size of the program, to have more than one assistant director.

Locker and Equipment Personnel (3)

Locker and equipment personnel deal primarily with the students and have to be diplomatic and personable. Often, a student judges the entire intramural program on the basis of his contact with the locker and equipment personnel. These persons issue equipment for contests and recreational free play, maintain the equipment, keep an inventory, and issue lockers.

Office Secretary (4)

The office secretary serves as a receptionist, answers the phone, takes dictation, maintains office records and files, schedules the director's appointments, and is often the only paid staff member in the office when the director and assistant director are busy elsewhere. Because of her direct contact with students and other people, it is extremely important that she be as personable as possible with everyone she meets.

Athletic Councils (5–8)

Intramural athletic councils are composed of representatives of the various participating student organizations—academic and professional fraternities, dormitories, and independents. For example, the academic fraternities' athletic council consists of an elected manager from each academic fraternity. The council meets at the beginning of each sport season, bi-weekly, monthly, or upon call of the intramural director. The intramural director or assistant director presents the proposed activity program; explains how tournaments are conducted, where played, and what equipment is needed. Within the limitations of time, facilities, and equipment, the council can be given a choice as to the type of tournament—single or double elimination or round-robin. The representatives, in addition to assisting future tournament planning, can evaluate past tournaments, officiating, eligibility rules, number of forfeits, and tournament structuring. The director usually distributes schedules or other communications at these meetings.

The council representatives serve as an important link between the intramural office and participating teams. Information is transferred from the intramural office to the teams through the council representatives. Conversely, the council manager usually is the fraternities' athletic chairman who in turn relates information to subunit managers or captains for the various sports. Numerous suggestions are channeled to the intramural director through the council. From student reactions, as reported by the councils, the director partially evaluates the quality of the program—"to what extent are the customers satisfied." The council has no part in conducting the intramural program other than in an advisory and liaison capacity.

Graduate Assistants (10–12,15–17)

Numbers 9 through 18 on the organizational chart shown in Figure 1 indicate the areas of program activity. These areas should be arranged to encompass the physical recreation needs of students and staff members. In college, the graduate assistant is an important key to the success of an intramural program. These assistantships or fellowships are comparable to those offered for teaching and doing research.

Graduate assistants conduct or assist in one or more phases of the program, such as the faculty and corecreation programs. They sometimes aid the intramural department by providing expert help in sports such as weight lifting, skiing, fencing, boxing, and wrestling in which full-time staff members are not proficient. The graduate assistants who have special talent in a sport can conduct tournaments and meets, offer instruction, and use safety precautions during workouts. Because of their greater experience and more mature judgment, graduate students assume greater responsibility than undergraduates. They lend stability and prestige to the program. In addition to invaluable intramural education, the assistants receive financial remuneration commensurate to their areas of responsibility.

Student Club Instructors (9, 13, 14, 18)

Sports clubs assist the general promotion of the intramural program as well as specific promotion of specialized sports. The better-than-average-ability students band together to form clubs in judo, archery, fencing, weight lifting, handball, squash, and other sports. Usually, the best performer in the group serves as student instructor. His services are on a voluntary basis but he could receive a complimentary locker or be awarded a monogram for his contributions to the program.

Clubs elect officers and are advised by faculty members or graduate assistants. Clubs assist in conducting specialized sports tournaments and also give exhibitions. Expert performers compete regularly with others of advanced ability and teach sport techniques to new members who need only desire and enthusiasm to gain admittance to the club.

Field Supervisors (20–21)

Field supervisors are needed if a number of games take place at the same time. They are then directors in charge of the playing fields or gymnasium courts. They see that teams are properly assigned to their respective fields or courts; that referees, scorekeepers, and timers are appointed; that scores are properly tabulated and turned into the central office; and that equipment is returned following the games. Securing and training student officials and handling protests on the field or court are two other important duties. The field supervisors need not be employed on a full-time basis. Usually, either undergraduate students with athletic experience or graduate assistants work part time after class hours. Their work is necessary when several activities are conducted at the same time at different places; for instance, basketball, hockey, swimming, and wrestling are often all conducted simultaneously and each needs someone present in an official capacity. Most schools have more than one field supervisor; others get along with one field supervisor for the most important seasonal activity and depend upon student managers to take charge of the rest.

Student Officials (25)

An efficient staff of student officials (referees, umpires, timekeepers) contributes to the quality of the intramural program. Numerous time-consuming protests are avoided by good officiating. Officials take practical and written tests under the direction of field supervisors. Officials are customarily paid by the hour or game. In some high schools, colleges, and universities, volunteer students officiate.

Officials can be varsity athletes, physical education majors, or other students. Men with varsity experience usually are good officials because of their experience and prestige. Physical education majors who are required to take a sports-officiating course are a good source. Good officiating is furthered through intramural officials' clubs and associations.

Senior Managers (19, 22)

There are two types of student managers in the intramural program—individual unit or team managers and over-all program managers. Individual unit or team managers are students who organize teams and enter them in intramural leagues and tournaments. Over-all program managers are usually organized on a graded scale—seniors, juniors, sophomores.

Senior managers are in charge of a corps of student assistant managers. These managers relieve the intramural director and assistant director of numerous program administration details. The chief duty of the senior manager is to assign work to the various junior and sophomore managers. This work includes assisting in making out schedules, notifying participants of playing time, recording scores and maintaining other office records, and helping graduate assistants supervise play areas. Senior managers, with the aid of their subordinate managers, organize and promote some individual or dual tournaments. Final approval of the tournament structures rests with the intramural director or assistant director. It is important that the director assign only duties that have educational value rather than tasks such as cleaning basketballs or mending badminton nets.

Managers are advanced from year to year if their work merits promotion. The two senior managers are selected from the junior managers by a committee consisting of the intramural director, assistant director, and outgoing managers. The senior manager's position is comparable to the varsity manager, with the exception that varsity managers perform their duties only while the varsity sport is in season, whereas intramural managers hold their responsibilities for the entire school year. Managers are not paid but may receive yearly awards, complimentary lockers, and equipment privileges. In addition to educational experience, senior managers receive a manager's letter and sweater. They retain all rights and privileges of the official varsity letter club of the school.

Junior Managers (23, 24, 26, 27)

Junior managers are selected by the intramural director, assistant director, and the senior managers from the sophomore manager's staff and are students who demonstrated proficiency in carrying out their assignments. The number of junior managers varies with the size of the school but is usually twice the number of senior managers and half the number of sophomore managers. In larger programs, junior and sophomore managers who do not qualify for promotions can stay on the staff as paid student officials, assistants to the field supervisor, or in some other capacity. The junior managers receive minor intramural letters or monograms in addition to the usual department privileges.

Sophomore Managers (28–35)

Sophomore managers are picked by the selection committee from students who are interested in "trying out" for the managerial positions. The major requisite for any candidate is desire and enthusiasm. Sophomore managers are oriented by the intramural director but receive most of their on-the-job training from the senior and junior managers. Intramural numerals are awarded to the sophomore managers. In large programs, freshman managers often prove useful.

Not all managers are good ones. When a good manager is found, however, it is difficult to evaluate his services, which would require considerable expenditure of money if he were on a paid basis. As a department grows and a larger paid staff is available, the responsibilities of the student managers lessen. However, the manager's position is still of vital importance to the success of a smooth-operating department.

Sport Managers

At some universities, sport managers take charge of a particular sport or group of sports. The usual plan is to have a sport manager in each of the "major" sports which involve the most work and a different sport manager to conduct the "minor" sports in the fall, winter, and spring, respectively. This method of handling the sport managers gives more prestige to their work. It gives them a job with a definite responsibility and they do not feel they wasted time if they are not elected to senior or junior managerships.

Intramural Advisory Committee

This is a body which it may prove well to organize though it meets but a few times each year. Members appointed to this committee by the school administration are faculty men and students interested in the intramural program. In a practical way, their services amount to little; but, in such matters as policies and influence with the school proper, their support is very helpful. At any special function of the intramural department, such as an annual banquet, the presence of faculty members makes the occasion more worthwhile for the students.

SUMMARY

1. The intramural department, while maintaining a separate identity, seldom exists as a separate administrative unit.
2. In high schools, the intramural program is usually administered by the physical education department.
3. In colleges and universities, the intramural program is usually administered by the physical education department, the intercollegiate athletic department, a separate unit primarily controlled by students, or an administrative unit which governs all activities relative to physical education, varsity athletics, and sometimes health.
4. Intramural programs are administered by students, physical education directors, varsity coaches, or intramural directors.
5. Centralizing the intramural program duties in one man is the most efficient method of control.
6. An intramural director should have a general knowledge of all sports, should be a good organizer who has close regard for details, and should be strictly impartial.
7. An assistant director, who usually supervises the paid and voluntary workers and the program of activities, relieves the director of many organizational details.
8. An office secretary and locker and equipment personnel are also important paid staff members in the centralized plan.
9. Intramural athletic councils are composed of representatives of the various participating student organizations and serve as an important link between the intramural office and the participating teams.
10. Graduate student assistants are often assigned to conduct or assist in phases of the program such as the faculty and corecreation programs.
11. Sport clubs of above-average-ability students in a particular sport such as judo assist the general promotion of the intramural program as well as specific promotion of their specialized sport.
12. Field supervisors are directors in charge of the playing fields or gymnasium courts. They train and assign officials and handle protests on the spot.
13. An efficient staff of student officials is necessary for a good intramural program.

14. Student managers in the intramural program are either team or individual unit managers or over-all program managers based upon class in school—senior, junior, sophomore.
15. Senior managers are in charge of the corps of student managers and assist the director and assistant director with administrative details.

4

Scope of Administrative Details

Administrative details within an intramural department are varied and require careful organization and study. The intramural sports program is spectacular in the size and magnitude of the numbers of participants it encompasses and the variety of events it offers. The larger the intramural organization grows, the more impersonal it becomes. Staff members must serve the interests of more students; they have less time to devote to the interests of the individual.

In a high school or small college or university, where one staff member usually handles most of the administrative details, the intramural program can be just as complete and extensive for that particular school as the program conducted at a large university or college or the high school employing a full-time intramural director. Responsibility is divided in the large program; in the small program, responsibility for all aspects of the program comes under the same director.

The primary difference between the large university intramural department with perhaps three or four full-time staff members and the small college or high-school intramural department directed by either a full- or part-time member of the physical education staff is the extent to which these administrative details are carried out. Programs embracing hundreds, even thousands of students, naturally require more attention to details. For, without attention to these details, many of which are outlined in this chapter, the program loses much of its vitality and completeness and decreases its primary function—to provide wholesome, recreative, and competitive sports for everyone.

Beneath the staff of permanent intramural personnel that is superimposed to give permanence and experienced direction to the over-all staff of a university intramural department, there is a group of student workers arranged in a hierarchy (see Fig. 1). There are student officials, managers, assistant managers, assistants to the assistant managers, and unit managers representing each team, which, in turn, represents a class, fraternity, dormitory, military company, or sport club. These students help organize and direct other students in performing numerous details.

Generally, the policies of an intramural department should be to: (1) serve the recreational needs of the students through a planned program of athletics and other forms of physical recreation; (2) sponsor as many different worthwhile and beneficial recreational activities as possible, thereby reaching the largest number of individuals; (3) sponsor as many leagues and tournaments as are needed to take care of all individuals desiring organized forms of competition; (4) conduct all activities in such a manner that the best results in the way of enjoyment, health, social contacts, and sportsmanship are gained by the participants; (5) emphasize those activities that have carry-over value, that is, the games which if learned while at school are used advantageously in later years of life; (6) create and maintain at all times the best of good will and sociability among all students and staff members participating in the program; (7) conduct each event on the program as efficiently as possible; (8) give individual instruction whenever possible without any special charge; and (9) encourage participation for the sake of the activity rather than for the award.

The administrative details necessary to assure successful completion of these policies, and thus of the entire intramural program, are outlined in this chapter. The outline presented is that for a large university intramural department such as the one illustrated in the "Organizational Plan for a University Intramural Department" (see Fig. 1).

Any department can select and adapt those features of this comprehensive plan which are applicable to its own particular situation.

A similar analysis of administrative details and the outline of procedures for basketball, also in this chapter, can be utilized to advantage by the junior high school, senior high school, or small college or university intramural director. Initial reports are not complete in listing all items that fall to the attention of the intramural department; nevertheless, such an attempt at compilation serves as a useful outline to which other items can be added. In this way, a most valuable source book for reference is built up for the use of individual departments.

Though the varied details mentioned in this chapter can be handled differently in different departments and some may be missing in small schools, the nature of the many responsibilities of a university intramural department can be studied to advantage by the student of intramurals. Such a collection of data proves to any observer that efficient operation of an intramural program involves considerable hard work which is not evident on the surface. The apparent simplicity of a successful intramural program is often a tribute to an unusually effective administration.

Regardless of the size of the intramural program or the number of staff members or participants, one fact remains constant. The successful promotion and completion of any intramural program requires attention to a myriad of administrative details by one or all staff members.

OUTLINE OF ADMINISTRATIVE DETAILS

1. *Executive*
   a. Assignment of staff to various duties
   b. Rules and regulations for sports
   c. Rules and regulations for managers
   d. Rules and regulations for building
   e. Purchase of equipment and supplies
   f. Care and upkeep of fields and courts
   g. Preparation of budget
   h. Office management

i. Administrative conferences
j. Special events and exhibitions
k. Charges and fees

2. *Professional*
   a. Writing articles for professional publications
   b. Giving addresses before educational groups
   c. Serving on school committees
   d. Working with allied departments—required physical education, interscholastic or intercollegiate athletics, health service, and teacher education
   e. Showing co-operative interest in local professional societies—education, health, physical education, athletics, and recreation
   f. Holding membership in local, district, and national professional organizations
3. *Community Services*
   a. Talk to various groups on subject of intramurals
      (1) Civic clubs
      (2) Parent-teachers' clubs
      (3) Radio-television
      (4) Athletic assemblies and banquets
   b. Work with community recreation department—also religious, civic, and industrial organizations sponsoring recreational activities
4. *Instruction and Research*
   a. Offer free instruction when possible
   b. Teach physical education classes
   c. Coach varsity and freshman teams
   d. Conduct intramural research
5. *Counseling and Guidance*
   a. Confer with managers on postponements, eligibility rules, protests, awards, and other managerial problems
   b. Advise students on remedial activities
6. *Conferences*
   a. With staff members
   b. With managers staff
   c. With student officials
   d. With athletic councils
   e. With other departments in interdepartmental conferences
7. *Student Contacts*
   a. Dissemination of information

   b. Office conferences and informal discussions
   c. Faculty-student councils and committees
   d. Supervision of participation
   e. Sports instruction
   f. Sports clubs
   g. Visits to fraternities, dormitories, etc.
   h. Banquets and other occasions of fellowship
   i. Orientation of new students
   j. Corecreation

8. *Office Management*
   a. Appointments
   b. Phone calls
   c. Information service
   d. Secretarial and clerical services—typing, mimeographing, sign making, bulletin upkeep, filing, addressing, mailing
9. *Correspondence*
   a. Information requests from other schools
   b. Professional questionnaires
   c. Committee work
   d. Recommendations for positions for students and teachers
   e. Information on playing equipment
   f. Information on new games and rules
   g. General communication
10. *Finances*
   a. Keep forfeit fee records
   b. Handle locker and towel charges
   c. Rent equipment
   d. Buy equipment and supplies
   e. Purchase awards
   f. Administer department budget
11. *Publicity*
   a. Student radio and newspaper
   b. Publication of annual intramural handbook
   c. Preparation of news releases
   d. Section in the school annual
   e. Articles in alumni magazine
   f. Intercollegiate programs
   g. Radio and television appearances
   h. Mimeographed intramural information sheets
   i. Bulletin boards and trophy cases

j. Posters depicting history, rules, records, recent champions, and unusual events
k. Orientation Week folders

12. *Recording Results*
a. Record of individual and team events
b. Record of winners of each event
c. Record of newspaper clippings
d. Record of pictures
e. Record of unusual events
f. Record of points earned by teams; by individuals
g. Records of winning times, distances, and points

13. *Participations*
a. Record of number of individuals using facilities
b. Total number of entries in all sports
c. Total number of different individuals in all sports
d. Total number of students entered in each organized sport
e. Staff participations
f. Comparative totals by years
g. Record of each student's participation
(1) Separate card for each student
(2) Separate check for each sport
(3) Total of competitions in each sport
h. Total number of athletic events
(1) Tournaments
(2) Meets
(3) Games

14. *Health and Safety*
a. Care of injuries
b. Injury reports
c. Health examinations
d. Issuance of medical regulations
e. Safety precautions
(1) Facilities
(2) Lifeguards in pool
(3) Spotters for gymnastics
(4) Special rules and regulations for certain sports

15. *Organization of Leagues*
a. Decide upon dates
b. Decide upon playing rules
c. Distribute entry blanks
d. Phone to check teams not entered

e. Record forfeit fees
f. Keep records of health examination status
g. Seed players and teams
h. Make up schedules
i. Notify about contests and games
j. Assign practice periods
k. Prepare score cards
l. Check equipment
m. Distribute schedules
n. Preserve after-game records—scores, participation points

16. *Field Supervision*
a. Assign officials
b. Supervise teams and equipment
c. Supervise central timing
d. Arbitrate protests

17. *Officiating*
a. Intramural officials' club or association
b. Interpretation meetings
c. Officiating techniques
d. Uniforms
e. Assignments

18. *Locker and Equipment Supervision*
a. Equipment maintenance
b. Locker assignments
c. Deposit fees and refunds
d. Towel service
e. Locker and equipment inventory
f. Lost and found

19. *Special Events*
a. Open houses
b. Sports clinics
c. Invitation tournaments
d. Athletic demonstrations and exhibitions
e. Faculty-student competition
f. Outside, nonuniversity activities

20. *Building Supervision*
a. Building maintenance
b. Building hours
c. Supervision—swimming pool and other special areas
d. Court reservations—recreational and competitive

In the foregoing outline, an idea was given of the many details and responsibilities of the intramural department which are not all apparent to the casual observer. Intramural administration in a large university demands many contacts and co-operative assignments with other departments, particularly those in related fields, such as physical education, intercollegiate athletics, health service, teacher education, and buildings and grounds. Much give and take is necessary if these relations are to be carried on harmoniously and in the best interests of the intramural program.

As an additional aid to the student or intramural worker, A Summary of Administrative Details is presented to illustrate the areas of the previous outline to which each member of the intramural staff is assigned (see Fig. 6). The intramural staff in this example includes all the workers, both volunteer students and paid staff members, shown in the Organizational Plan for a University Intramural Department. (See Fig. 1.) The extent of staff responsibility for each detail depends on the number of staff personnel, number of participants, experience, training, and capabilities of staff and student workers and local needs (finances, facilities, equipment).

ADMINISTRATIVE DETAILS FOR A SPORT

Not all of the many details of administrative responsibility are covered in the preceding outline. A complicated procedure for each sport is necessary if the sport is to be conducted with a maximum degree of interest and efficiency. The observer who looks at an intramural bulletin board and thinks that all that is necessary to conduct a successful tournament is to tack an entry sheet on the board, let the contestants sign their names, and then fill in their scores, is as far from the truth as the traveler who hurries through a strange country and then tries to relate a meaningful picture of the customs of the people.

To illustrate the necessary procedure, basketball is selected as an example. A check list can be prepared for each

ADMINISTRATIVE DETAILS	DIRECTOR	ASSISTANT DIRECTOR	SECRETARY	GRADUATE ASSISTANTS	FIELD SUPERVISORS	SENIOR MANAGERS	JUNIOR MANAGERS	SOPHOMORE MANAGERS	VARSITY COACHES	LOCKER-EQUIP. PERSONNEL
1. EXECUTIVE	X	X								
2. PROFESSIONAL	X	X		X					X	
3. COMMUNITY SERVICES	X	X		X					X	
4. INSTRUCTION AND RESEARCH	X	X		X					X	
5. COUNSELING AND GUIDANCE	X	X		X						
6. CONFERENCES	X	X		X	X				X	
7. STUDENT CONTACTS	X	X	X	X	X	X	X	X	X	X
8. OFFICE MANAGEMENT	X	X	X	X		X				
9. CORRESPONDENCE	X	X	X	X						
10. FINANCES	X	X	X							X
11. PUBLICITY	X	X	X	X		X				
12. RECORDING RESULTS			X	X		X	X	X		
13. PARTICIPATIONS				X		X	X	X		
14. HEALTH AND SAFETY	X	X	X	X	X	X	X	X	X	X
15. ORGANIZATION OF LEAGUES	X	X		X		X	X	X		
16. FIELD SUPERVISION		X		X	X	X	X	X		
17. OFFICIATING		X		X	X					
18. LOCKER AND EQUIP. SUPERVISION					X	X	X	X		X
19. SPECIAL EVENTS	X	X		X	X	X	X	X	X	X
20. BUILDING SUPERVISION	X	X	X	X	X	X	X	X		

Figure 6. Summary of Responsibility for Administrative Details.

sport. (See Fig. 7.) A chart and description of items follows. "Initialed by" on the chart indicates the staff member responsible for completion of each item. When organizational details are outlined in check list form and followed according to schedule, efficient program operation is assured. Use of the check lists enables the office staff to perform many duties that otherwise would consume the director's time.

I-M BASKETBALL CHECK LIST			
Date of Completion	Procedural Details	X	Initialed by Staff
Nov. 1	1. Arrange dates	X	DJM
Nov. 1	2. Review playing rules	X	DJM
Nov. 3	3. Acquire and display awards	X	DJM
Nov. 3	4. Prepare equipment and facilities	X	DJM
Nov. 5	5. Issue advance publicity	X	DJM
Nov. 10	6. Send out entry blanks	X	JAE
Nov. 20	7. Telephone the final notice	X	JAE
Nov. 21	8. Receive and classify entry blanks	X	JAE
Nov. 22	9. File the forfeit fee, record and receipt	X	JAE
Nov. 23	10. Seed the teams	X	DJM
Nov. 23	11. Draw up the schedules	X	DJM
Nov. 23	12. Assign practice periods	X	DJM
Nov. 24	13. Send items to the news outlets	X	DJM
Nov. 25	14. Distribute schedules	X	JAE
Nov. 26	15. Prepare daily schedule sheet	X	JAE
Nov. 27.	16. Meet with student officials	X	DJM
Nov. 28	17. Check health status and eligibility	X	JAE
Nov. 28	18. Make out score cards	X	JAE
Daily	19. Assign officials - make out officials' rating cards	X	LAM
Daily	20. Check score sheets following games	X	JAE
Daily	21. Record scores, officials, sportsmanship ratings	X	JAE
Daily	22. Record participation	X	JAE
Feb. 25	23. Tabulate all-year participation points	X	DJM
Feb. 28	24. Record results in permanent records	X	JAE
Mar. 1	25. Distribute awards	X	DJM
Mar. 1	26. Send out final publicity	X	DJM

Figure 7. I-M Basketball Check List.

BASKETBALL PROCEDURE

1. *Arrange dates.* Make out calendar giving the dates for the different leagues and tournaments. Include dates upon which entries close.
2. *Review playing rules.* Follow regulation playing rules whenever possible. Adapt rules to local circumstances if necessary. Post rules on bulletin boards. Distribute them with schedules.
3. *Acquire and display awards.* Order awards and display them upon arrival.
4. *Prepare equipment and facilities.* Have available balls, baskets, nets, whistles, timing and scoring devices, and playing courts.
5. *Issue advance publicity.* Send announcements of events to student newspapers and radio stations. Post announcements on bulletin boards.
6. *Send out entry blanks.* Draw up blanks giving the regulations of the tournament and the rules of play. Offer managers the opportunity to state preferred playing times.
7. *Check and telephone final notices.* When entry blanks are returned on the closing day, check the lists of teams and phone those not having an entry blank to determine if the entry is still intended.
8. *Receive and classify entry blanks.* Classify the entry blanks according to units of competition and preferred playing times. Record the entries and times together with the name, address, and phone number of the manager for the particular team.
9. *File forfeit fee record and receipt.* Whenever a forfeit fee is required at the time of the entry, make out a receipt. Fee is returned if the team goes through the schedule without a forfeit or it can, upon conclusion of the sport, be transferred to the credit of another sport.
10. *Seed the teams.* Classify teams into leagues. Consider previous league structure, champions, and anticipated strength of teams.
11. *Draw up schedules.* Announce dates, hours, and courts for the respective games. If a group is playing in two or more sports which come during the same season of the year, care must be taken that the group does not have two activities scheduled the same day.

12. *Assign practice periods.* Set aside hours for practice periods. Assign the courts to the teams. The notice is included on the schedule which is sent to each team.
13. *Send items to news outlets.* Send publicity items of interest to the newspapers and radio stations. Include last year's winners, favored teams for this year, outstanding players, general rules, numbers of teams entered, and the schedule.
14. *Distribute schedules.* Mimeograph the schedule for each team. Either mail it or hand it to the team manager. Send copies to the student newspaper and radio station.
15. *Prepare daily schedule sheet.* Include the teams playing, the time assigned to them, the courts assigned to them, names of opponents, and assignments of officials.
16. *Meet with student officials.* Discuss the rules so that all officials have the same instructions and understand the game's interpretations.
17. *Check health status and eligibility of participants.* Use Health Service and probationary lists.
18. *Make out score cards.* Fill out printed or mimeographed basketball score cards with date, time, court, names of teams, and names of officials. The floor supervisor distributes the cards to the officials at game time.
19. *Assign officials and make out officials' rating cards.* Have field supervisor assign officials and make sure officials' rating cards accompany score cards. Have team captains rate the officials and the officials rate the teams for sportsmanship.
20. *Check score sheets following games.* At the conclusion of the game, the officials check the score card for completeness and accuracy.
21. *Record scores, officials, and sportsmanship ratings.* Record scores on the league schedule sheet in the office and on the bulletin board. Tabulate officials and sportsmanship ratings. Make available scores and game details to campus news outlets.
22. *Record participation.* Following each game, record the names of all players on participation cards which show the individual athletic record of each student. Record team participations.
23. *Tabulate all-year participation-achievement totals.* Tabu-

late cumulative participation-achievement point totals during and following play-offs.

24. *Record results in permanent records.* Following the season, record all league and play-off results in permanent record files in the office for use in the intramural handbook and yearbook. File written summaries and suggestions about the past season as aids for the next season.
25. *Distribute awards.* Use blank form to record full information about the award for the particular sport, such as cost, style, recipient, etc. Have each person receiving individual awards sign his name as a receipt on this sheet. Have the captain sign for team awards.
26. *Send out final publicity.* Send a mimeographed sheet to the hometown paper of each member of the winning team stating that each student was a member of the winning intramural basketball team at his school. Include points of interest such as name of the team, the number of teams participating, and the score of the final game.

SUMMARY

1. Administrative details within an intramural department are varied and require careful organization and study.
2. The small school or one-director intramural program, to be complete, has almost as many administrative details to be attended to as the large school program.
3. Administrative responsibility is divided in the large intramural program; in the small program, responsibility for all aspects of the program comes under the same director.
4. The extent to which administrative details are carried out is the primary difference between the large university intramural department and the small college or regular high-school intramural department.
5. Though the varied details mentioned in this chapter can be handled differently in different departments and some may be missing in small schools, the nature of the many responsibilities of a university intramural department can be studied to advantage by the student of intramurals.
6. The successful promotion and completion of any intramural program requires attention to a myriad of administrative details by one or all staff members.

7. Intramural administration demands many contacts and co-operative assignments with other departments of a large university, particularly those in related fields such as physical education, intercollegiate athletics, health service, teacher education, and building and grounds.
8. The extent of responsibility for each administrative detail in an intramural department depends on the number of staff personnel, number of participants, experience, training and capabilities of staff and student workers, and local needs (finances, facilities, equipment, etc.).
9. When organizational details are outlined in check list form and followed according to schedule, efficient program operation is assured.

5

Finances, Facilities, and Equipment

Three separate yet interrelated aspects of the intramural sports program are finances, facilities, and equipment. The program's entire operation and scope depend on the amount of money available. This dollars and cents aspect, in turn, determines the type and extensiveness of facilities and the amount of equipment.

Without adequate funds, an intramural program cannot support a well-rounded sports and recreation calendar. Of necessity, many of the so-called "minor" sports have to be excluded. Without adequate funds, intramural programs are penalized by not having their own facilities and sufficient equipment for all who wish to participate.

FINANCES

Financing the intramural program is a major problem for the intramural director. Available funds often determine the quality and quantity of the program. A reasonable formula is "dollars and cents = staff, facilities, and equipment = program." An intramural program cannot be effective unless it is on a sound financial basis.

The financial needs of the program should be met with the same consistency and stability as any other phase of education. Intramural sports are not expensive. In a well-planned and well-directed intramural program, the value received is extraordinarly large compared to the low cost per individual participant, which can average as little as $1.00 to $2.00 yearly.

Sources of Income

Intramural programs are generally financed by one of the following methods:

1. *Physical education budget.* This method allocates funds for intramural activities from the total physical education budget. It is a satisfactory method provided a specific budget is in effect for intramurals and the original source is reliable.
2. *Athletic gate receipts.* When this source of revenue is used, gate receipts should be placed in the general school fund and then separate budgets should be approved for the intramural program and the varsity athletic program. (With this method, the existence of the I-M program depends upon adequate athletic gate receipts.) Complete reliance on gate receipts hinders the growth and development of the intramural program. When funds are inadequate the non-fund-producing program of intramurals suffers retrenchment. It is important to note, however, that many facilities used for the conduct of the intramural program are built with funds accumulated from gate receipts.
3. *Student activity fees.* This method is becoming increasingly popular, especially in colleges and universities. Students pay an activity fee at the beginning of each quarter or semester. A portion of this fee is budgeted for such activities as the student newspaper, student government association, student union program, and intramural programs for men and women. In a few large universities, the activity fee is used not only to maintain the program but also to help finance the construction of intramural buildings and recreational gymnasiums. If the intramural program cannot be financed by general school revenue, this activity fee method is more advantageous than allocations from athletic gate receipts.
4. *Entrance and forfeit fees.* Some intramural departments augment appropriations through charging entrance fees or forfeit fees. Entrance fees are charged at the time an individual or team registers for participation in a particular activity. The cost might range from $.50 for individual and dual sports to $2.50 for team sports, or approximately those amounts. In addition, an entrant might have to pay

a forfeit fee which is returned to him if he plays but which he loses if he forfeits the game. Entrance and forfeit fees violate one of the basic principles of intramural sports, namely, that the program should be "free and voluntary." Entrance fees are an obstacle for some students and discourage mass participation. They also are a nuisance to both the administration and the participant. Forfeit fees are a negative means of forcing students to participate. There should be no concern about forfeits if the intramural program is effectively and efficiently administered.

5. *Admission charges.* An additional way to obtain funds for the intramural program is to charge admission for intramural events such as sports nights, sports carnivals, faculty-student nights, corecreation sessions, exhibitions, or championship games. In general, this method of raising funds is not advisable. An intramural program should place emphasis on participation and not on general attendance at revenue-producing events. Much time is required to promote and administer such "shows" properly. Therefore, less time is available for the regular activities in the intramural department.
6. *Dues.* A method of defraying expenses within a department is to charge dues for membership in the recreation association or athletic councils. Cost of awards is sometimes defrayed through payment of dues by participating organizations such as fraternities, clubs, or dormitories.
7. *Other sources.* Additional funds can be raised for intramural program expenses through special fund-raising projects. Student sports clubs, associations, and athletic councils usually organize and administer these functions. The following list suggests types of activities which can be used for this purpose:

   a. Sports films
   b. Paper drives
   c. Concessions at games
   d. Athletic equipment sales
   e. Car washes
   f. Donkey basketball games
   g. Scrap metal drives
   h. Sales from athletic programs
   i. Bottle collections
   j. Sports tag days
   k. Magazine subscriptions
   l. School stationery sales

Some departments may be financed by a combination of two methods. For example, the facilities might be maintained from funds from athletic gate receipts and the program financed by funds from student fees. Ideally, the intramural department should have a separate budget financed by funds from the general revenue of the institution.

Budget Allocations

In preparing the budget, the intramural director must consider both *future* and *immediate* departmental expenditures. *Future* items include capital outlay for new facilities and maintenance of the present facilities. In most schools, future items are covered in the over-all athletic or physical education department budget or the over-all school budget. The intramural director should be familiar with all budget plans for capital outlay for new facilities. He may have little familiarity with allocations for maintenance of the facilities. When the question is asked, "How much does it cost to conduct intramurals in your school?" maintenance costs are often omitted in the answer because the director is not informed in this area. If facilities are used jointly for physical education classes, varsity athletic practices and games, and intramural programs, use by each division determines what percentage of the maintenance budget should be assigned to the respective programs.

The director is usually completely responsible for making up the *immediate* budget. Accurate participation records help predict increases or decreases in participation in various activities for next year; this assists in determining the budget requests. Items in the immediate budget should be relatively stable. For example, the past year's number of games played, plus the expected increase for the following year, times the rate of pay for officials and number of officials used per game should equal a reasonably accurate officials' budget figure. Funds must be budgeted for other items such as equipment, supplies, awards, staff salaries, and publicity. From year to year, these figures are easily adjusted by considering general cost increases and program expansion. The budget should not be padded, but every precaution should be taken to assure adequate funds to prevent program cutbacks.

FACILITIES

When considering the "unlimited potential" of the intramural sports program, the generalization can be made that all intramural facilities are inadequate. Obviously, some institutions have more ideal facilities than others. When increased student enrollments are taken into account, it is questionable if facilities can provide for the qualitative and quantitative objective of "a sport for everyone and everyone in a sport," particularly when some schools have difficulty securing adequate classroom space.

However, there are certain tendencies which are encouraging for the growth of intramurals. New school plants have better athletic facilities than the schools in the past. New construction and expansion of stadiums, field houses, and gymnasiums makes possible increased intramural activity. In some schools, old varsity athletic facilities are turned over to the intramural department.

One of the most encouraging trends is the construction of a special facility or gymnasium for intramural sports. A few large universities have already constructed them or are including them in their expansion plans. There are two major plans: (1) buildings used exclusively for intramurals on a corecreational basis; (2) buildings used predominantly for intramurals but not to the exclusion of physical education classes and varsity practices. One of the most important functions of the intramural program is to encourage students to make sports a daily habit through nonorganized "free play" activities. This objective is best attained with the corecreational building in plan one.

In the larger school system, physical education classes and varsity practices cause a restriction in the free-play activities of sports such as swimming, tennis, handball, paddleball, squash, basketball, trampoline, golf, badminton, archery, and weight lifting. Those students who do not have a continuous class schedule may desire to go to the gymnasium for a workout during a free period. Students at commuter schools often work out in the afternoon following their last class. Physical education classes and varsity practices sometimes prevent a facility from being available for free play at the right time. If a student finds the gymnasium unavailable once or twice, he might seek some other form of recreation, too often sedentary in nature. Only the student who understands the importance of physical exercise seeks to alter his schedule to conform to the availability of the facility.

An intramural sports building serves the campus as a center for physical recreation just as the student union building serves the campus as a center for social recreation. Whenever possible, indoor and outdoor facilities should be located close to student living units such as dormitories and fraternities. Properly located, attractive facilities encourage students to participate in physical recreation activities.

Indoor Facilities

In planning for new facilities, it should be remembered that substandard facilities mean a substandard program. For all games and sports, official court and field dimensions should be used whenever possible.

The following list indicates the types of areas which should be considered in planning an intramural sports building for men and women.

1. *Main gymnasium*
   –regulation basketball courts with dividing nets
   –regulation volleyball, badminton, and indoor tennis courts
2. *First auxiliary gymnasium*
   –regulation basketball, volleyball, badminton, and indoor tennis courts
3. *Second auxiliary gymnasium*
   –gymnastic area

–regulation basketball, volleyball, badminton, and indoor tennis courts

4. *Swimming pool*
   –L-shaped pool with beginner's area and special diving pool or 50-meter pool
5. *Wrestling and judo room*
6. *Boxing and punching-bag room*
7. *General exercise room*
   –weight lifting equipment and rowing machines
8. *Handball (and paddleball) courts*
9. *Squash courts (singles and doubles)*
10. *Golf driving-space*
    –driving nets
11. *Rifle range*
12. *Archery range*
13. *Game room*
    –table tennis tables, shuffleboard space; adequate room for darts, box hockey, box soccer
14. *Athletic council meeting room*
15. *Audio-visual room*
16. *Administrative offices*
    –director, assistant director, secretaries, I-M managers, sports club supervisors, others
17. *Lounge and lobby*
    –bulletin boards and trophy cases
18. *Training room or first aid room*
19. *Men's and women's locker rooms*
    –full and half lockers and basket combinations
20. *Men's and women's shower rooms*
21. *Faculty locker room*
22. *Steam and dry heat rooms*
23. *Equipment rooms*
24. *Janitorial storage and engine room*

A public address system is essential for a large recreational building to permit finding individuals in case of emergency or other reasons. Closed circuit television is helpful in supervising areas from a central location. A good lighting system eliminates the necessity of numerous colored lines on the gymnasium floor. Most gymnasiums have a different colored line for each court such as black for basketball, red for volleyball, white for tennis, and green for badminton. This maze of lines is confusing for the players. Lights built in the floor produce specific court lines which illuminate when the corresponding wall switch is turned on.

Outdoor Facilities

Accessibility to intramural facilities is extremely important for increased participation. Whenever possible, outdoor play areas should be located adjacent to indoor facilities. Outdoor intramural areas include the following: touch football fields; soccer and speedball fields; softball diamonds; baseball diamonds; tennis courts; volleyball courts; basketball courts; handball courts; horseshoe courts; track space; golf course; and skating rink.

Some areas can be used for dual purposes; for example, the field used for touch football in the fall can be used for softball in the spring; tennis practice boards can be used for one-wall handball. Blacktop areas can be used for tennis, basketball, or volleyball in the summer and for ice hockey and general skating in the winter.

Lighted fields for touch football, softball, and baseball offer an answer on campuses where space is limited. From 4:30 to 10:30 P.M., 24 one-hour touch football games can be played on 4 lighted fields; it would take 24 fields to care for the same programs were the games scheduled in daylight. In some sections of the country, only one game can be scheduled in the late afternoon because there are too few daylight hours. Where lighted fields are available, some students request playing under the lights because it is more attractive.

Co-operative Use of Facilities

In some schools, the same facilities are used for both the intramural program and physical education classes, or for intramurals and varsity athletic games and practices, or for all three programs. With joint usage, it is necessary to have a scheduling supervisor to clear all activities. Co-operation by all divisions is essential to avoid conflicts. Nothing is more discouraging to the participant than to show up for an intramural basketball game which has been canceled because of a previously scheduled varsity wrestling match.

One of the disadvantages of co-operative use of facilities is that intramural sports, because of lack of prestige, are often assigned the least desirable times. Where facilities are inadequate and there is conflict between intramurals and physical education or varsity athletics over use of certain areas, intramurals usually give way to the other programs. This is the reason two-way co-operation is imperative.

It is often necessary to rent commercial facilities for sports such as bowling, golf, roller skating, and ice skating. Rentals should be handled in a complete, business-like manner to assure the success of the immediate activity and future programs. Bonded carriers should be used when transporting participants to off-campus recreation.

EQUIPMENT

The extent to which intramural departments should furnish equipment for the various activities is debatable. Ideally, all of the equipment necessary for the conduct of the activities should be provided by the department. Realistically, most departments do not have sufficient funds to purchase all essential equipment. Some schools use equipment previously used by the varsity teams. At other schools, the physical education and intramural departments share the equipment. The objective of administering an efficient and attractive program should be kept in mind when deciding equipment policies. Obviously, students will be more likely to participate in an intramural program if they do not have to buy expensive equipment. Since the ideal situation seldom exists, the following policies can serve as a guide.

General Equipment Policies

For team games, it is customary for the intramural department to furnish team equipment such as the balls, bases, nets, and bats. But the department seldom furnishes personal equipment such as tennis shoes. Some student organizations have their own bats, gloves, racquets, shoes, jerseys. When possible, some intramural department equipment should be available on a check-out basis for teams and individuals who cannot afford to supply their own and thus would not be able to participate unless equipment were available to them.

A method of assuring new balls for single-elimination contests, for example, in tennis, is to have each contestant furnish three new balls. The loser of the match keeps the three balls used in the game; the winner of the match gets three new balls from the supply. With this system, each participant in the tournament buys only three balls and new balls are assured for every match.

The restriction on furnishing individual equipment for each member of the team should not apply to sports such as tackle football. Schools have the responsibility to protect players in contact sports, and seldom can players afford the expensive outfits used in contact sports. When trained varsity men find it necessary to use protective equipment, it is reasonable to say that the less highly trained intramural players should be similarly safeguarded.

The intramural department should furnish equipment for those individuals playing a specific position in a sport. For example, a baseball catcher should be furnished his outfit because this position requires protective equipment not necessary for the other eight positions on the team. Similarly, in hockey, the special protectors needed by goalies should be furnished. By recognizing these special needs, the intramural department aids the individuals whose particular playing position is hazardous and thereby keeps injuries to a minimum.

Nonscheduled or free-play recreational activities are greatly enhanced if participating groups are loaned the necessary equipment. This situation often arises when student or faculty groups have picnics or challenge games. Obviously, it is not advisable for them to buy materials that they would use only once or twice. The intramural department gains many friends by helping make these worthwhile occasions a success.

The formation of new clubs can be encouraged in sports such as judo, weight lifting, archery, and fencing, if equipment for these activities can be loaned or rented to participating individuals or teams. Such innovations depend upon the supply of adequate equipment for their successful introduction.

When the varsity and intramural departments work closely together, the intramural group can save considerable expense by using "secondhand" varsity equipment for I-M practices and games. When athletic authorities realize that the equipment receives a double use, balls, bats, and gloves will be turned over to intramural teams while still in good condition. As varsity departments pass on their older equipment to intramural departments, so the latter often contribute their worn materials to charitable organizations for their athletic programs.

Purchase of Equipment

An up-to-date inventory is the forerunner of an equipment purchase. The inventory report should be as simple as possible and include information about the type, quantity, and condition of the equipment in stock. It should also show what materials should be destroyed, repaired, and reordered. Figure 8 illustrates the kind of inventory report which should be taken in order to be fully aware of the equipment on hand.

In purchasing athletic equipment, consideration should be given to quality and design of the material, safety factors, cost of purchase and maintenance, and source of supply. Purchasers should not buy on price alone. Most equipment experts agree that it is more economical to spend more money for quality material than to purchase inexpensive merchandise. For example, poor-grade softball bats necessitate numerous reorders due to breakage, are less safe for the participant, and result in "unsatisfied contestants and cus-

Item	Size	Quantity	Poor	Good	New	Lost	Repair	Destroy	Replace
Baseballs		56	36	10	10				36
Baseball Bats		18	6	12					6
Basketballs		33	11	20		2			13
Boxing Gloves	Small	10	1	9			1		
Boxing Gloves	Medium	12	3	9					3
Boxing Gloves	Large	11	1	8	2			1	1
Catcher's Masks	Medium	2		1	1				
Catcher's Masks	Large	5	1	3	1		1		
Footballs		18	2	9	6	1			3
Hockey Pucks		24	18	4	2	2			26
Hockey Sticks		80	15	63	2			11	11
Horseshoes		40		40					
Hurdles		18	3	14	1		3		
Ice Skates	8	24	2	16	4	2			4
Ice Skates	9	6	1	4	1		1		
Ice Skates	10	15		12	2	1			1
Ice Skates	11	10	1	9			1		
Ice Skates	12	5		5					
Soccer Balls		12	1	10		1		1	2
Softballs		72	40	20	7	5			45
Squash Racquets		21	5	15	1				5
Squash Ball		48		40	8				
Table Tennis Nets		10	2	4	4		2		
Table Tennis Paddles		20	2	8	10				
Tennis Balls		72	47	19		6			53
Volleyballs		9	2	7					2
Volleyball Nets		5		5					
Wrestling Mats		2	1		1		1		

Figure 8. Intramural Equipment Inventory.

tomers." Most students, particularly at the college level, are good judges of superior and inferior equipment. Many problems in the equipment area are eliminated if orders are placed with reputable sporting goods dealers.

Some school systems require that bids be submitted on items of equipment. This method saves considerable money when buying from the lowest bidder, but there is some danger of receiving low quality merchandise. To eliminate this danger, intramural directors must exercise extreme care in preparing orders. The specifications of each item must be clearly outlined, with particular emphasis on the degree of quality desired. Where schools do not use the bidding system, it is wise for the purchaser to compare prices carefully and, if possible, to secure a sample of the item to be purchased. For the limited budget, the practice of buying "seconds," "closeouts," or reconditioned equipment is a practical means of getting fairly good material at low cost.

Sporting goods companies are quick to point out the value of ordering early. Early orders mean early deliveries and allow plenty of time to make necessary adjustments or revisions. Blanket requisitions, covering a specified amount of money for a limited period of time, assist departments in making minor or hurried purchases and in overcoming order and voucher delays.

Care of Equipment

Because the cost of equipment represents a sizable portion of the department budget, definite policies should be established to protect this investment. In small schools, the maintenance and issuance of equipment might be assigned to a faculty member who perhaps could receive extra compensation. Universities and colleges employ full- or part-time equipment managers who are responsible for cleaning, repairing, and issuing equipment and assigning lockers. Student managers often assist the staff manager.

Whenever possible, the equipment room should be large enough to house all intramural athletic equipment. This room should have adequate bins and racks to assure storage of equipment in a cool, clean, and dry environment. Good air circulation is extremely important for storing off-season athletic goods. Equipment stored without proper ventilation often rusts or mildews. All equipment should be clearly marked for size and identification with India ink, electric needle, or a special paint. An equipment room which is systematically arranged reduces the number of man-hours necessary to issue and care for equipment.

All equipment must be carefully checked out. Each student desiring to use equipment should fill out a requisition slip which includes the following information: (1) student's printed name, address, telephone, and locker number; (2) quantity and name of each item desired; (3) identification number of each item; (4) date and time of check-out; (5) date and time of return; and (6) a statement which says in effect that the equipment is loaned by the Intramural Department and the borrower agrees to pay for any unreturned or carelessly damaged equipment. Some locker room check-out systems require a deposit until the equipment is returned. This deposit can be money, a fee statement, ring, watch, or a shoe (particularly when the student changes to gym shoes).

It might be necessary to place a restriction on the length of time an individual can retain the equipment. The length of this time period depends on the amount of available equipment. Some departments require loaned equipment to be returned immediately following the game and others by noon of the following day. Unless this regulation is enforced, participants might keep the equipment for the entire season, thus preventing maximum use.

Sometimes it is possible to have the field or floor supervisor check out all the equipment used for a specific set of games. In this case, he reissues the equipment to the individual team managers who subdivide the responsibility. Each referee or umpire is held accountable for materials used in his respective games.

PROVISIONS FOR SAFETY

Schools have a moral obligation, if not a legal responsibility, to provide safe facilities and equipment. However, the school is relieved of liability if it adequately proves certified and competent staff members are employed. Individual teachers and coaches have greater responsibility than their school when they are proved negligent in conducting school activities.

The intramural director or supervisor must develop a sense of safety responsibility. Negligence can be avoided if safety precautions are constantly applied in program planning and administration. Emergency phone numbers should be posted on all I-M bulletin boards.

The major problem is to avoid or minimize injuries. It is estimated that approximately 50 per cent of all the injuries could be avoided if proper precautions were utilized. Injuries occur because of lack of conditioning, improper medical care, hazardous play areas, inadequate equipment, and poor officiating. Unfortunately, some injuries occur regardless of safety precautions.

Some schools have had to discontinue certain activities because of injuries which received inadequate treatment or bad publicity and which subsequently created unfavorable impressions on the school administrators. In these situations, it is important to compare the number of participants or exposures to injury with the actual rate of incidence. A good analogy is the small number of airplane accidents that occur in the millions of safe air miles flown.

The following safety check points should be set up to assist the intramural supervisor in overcoming negligence:

1. *Facilities.* All facilities should be inspected regularly and systematically. Padding should be installed on gymnasium walls and around poles or projecting obstacles. Fields should be level and free from holes, metal plates, and wooden softball bases (on touch football fields). Floors should be checked for slipperiness, particularly after a school dance. Teams should not play in crowded areas or outdoors during inclement weather. For example, if two softball diamonds are adjacent, ample room should be allowed to avoid collision of outfielders.
2. *Equipment.* If possible, all equipment should be provided and should be kept in good condition. There is a tendency

for players to play with less protective equipment, especially when players furnish their own or use hand-me-down, substandard material. Providing baseball catchers' and hockey goalies' equipment greatly minimizes injuries. Checking out track shoes for meets offers better traction for runners and reduces falls caused by gymnasium shoes on a cinder surface.

3. *Medical examination.* Each participant should have a yearly health examination before competing in the I-M program. Students who fail the health examination are not eligible for intramural play and should be checked with extreme care.
4. *Play supervision and officiating.* Supervisors should be in attendance at all contests and know exactly what procedures to follow in case of injury. Entrants should be encouraged to condition before participating and should not be eligible to compete in sports such as wrestling, boxing, track, and cross country without completing a required number of workouts.

Student officials must be made aware of the important role they play in preventing injuries. In touch football, numerous injuries occur because of unnecessary roughness in blocking and tagging or touch tackling. Strict officiating alleviates needless injuries. Officials must insist that players wearing glasses also wear plastic eye guards. Rules can be modified to eliminate hazardous conditions. Examples in touch football include declaring the ball dead when a dropped ball hits the ground and prohibiting players from leaving their feet when administering a tag.

Intramural directors should not promote activities unless safe playing areas and protective equipment are available. Safety policies and procedures must be clearly defined and effectively administered. Accurate accident reports provide important data for revising and keeping up-to-date safety rules and regulations.

SUMMARY

1. Available funds often determine the quality and quantity of the intramural program. A reasonable formula is "dol-

lars and cents = staff, facilities, and equipment = program."

2. Intramural sports are not expensive. In a well-planned and well-directed program, the cost per participant averages as little as $1.00 to $2.00 yearly.
3. Intramural programs are most frequently financed by the physical education budget, athletic gate receipts, student activity fees, entrance and forfeit fees, admission charges, and dues.
4. In preparing an intramural budget, consideration should be given to the *Immediate* and *Future* expenditures of the department.
5. The budget should not be padded, but every precaution should be taken to assure adequate funds to prevent program cutbacks.
6. When considering the "unlimited potential" of the intramural sports program, the generalization can be made that all intramural facilities are inadequate.
7. Encouraging to the growth of intramurals is the construction or planned construction of intramural sports buildings or recreational gymnasiums.
8. Buildings used exclusively for intramurals on a corecreational basis are most satisfactory to an adequate intramural program.
9. Intramural sports buildings or recreational gymnasiums should include areas and facilities to handle as many different types of sports and activities as possible.
10. Whenever possible, outdoor play areas should be located adjacent to indoor facilities to stimulate participation through accessibility.
11. Where facilities are used co-operatively by the intramural, physical education, and varsity athletic departments, supervised scheduling and interdepartmental co-operation are essential.
12. The extent to which intramural departments should furnish equipment is debatable.
13. Usually, team equipment is provided while individuals must equip themselves.
14. Nonscheduled or "free play" recreational activities are greatly enhanced if such groups are loaned the necessary equipment.
15. When the varsity and intramural departments work closely

together, considerable expense is saved by using second-hand varsity equipment for I-M practices and games.

16. An up-to-date inventory is essential before purchasing equipment.
17. In purchasing equipment, consideration should be given to quality and design, safety factors, cost and maintenance, and source of supply.
18. Equipment should be carefully supervised, if possible by a staff member, and stored in a properly ventilated room.
19. A check-out system should be used to insure proper return of equipment.
20. Schools have a moral obligation, if not a legal responsibility, to provide safe facilities and equipment.
21. The major problem is to avoid or minimize injuries.
22. Safety is emphasized by regular inspection of facilities, use of proper equipment, annual medical examinations, competent officiating, and adequate supervision of play.

6

Units of Competition

The selection of units for the successful promotion of intramural competition differs according to the size and type of institution. The ties of connection among the students attending school in their home city are much different from those that exist when college students live away from home or on campus. In some schools located in large metropolitan areas, the commuter student presents special problems. Even in colleges and universities there are many differences, for some have dormitories and fraternities and others do not. It is evident, therefore, that the matter of what units to use is one for each institution to decide after making a careful survey of its local situation—age interests, group connections, size of school, and facilities.

A number of sports, such as track, tennis, wrestling, bowling, swimming, handball, squash, archery, and badminton, are individualistic in nature and, consequently, do not depend entirely upon a group spirit. For this reason, it is not necessary to base the promotion of these sports about any particular unit; and many departments conduct, instead, the *all-campus* tournaments which are open to all eligible students regardless of affiliation. This, in reality, makes of each individual a unit by himself.

Despite the close dependence of units upon local conditions, the class unit—freshman, sophomore, junior, senior—is frequently used. Its popularity, however, is more in evidence in smaller schools. In larger schools, classes are larger and thus may become too unwieldy to use as a unit. As this situation develops, smaller, more solidly organized units, such as the fraternity or the high-school homeroom, are a more effective means of bringing about rivalry and increased participation.

In general, the larger the unit is in size, the more difficult it is to organize for competition. An impersonal relationship exists between the members of the unit, so that they must be continually encouraged by efforts of the intramural authorities and class managers. A large group has more candidates for the one team and this means extra work to select team members. Such a situation is not difficult to handle when there is a staff of coaches on hand, such as the varsity possesses; but intramural authorities are limited in the amount of personal help they can give the student teams and cannot depend on student managership entirely to handle the large unit.

The unit based upon a common residence, such as the fraternity, dormitory, or homeroom, is usually the most successful. The one great advantage this type of unit has over the class unit is that it provides a common and regular meeting place where announcements are made, discussions held, group spirit aroused, and trophies displayed.

Inasmuch as the relative importance of a unit is seldom the same in each institution, the units of competition are discussed in their relation to the small and large college and university, senior high schools, junior high schools, elementary schools, and women's programs.

COLLEGES AND UNIVERSITIES

More units of competition are available in colleges and universities than in high schools and elementary schools. Many schools and universities are large enough to use a considerable number of units but are handicapped because of limited facilities. In this case, the larger and more democratic units should be utilized so that a maximum number of students use the facilities.

SMALL COLLEGES	LARGE COLLEGES AND UNIVERSITIES
Class units	Class units
Fraternity units	Fraternity units
Dormitory units	Dormitory units
Independent groups	Independent groups
Geographical units	Geographical units
Department groups	College and department groups
Sport club units	Sport club units
Boarding club units	Boarding club units
Graduate-student groups	Military units
Corecreation groups	Religious groups
Individual student groups	Foreign-student units
Faculty groups	Graduate-student groups
Summer-session groups	Corecreation groups
	Individual student groups
	Faculty groups
	Summer-session groups

CLASS UNITS. This type of unit works well in both small and large schools but relatively more so in smaller institutions. Here, the limited size of the classes helps make members well acquainted with their classmates; this leads to a strong class unity, which, in turn, means spirited competition between the classes. A drawback in the larger schools is the small number of players for which the class unit provides.

The class unit is the most democratic unit; it draws no social distinction. Class traditions already exist so that a class spirit, similar on a small scale to the so-called "school spirit," can be aroused. With increasing enrollments, class morale is exceedingly difficult to develop. Furthermore, the class teams, because of the many candidates from which they draw, generally provide the most skilled intramural competition. The organization of the class teams is thus a selective process. The knowledge that the class team is the highest achievement in intramural competition offers an incentive for players on other teams to improve their abilities.

FRATERNITY UNITS. In practically every institution of higher education in which they exist, fraternities are a most successful unit for intramural competition. They are already well organized and loyalty is present to a high degree. It is relatively simple to carry over this spontaneous loyalty into a program of athletic competition.

Fraternity competition is so popular that even Class "B" leagues are formed in the leading intramural sports. These leagues provide for men who do not have the skill required to make the first team and yet are eager to play. In a sense, they are comparable to the second teams of high schools. Rules must be provided so that while players of Class "A" teams do not interchange with Class "B," Class "B" players can move up to Class "A" teams.

This scheme of permitting the organization to enter two or more teams, graded on the Class "A," "B," and "C" plan, is only practical where the candidates are well known to each other, such as in the fraternity, or where a very close supervision is exercised, such as the varsity and second team. The method of classification in itself is preferable to methods such as weight, for it automatically provides a division of players according to their respective abilities.

The permanency of fraternity groups makes them well adapted for competition that carries over the whole year. Some intramural systems conduct separate leagues for the national and local fraternities; the more common practice opposes any differentiation. However, it is common and good practice to provide separate competition for professional fraternities, for their representatives are on the graduate level.

DORMITORY UNITS. Where dormitories exist, it is relatively easy to develop a spirited athletic rivalry between them. Dormitories have some of the advantages of the fraternity, i.e., loyalty and social tradition already exist, communication is easy between the members, team trophies are enjoyed by all, and there is the permanency that is important in the success of point systems which evaluate all-year efficiency. The social relationship of the dormitory also brings about an interest in the younger members on the part of the more experienced upperclassmen; in actual practice, this interest encourages more men to try out for sports and offer coaching advice.

There are many methods of organizing competition using this unit. The simplest of these chooses one representative team from each dormitory. The more complicated plans secure more teams by combining the dormitory idea with some other combination, such as the class, weight classification, or "A" and "B" differentiation. If a combination plan is used, this does not necessarily mean that having one representative team from each house must be abandoned. The minor leagues can be run preliminary to, or following, the choosing of the major team. Another innovation in dormitory competition is the use of houses, wards, blocks, or floors of the dormitory as units of competition. For example, eight basketball teams represent the third floor of Dormitory C. A similar number of teams are organized on the second floor and these teams compete with each other.

INDEPENDENT GROUPS. The intramural program faces one of its biggest problems in attracting the students not belonging to any fraternity, society, dormitory, or regularly organized group. Many "independents" are reached by using the school units, such as class or department, but usually these are the ones possessing considerable athletic skill. Again, many independents are reached through other leagues (military, religious, geographical) which bring fraternity men and independents together on a common footing. There still remains a large number of independents, however, who are not skilled players and not socially enough inclined to join some organization. These individuals are most effectively reached through required physical education classes. Some departments conduct independent leagues in the more popular activities and open these leagues to any informal group that submits a list of eligible players. The ability of the leaders of these groups largely determines their measure of success. These groups never arouse more than a temporary interest and a few defeats often cause the team to disband. Nevertheless, this unit provides good training for many individuals who would otherwise be neglected, and who, as a rule, are the ones needing it the most.

Intramural departments in large universities are frequently criticized because their programs feature fraternity and dormitory sports to an extent that outwardly signifies favoritism when compared with the activities of nonfraternity-dormitory students (independents). Greater proportions of fraternity and dormitory students are reached than nonfraternity-dormitory students; but the situation does not reflect intentional favoritism. Intramural authorities are interested in all groups, but fraternities and dormitories are already organized and easily accessible. On the other hand, the independents must be stimulated to organize themselves before they participate. Even then, their organization lacks the permanency, loyalty, and convenience which are the prominent factors in making the fraternity and dormitory units so successful. Fortunately, independent groups are becoming better organized and more cohesive.

One of the major problems in intramural administration is to develop a tradition in these independent groups which results in some permanency of competition. The independent groups might carry their interest over from year to year if a greater group spirit is developed. When this is done, independent groups can enjoy the use of the group-scoring plan which applies to fraternities, dormitories, and other highly organized units.

Geographical units. At certain schools, clubs representing counties or school districts develop considerable spirit and respond well to the intramural program. Students coming from a certain city can organize a high-school alumni club. These groups have an advantage. The members are usually acquainted with each other and therefore know each other's athletic ability.

Other units of this type, as found in the larger universities, are state clubs and larger sections in which several states are combined. The latter case is often associated with the activities of freshman classes; the classes are divided geographically and the members of one section are assigned to particular upperclass advisors.

In general, the close relationship between students in these geographical units, which is so essential for an enthusiastic, permanent competitive group, is lacking. Nevertheless, in some schools, these groups are highly organized units in the intramural program.

Much of the interest displayed by district or sectional organizations depends upon the frequency with which they meet for other business and social purposes. As a general rule, much follow-up work is needed to keep the athletic interest alive.

Another geographical unit is the campus zone. The campus is divided into a number of zones from which intramural teams are organized. Population rather than area should determine the size of the zone.

College and department units. Competition between teams representing various colleges of the university or departments of a college can be substituted for interclass games or are promoted in addition to the interclass program. Competition between departments of a college can attain an important place in the intramural program of a smaller school where departments assume the same role that colleges do in a large university. While the interdepartment league is also found in large universities, it occupies a position of secondary importance owing to the existence of the larger intercollege unit.

Sometimes a preliminary league is conducted within each college to pick a representative college team. This league is by classes within the college or by departments. The class is preferable because it draws more definite eligibility lines. While a player's class is easy to establish, his department may not be because the educational training of the underclassman is general in nature and often he does not choose his department of specialization until his junior year.

Sport club units. Sport clubs are most popular in small colleges. An arbitrary number of clubs is designated, and interested incoming students are assigned to them. Students are members of the same clubs throughout their collegiate days. College nicknames, major league baseball nicknames, or colors are often used as club names. The main advantage of sport clubs is that they provide cohesion and group loyalty.

The sport club idea is also successful in certain specialized activities where there is a small but enthusiastic group of followers. Sociability is stressed along with interest in the sport. Outing clubs where picnics are part of the program are an example. Skiing, figure skating, archery, canoeing, sailing, riding, badminton, rifle shooting, and weight lifting are sports that lend themselves well to the formation of sport clubs.

Boarding club units. Boarding clubs or eating co-operatives are units which meet with considerable success. The tie that holds the team members together is mainly one of friendship from frequent association at meal times. This common meeting place gives the boarding house an advantage over the groups that are similary based on social acquaintance but which are scattered and do not meet except for practice or a game. Interest in these leagues is greatly furthered when the boarding club gives a banquet for its players at the close of the season.

Military units. In military schools and colleges and universities which provide branches of military and naval training, competition is frequently organized among companies, batteries, or troops. The attitude of the military authorities largely decides whether this plan is successful. If their co-operation is not secured, the leagues usually lose their student support. Much success is attained if the military authorities sympathize with competitive athletics.

There should be complete co-operation between the military authorities and the intramural department. If military unit winners compete for all-school championships, the intramural department should maintain greater control in coordinating the program.

The group-scoring point system can be introduced very successfully with the intercompany type of competition, for these units preserve their identity throughout the whole year.

Religious groups. In many college communities, churches conduct student denominational clubs, and it is possible to arouse athletic interest in these groups. The success of such a league depends largely upon a strong leadership in each of the clubs. It is well to get the co-operation of the Students' Religious Association in this enterprise, for it is usually in close touch with the groups concerned and acts in a centralizing capacity. The church unit is primarily successful with popular sports such as basketball, baseball, and touch football. The group's natural interests determine what other sports can be conducted successfully.

Foreign student units. In some schools, where the number of foreign students is sufficient, separate units are organized for them. Often these students are sensitive to their shortcomings in American sports. For this reason, activities should be adapted to the students. Soccer and volleyball are two team sports in which they usually excel.

Graduate student groups. In large universities, the intramural department provides competition for students doing advanced study. Individual, rather than team sports, usually have greater appeal for graduate students since it is difficult for large numbers to get together at regular intervals for team competition. These older students often prefer less vigorous sports.

Corecreation groups. One of the most progressive developments in some intramural programs is the inclusion of corecreational activities. College men and women participate in badminton, swimming, tennis, golf, table tennis, archery, volleyball, and bowling. Advantages of the corecreational trend in intramural athletics are: (1) contributing new and wholesome opportunities for congenial companionship; (2) resultant ease of adjustment in mixed social groups; (3) enhanced self-expression and happiness from participation in athletic, social, and creative activities; and (4) increased self-confidence and assurance from better skill in performance and ease of group adjustment that such participation engenders.

INDIVIDUAL STUDENT GROUPS. Students who are not affiliated with any particular group are urged to sign up individually for intramural activities. These students can be assigned to teams at a mass meeting. Team managers and team names are selected at these meetings. This method is particularly effective at large universities.

FACULTY GROUPS. Intramural authorities often promote competition for faculty members. Rarely, in small schools, are there ever enough faculty athletic enthusiasts to form a faculty league. The prevailing situation is to find one faculty team—usually made up of younger men—who play challenge games with student teams or with other adult teams chosen from representative clubs of the city. Where there are facilities for individual sports, however, the faculty usually uses them with enthusiasm. In the larger schools, some faculty competition is possible, usually between the faculties of the different colleges.

SUMMER SESSION GROUPS. With increased registrations in summer sessions at colleges and universities, intramural departments have increased responsibilities. Graduates, who actively participated in intramural or varsity programs during their college days, feel that some activity should be indulged in for relaxation and recreation, as a chance to "get away from the books."

Originally, only a small group of students indulged in play activities. However, the chance to get out of doors in the sunlight lured many more.

Because of the rather loosely knit organization of the summer session, and because of the short intensive period of study, it is rather difficult to set up definite lines of demarcation for units in summer sessions. Consequently, schemes must be devised to fit local needs. Teams usually consist of representatives of various departments, organizations, faculty groups, and independent groups. These teams play in the same league or tournament.

The team sport that particularly lends itself to a summer-school recreation program is softball. One method of organizing the summer-school students into a softball league is to have it comprised of superintendents, principals, high-school teachers, and university faculty members. This four-team league is very successful. If desired, the league could be enlarged to six teams by adding teams from undergraduate students and graduate students, respectively. Another practice is to have a separate four-team student league and have the champions of the two leagues play off in a summer-school "World Series."

Considerable interest is shown in purely recreative and more individualistic activities such as golf, tennis, badminton, swimming, horseshoes, table tennis, handball, and squash. The tournaments in these activities are run on a regular elimination basis.

SENIOR HIGH SCHOOLS

Senior-high units are based primarily on school divisions instead of the miscellaneous type used in junior-high and elementary grades. Because of the diversification of interests among high-school students and the fact that they are individually classified for various curriculum units rather than by groups as they are in lower grades, it is more difficult to reach a large portion of the student body through intramurals. For this reason, the director spends much time on promotional work in addition to the organizational phases of the program. Since this situation is comparable to that which exists in colleges and universities, a high-school intramural director should study collegiate program techniques.

The relative order of importance of intramural units in the senior high school is as follows:

1. Grade or class units
2. Homeroom units
3. Physical education sections
4. Residential or geographical units
5. Arbitrary units
6. Departmental units
7. Prevocation units
8. Corecreation groups
9. Society units
10. Military units
11. Faculty groups

GRADE OR CLASS UNITS. In the smaller standard four-year high schools, teams representing the four classes—freshman, sophomore, junior, and senior—are most prevalent. This is especially true in school systems that have the ninth, tenth, eleventh, and twelfth grades together; that is, they either do not use the junior high school plan at all or use the 6–2–4, which only includes the seventh and eighth grades in the junior high school. The four classes are as many as can be accommodated in many high schools. In the larger systems, it is advisable to adopt a classification revision which results in more teams, such as following the two-semester plan in which there are two teams from each class (11A, 11B, 12A, 12B, etc.). If there are three grades in the school, the plan produces six teams—10A, 10B, 11A, 11B, 12A, and 12B.

HOMEROOM UNITS. In the homeroom, students are assembled under one teacher for purposes of studying and holding classes. Students report to these rooms at the beginning of the morning and afternoon sessions and during periods when they do not have classes. Homeroom leagues are often called "session room," "house," or "study room" leagues. Friendly rivalry between the different homerooms is easy to foster because of a common assembly place. This provides a feeling of unity, facilitates making announcements, and arouses pride in the possession of group awards.

PHYSICAL EDUCATION SECTIONS. Teams are organized according to physical education sections. This procedure works well if all students in the school take physical education. However, in many high schools, facilities are not sufficient to handle all students and in others, eleventh- and twelfth-grade students do not take physical education because it is elective rather than required. When teams are formed for competition, they should play their games outside of and not during the physical education period. Class time should be spent teaching students physical skills which they can voluntarily utilize in the intramural and other community recreation programs. Because older students do not devote much time to physical education classes and many have increased interests outside of school, a stronger bond than the gymnasium section is needed to create enthusiasm for participation.

Residential or geographical units. Another method of selecting teams is to group players from the districts or areas in which they live. These sections can be determined by plotting school attendance on a map and making equitable divisions of the school district. In making these divisions, it is desirable to follow natural boundaries, if they permit fair competition. Because of the large drawing area of a senior high school, many districts or wards are apt to be represented, and consequently there are more teams. At the same time, however, there could be a lessening of student interest in units of this type. This unit is often used to reach students who do not compete with other units of competition. Students are sometimes grouped according to school bus routes.

Arbitrary units. This unit, sometimes called the independent unit, includes teams which are formed by lot and designate captains from a miscellaneous group of students. Division of players can be made alphabetically, by numbers or by choosing sides. It is frequently used in combination with other units to involve students not included in other categories. While competition under this unit is enjoyable, it is frequently harder to organize activities of continuing interest. There could be a lessening of enthusiasm for participation based on the "pick-up" team idea. It is necessary, therefore, to encourage players to band together, form sports clubs or athletic clubs, and participate with the same group throughout the entire school year. Units which have a strong tie of loyalty are best able to overcome lack of enthusiasm and succeed.

DEPARTMENTAL UNITS. This grouping is on the basis of the curriculum of studies: college preparatory, industrial, commercial, agricultural, and specialized trade. The method, though not used extensively, does offer another way of reaching more students in large high schools. One disadvantage is that it can create undue rivalry among groups who are not on comparable intelligence levels.

PREVOCATION UNITS. Another unit which can be used in the vocational high school or in secondary schools which have prevocational departments is the prevocation unit. For example, students majoring in tinsmithing can form one unit; electricians, another; patternmakers, another; mechanics, still another, and so on. Students from each area of study can enter teams in regular school intramural leagues.

CORECREATION GROUPS. Although not used as extensively as it might be, the corecreation unit for high schools is completely desirable. It is at the high-school age that boy-girl relationships are often not understood. The reader is directed to the discussion on corecreation in Chapter 13 which applies to high-school and college students. Numerous activities can be conducted on a coparticipation basis to give students meaningful experiences in a wholesome atmosphere.

SOCIETY UNITS. Some success is gained in organizing competition based on the various societies of the school—literary, debating, science, glee, and radio clubs and dramatic associations, orchestras, and honor groups are the most prominent. However, members of these groups are usually so devoted to their own specialized fields that they have little time for intramurals. For this reason, these students should be encouraged to participate in physical recreation.

MILITARY UNITS. High schools that have military programs can use regiments, battalions, divisions, companies, squads, etc., for units of competition. These are excellent means for creating rivalries because military authorities usually arrange nonathletic competition among these units and consequently there is a natural arrangement for intramurals. Often, it is only necessary to provide facilities, officials, awards, and equipment, while actual control of participation remains with the military officers.

FACULTY GROUPS. Only large high schools have enough faculty members for intramural competition among themselves; all high schools have enough staff personnel to conduct faculty-student competition. Although the high-school student is much younger than the faculty, he can hold his own in competition because of better conditioning and training.

JUNIOR HIGH SCHOOLS AND ELEMENTARY SCHOOLS

In junior high schools and elementary schools, age interests do not demand the high specialization in play that can only be maintained in a sharply defined and permanent group. Participation in the primary grades is usually on a free-play basis, but for the fourth, fifth, and sixth grades, play can be on an intra- or intergrade basis. For these grades, and particularly during junior high years, the gang spirit is so strong that teams are formed almost at will by the instructor, whereas with older students there is a greater necessity for loyalty ties that bind members together. Players of this age spend much time together and know each other well; hence, a good *esprit de corps* is quickly aroused with little effort by the intramural director. For this reason, it is not as necessary to define units of competition at this school level. All units usually work well because students are basically interested in belonging to and playing with a group.

Specific units of competition used successfully in junior high schools and elementary schools are listed below:

1. Grade or class units
2. Homeroom units
3. Physical education sections
4. Residential or geographical units
5. Arbitrary groups
6. Boy Scout troops
7. Corecreation groups

GRADE OR CLASS UNITS. Teams representing various grades, such as fifth, sixth, seventh, and eighth grades, are successful for conducting intramural competition. One objection to competition between grades is that higher grades have an advantage because of the rapid physical development of pupils at this age. This disadvantage is offset by classification and handicapping methods. Students in higher grades often lose interest in participating because of other available activities as they progress toward graduation. Enthusiasm among lower-grade students compensates for lack of skills.

HOMEROOM UNITS. One team can represent each homeroom or, if facilities and group size permit, players can be classified so that two or three teams are entered from each homeroom. This is an excellent method for forming teams because of close-knit friendships developed in the homeroom. It is also easy to inform teams when they play, etc., because this information is given to the players together with other general school announcements. Another method has one team organized in each homeroom and remaining players play in another league which is conducted independently on a weight classification plan. Captains are appointed and teams are formed regardless of homeroom connections.

PHYSICAL EDUCATION SECTIONS. This unit works well in elementary schools and junior high schools because almost all students take physical education. One or more teams are organized from each physical education class (such teams do not participate as teams in the classes). As mentioned in the discussion of senior high school units, physical education class time should be used for teaching purposes and not intramurals.

Gymnasium section members are divided into as many teams as the class size warrants, and a series of competitions takes place among these representative teams outside of class time. Team names can be assigned on the jungle idea; animal names are used, e.g., bears, lions, tigers, wolves. Frequently, teams are named for large universities, e.g., Harvard, Yale, Princeton, Stanford, or for big league baseball teams, e.g., Yankees, Cubs, Indians, Giants, Braves. Teams are placed under the direction of student leaders from the respective physical education classes who serve as team managers or team captains.

Residential or geographical units. This is the same method used in senior high schools where teams are organized by residential areas in which members live. If a school includes several wards of a city, it is feasible to use the official boundaries of these wards. Where sharp social distinctions exist between sections of a city, care must be exercised in using this unit or feelings of antagonism could be intensified.

Arbitrary units. This unit can be used in combination with other units or independently. The intramural director can call a meeting of all students desirous of belonging to a team and at that time organize as many teams as possible. As in the physical education sections, teams can be named for animals, universities, big league teams, colors, etc. Some schools arbitrarily place all students in one of two color divisions for intraschool playdays. Each student maintains his identity with his color team throughout his school career. School colors are usually chosen. Field-day events are set up with modified rules for boys and girls. On prearranged dates, perhaps once during fall, winter, and spring, classes are dismissed for participation in the playday and the color winner is determined by meet points.

The intramural director can divide students into arbitrary groups or appoint or elect captains and have them choose teams. It is essential to distribute the players' talents evenly. Captains choose players alternately until four, six, or eight players are chosen. Then, the captain who had last choice picks the fifth, seventh, and ninth players, respectively, according to the number of players in each group, until all participants are selected. In other words, the captains reverse the order of their choice after a certain number of contestants are selected. From a mental hygiene standpoint, it is advisable to have the "choosing up" done when the players are not present so poorer performers are not subjected to the humiliation of being selected last.

BOY SCOUT TROOPS. Schools in which Boy Scout troops are organized can promote group competition in both athletic and scouting activities. When this unit is used, it is very important that intramural and scouting authorities should co-operate closely. The athletic program should not be stressed so it overshadows the interest in other types of scouting education. Intramural workers find this unit leads to much individual interest and practice, for considerable proficiency is required to pass scout tests in athletics, physical development, and health.

CORECREATION GROUPS. Most physical education activities in elementary schools are conducted on a coeducational basis. Therefore, corecreational intramural activities are a logical extension of physical education classes. Unfortunately, this is not as true in junior high schools and it is most desirable to promote corecreation activities as much as possible. It is never too early to clarify many of the relationships which exist between boys and girls.

WOMEN'S DEPARTMENTS

Practically all units mentioned in this chapter are suitable for the girls' and women's program. A few, however, are especially appropriate for girls' intramural activities. The class unit is usually of greater importance to women than men because varsity-type athletics are not prevalent and class teams are often the best coached and most proficient. In colleges and universities, housing conditions encourage dormitory, sorority, and boarding club units of competition. Obviously, the units must be adapted to fit their own usage.

Another method which is extremely popular in many areas is the Girls' or Women's Athletic and Recreation Association. These associations are closely knit groups of sports clubs, each with a specialized interest. They sponsor all-campus tournaments as a service to the entire student body and they conduct closed tournaments for their particular club. If the latter, it is necessary for the women's intramural director to conduct a tournament for nonmembers of the club.

A few intramural programs are arranged on a corecreational basis with many activities for both boys and girls and some separate tournaments for boys and others for girls.

SUMMARY

1. The selection of units for the successful promotion of intramural competition will differ according to the size and type of institution.
2. A careful survey of the local situation, including age interests, group connections, size of school, and facilities will be valuable in determining what units of competition to use.
3. The larger the unit is in size, the more difficult it becomes to organize.
4. The interclass unit is successful in both small and large schools but relatively more so in the smaller institutions.
5. Fraternities, where they exist, are a highly successful unit of competition because of their close organization.
6. Dormitories, where they exist, also are successful units of competition, possessing many of the same qualities as fraternities.
7. Where groups are large enough it is often feasible to subdivide them for intramural participation by means of class differentiation, "A" and "B" groups, or by a simple weight classification such as lightweights and heavyweights.
8. The intramural department has a major responsibility to attract students not belonging to any organized group such as fraternities and dormitories.
9. At certain schools, clubs representing counties or school districts have proved successful for intramural competition.
10. Competition between teams representing the various colleges or departments of a school are often successful.
11. Sports clubs, boarding clubs, military units, religious groups, foreign students, and graduate groups, where they exist, are often successful units of competition.
12. Corecreation is one of the most progressive developments in intramural programs.

13. Faculty members should be encouraged to participate in intramural activities, either as teams or as individuals.
14. Fewer units of competition are available for use in elementary schools and junior and senior high schools than in colleges and universities.
15. Senior high-school units include grades or classes, homerooms, physical education sections, residential or geographical, arbitrary groups, departmental, prevocational, corecreation, societies, military units, and faculty.
16. In junior high schools and elementary schools, age interests do not demand a high specialization of play.
17. Specific units of competition for junior high schools and elementary schools include grades or classes, homerooms, physical education sections, residential or geographical, arbitrary groups, Boy Scout troops, and corecreation.
18. Classes, boarding clubs, dormitories, and sororities are successful units of competition for girls' and women's intramural programs.
19. Girls' and Women's Athletic and Recreation Associations conduct intramural-type programs in many schools.

7

Program of Activities

The intramural program of activities varies according to local conditions. Some sports, such as basketball, baseball, and track, are popular with all schools; other sports are peculiar to different localities. Lacrosse, squash, soccer, fencing, and rifle shooting are carried on to a much greater extent in the East than in the central states or the far West. Hockey and other ice sports are usually confined to the northern sections. A number of institutions throughout the country have indoor rinks which make possible the inclusion of ice hockey in the intramural program. Ice carnivals are annual occasions in some schools.

Team games are more popular with the average school participant than games emphasizing individual ability. Students also prefer games which do not require long preliminary practice or a great amount of equipment and expense. Basketball is ideal as an intramural game and proves to be the most successful sport in almost every locality; softball is a close second. It is observed that the average intramural player does not train for a sport. While desiring to see his team win, he does not subject himself to an intensive training schedule to facilitate winning. In certain sports (wrestling, for example), the intramural champion can be recognized as one of the outstanding participants in the school. In such cases, there is the incentive to train and win this recognition.

Sports chosen for general promotion among the student body should arouse a spontaneous interest and provide invigorating exercise without resulting in complete exhaustion. The trend is to expand the original program of developmental sports to include recreative sports and, finally, novelty sports as well. The so-called "rugged sports," which require careful training and leave the untrained player chiefly concerned with his bruised and exhausted condition, do not meet the situation as successfully as the more recreative types. When the more vigorous sports are included in the intramural program, it is extremely important to adhere to strict training rules and regulations. In general, the intramural player prefers games which provide active fun without depleting his whole reserve power.

In selecting sports, the size of the school and the age of the students should first be considered, and then attention should be given to local facilities and desires. The greatest variety can be promoted in the large collegiate institutions where students come from all sections of the country. Such a cosmopolitan group is sure to have some of its members interested in almost any conceivable branch of athletic activity. A few sports well promoted, however, constitute a better program than a hodgepodge of many sports which are not popular enough to warrant encouragement.

The program should keep pace with the changing and developing desires of the student body. A new intramural department should limit itself to the few sports which are popular and later introduce other sports as their desirability becomes evident. Where the budget is limited, the activities which reach the greatest number in proportion to the amount expended should receive first attention.

The number of sports that can be offered by any one school depends upon the available facilities, staff, and equipment. The following comprehensive list includes activities used in various elementary, high-school, and college intramural programs:

aerial darts
archery
badminton
baseball
basketball
bike racing
billiards
blitzball
board track relays
boat pulling
bowling
box hockey
boxing
canoeing
cards
checkers
chess
codeball
cricket
croquet
cross country

curling
deck tennis
endball
fencing
field floor hockey
field hockey
figure skating
flag football
fly baitcasting
football agility test
free throw contest
golf
golf putting
gymnastics
handball
hexathlon
hockey
hole-in-one golf
horseshoes
ice carnival
indoor baseball
judo
kickball
lacrosse
life saving
150 lb. basketball
outdoor volleyball
paddleball
paddle tennis
pistol shooting
pushball
racquet tennis
relays
riding
rifle shooting
rowing
roller hockey
sailing
shuffleboard
Sigma Delta Psi
six-man football
skeet shooting
skiing
soccer
softball—fast pitch
softball—slow pitch
speedball
speed skating
splashketball
squash
steeplechase run
sweepstakes
swimming
table tennis
tackle football
tennis
touch football
track and field
tumbling
turkey run
twenty-one
two-man volleyball
volleyball
water basketball
water polo
weight lifting
wrestling

Sports tend to group themselves naturally into the three seasons of the school year—fall, winter, and spring. It is by seasons that they can be most advantageously discussed. Some are adaptable to more than one season and should be promoted accordingly, but for the most part the divisions are seasonal.

Students attending school during the summer months desire a recreational program, and it is the responsibility of the intramural department to provide one for them. A discussion of the program for the summer session, therefore, has been included following the fall, winter, and spring activities. Only the principal sports on the seasonal calendar are discussed in this chapter.

FALL

With the exception of touch football, there are few universally popular fall games. In addition, the number of sports from which a selection can be made is smaller than in either of the other two seasons. However, to prevent overactivity during a particular season, it is essential to arrange an equal number of activities during each season.

Touch Football

Touch football is the most popular fall sport. It capitalizes on the students' natural interest in football, and requires little skill, training, or equipment. Strict field supervision and good officiating will reduce injuries in this game to a minimum.

Touch football is played under modified rules at most schools. For example, the number of players on a team varies from six to eleven. The method of touch-tackling can be with one or two hands on a certain area of the body. Another method consists of pulling out a small cloth strip or flag from under the runner's belt.

To eliminate ties in touch football the number of downs can be counted, the team with the most downs, the winner. If score and downs are the same, then starting on the 50-yard line, run eight alternating plays. At the end of the alternating plays, the team that has the ball on the opponent's side of the 50-yard line breaks the tie and the score for the penetration series is 1–0. Thus, the scores 6–4d–1 to 6–4d–0. Figure 33, page 230, shows this system of scoring in use.

A committee of the College Physical Education Association has surveyed touch football modifications in an attempt to standardize the rules. These high-school and college rules have been published by The Athletic Institute under the title *National Touch Football Rules Handbook*.

Tackle Football

While tackle football is one of the most popular varsity sports, it has fallen into disfavor as an intramural game for several reasons. In the first place, the game requires intricate plays and teamwork which cannot be acquired without a considerable amount of practice time. Furthermore, the department can rarely afford to furnish proper coaching for the teams, and therefore the men enter the games insufficiently trained for such strenuous activity.

Another difficulty is the prohibitive expense of equipping all the players. Adequate equipment for the varsity player is expensive and it is not justifiable to permit the untrained individual to compete with less complete protection. As might be expected, untrained and poorly equipped players are injured far more frequently and seriously than are the varsity men, and in some places, it was decided that the benefits do not justify the risks.

In small schools where there are few teams and it is possible to train and equip them in adequate manner, football can more safely be given a place on the intramural program, but its use in large institutions is rarely desirable except for a small number of teams that can be supervised.

Football Field Meet

A football field meet is always an appealing activity for boys especially during the regular football season. Some activities are suggested as possible events for such a meet.

1. Forward pass for distance
2. Forward pass for accuracy
3. Punt for distance
4. Drop-kick for goal (number of goals kicked in five or ten attempts)
5. Place-kick for goal (number of goals kicked in five or ten attempts)

Soccer

The popularity of soccer varies greatly with the locality and particularly with the students' nationalities. Where a large proportion of the students are of English or Canadian descent, or are foreign students who have played the game in their native lands, soccer is usually the choice for fall activity. In Europe and to some extent in the Far East, soccer has the same appeal as baseball does in this country.

Introducing soccer as a part of the regular physical education instruction program helps to popularize the game for intramural play. From the standpoint of the intramural department, soccer has a serious fault—the infrequency of scoring. This makes tie games—often scoreless games—very common, and the schedules are held up by the necessity of playing the tie games over again. One scheme which can be used to avoid tie games is to score one point for a corner kick and two points for a goal. Another scheme is to score one point for fouls which result in free kicks. This scheme tends to limit bodily contact which is the cause of most fouls in soccer.

For an intramural activity, soccer meets other needs quite well. It is extremely economical because gymnasium uniforms are a prescribed part of the clothes budget, a sweater or a sweat shirt can be added, and local rules can proscribe use of other than regular gymnasium shoes or sneakers. A ball is the only necessary equipment. Where expenses are an item of much concern, soccer can be added as an economic necessity.

Speedball

Speedball is especially adapted to intramural competition in that the rules are few and easily mastered and team play is not too complicated. The skills are largely borrowed from soccer and basketball, with a few from football, and thus are already well known to most participants. As a consequence, the game is enjoyed by players who have never seen the game played before their initial attempt. Speedball permits the hands to be used. Players enjoy the variety that comes from the combination of ground and overhead play. This variety also permits more scoring possibilities so that tie games are rare.

The cost of equipment is almost nothing, both from the standpoint of the intramural department and of the players themselves. Such injuries as occur are not apt to be serious in nature.

Cross Country

This sport is popular with some students who are not adept at team games. Even though free from the element of physical contact, cross country is a very strenuous sport and each contestant should have a careful health examination before being allowed to compete. A minimum number of practice runs should be required as a prerequisite to entering any of the championship meets. Having a coach or varsity runner to run with and instruct the men helps stimulate enthusiasm and improve form.

In meets, all contestants should be plainly numbered before the race begins so that the judges can determine the order of finishing without confusion. This also lightens the duties of any checkers who are needed along the course and definitely settles any disputes regarding "short cuts." For intramural purposes, a course of two or three miles is sufficiently long.

The cross-country meet can be handled either as an open meet or as a team affair. If the latter method is adopted, five men are usually picked for large units like the class and three for small units like the fraternity. As many men as desire can run for their class but only the first five to finish are considered as the class team (first three in the case of the fraternity race). Their respective places of finish in the race are taken and added together; the total is then compared with that of other teams likewise chosen and the lowest total is the winner. For example, if the five best men of a team finished 1, 3, 4, 7, 8, the total of this team would be 23 and it would be a victor over teams possessing a higher total.

"Turkey Days" or "Turkey Trots" are increasingly popular as a Thanksgiving feature. In this cross-country race, the prizes are a turkey for the winner, a goose for second place, a duck for third, and a chicken for fourth.

Rifle Shooting

Rifle shooting can easily be promoted wherever an ROTC unit is established. Co-operation with the military authorities is usually appreciated, for the intramural awards help to stimulate interest in trying out for this form of competition. It is sufficient to conduct meets and open tournaments. Quite often, telegraph or mail matches are held with other institutions and in such cases the intramural meets form the basis for the selection of the competing teams.

Table Tennis

Table tennis lends itself well to noon hour, corecreational, and adult programs. Individual and dual championships can be sponsored as well as team matches. Matches are often played on tables in fraternities, dormitories, recreational gymnasiums, student unions, and intramural buildings.

Bowling

The promotion of bowling depends almost entirely on the character of the available bowling establishment. With the advent of air-conditioned alleys, soundproof walls, automatic pinsetters, and attractive rates for school groups, the activity is becoming very popular. Proprietors often offer special reduced rates for afternoon play when the alleys are not so busy. They also have in mind the advantages of developing interest among younger players, who, after graduation, may continue to be regular patrons.

Some colleges have nearby a commercial recreation hall that caters almost exclusively to student trade and the standards are usually kept high. Some of the larger institutions have alleys connected with the gymnasium or with a student union building. Bowling has the advantage of reaching some of the older students who cannot be induced to take part in other competitive sports.

Open singles and doubles tournaments can be held, but the big interest centers around the four- or five-man team events. If no difficulty is encountered in securing alleys, the entry list can be broken up into small leagues to be followed by an elimination of the league winners. If the use of the alleys is restricted, it is best to conduct the sport on a qualification basis, picking a certain number of the high-score teams to compete in a final elimination series.

A new idea is that of interschool competition by mail or telegraph. It works well in fraternity competition with the various chapters of the same fraternity bowling on the same day.

Various methods of interesting new bowlers and poor bowlers in team competition have been devised. One of them is "overaverage" or handicap bowling. The "overaverage" method is a handicapping procedure, as used in golf, to equalize the competition.

An average is determined by adding the total number of pins and dividing by the number of games. The result is subtracted from a scratch score (170, 180, 190, 200) which is usually 10 pins higher than the highest individual average in the league. A percentage of the difference is the handicap. This percentage may be 66⅔, 70, 75, or 80 per cent, depending on the ability of the bowlers in the league. For example, the average for 25 games is 152 (3,800 pins ÷ 25 games). One hundred fifty-two subtracted from 170 (scratch score) is 18. Sixty-six and two-thirds of 18 is 12. The handicap is then 12 for each game, which is added to the total number of pins, or if a bowler rolls 158 in the first game, the score is 170 for the game; if in the second game 144 is scored, the score is 156; and in the third game 148, the game score is 160. The handicaps in this system change each week according to the results of the tabulated averages. Handicaps can be figured on a team as well as individual basis. Figure 68 shows three individual handicap charts which can be used in determining averages. Additional bowling charts and information are available from the American Bowling Congress, Milwaukee, Wisconsin.

Other promotional devices include posting of high averages, high single-game totals and high-three-game totals for teams and individuals, and the use of the four-point system. In the latter, one point is allowed for each of the three games bowled and a fourth point is awarded to the team with the higher three-game total.

Paddleball

Paddleball is played on a handball court and is similar to handball except that paddles are used. The paddles are attached to the wrist with a leather thong. The rubber ball is the same size as a tennis ball. Paddleball is popular at all levels of ability. Most students find paddleball requires less skill than handball or squash. The game can be played according to one-wall or four-wall rules. Where handball courts are unavailable, a gymnasium wall can be substituted for one-wall paddleball.

Badminton

Badminton is an unusually fine sport for high-school and college students. This sport is readily adapted to men and women and boys and girls. Its major disadvantages as an intramural sport are (1) the expense of equipment, and (2) the limited number of players that can be used. Badminton is now one of the most popular corecreational activities.

Other Fall Sports

The local situation determines what other fall sports can be conducted successfully at any given school. A number of schools find lacrosse popular with class and department teams. Softball is another sport that is promoted with fair success, although its popularity begins to wane after having been played throughout the spring and summer.

A number of winter sports can be started indoors in the latter part of the fall season. For example, a pre-Christmas open basketball tournament can be started in late November. This tournament gives teams a chance to organize and practice in advance of the regular winter leagues and tournaments. Weight lifting, judo, and water polo can also be organized in the fall and continued throughout the winter. Corecreation and informal or "free play" activities should be started in the fall and continued throughout the school year. The "free play" activities are those in which students utilize facilities and equipment on an informal basis.

WINTER

The winter season usually provides the best conditions for the development of intramural sports. With the exception of some outdoor winter sports, inclement weather does not interfere with schedules and a complete program for all sports can be prepared at the start of the season. Furthermore, contestants have more time to prepare for their favorite sports. The basketball teams can be organized toward the close of the fall season. The swimmers and wrestlers have several months in which to train before their final championship meets and are usually in good condition by that time. When playing facilities are crowded, the schedules in such sports as handball and volleyball can be started late in the fall and continued, without interruption, into the winter.

All these advantages stand in marked contrast to the short fall and spring seasons, when schedules must be started with the opening of the seasons and rushed to completion with little opportunity for preparation or practice.

Basketball

As mentioned before, basketball is an ideal intramural game and practically everywhere is the most popular event on the year's program. The expense of equipment is small. Basketball does not require a great deal of preliminary practice to develop teamwork and nearly every student has played the game enough to enjoy it. The number of players required for a team is small and they can readily be assembled. Leagues can be promoted successfully with practically any type of unit, the amount of available playing time and space usually being the only limitations to the program.

The games can be played in quarters of from 6 to 10 minutes or halves of from 12 to 20 minutes. Games can either have time-out periods or be played in straight running-time. If teams agree, championship games can be played according to regulation high-school or college basketball rules. Where facilities include adjacent basketball courts, a central timing device can be used to time several concurrent games on straight running-time.

It is quite important that competent referees be secured for all basketball games, as most of the players are fairly well versed in the rules, and this sport, more so than almost any other, depends for its success upon good officiating. Good officiating prevents many disputes and eliminates the tendency to introduce rough tactics.

Free Throw Contest

Free throw contests are an outgrowth of intramural basketball. While there is little exercise connected with this activity, it promotes considerable interest. In some schools, several thousand students participate in these contests.

If the basis of the tournament is 100 tries, winners usually average between 70 and 85 successful attempts. It is evident that with a large number of entries the task of supervising the full number of throws on the part of every candidate is almost endless and therefore a qualification plan should be adopted. Supervision is facilitated if participants on competing teams keep each other's scores.

One means of conducting the qualifications series is as follows: all candidates take 25 free throws and those making 15 or more qualify; then, those who have successfully passed the initial test shoot 25 more times (making 50 attempts in all) and the 10 high men are chosen; then, 10 high candidates are permitted 50 more totals, with the winner judged on the basis of 100 total attempts.

The various units can follow the same procedure in determining team victors. Often, a team uses the same five men that compose its regular basketball team in the free throw contest. This makes the conducting of the contest easy, as the men do their shooting the same night they play a game. Certain schools allow all unit members to take part and the total score of the five high members constitutes the team record.

BASKETBALL FREE THROW CONTEST

TEAM OR ORGANIZATION________________________

I agree to follow regulations and pledge my honor in shooting and checking free throws.

Print Name________________________

Signature________________________

Shoot two rounds of 25 free throws:

As soon as the 10 practice throws are completed, the contestant should advise the checker he is ready to start. The count begins when the first free throw is made. Under no circumstances should a checker accept successful throws that are made during the practice period. These two rounds are the only ones that count toward team scores.

SAMPLE ROUND

1	2	3	4	5	6	7	8	9	10	11	12	13	14	15	16	17	18	19	20	21	22	23	24	25	Total
1	X	X	2	3	4	X	5	X	X	6	7	8	9	X	10	X	X	11	X	12	13	X	14	X	14

X Equals a Miss -- Numbers indicate the running score.

FIRST ROUND

1	2	3	4	5	6	7	8	9	10	11	12	13	14	15	16	17	18	19	20	21	22	23	24	25	Total

SECOND ROUND

1	2	3	4	5	6	7	8	9	10	11	12	13	14	15	16	17	18	19	20	21	22	23	24	25	Total

1st and 2nd round totals____

Note: Checker must not be a Teammate of contestant.

Signed by Checker________________________

Checker's Team________________________

All-U Champions

Any contestant making 40 or more free throws in the first two rounds will receive 50 additional throws if he desires to try for the All-U Individual Title. These throws are to be recorded below in rounds three and four.

THIRD ROUND

1	2	3	4	5	6	7	8	9	10	11	12	13	14	15	16	17	18	19	20	21	22	23	24	25	Total

FOURTH ROUND

1	2	3	4	5	6	7	8	9	10	11	12	13	14	15	16	17	18	19	20	21	22	23	24	25	Total

Grand total____

Signed by Checker________________________

Checker's Team________________________

Figure 9. Basketball Free Throw Contest Score Sheet.

Another way to complete the contest in one day is to give each contestant 2 rounds of 25 shots. Then the 10 best rounds are put together for a team score. Two rounds, or just 1 round, of any 1 player can be counted in the best 10 rounds. The highest possible team score is 250. The players can compete any time during the day or evening. Figure 9 shows a basketball free-throw contest score sheet.

Volleyball

Although volleyball lacks physical contact, experience shows the game appeals to many students. It is being added to school programs for several reasons. The physical education classes in junior and senior high schools include volleyball as a regular class activity; thus, the science of volleyball has advanced to the point where it challenges players. And, it can be played for many more years than basketball. Continuous activity and alertness are keynotes of volleyball.

The growth of volleyball is phenomenal. Practically every YMCA in the country has organized junior and senior volleyball leagues. The senior team usually enters regional or state tournaments, with the ultimate goal to qualify for the national championship. In addition, every businessmen's class devotes part of its workout period to volleyball. It is through the YMCA that volleyball enjoys its current popularity, although schools are including the game more and more in their physical education programs.

Volleyball is especially adapted to faculty groups where less strenuous exercise is usually preferred. Foreign students attending American universities show unusual interest in and adaptability to the game. The skills of striking the ball are learned much more readily than the catching and throwing so predominant in other American games.

Playing-rule modifications are frequently used to adapt volleyball to the intramural program. Beginning players are permitted to assist on serves and to have additional taps on each side of the net. Official volleyball rules provide for the scoring of a point only by the serving team. Under this rule, the length of playing time for a game varies considerably. Scoring a point on each serve is a modification which standardizes playing times. Time limits on length of games also increase standardization for scheduling purposes.

Volleyball, with three men and three women on each side, is an excellent corecreational activity.

Swimming

Where facilities permit, swimming should be one of the main features of the winter program. A variety of dual, triangular, quadrangular, open, and novelty meets can be conducted. One popular novelty meet is the sweatsuit race in which contestants wear sweat shirts and pants. To prevent a few outstanding performers from dominating a meet, the number of events in which any individual can enter should be limited to two, possibly three. Awarding points for at least six places in each event also stimulates the less skilled participants, especially when teams from organized units are competing. Records should be maintained from year to year to add interest to the sport.

Unless other agencies are handling the situation, the intramural department can satisfy a popular desire by furnishing instruction at scheduled times in swimming and life-saving. This can be very informal or can be done in classes with graded instruction permitting the student to join any group according to his proficiency. Water polo is popular in a number of schools that have facilities. It is, however, a sport that requires a considerable amount of endurance; a training regimen should be a prerequisite. Splash parties for men and women are a popular corecreational activity.

Hockey

The weather plays an important part in a successful hockey program. In some sections of the country, this sport cannot be promoted at all. Many schools that conduct hockey schedules have a constant battle against the elements, and not infrequently tournaments fail to be completed before warm weather permanently ruins the ice. Where weather conditions are favorable, hockey has no peer as an invigorating game. With more and more rinks being provided for college and high-school student use, weather becomes less a problem. Because of its strenuous nature, hockey periods can be shortened to ten or twelve minutes each of straight running-time. It often helps inexperienced players if the off-side rule is temporarily disregarded.

To allow more games to be played in the allotted time, periods of two separate games can be dovetailed: teams A and B play their first period, followed by teams C and D playing their first period; then, A and B play their second period, C and D play their second period, and so on.

Schools that find difficulty in maintaining ice may limit their intramural competition to a few teams composed of the best players, and, if necessary, play a straight elimination series, with a consolation series for the first-round losers.

Indoor Track

To encourage the less expert contestants, indoor track meets should follow the restrictions suggested for swimming, i.e., no individual should be allowed to enter more than a limited number of events and at least five places should be awarded in each event. It is also advisable to prohibit any man from entering more than one run above 440 yards. Inasmuch as the indoor pole vault takes a considerable amount of time and is rather dangerous, it is advisable to omit it from the intramural meet.

Novelty races and events are often very popular, particularly if they are repeated annually and well publicized. The relay race, pentathlon, tug-of-war, and chariot race are excellent events to include in an intramural meet, but because of the difficulties in handling them during the meet, they are often conducted on separate occasions.

Wrestling

Contestants in wrestling should be required to train under a competent instructor before competing in the championship tournaments. All meets in colleges and universities can be conducted by weight classes (115, 123, 130, 137, 147, 157, 167, 177, and 191 pounds and heavyweight) as specified in the intercollegiate wrestling regulations and, except for the duration of bouts, these official regulations should be used to govern all meets. It is advisable to limit bouts to four or five minutes each in the preliminary rounds of a tournament and to six or seven minutes each in the semifinal and final events. In case of draws, the referee's decision should determine the winner. The time requirement for "advantage" can be lowered proportionately.

In intramural wrestling in the high school, the following weight classes are used: 95, 103, 112, 120, 127, 133, 138, 145, 154, 165, and 175 pounds and heavyweight. One to three pounds overweight in each class can be allowed. Whatever the limit set, it should be rigidly enforced and all contestants, except where they compete more than once during the same day, should be required to weigh in before each bout. If this is not enforced, the objection arises that a man entering a four-day tournament can train down to a low weight before the first match and yet be as much as ten pounds overweight for the final bout.

In high schools, equalization of competition should be observed. Otherwise, it is possible that a boy of sixteen may weigh only 115 pounds and be scheduled to compete against another boy of twelve or thirteen who weighs the same. The variance in age is at once apparent and the obvious advantage of the sixteen-year-old is seen.

Extreme caution and well-qualified adult supervision are essential to the safe use of wrestling as an intramural sport in the high schools.

Boxing

Whether or not boxing should be sponsored in the intramural program is open to question. Boxing requires careful training and should only be promoted as an intramural sport when proper conditioning can be required and supervised.

Three rounds of two minutes each, with one-minute intermission periods, are advisable for tournament bouts. Weight classifications are 119, 126, 132, 139, 147, 155, 165, and 178 pounds and heavyweight.

An experienced referee is necessary and judges should be carefully selected; the determination of the winner in a close bout requires keen judgment of boxing; and a tournament is handicapped by poor decisions. Many schools require the written consent of the parents before a minor student is permitted to engage in a scheduled boxing match, particularly so if the boxing events are part of an exhibition for which admission is charged. As in the case of wrestling, to be safely and successfully used in school programs, boxing necessitates well-qualified adult supervision.

As a precaution for safety in actual practice and competitive bouts, large gloves should be used. With the 12-ounce and 14-ounce glove for college intramural matches, little permanent damage can be done. For high-school and junior high-school class activity and camp boxing, 16-ounce gloves are suggested.

Handball

If enough courts are available, handball usually attracts a large number of participants. Open tournaments of singles and doubles matches are easily conducted because players can usually be relied upon to decide their own points and keep their own scores. As in tennis, final dates should be set and matches completed on or before these dates.

In tournaments between various units, the simplest plan has one or two men representing each unit. Handball is such a popular game, however, that many departments secure larger representations by requiring four-man teams, each consisting of two singles players and two doubles players. In this case, the winning of each match counts one point. For example, the number one singles players play three matches (not the best two of three), totaling three points. Matches involving the number two singles players and the doubles players are also worth three points. Total number of possible team points is nine, thus permitting scores of 9–0, 8–1, 5–4, etc. Five-man teams are another alternative, with two doubles players (counting two points for the match) and three singles players (each match to count one point). This team plan of competition can also be utilized for paddleball, and other individual and dual sports.

Gymnastics

Apparatus work and tumbling are not as attractive to the average student as the team games. The success of gymnastic meets depends largely upon the response which gymnasium instructors secure from their classes. There are seldom enough proficient gymnasts in the average intramural unit to hold team meets; but individual championships are advisable and should be given a place in the intramural program. Schools that have a department for the training of physical education teachers find it much easier to arouse interest in gymnastics.

Squash

Squash is an extremely fast game which requires limited equipment and special courts. Because of lack of courts, the game is often limited to larger schools. In general, fewer squash courts than handball courts are available. Squash can be played in singles, doubles, or team events.

Other Winter Sports

In northern schools, speed and figure skating, curling, skiing, and tobogganing are popular winter sports. Many of these schools have organized outing clubs and their winter outdoor carnivals are outstanding events of the school year. In addition, deck tennis, twenty-one, darts, basketball golf, shuffleboard, codeball, and box hockey are popular indoor winter intramural sports.

SPRING

The spring season usually makes its debut with a rush and is quickly terminated by the advent of final examinations. Schedules must be started almost as soon as the weather permits outdoor work. Very little preliminary practice can be allowed. It is always necessary to reserve several dates for the games and matches which have to be postponed because of inclement weather or wet grounds.

In spring, a student's interest in intramural sports may be at a low ebb unless his team is a strong contender in the year-round standings. This is partly due to the usual listlessness that comes with spring weather and partly to the fact that the student's time is crowded with the many school functions that precede the close of the school year. On the other hand, there are plenty of popular sports from which to choose a program.

Baseball

The main difficulty in promoting baseball on a large scale in intramural work is the amount of space it requires. This need for space makes it necessary to carefully plan the use of available fields. Lack of sufficient space for play has made many schools limit baseball to class leagues and introduce softball for the great majority of students.

For intramural use, a game shortened to five to seven innings or limited to an hour and a half is preferable to the regulation nine-inning game.

Baseball Field Meet

An appropriate spring activity is a baseball field meet. It is conducted in the same manner as a football field meet or track meet. The events which can be used are:

1. Running bases
2. Catcher's throw for accuracy (to second base)
3. Baseball target throw
4. Baseball pitch
5. Throw for distance
6. Fungo hit
7. Bunt and run

Softball

In many schools, softball is the most popular spring sport. One reason is that the mediocre player is not so noticeably outclassed by the more experienced teammate or opponent as he is in baseball, and he therefore gets more enjoyment out of the game. In addition, a player can enter the game with no other equipment than his old clothes and a pair of tennis shoes and, hence, impromptu practices can be staged at any convenient time.

At the present time, softball stands next to basketball as a leading intramural activity, both in the number of institutions promoting the game and also the number of participants.

Softball has an advantage from the administrative standpoint in that each diamond requires considerably less space than in baseball. By careful planning, three or four softball diamonds are included in the same area that would be needed for one baseball diamond. Teams can hold practices in vacant lots where the space is too limited to play baseball and this is of considerable assistance where the playing fields are not readily accessible to all teams. In this connection, there is much impromptu competition in softball between fraternities and other social groups.

A popular modification of regular softball is slow-pitch softball. Emphasis in this game is on running, hitting, fielding, and throwing. Slow-pitch softball is played according to regular softball rules with the exception that the pitcher must deliver the ball with a perceptible one-foot arch. Slow-pitch can also be played using the following modifications: (1) 10 players per team; (2) 45–50-foot bases; (3) 36–40-foot pitching distance; (4) pitches thrown with too much speed and spin are called balls; (5) stealing and bunting are prohibited; and (6) the batter is automatically out on a dropped third strike.

Outdoor Track

Practically the same suggestions given under "Indoor Track" apply to the sport when conducted out of doors. There is often much discussion as to whether the javelin and discus throws, which cannot be used indoors, should be included in outdoor meets. This question must be decided locally, depending chiefly upon whether the competitors are given any training in these events before the meet and whether the event can be conducted without danger. The one- and two-mile run should not be considered unless the competitors have undergone a carefully supervised course of training. Novelty events and relays can be introduced if desired.

Tennis

Tennis is becoming increasingly popular, and the chief problem of most institutions is to secure enough courts to accommodate all who desire to play.

Spring tournaments require continual attention and stimulation if they are to be completed before the close of the school year. Rain and wet courts constantly interrupt the schedule. A final date should be set for the completion of each round and inclement weather accepted as the only excuse for postponement. All-school singles and doubles tournaments are usually successful and team championships can be decided between fraternity, independents, graduates, or other units. When possible, the team basis for fraternities and independents should be made stronger by having four or more men comprise a team. The match is decided by scoring one point per match to the winners, as suggested for handball.

Horseshoes

Horseshoes or "barnyard golf" has an advantage as an intramural sport because courts require comparatively little space and can usually be laid out in space otherwise idle. Horseshoes also attracts students who are physically incapable of strenuous participation. The tournaments should be conducted as in tennis, deciding all-school singles and doubles champions and team championships between such units as are matched in other sports. The unit championships can be decided by teams of six men, making three doubles matches, with the winner securing two victories out of the three matches played. Regulation 14-inch stakes at 40 feet should be used and no shoes allowed that do not meet the official specifications. Team-scoring methods used in handball, tennis, etc., can also be used in horseshoes. Contestants can usually decide their points satisfactorily but it is advisable to furnish officials for championship games. The cancellation and count-all points methods of scoring can be used. The general practice is to play the best two out of three games to determine a match.

Archery

This sport, while of considerable interest to men, is especially fitting for young women and girls. The muscular effort involved can be strictly controlled by the use of a variety of bows. The postural values of archery are widely recognized. Students' interest can be enhanced by formation of clubs and by the increasing use of the bow and arrow in hunting. Roving archery, clout shooting, and archery golf are popular club activities.

Disadvantages include expense of equipment and possible danger resulting from carelessness. Students must often furnish their own equipment. Target areas should be carefully selected and supervised.

Fencing

Fencing is generally conducted on a club basis. Divisions include foil, saber, and épée. Equipment is expensive and students must often provide their own. Beginning, intermediate, and advanced groups should be organized to encourage equalized competition. Ladder tournaments are effective in developing tournament-contesting, -judging, and -directing. Practice and meet areas are provided by using removable rubber mats on gymnasium floors.

Golf

More Americans are becoming interested in golf each year and student tournaments need very little stimulation. Unfortunately, it is impossible in most institutions to provide courses to meet the popular demand. The construction and maintenance of a golf course are expensive. Some departments conduct tournaments on private courses by paying the "greens fees" of the participants. If the intramural department cannot defray the fees of the contestants, it can offer the trophies for the winning players. This could result in only a few students being able to play golf, but this situation would be quite true even though the intramural department did not promote a tournament.

The way in which a golf tournament is conducted depends upon the group, the facilities, and the length of time necessary to complete the matches. There is the general method of championship golf tournaments to determine the qualifying players. This is known as *medal play.* Medal play is the actual stroke score for a complete round. Each player posts the total number of strokes necessary for the round. The lowest scorer is the winner. Medal play can be said to be an attempt to beat par. The results of medal score determine the various tournament flights or classes for match play.

A second method, *match play,* involves competition between two players; each attempts to win the larger number of holes, by lower stroke score per hole. If the score is posted as 1 up, this means that one player won only one hole more than his opponent; if the score is 2 and 1, this means one player has won two holes more than his opponent, with only one hole left to play. The winner of the tournament in match play is decided after the usual elimination round.

If a tie results at the end of 18 holes, single holes are played until the tie is broken.

Team matches are generally played according to the *Nassau system.* Players are matched for team play in the usual manner with the number one players of each team playing against each other, number two players paired together, etc. The Nassau system awards three points for each match on the basis of the number of holes won. One point is awarded to the winner of the first nine holes, one point to the winner of the second nine holes, and one point to the player who wins the greatest number of holes for all 18 holes. Thus, it is possible for A to defeat B 3–0, 2½–½, or 2–1. The score of 3–0 indicates A won the first 9 holes, second 9 holes, and the total 18 holes. In the case of ties at the end of 18 holes, winners can be determined by playing extra holes. A variation of this system is used for medal play, intramural golf tournaments. Similar point-awards are given to the player with the low medal score at the end of each 9 holes and at the end of 18 holes.

HANDICAPS FOR SEASON OR LEAGUE PLAY. Handicap matches can be played with predetermined handicaps for each individual. One method of determining the handicap is to post three 18-hole scores, attested to by another player, from which an average round is figured. Three fourths of the difference between the average score and par is handicap. For example, scores for 18 holes are posted as 93, 95, and 88, a total of 276. The average round is 92. Three fourths of the difference between 92 and 72 is 15, the handicap. In match play these 15 strokes can be used as indicated on the score card handicap columns 1 through 15. Thus, a handicap cannot be utilized at convenient times. In the event of a tie at the end of 18 holes, another 18 holes should be played to determine the winner. However, if players mutually agree, a sudden death play-off can be used. In sudden death, handicaps are applied only as they fall in line on the score card handicap columns. For medal play, the number of handicap strokes (15) is subtracted from gross score (92) to equal the net score (77).

ONE-DAY TOURNAMENT HANDICAP SYSTEMS. To encourage good turnouts, competition for one-day golf tournaments should be equalized. The Peoria, Callaway, and Horner handicap systems can be used. For example, the Horner system encourages consistent scoring, is simple, and can be calculated from the score cards as they are turned in. All 18 holes are classified as birdies, pars, 1 over par, 2 over par, and so on. For golfers whose gross scores are 100 or less, the system works as follows:

1. Select the best nine holes (lowest scores).
2. Count the number of strokes over par on these nine holes to arrive at a differential.
3. Double this differential.
4. Subtract this figure from the actual score to determine the net score.

For players scoring 101 or more, the procedure is the same with the exception that 10 holes are used instead of 9 holes to determine the number of strokes over par explained in (1) above.

One method of team scoring enables a fraternity or an independent group to enter five players in a match with the four lowest scores added for the team score. Thus, the team with the lowest total is declared the winner.

Another method of team scoring is to have fraternities or independent groups enter as many players as they wish. Each posts his score at the end of 18 holes and the total of the five lowest scores is added for a team total, with the lowest aggregate score being declared the winner.

The *blind bogey* golf tournament is exceptionally good as an intramural activity because anyone can win, regardless of ability. It can be conducted as a separate tournament or concurrently with a medal play tournament.

Participants record their estimated handicaps with the starter before teeing off. If the individual's actual score minus the guessed handicap equals blind par, he is one of the tournament winners. Blind par is established by drawing a number between 70 and 80 after all participants have left the first tee. In estimating handicaps, golfers should think of what number subtracted from what they are going to shoot equals the number which will be drawn out of the hat. For example, 110 (actual score) minus 36 (guessed handicap) equals 74 (blind par drawn from a hat). If it is desirable to give away numerous prizes, more than one blind par can be drawn.

A *flag match* is often run as a novelty on holidays, reunions, or other special occasions. By adding the usual handicap of the individual to par for the course, the number of strokes for the day is determined. Each entrant then plays a regular round and places his flag wherever his ball stops on the last of the allotted strokes for the day. Ordinarily, this should bring the flags close to the 18th green. For example; A has a handicap of 15 strokes. Fifteen strokes added to a par of 72, would be 87 strokes. After the 87th stroke, A places his flag. B has a handicap of 20. Twenty strokes added to 72 is 92. B has a good day and makes the 18 holes in 87 strokes. He still has 5 strokes to go, which could bring him 1 stroke beyond the 19th hole, where he places his flag. The distance of the flags beyond the 18th hole determines the winners.

Another variation of the flag match is *par golf*. Each contestant is permitted 72 (par) strokes. Flags are placed in relative positions and the player whose flag is farthest advanced is the winner.

Other Spring Sports

There are other spring sports that are successful. Where proper facilities are available, aquatic sports, especially sailing, water skiing, bait and fly casting, and canoeing and rowing, are very popular.

SUMMER

Certain factors should be considered in formulating the program for the summer session. As a rule, students are older and less competitive-minded. The more individualistic sports appeal to them, although softball is extremely popular, and units are easily found on which to base the competition.

An all-important consideration is that of weather. It is recommended that activities be scheduled late in the afternoon when cooler temperatures may be expected. Scheduling games and matches from four-o'clock on is also less likely to interfere with classes or time for study.

Many summer students play golf, tennis, and swim when it is convenient. The students often borrow materials and equipment for outings and picnics.

The following list covers the scope of activities which can be offered during the limited period of a summer session.

SUMMER SESSION PROGRAM OF ACTIVITIES

Archery	Handball	Sigma Delta Psi	Swimming
Badminton	Horseshoes	Softball	Table tennis
Bowling	Outings	Squash	Tennis
Golf			

Sigma Delta Psi Activities

Many colleges and universities have established chapters of Sigma Delta Psi, national athletic honorary fraternity. The trials for meeting the requirements for membership are usually conducted by the intramural department. Publicity concerning the society and its requirements should be distributed when the fall season opens so that candidates can begin their practice and pass the tests at any convenient time throughout the year. Sigma Delta Psi originally established a junior division which, though intended for college students of lesser skill, has standards well adapted for use by high schools that wish to establish an honorary society of this type. To promote interest, yearly records of individual performances should be maintained.

As a competitive activity on a team or group basis, Sigma Delta Psi has excellent possibilities. It can be used in the form of a field day or track meet, as for instance, the modern decathlon, by awarding points of 5, 3, 2, 1 for place-winners in each of the events. Or it could be held on a series of days when three or five of the activities are contested.

Another method of team scoring allows the entrants to take the test in the usual manner. Then, points are awarded for achievement according to national scoring tables. Scores of the best ten entrants are compiled and the high total determines the winner. Sigma Delta Psi tests, requirements, and scoring tables are reproduced in Appendix B.

SUMMARY

1. The program offered by the intramural department must necessarily vary according to the local conditions.
2. The average school participant is more strongly attracted by the team game and activities which do not require long preliminary practice or a great amount of equipment and expense.
3. The sports chosen for general promotion among the student body should arouse a spontaneous interest and provide invigorating exercise without resulting in complete exhaustion.
4. Sports tend to group themselves naturally into the three seasons of the school year.
5. To prevent overactivity during a particular season, it is essential to arrange an equal number of activities during each season.
6. Major fall activities include touch football, tackle football, football field meets, soccer, speedball, cross country, rifle shooting, table tennis, bowling, paddleball, and badminton.
7. The winter season usually provides the best conditions for the development of intramural activities.
8. Major winter activities include basketball, free throw contests, volleyball, swimming, hockey, indoor track, wrestling, boxing, handball, gymnastic meets, and squash.
9. Major spring sports include baseball, baseball field meets, fast and slow pitch softball, outdoor track, tennis, horseshoes, archery, fencing, and golf.
10. Summer session activities include softball, swimming, Sigma Delta Psi, tennis, golf, outings, table tennis, horseshoes, bowling, badminton, handball, archery, and squash.

11. In selecting sports, the size of the school and the age of the students should first be considered, and then attention should be given to local facilities and desires.
12. A few sports well promoted constitute a better program than a hodgepodge of many sports which are not popular enough to warrant encouragement.
13. The number of sports that can be offered by any one school depends upon the available facilities, staff, and equipment.
14. Certain sports, such as golf and bowling, lend themselves to handicapping procedures and, when organized for competition, have special methods unique to themselves.

8

Time Periods and Scheduling

Time enters into every phase of the intramural sports program. The person in charge of the program must carefully choose time and completely co-ordinate I-M activities with all other phases of the school program. Finding time periods for intramural sports depends on the local situation. It is important to the success of the program because the student's ability to participate frequently is determined by when the activities are offered.

The season of the year is important in the division of activities. The program is usually arranged according to fall, winter, spring, and summer. Available time often determines the type of competition to be used. For example, in order to complete schedules quickly, a single elimination tournament can be scheduled rather than a round robin tournament.

Time is important from another standpoint—lack of it on the part of faculty I-M supervisors. These individuals are often too busy, particularly in high schools, coaching varsity athletics or teaching classes to give sufficient time to the intramural program. If the gymnasium or outdoor facilities are used co-operatively by men's and women's programs—varsity, physical education, and intramural—they may not be readily available for intramural sports. In any case, the intramural director must anticipate all possible time problems in preliminary planning. Figure 10 illustrates a monthly calendar of events set up by an intramural director. Exact times for conducting each of the activities can be entered as the event approaches.

INTRAMURAL DIRECTOR'S MONTHLY CALENDAR

MONTH January YEAR 1966

SUN	MON	TUE	WED	THU	FRI	SAT
2	3 Classes Begin	4 Independent Athletic Council Fraternities Athletic Council	5 Dormitory Athletic Council	6 I-M Officials Association Meets	7 Corecreation	8 Varsity Basketball
9 STAFF-FAMILY RECREATION	10 Leagues Begin Independent Basketball Dormitory Bowling	11 Leagues Begin Fraternities Basketball Independent Hockey	12 Leagues Begin Independent Bowling Dormitory Basketball Fraternities Hockey	13 Leagues Begin Fraternities Bowling Dormitory Hockey	14 Corecreation	15 Varsity Hockey
16 STAFF-FAMILY RECREATION	17	18 Faculty Bowling Begins	19 Judo Club Meets	20 Mixed Bowling Begins	21 Corecreation	22 Varsity Basketball
23 STAFF-FAMILY RECREATION	24 Varsity Basketball	25	26 Archery Club Meets	27	28 Corecreation	29 Varsity Hockey
30 STAFF-FAMILY RECREATION	31 I-M Officials Association Meets	1 Free-throw Contest Begins	2 Faculty Volleyball Begins	3 Handball Begins	4 Corecreation	5

Figure 10. Intramural Director's Monthly Calendar.

TIME PERIODS

Discussion of evening, after school, noon hour, and other time periods is helpful in understanding the importance of time in I-M scheduling.

Evening Hours

Scheduling intramural contests in the high school during evenings is not always a satisfactory procedure. Parents often object to such evening programs because they want their children home at night. However, with increased evening extracurricular activities in high schools, some directors have success with early evening programs, particularly if daytime hours are not available. Many interscholastic games are played during the evening hours, so there should be little objection for intramurals.

There are other factors which make it impractical to schedule games in the evenings. Varsity contests and municipal recreation activities often occupy the facilities. The opening of the school building for adult education sometimes precludes the use of the building for regular school activities. If the coach or physical education teacher also serves as intramural director and community recreation leader, he often schedules adult recreation or recreational activities of a nonathletic nature in the evenings. Some recreational leaders feel that students have use of the school facilities during the day and therefore nights should be reserved for community-wide recreation. If evening hours are used for intramurals, teams should not be required to play more than once or twice a week.

Intramural scheduling in colleges and universities is somewhat standardized. The majority of the departments conduct their programs during the late afternoons and evenings. This time seems most convenient for students and most satisfactory for securing facilities. When varsity teams and physical education classes use the same facilities and have preference, as is the case in most schools, the evening is the only time that facilities are available for intramural sports. With increased enrollments, it may be necessary to schedule activities throughout the day and evening. Students with afternoon and evening classes could play games in the morning.

After-School Hours

Perhaps the most satisfactory time for intramural sports in the high school is the period immediately following afternoon classes. The majority of students are present and there is no need for transportation or going home and returning to school at a later hour. Building maintenance costs are not as extensive as in the evening since electric lighting is seldom needed. Faculty supervision is more easily secured for afternoon hours. Parents usually are pleased to have their children play under supervision in a safe environment during after-school hours.

After a full day of comparatively sedentary work in classes, the student participating during after-school hours enjoys the opportunity to "let off steam." The exercise and play of such a program is truly recreative. The main objection to the late afternoon intramural program comes from those students who must do tasks at home or who are employed then. It is helpful to schedule activities on the same day at the same time so students are able to plan their work accordingly. It is highly possible, however, that the employed students cannot participate to any great extent in either the afternoon or evening no matter what time games are scheduled.

Students in many consolidated schools must use scheduled bus transportation and cannot participate during after-school hours. For such students, evening participation is usually ruled out. In these schools, the program is scheduled during the noon hour or a special activity period.

Late afternoons during fall and spring are ideal for outdoor activities in colleges and universities. However, where lighted fields are available, students often prefer to play in the evenings. At large commuter campuses, late afternoon schedules should be arranged so students are not required to drive back to the campus in the evening. The summer session intramural programs are confined almost entirely to the late afternoon to avoid class conflicts and to avoid the heat of the earlier part of the day.

Noon Hours

Noon-hour intramural programs are popular in high schools and elementary schools. School administrators appreciate the supervision of the many students who do not go home for lunch. This plan permits students who must work after school to participate in the program. The noon-hour program is particularly well adapted to schools in rural communities where the majority of the student body cannot get home for lunch.

The use of strenuous activities in noon-hour intramurals is not recommended. Activities should be selected for their social rather than physical values. Sufficient time should be allowed so students can eat their lunches leisurely. The intramural program should begin at the same time each day. There is often a tendency for students to rush through eating in anticipation of starting play as soon as they finish their meals.

Basketball, volleyball, track, soccer, swimming, touch football, and hockey fall into the category of strenuous activities. It is argued that since many boys strenuously roughhouse and romp after lunch, it is better to promote an activity in which ten to twenty engage while others watch than to have all students participating in unorganized play. Such activities can cause parental criticism and should be used with discretion. If activities of this nature are promoted, rules should be modified to eliminate or reduce strenuous aspects of the games.

Suggested activities for the noon-hour program follow:

archery
badminton
billiards
bombardment
bowling
box hockey
box soccer
checkers
chess
circle games
croquet
curling
dart games
deck tennis
dodgeball
end ball
fencing
floor baseball
free throw contest
golf putting
hand tennis
horseshoes
loop and aerial tennis
newcomb
nine pins
novelty relays
paddle tennis
pin ball
shuffleboard
smash
social and square dancing
softball
stunts
table and card games
table tennis
tetherball

The noon-hour program is an excellent place in which to start or conduct a corecreational program of activities. Because activities should be of a recreational nature and less strenuous for health reasons, girls and boys enjoy playing many of them together. Obviously, noon-hour activities should be of the outdoor variety whenever weather and facilities permit.

In some schools, the noon-hour program is arranged so that activities start at the beginning of the lunch period. Games are followed by a shower and sufficient time is provided for lunch. This plan is favored over the "eat lunch and then play" plan. It is particularly effective in schools that have a long lunch period. Some schools have free periods before and after lunch. Such an arrangement allows more time for eating and playing games if the students are permitted to shower and dress during the free-hour period. In large schools that have split shifts or split lunch periods, it is necessary to carry on two separate noon-hour intramural programs.

School Hours

Many high schools conduct the intramural program during school hours because students use school busses or the staff is not adequate to promote afternoon or evening intramural programs. The available physical education and coaching staff members are often busy with other duties.

Gymnasium classes. While many schools use certain gymnasium periods for intramural competition, physical education authorities advocate that the class period should be primarily for instruction and not a period for actual competition. However, if the gymnasium periods afford the only opportunity for intramurals, then such arrangements are justified. This can be done in several ways: (1) using squads for units of competition during the regular period; (2) setting aside one of the allotted physical education periods each week; (3) arranging an additional period expressly for intramural competition.

Free periods. Another possible time for intramurals during the school day, particularly in the small high school, is the students' free or study period. Competition can be arranged for these times if there is no objection from school administrators. This plan is particularly effective if free periods are scheduled the last hour of the morning and the last hour of the afternoon.

The difficulty of the free-period method is the possible conflict in the use of facilities. Physical education facilities are usually completely scheduled throughout the day with boys' and girls' classes and varsity team practices. When free periods are scheduled at different hours throughout the day, there is considerable conflict in the use of the gymnasium. If staff, facilities, and equipment are sufficient to take care of all groups, free-period intramurals work effectively. Often, interested teachers in other areas volunteer their services to assist in certain intramural activities.

Club or activity periods. The club or activity period is another effective time for intramural sports. Many high schools have one period each week when students choose club activities such as music, dramatics, woodwork, food preparation, sewing, art, aeronautics, space probing, or sports. Sports clubs should be prominent in the school club program. They can be centered around specific sports such as weight lifting, judo, wrestling, tennis, golf, swimming, tumbling, and archery, or there can be an intramural sports club which promotes regular tournaments. The length of the club or activity period usually determines the success of this method.

Other Periods

SATURDAYS. In nearly all elementary and high schools, there are a number of students who have paper routes, delivery jobs, and other part-time employment after school hours that prohibits participation in the intramural program. Many of these students would return to school to participate if activities were scheduled at a convenient time.

Because of this need, and with an assured group of interested participants, programs are scheduled for Saturday mornings and afternoons with good success. For the benefit of the intramural groups returning for participation, it is possible to secure the services of varsity squad members for officiating. After regular Friday afternoon or evening games, they are free and enjoy the leadership responsibilities. Coaches are usually interested to have the "day-after-game soreness and fatigue" worked out in this constructive manner.

At the college level, Saturday is or is not a good time for intramurals, depending on the local situation. In large colleges and universities, classes, commuting, student employment, and conflict with other campus activities hinder Saturday intramural schedules. Saturday home-football-games and other varsity contests conflict with the use of facilities and student interests. Even if facilities are available, it is inadvisable to schedule intramural events when varsity teams are playing at home.

MONDAYS AND FRIDAYS. Facilities ordinarily used by varsity teams are often available on Mondays and Fridays for intramural activities. A day of rest is usually prescribed for Mondays after the varsity game, and Friday afternoons preceding varsity games are rarely used for practice. Intramural participants like to use varsity facilities and this is an added incentive to the program.

Friday is not a good day in colleges for the same reasons mentioned previously for Saturday. Many students like to go home for the week-end and leave immediately after Friday classes conclude. College dances and fraternity parties are often held on Friday evenings. However, intramural departments on larger campuses easily compete with such activities because of the wide variety of student body interests. Friday or Saturday night is often the best time for corecreation sessions. Scheduling intramural games on Monday night is difficult on campuses where fraternities hold meetings every Monday night. In this situation, dormitories or independent groups can usually be scheduled for Monday.

VACATION PERIODS. School holidays—Christmas vacation, spring vacation, Easter vacation, Thanksgiving, Lincoln's birthday, and Columbus Day—afford additional opportunities for intramural tournaments. This is a particularly convenient time for extramural sports when I-M teams from different schools meet in tournament play.

FREE CHOICE PERIODS. When only a comparatively few individuals are entered in a tournament for golf, tennis, horseshoes, handball, table tennis, paddleball, squash, or badminton, times are arranged by the participants for their own convenience. With this type of scheduling, a deadline is set to indicate the date on or before which the matches must be played.

EARLY MORNING HOURS. Some schools find early morning hours, starting at 7:45 or 8:00 before classes begin, a satisfactory time for intramural contests. As mentioned previously, increased enrollments may necessitate intramural morning-leagues and -tournaments.

SPECIAL DAYS. School administrators are often willing to set aside regular class time so an entire school can participate in a field meet, track meet, play day, or sports day. Usually, the afternoon classes are suspended and the entire school assembles for sports activities. The holiday from classes adds enthusiasm and interest to such programs. Half-days are set aside during fall, winter, and/or spring, with outdoor activities promoted in fall and spring and indoor activities emphasized in winter. All students in the school are assigned to blue or gold teams. Both boys and girls are included, and team scores are recorded from year to year. To add tradition and interest, students are identified with the same color each year. As new students are enrolled they are assigned to one of the two groups, with some consideration given to equalizing competition on the basis of the previous year's records and knowledge of probable individual performances. Colors or names are used to identify the two main groups. This type of competition requires detailed planning and administration but it is extremely worthwhile.

From the previous discussions, it is easily understood that intramural time arrangements are indigenous to localities and attitudes of sponsors interested in the program of athletics for all. The enthusiastic intramural director will find some time to conduct an intramural program in his school.

SCHEDULING

A well-planned and -administered schedule often means the difference between a highly successful intramural program and one that looks good on paper. The following discussions deal with scheduling factors such as entries, notification of participants, and postponements. (The mechanics of structuring leagues, meets, and tournaments are considered in Chapter 9.)

Entries

There are numerous types of entry blanks, but in general they are classified three ways: (1) team entries, (2) individual and dual entries, (3) meet entries. A team entry blank for team managers to fill out (see Fig. 11) is used for

Date ____________ Checked by ______
Scheduled ______

TEAM SPORTS ENTRY BLANK

SPORT ______________________

TEAM ______________________ (print) MANAGER ______________________ (print)

ADDRESS ______________________ MPLS. ___ ST. PAUL ___ TEL. __________

CIRCLE HOURS YOUR TEAM CANNOT PARTICIPATE. DRAW A LINE UNDER PREFERRED PLAYING TIMES.

MONDAY	4:00-5:00	5:00-6:00	6:00-7:00	7:00-8:00	8:00-9:00	9:00-10:00
TUESDAY	4:00-5:00	5:00-6:00	6:00-7:00	7:00-8:00	8:00-9:00	9:00-10:00
WEDNESDAY	4:00-5:00	5:00-6:00	6:00-7:00	7:00-8:00	8:00-9:00	9:00-10:00
THURSDAY	4:00-5:00	5:00-6:00	6:00-7:00	7:00-8:00	8:00-9:00	9:00-10:00
FRIDAY	4:00-5:00	5:00-6:00	6:00-7:00	7:00-8:00	8:00-9:00	9:00-10:00

- TEAM ROSTER -

1. ______________	11. ______________
2. ______________	12. ______________
3. ______________	13. ______________
4. ______________	14. ______________
5. ______________	15. ______________
6. ______________	16. ______________
7. ______________	17. ______________
8. ______________	18. ______________
9. ______________	19. ______________
10. ______________	20. ______________

- ELIGIBILITY -

THIS CERTIFIES THAT I KNOW AND UNDERSTAND THE INTRAMURAL ELIGIBILITY RULES AND HAVE COMPLETELY CHECKED THE ELIGIBILITY OF ALL THE PLAYERS ON MY TEAM. IF THERE IS ANY DISCREPANCY, I WILL ASSUME FULL RESPONSIBILITY. FAILURE TO COMPLY WITH THESE RULES WILL RESULT IN DISCIPLINARY ACTION AS OUTLINED ON PAGE 10 OF THE I-M SPORTS HANDBOOK.

____
Manager's Signature

Figure 11. Team Sports Entry Blank for Team Manager's Use.

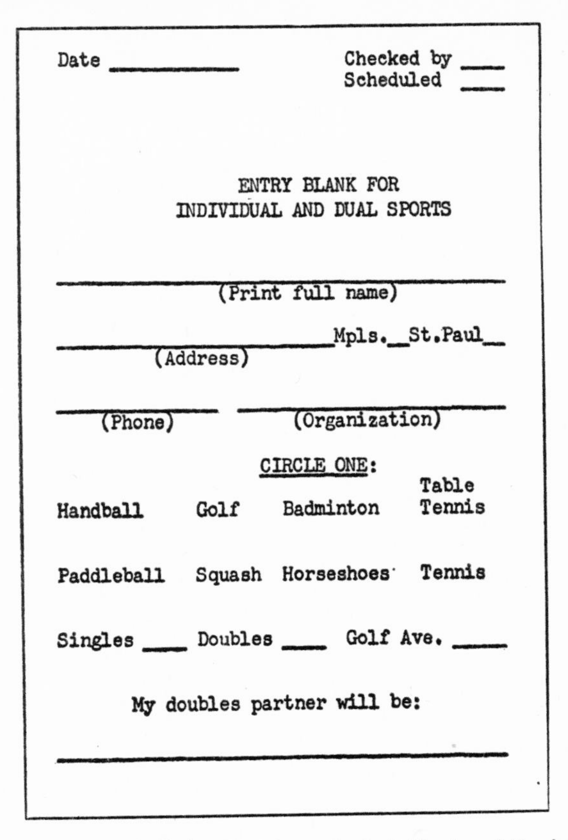

Date ________ Checked by ___
Scheduled ___

ENTRY BLANK FOR
INDIVIDUAL AND DUAL SPORTS

____
(Print full name)

______________________ Mpls.__ St.Paul__
(Address)

__________ ______________
(Phone) (Organization)

CIRCLE ONE:

Handball	Golf	Badminton	Table Tennis
Paddleball	Squash	Horseshoes	Tennis

Singles ___ Doubles ___ Golf Ave. ____

My doubles partner will be:

____

Figure 12. Entry Blank for Participant in Individual and Dual Sports.

sports such as basketball, touch football, softball, and volleyball or individual and dual sports such as tennis, handball, and golf which are promoted on a team basis. The individual and dual sports entry blank (see Fig. 12) is used by the individual participant for squash, badminton, table tennis, horseshoes, paddleball, handball, and tennis when promoted on a nonteam basis. Meet entry blanks are used for swimming, wrestling, and track meets, when students enter individual events such as the 100-yard dash, 220-yard dash, high jump, shot put, and broad jump.

Entry blanks should request information which facilitates effective scheduling. The following list indicates the items which should be included on entry blanks:

1. Name of the sport
2. Name of the entrant
3. Manager's or captain's name, address, and telephone number
4. Specified hours the participant(s) CAN or CANNOT participate
5. Date of entry
6. Alphabetical listing of team roster or positioning of players in appropriate events
7. Signed statement of eligibility
8. Space for office checking and scheduling

The signed statement of eligibility places the responsibility of understanding and checking the team's eligibility on the manager or captain.

Rules pertaining to tournament or meet procedures are sometimes included on entry blanks. However, a less complicated and neater appearing entry form results if rules are published on supplemental sheets. To avoid possible misscheduling, one entry blank should be filled out for each team when organizations enter more than one team. When entries are received, they should be carefully checked for errors and properly classified. If students are asked to return entries to the office in person instead of by mail, the office staff can eliminate inconsistencies by immediately checking the entry and eligibility status of the participants. In addition, important office-student relationships are established if the staff is helpful in answering questions and letting individuals know the I-M department is ready to be of service to assure satisfactory experiences on the part of entrants.

There are two different opinions on setting entry deadlines. One group feels that deadlines should be set for all entries and the other group thinks an open-end deadline should be utilized. The open-end deadline suggests that entries are due by a certain date but additional entries are accepted if they can be worked into the tournament. In large schools, there may be drop-outs, and late entries are substituted to eliminate forfeits. One of the disadvantages of the latter method is that it encourages late entries. Entry deadlines strictly adhered to, combined with program publicity which informs all students, should develop a sense of student responsibility which helps eliminate late entries and reduce drop-outs.

In some highly organized intramural programs, the intramural director automatically enters one team from each fraternity, or other stable unit, for each sport. The fraternity notifies the I-M office if they want more than one team or do not want any teams. Still another method is to send a card to each campus group requesting that they return the card if their organization intends to enter a specific sport. After checking the entries against the list of teams that usually enter, it is wise to call the nonentered organizations before the final deadline to check if they are entering a team. However, this can have a negative effect comparable to allowing late entries in that it encourages groups to be delinquent; they know they will be called if they fail to enter a team.

Arrangements

Perhaps nothing is more detrimental to the intramural program than poor scheduling. If a team is told to report for a contest and its opponent or the officials fail to appear, it results in demoralized participants. If this condition exists even occasionally, the students soon lose interest, and pride in the intramural program is destroyed.

There are several factors which must be considered before schedules can be completed. Attention must be given to: (1) time allotted for the league or tournament; (2) available equipment and facilities; (3) number of entering individuals and teams; (4) number of games necessary to complete the schedule; (5) conflicts with other campus activities; (6) allowance for possible postponements because of inclement weather; (7) seeding of exceptional performers or last year's winners; and (8) assignment of practice games.

To avoid all possible conflicts, the intramural director should utilize yearly, monthly, and weekly calendars. If activities on the yearly calendar are arranged during the same period from year to year, students learn to anticipate tournaments. The establishment of traditions is very important to successful intramural programs. Calendar worksheets or large cardboard calendars with write-on and wipe-off grease pencils are extremely effective aids in co-ordinating intramural activities.

When possible, specific dates and times should be set for a tournament match or league game. Some tournaments require participants to set their own times, with the provision that games must be played on or before a certain date or with instructions to play one game per week. This flexibility is often necessary for faculty competition but it is difficult to attain success without constant supervision and reminders from the intramural staff. Entrants wait for their opponents to call, and before long the tournament is behind schedule or is on schedule with several forfeits. Slow tournaments and forfeits result in unsatisfied participants. This type of scheduling is most effective when competitors are enthusiastic and do not require prompting to play a match in ladder, pyramid, or funnel-type tournaments.

Schedules should be arranged as far in advance of actual playing dates as possible. However, time may restrict advance scheduling because entries are not available until a few days before games begin. This is particularly true of activities which begin the first or second week of school. Some directors feel it is advantageous to make up a partial schedule covering first-round games and then complete the schedule, eliminating forfeiting teams and drop-outs. This also permits partial seeding if first-round, undefeated teams are not scheduled to meet until the final round of league play.

Another important consideration in arranging schedules is that teams should be scheduled to play the same night each week. This permits students to arrange their other school activities accordingly. If two or more sports are sponsored at the same time, care must be taken to schedule them on different nights for the same units. For example, fraternities could bowl on Tuesdays and play basketball on Thursdays to eliminate conflicts if some member plays on both teams.

Whenever feasible, preferred playing times should be honored in drawing up schedules. Eventually, some teams have to play on a different night in order to meet winners of other divisions in the play-offs. It is possible that two teams that would not ordinarily play according to preferred times listed on their entry blanks are required to meet in the play-down. When this occasion arises, the managers have to agree on a time even if it is as unusual as 7:00 A.M.

Schedule Forms

Actual schedules can take one or all of several forms: original work schedules, office master or daily schedules, mimeographed or dittoed schedules, card schedules, student newspaper schedules, or daily schedules posted in the playing area. Original work schedules are prepared from entry blanks. Samples of types of entry blanks appear on pages 140, 141, and 156. The master or daily schedule is drawn from the work schedule. This schedule includes the sport, time, date, court or field, opponents, officials, and a telephone check column or name of the person notified about the game. Figure 13 illustrates two types of intramural daily schedules. The advantage of Type I is that duplication of games on a court or field is easily discernible. A disadvantage is that a separate form must be used for each sport. Several sports can be scheduled on the Type II form.

Schedules can be mimeographed or dittoed and given to team captains. These schedules should include opponents, date, time, sport, court or field, blanks for score, parentheses for final league position, and simple directions. Figure 14 shows a schedule for independent teams in the touch football league. Card schedules offer comparable information

INTRAMURAL DAILY SCHEDULE

SPORT Softball | Type I | DATE Tues., May 3

TIME	FIELD VI	FIELD VII	FIELD VIII
4:30	Arrow Inn Chateau Club		Centennial 10 Centennial 7
6:00	Alpha Delta Phi Kappa Sigma	Tiger A.C. Amigo Club	Pioneer 6 Pioneer 2
7:30	Phi Beta Pi Psi Omega	Zeta Psi Sigma Chi	Standard Deviates Combo's
9:00	Newman Club Sad Sacks		
UMPIRES	Anderson & Tutt Bailey & Roeder	McCarthy & Buendorf	Schoenke & Siegel

INTRAMURAL
SCHEDULE FOR TODAY

Type II | DATE Wed., Jan. 20

SPORT	TIME	COURT	TEAM	NOTIFIED	VS	TEAM	NOTIFIED
Basketball	7:00	1	ACACIA	Olson	VS	CHI PHI	Smith
"	"	2	SIGMA NU	Parr	VS	THETA XI	Donnelly
"	8:00	3	THETA CHI	Bye	VS	BETA THETA PI	Reed
"	"	4	TRIANGLE	Larson	VS	DELTA CHI	Kaiser
					VS		
Volleyball	4:15	6	MERRITT 1	Hass	VS	ANDREWS 6	Fox
"	"	8	MC LEOD 3	Miller	VS	CARVER 5	Grewe
"	7:30	6	SWISHERS	Sans	VS	PUFFIN 6	Nibbe
"	"	8	VALLEY FIVE	Johnson	VS	MERCURY'S	Luger
"	8:30	6	2 - 4 - D's	Case	VS	WHIZ KIDS	Peller
					VS		
					VS		

Figure 13. Types of Intramural Daily Schedules.

but only for the team involved. Duplicated schedule sheets carry several divisions and give players an opportunity to follow the play of other teams in the league. These schedules are distributed to team managers through the mail, athletic council meetings, student post office boxes, or intramural information boxes reserved for each manager.

Student newspapers often carry a daily schedule of intra-

TOUCH FOOTBALL

INDEPENDENT SCHEDULE

DIVISION I

Team	Score	Team	DATE	FIELD	TIME
EVANS SCHOLARS (3)	12 vs 20	RICHFIELD A.C. (1)	10-7	1	6:10
WASH. AVE. BUMS (0)	6 vs 8	NEWMAN "BLUE" (2)	10-7	3	7:50
EVANS SCHOLARS	7d vs 2d	WASH. AVE. BUMS	10-14	2	9:30
RICHFIELD A.C.	7 vs 6	NEWMAN "BLUE"	10-14	2	7:00
EVANS SCHOLARS	14 vs 21	NEWMAN "BLUE"	10-21	4	8:40
RICHFIELD A.C.	18 vs 12	WASH. AVE. BUMS	10-21	4	7:50

DIVISION II

Team	Score	Team	DATE	FIELD	TIME
MILLARDERS ( )	__vs__	COFFMAN BOMBERS ( )	10-8	1	7:50
WRONSKIANS ( )	__vs__	TIGER A.C. II ( )	10-8	1	7:00
MILLARDERS	__vs__	WRONSKIANS	10-15	2	8:40
COFFMAN BOMBERS	__vs__	TIGER A.C. II	10-15	2	7:50
MILLARDERS	__vs__	TIGER A.C. II	10-22	3	8:40
COFFMAN BOMBERS	__vs__	WRONSKIANS	10-22	3	7:00

DIRECTIONS

Fields 1, 2, 3, and 4 are located north of the railroad tracks on Delta Field.

NOTE: At the completion of the divisional round robin, undefeated teams compete in single-elimination All-U Class A Play-offs. Teams with one loss enter the All-U Class B Play-offs. Teams with two losses play in the All-U Class C Play-offs. Winless teams compete in the All-U Class D Play-offs.

Figure 14. Independent Touch Football League Schedule.

mural events. This schedule is derived from the master schedule in the office, and someone should be charged with the responsibility of relaying correct information to the newspaper. In addition, daily schedules can be posted in the lobby of the gymnasium building or on a portable black board or bulletin board in the area of play. For added interest, the league position of the teams should be placed in parentheses after the team name. For example, Alley Cats (4) *vs.* Pinsplitters (2).

In addition to notifying teams via schedules, some intramural directors advise making reminder calls or sending reminder cards. These reminders should be given at least two days in advance of the game. When teams are called, a check mark should be placed behind the team name on the master schedule or the name of the person taking the call should be recorded in case there is a question of who failed to relay the information. Students have a tendency to blame the intramural office when inconsistencies occur.

Other directors prefer to send out just one schedule indicating to the manager this is the only notification. This places responsibility on the team manager. In large schools where students have numerous activities, it is advisable to use combination methods of scheduling and notification such as daily newspaper schedules, mimeographed schedules, and telephone or card reminders. If these combinations are used, extreme care must be exercised to avoid providing conflicting information. Each intramural supervisor has to decide which procedures insure an efficient and effective program in his school.

Postponements

Postponements are inevitable in intramural work and must be adequately handled. Indoor winter activities do not cause much trouble in this respect, but fall and spring outdoor sports encounter schedule changes because of inclement weather. One rainy day can postpone an entire schedule of games and result in twice as much staff work in rescheduling. Two days could be lost, depending on the amount of rainfall and the drainage of the playing fields. Other obstacles include campus-wide functions and varsity athletic contests which many students attend.

Insofar as possible, the factors that cause postponement should be predetermined. For instance, the dates of varsity games and school functions should be omitted from intramural schedules. The larger the school, the more difficult scheduling is and it is necessary to exercise more flexibility in this type of postponement request. Inclement weather cannot be foreseen. An intramural staff member should be the judge of playing conditions rather than the competing teams. Teams should be required to contact the intramural authorities and obtain their decision on questionable games.

If the weather is such that postponement is determined several hours before game time, the I-M office can perform a valuable service by notifying all of the teams. In general, it is advisable to establish a cancellation deadline, and if games are not called by this time, they are canceled at the field of play. This assures completing the games and eliminates any possible mistake of canceling too early. After teams are at the field and conditions become worse, the decision to continue or terminate the games rests with the intramural supervisor or officials.

The previous discussion dealt with *bona fide* postponements, those resulting from weather and school functions requiring school attendance by the general student body. These are not the only situations in which game delays are requested. It is not unusual for a team to ask for a postponement because one or more members are ill or out of town. Some of these are not valid requests and the director has to consider each situation on its own merits.

In colleges and universities, social groups, such as fraternities, often find that a certain scheduled game interferes with some social event they are planning. This can be true of homecoming preparations, an exchange dinner, or a founder's day banquet. This type of request usually is denied. If intramural schedules are continually changed to meet all situations and favor all teams, it is next to impossible to complete the schedules. Such organizations should be encouraged to make a choice as to which activities are most important to them. Scheduling games on the same night of the week for a particular team gives them an opportunity to arrange their social calendar around intramural activities.

There are times when both teams mutually desire to postpone their game. Each team should officially notify the

I-M office of its intention. Otherwise, one team could call the other and imply that the I-M office is postponing the game. This case is different from the one in which only one team wants a change. To permit the change in the latter instance is unfair to the team willing to play as scheduled. The mutual request is often granted when it is possible for the game to be played at another time without disrupting the schedule. It is important that the request be made as early as possible so the I-M office can substitute another game. The substitute teams should have at least two days' notice.

Following a postponement, an arrangement must be made to reschedule the game(s). Different methods are used with elimination tournament and league games. In the elimination series, the games are simply postponed a day. This is the only feasible method because future games are contingent on winners of previous games. In the league series, where a schedule is made out in advance to cover the entire season, the previous method is impossible because games are already scheduled for the days succeeding the one on which the games are postponed. Therefore, the schedule must go ahead as previously arranged and the postponed games must remain undecided until the schedule permits an open date.

Postponed games are usually rescheduled at a time other than the regular playing time. To save office time in rescheduling, it is advisable to have the two managers arrange a mutually agreeable time. Both managers should contact the I-M Office to confirm the new schedule. This eliminates numerous "middle" calls by the staff.

Experience of people in intramural work indicates that as many reasons as possible for postponements should be anticipated beforehand and avoided. Unless absolutely necessary, postponements should not be accepted later than 24 hours prior to game time and not at the inconvenience of one team. If postponement policies are not consistently enforced, players are encouraged to seek a game change for the slightest reason and intramural sports lose prestige.

SUMMARY

1. The person in charge of intramurals must carefully select time and completely co-ordinate I-M activities with all other phases of the school program.
2. Time of day, season of the year, availability of buildings, fields, and courts, and amount of time that the I-M supervisor can devote to the program, all determine I-M scheduling.
3. Evening schedules are usually not desirable in high schools while they are common in colleges and universities.
4. Late afternoons, following classes, are popular in both high schools and universities and colleges for I-M participation.
5. Noon-hour I-M programs are popular in many high schools and elementary schools but emphasis should be placed on less strenuous activities.
6. The noon-hour program is an excellent place in which to start or conduct a corecreational program of activities.
7. Many schools conduct their I-M programs during free periods or club or activity periods during the school day.
8. Additional times for intramurals in either high schools or colleges and universities are Saturdays, Monday, and Friday afternoons and evenings, vacation periods, early mornings, and special days.
9. Regardless of obstacles and local conditions, the enthusiastic intramural director will find some time to conduct an I-M program in his school.
10. A well-planned and -administered schedule often means the difference between a highly successful intramural program and one that looks good on paper.
11. Entry blanks are generally classified into three types: team, individual and dual, and meet.
12. Entry blanks should request information such as name of sport, entrant's name, manager or captain's name, phone and address, preferred hours for competing, team roster, signed statement of eligibility, space for office checking and scheduling, etc., which facilitate effective scheduling.
13. Entry deadlines encourage student responsibility and help eliminate late entries and reduce drop-outs.
14. To insure proper schedules, attention must be given to time needed for completion, available equipment and facilities,

number of entries, maximum number of games necessary to complete the schedule, conflicts with other campus activities, allowance for possible postponements, seedings, and practice games.

15. Specific dates and times for events should be set as far in advance as possible.
16. Teams should be scheduled to play the same night each week.
17. Actual schedules can be original work schedules, office master or daily schedules, mimeographed or dittoed schedules, card schedules, student newspaper schedules, or daily schedules posted in the playing area.
18. Schedules should include opponents, date, time, sport, court or field, blanks for score, parentheses for final league position, and simple directions.
19. Postponements are inevitable in intramural work and must be adequately handled to insure a smooth-running program.
20. Inclement weather cannot be foreseen, but such factors as school functions and varsity athletic contests at home should be taken into account when scheduling to avoid future postponements.
21. Postponed games are usually rescheduled at a time other than a regular playing time.
22. Unless absolutely necessary, postponement should not be accepted later than 24 hours prior to game time and not at the inconvenience of one team.

9

Meet, League, and Tournament Methods

One of the most important elements in a successful intramural program is proper selection of meet, league, or tournament methods to use in conducting a particular sport. Meets, leagues, and tournaments are well-developed plans for providing organized and impartially scheduled, competitive participation in a sport usually designed to select one or more winners. The ideal competitive plan for intramurals should: (1) determine a true champion; (2) offer equal or well-matched competition; (3) insofar as possible, require participants to play an equal number of games or matches; (4) not be too short or, conversely, be played over too extended a period of time; (5) involve as many teams or players as possible; and (6) provide keen rivalry for all participants including those who lose several games.

In selecting the competitive method, it is necessary to consider what the activity is and why it is conducted—the purpose of the tournament or league. If it is an individual or dual sport, it requires a different plan than a team sport. An individual sport may also be conducted on a team basis. In addition to the purpose and nature of the activity, attention must be given to the age, interests, and abilities of the participants. Other considerations include: (1) time, facilities, and equipment available; (2) number of winners desired; (3) accuracy with which players rank in order of finish; and (4) personnel available to supervise and officiate the competition.

Discussion of methods of organizing participation is centered on meets, leagues, tournaments, and ways of equalizing and classifying competition.

MEETS

Meets are customarily used for contests which include a number of separate events and which must be completed within a day or so—possibly within an afternoon or evening Meets are especially suitable for track, swimming, gymnastics, and ice skating and for field days or sports festivals. A complete schedule should be arranged in advance and each event run off at the designated time.

Track and Field Meets

Track and field meets are held during the outdoor and indoor seasons with events adapted to each situation. Sample schedules for both meets are included in this chapter.

OUTDOOR MEET. A well-arranged schedule is a necessity if trial heats in the dashes and hurdles are scheduled. Time reserved for trial heats in each event must be determined by the number of entries. The finals usually take the same length of time. In field events, one must consider the number of entries and how many events can be carried on at the same time with available space and jumping pits. The high jump and pole vault are especially slow events and should be started as early as possible. To assure an efficient meet, starting and finishing points for track events and positions of the hurdles should be plainly marked, equipment stored in its proper place, and men stationed to remove and replace hurdles quickly.

OUTDOOR TRACK MEET

TRACK EVENTS

1. 120-yard high hurdles, trial heats .... 2:00 P.M.
2. 100-yard dash trial heats .... 2:20 P.M.
3. One-mile run .... 2:35 P.M.
4. 440-yard dash .... 2:45 P.M.
5. 100-yard dash, finals .... 2:55 P.M.

6. 120-yard high hurdles, finals .... 3:10 P.M.
7. 220-yard dash, trial heats .... 3:25 P.M.
8. 220-yard low hurdles, trial heats .... 3:40 P.M.
9. 880-yard run .... 4:00 P.M.
10. 220-yard dash, finals .... 4:10 P.M.
11. 220-yard low hurdles, finals .... 4:25 P.M.
12. Half-mile relay .... 4:45 P.M.

FIELD EVENTS

1. Pole vault .... 1:15 P.M.
2. High jump .... 1:15 P.M.
3. Shot put .... 1:30 P.M.
4. Broad jump .... 1:30 P.M.
5. Discus .... immediately after completing shot put

The above program is planned for a college intramural meet in which there are a large number of entries. Whenever possible, such a meet should take place over a period of two or three afternoons. Preliminaries can be scheduled for the first two days and finals on the last day or preliminaries and finals of several events can be scheduled each day. For example, on Monday, schedule the broad jump, shot put, 220-yard dash, and mile; Tuesday, high jump, discus, 120-yard low hurdles, and 880-yard run; Wednesday, pole vault, 100-yard dash, 440-yard dash, and half-mile relay. The two- or three-day schedule for a large meet is less strenuous for the competitors.

Teams should submit entries prior to a track meet to aid team managers in organizing their teams. However, it is not always advisable to arrange heats from these entries because there might be numerous "scratches" and heats would have to be rearranged. A method to overcome "scratches" requires each individual entrant to fill out a slip, similar to the one appearing in Figure 15, at the track for each event he intends to enter. Small pencils are provided at strategic places in the track area. The clerk-of-course or "heat arranger" calls for entry slips for the event before the start of each event. In the 220-yard dash, he calls for all individual slips for the "220" and proceeds to count and arrange heats a few minutes before the first "220" heat is run. After a heat is arranged and announced, a track supervisor

I-M TRACK ENTRY BLANK

Name (Print): ______________________
Last First

Team: ______________________

- - - - - - - - - - - - - - - - - -

Event (circle one)

100 Yd. Dash	220 Yd. Dash
440 Yd. Dash	Half Mile Run
Mile Run	Half Mile Relay
High Jump	________
120 Low Hurdles	________
Broad Jump	________
Shot Put	________

- - - - - - - - - - - - - - - - - -

HEAT ________ LANE ________

TIME ____ PLACE ____ POINTS ____

Figure 15. Entry Blank for Participant in Track and Field Meets.

takes the slips for that heat to the head judge or timer who in turn records the place and time of the winners. (This individual-entry procedure works well in swimming and other meets and in tournaments, such as wrestling, where entries are usually taken at the last possible moment in an effort to eliminate all "scratches" or forfeits.) This does not preclude preconditioning workouts but provides a true tournament draw for those present for the actual tournament.

Another procedure which is used when students are not competing for teams is to have all entrants line up according to height. For example, 32 students show up for the 220-yard dash; there are 8 lanes on the track. After lining up according to size, the participants "count off" by four's. The number one's run in the first heat, two's in the second, three's in the third, and four's in the fourth. Runners line up according to heats behind the starting line and are ready to run as soon as their heat is called. Arranging heats according to size provides a good distribution of fast and slow runners. If entrants are participating for teams, this method does not prevent all members of the same team from running in the same lane. This procedure can be used with teams if adjustments are made to alternate team members in different heats.

In public school competition, the previous track schedule can be followed but the events should be modified to meet the age and conditioning of the students. The fact that some of the events can be eliminated entirely usually permits a shorter program. Restrictions are usually placed on the number of events in which a student participates.

Several interesting variations can be devised for elementary- and secondary-school track meets. In field events, such as the broad jump and high jump, team points are assigned for achieving certain distances. Each team is represented by the same number of contestants. Points are awarded to each team member who clears a certain height or distance. The reverse method is also used with points assigned to contestants who fail to survive the trials and the team with the least points is the winner.

The broad jump can be conducted on a "match play" basis. For example, the number one jumper of team A is matched against the number one jumper of team B, number two of team A against number two of team B, etc. One point is awarded to the winner of each match jump. Team points are totaled to determine the broad jump winner and they can also apply to the over-all track meet winner.

Another variation adds all team members' standing-broad-jump distances and compares the total with the opposing team's total. After jumper A jumps, teammate B places his toes at the heel marks of jumper A and jumps in the same direction. Each team member jumps in this manner as do members of the other teams. The team which jumps the greatest distance wins. This type of comparison eliminates measuring distances.

Scoring in intramural track meets should be liberal with as many students as possible scoring or given the opportunity to score. Two commonly used procedures score all events including relays 10–8–6–4–2–1 or score 7–5–4–3–2–1 in all events except the relays which are scored 14–10–8–6–4–2.

The officials for the meet can include the following:

1 referee	1 announcer
1 starter	2 judges per place for track events
1 clerk-of-course	3 timers
1 scorer	1 judge per field event

For large meets, it is advisable to provide assistants to help the clerk-of-course, referee, scorer, and announcer. There should be at least two judges at the finish line for each place picked in the event.

It is important that care be taken in choosing officials. The referee and starter especially must be experienced and the clerk-of-the course and announcer should keep the events moving according to the time schedule. The varsity or assistant track coach can usually be secured as starter and members of the varsity team can serve in other capacities.

INDOOR MEET. In planning an indoor track and field meet, many of the same problems are faced as in the outdoor meet. The events must be adapted to indoor use and some distances are adjusted to fit local facilities. Some schools have a curved running-track in the gymnasium and enough floor space for a 50-yard straightway. Others have access to a field house with an eighth-mile track or comparable running area.

Where only a few teams are participating, a relay race can be included in the program, preferably at the end. In many intramural meets, the large number of entries makes it advisable, because of cramped facilities, to conduct relays at another time. A separate indoor relays meet can be

scheduled and the four top teams could later stage a preliminary race to a varsity indoor track meet.

INDOOR TRACK MEET

TRACK EVENTS

1.	60-yard dash, trial heats	7:30 P.M.
2.	One-mile run	7:50 P.M.
3.	60-yard dash, finals	8:00 P.M.
4.	70-yard high hurdles, trial heats	8:15 P.M.
5.	440-yard dash	8:30 P.M.
6.	70-yard high hurdles, finals	8:40 P.M.
7.	70-yard low hurdles, trial heats	8:50 P.M.
8.	880-yard run	9:05 P.M.
9.	70-yard low hurdles, finals	9:15 P.M.
10.	Relay	9:25 P.M.

FIELD EVENTS

1.	Pole vault	7:00 P.M.
2.	High jump	7:00 P.M.
3.	Shot put	7:00 P.M.
4.	Broad jump	8:00 P.M.

Swimming Meets

A swimming meet is easier to conduct than a track meet because only one event is contested at a time. However, to run an efficient meet requires detailed planning and almost as many officials as for track. Preliminary events are usually scheduled for one evening with the finals on the following evening. Officials consist of referee, starter, finish judges, diving judges, clerk-of-course, take-off judges, timers, scorer, and inspector of turns and swimming form. For intramural meets, the varsity coach or other experienced official can assume the duties of more than one official. For example, the coach serves as referee, starter, take-off judge, inspector of turns and swimming form, and one of the diving judges. Varsity swimmers and student intramural assistants can serve as timers, finish judges, and scorers.

Swimmers in the time trials who advance to the finals are selected on the basis of time and place of finish. Two finish judges and three timers should be assigned to each lane. Some intramural directors forego finish judges and rely on timers to determine who swims in the finals and then use both timers and judges for the final night. Picking places in a track or swimming meet can be very difficult, particularly in short races and if students or other inexperienced personnel serve as the finish judges. Occasionally, this job is even troublesome for the expert. Some mechanical scoring devices are available which record the contestant's time and place on a total board.

There is usually a wide range of ability in diving. Divers perform their required and optional dives on the one-meter board. The total number of dives depends on the ability of the divers but it is usually not more than eleven or less than five. As an example, two dives are required, such as the plain front and plain back dive, with three dives optional. Dives are divided into five categories: Group I, forward dive; Group II, back dive; Group III, reverse dive; Group IV, inward dive; and Group V, forward dive, one-half twist. Another method is to draw the compulsory dives from several or all of the foregoing groups and insist that voluntary dives represent at least three or four different groups.

Three judges should be appointed to judge the diving. If five judges are used, high and low awards should be canceled. Dives are judged on the following ten-point scale: very good = 9, 9.5, 10 points; good = 7, 7.5, 8, 8.5 points; satisfactory = 5, 5.5, 6, 6.5 points; deficient = 3, 3.5, 4, 4.5 points; unsatisfactory = 1, 1.5, 2, 2.5 points; completely failed = 0, 0.5 points. The sum of the three awards is multiplied by the degree of difficulty for a particular dive to obtain the total value. The diver with the highest point total wins the diving event. Diving score sheets and calculator can be obtained from the AAU in New York.

The following scoring chart can serve as a guide for assigning team points in an intramural swimming meet:

	MEDLEY AND FREESTYLE RELAYS	OTHER EVENTS
4 Lanes	10–6–4–2	5–3–2–1
5 Lanes	12–8–6–4–2	6–4–3–2–1
6 Lanes	14–10–8–6–4–2	7–5–4–3–2–1

It is customary to limit competitors to participation in any three events. Conditioning periods should be required, and, in addition, events should be shortened to accommodate abilities of the participants. The following program is suggested for intramural swimming meets:

INTRAMURAL SWIMMING PROGRAM

1. 200-yard medley relay (four swimmers on a team; each swims one-fourth of the distance continuously: first, backstroke; second, breaststroke; third, butterfly stroke; fourth, a stroke other than these three)
2. 50-yard freestyle
3. 50-yard butterfly stroke
4. 50-yard backstroke
5. 100-yard freestyle
6. 50-yard breaststroke
7. One-meter springboard diving
8. 100-yard individual medley (the first one-fourth distance is the butterfly stroke, the second one-fourth, the backstroke, the third one-fourth, breaststroke, and the last one-fourth any stroke other than the first three)
9. 200-yard freestyle relay (four swimmers on a team; each swims 50 yards continuously)

Gymnastic Meets

Gymnastic meets are generally arranged according to a schedule similar to track and swimming. Events usually include tumbling, horizontal bar, parallel bars, side horse, and rings. Judging the work on each piece of apparatus is similar to judging diving. The scale is based on 100 points instead of 10 and the degree of difficulty. Difficulty is figured in the judges' award with 60 points allowed for the degree of difficulty and 40 points allotted to form and execution of the exercise. Physical education instructors, coaches, and varsity team members are an excellent source of gymnastic judges.

If a meet consists of a large number of entries, team scoring can be based on ten places in each event, 11–9–8–7–6–5–4–3–2–1, or, for fewer entries, five places, 6–4–3–2–1. Another team scoring method is to total judges' awards of the top three team members in each event. The best individual performance for all-around and each event can be recognized as well as team performance. A gymnastic meet is particularly effective if it coincides or follows a physical education teaching unit on gymnastics.

Other Meets

Speed skating and ice carnivals are usually conducted on a meet basis. These meets are held indoors or outdoors, depending on available facilities. Events consist of long and short distance races, relay races, and novelty races.

Sports carnivals, field days, and festivals are also arranged on a meet basis. Some track and field events can be included as well as novelty and exhibition events. Competition can be scheduled between student and faculty teams or final matches of some intramural sports can be played. A more detailed explanation of these programs is found in Chapter 13.

LEAGUES

Many sports cannot be conducted on the meet plan. This is true of team games such as basketball, softball, touch football, baseball, volleyball, and hockey and a number of individual sports such as tennis, handball, and squash. For these, the method chosen depends largely on the time, facilities, and equipment available. Leagues are discussed in this section with attention given later to other short- and long-term tournaments.

In tournament structuring, the word "league" refers to grouping individuals or teams for competitive purposes. Broadly interpreted, it can include an entire unit such as the fraternity league, dormitory league, or independent league with the leagues subdivided into divisions or sections. In some programs, divisions and sections are referred to as leagues. A league is generally arranged with games scheduled on a round robin or partial round robin basis.

Round Robin Calculation

When there is sufficient time and space, each contestant should be allowed to play against every other contestant and the winner determined according to won and lost records or the percentage of victories. The round robin tournament, sometimes called the percentage plan, provides the most participation and is extensively used in intramurals. Although it is the most objective method of measuring the ability of the competitor, one of the disadvantages is the amount of time necessary to complete a round robin. It is particularly cumbersome when large numbers of teams or individuals enter competition. While it is a popular method with entries of eight or less teams, it is only in sports such as bowling that a league including more teams is practical.

Another disadvantage is that teams might finish with identical won-lost records. When this happens, teams can play off to break the tie, if time permits, or ties can be allowed to stand, in which case there are co-champions if the tie is for first place. In situations where time is not available for a play-off and it is necessary to determine places in the final league standings, it is possible to establish procedures which denote final positions. If two teams are tied, first place is awarded to the team that defeated the other team during league play. In bowling, a tie can be broken by crediting first place to the team that has the higher total pin fall for the entire season. Another method which is used is to settle two-or-three-way ties according to differences in teams' scores during league play. In basketball, points scored by and against the teams are added to take into account offensive and defensive ability. The difference between these two sums results in a plus or minus factor and the team with the highest plus factor is awarded first place or the highest place if the tie does not involve first place. For example, Teams A, B, and C are in a three-way tie for first place in a six-team league.

	TEAM A (W–4, L–1)	TEAM B (W–4, L–1)	TEAM C (W–4, L–1)
1st game scores	42–40	54–44	44–54
2nd game scores	41–38	38–41	50–47
3rd game scores	63–62	32–31	39–36
4th game scores	38–40	61–59	40–38
5th game scores	55–51	48–45	56–55
Total differential	239 −231=(+8)	233 −220=(+13)	229 −230=(−1)

According to the above tabulation, Team B has a plus factor of 13 and is awarded first place, Team A has a plus 8 and is in second place, and Team C has a minus 1 and is in third place. In an effort to prevent ties, some tournament directors seed teams on the basis of previous performance and complete the round robin schedule after the first round of games is played. This procedure gives them the opportunity to remove forfeiting teams and to schedule first-round winning teams so they meet in the final games, thus providing the best competition at the end of the schedule.

League standings can be listed on a percentage or nonpercentage basis. When the nonpercentage plan is used, teams are ranked according to their won and lost records; namely, 6–0, 5–1, 4–2, etc. In checking for accuracy of won and lost records, the sum of the won column should equal the sum of the lost column and at the completion of the round robin, each column should total the number of games played. Under the percentage plan, teams are ranked according to percentage of games won, as shown below. The percentage is found by dividing the number of games won by the number of games played. The division is carried three places to the right of the decimal.

$$\text{Example: } \frac{\text{Games Won}}{\text{Games Played}} \qquad \frac{(5)}{(6)} = 0.833$$

If teams play an equal number of games, the team with the highest percentage of games won is the league winner. When teams do not play the same number of games, the nonpercentage plan should be used.

INTRAMURAL SOFTBALL LEAGUE

TEAM NAME	GAMES PLAYED	GAMES WON	GAMES LOST	PERCENT-AGE	PLACE
1. Bulldogs	7	7	0	1.000	1
2. Badgers	7	6	1	.857	2
3. Beavers	7	5	2	.714	3
4. Bobcats	7	4	3	.571	4
5. Baboons	7	3	4	.429	5
6. Broncos	7	2	5	.286	6
7. Bears	7	1	6	.143	7
8. Buffalos	7	0	7	.000	8

Percentages are sometimes illustrated in picture form such as bar graphs, thermometers, or test tubes filled at different levels.

To determine the number of games a team is behind the leading team in leagues, add the difference in wins and losses of the two teams and divide the result by two. In the above softball league standings, the Bulldogs have won seven and lost none and the Broncos have won two and lost five. The difference in wins is five and the difference in losses is five. Five plus five is ten and ten divided by two is five. Therefore, the Broncos are five games behind the Bulldogs.

Before drawing up a round robin, it is necessary to determine the total number of games and rounds needed to complete a schedule in which all competitors meet each other. The term "round" refers to the degree to which the schedule or tournament is completed; it is a measure of tournament progress. In a league which has an even number of teams, the first round is completed when each team has played its first game, the second round consists of teams playing their second game, etc. In elimination-type tournaments, a round with eight teams remaining is called the "quarterfinals"; four teams, the "semifinals"; and two teams, the "finals." The number of rounds necessary to permit each team to meet every other team is equal to the number of teams in a league that has an uneven number of teams and is one less than the number of teams in a league that has an even number of teams.

To determine the number of games necessary to complete a round robin, the following formula can be used: $N\ (N - 1) \div 2$; N equals the number of teams. First, subtract 1 from the number of teams; then multiply this number by the number of teams entered and divide this figure by 2 to determine the number of games to be played.

Word formula:

$$\frac{\text{number of teams} \times \text{number of teams MINUS one}}{\text{DIVIDED by two}} \text{ EQUALS } \text{number of games}$$

Example: Number of teams equals 6

$$\frac{6\ (6 - 1)}{2} = \text{number of games}$$

$$\frac{6\ (6 - 1)}{2} = 15 \text{ games}$$

Another method sometimes used to determine the number of games necessary to complete a round robin is to record the number of entries in arithmetic progression, cancel the largest number and add the remaining numbers. Example for six teams:

1, 2, 3, 4, 5, 6 $\qquad 1 + 2 + 3 + 4 + 5 = 15$ games

To offset the disadvantage of excessive time to complete a round robin with numerous teams, it is possible to play a partial round robin. This means that each team does not play every other team because the number of rounds played is only equal to the amount of time available. Often, intramural and varsity leagues are arranged on a partial round robin basis, and, consequently, the league champion is not a true champion.

A more desirable method which can be used to overcome the "time" disadvantage is to divide the large number of teams into smaller leagues or divisions and have the respective league winners play off for the championship. This does not provide a completely true champion but the winner is more representative than the winner of a partial round robin. Some tournament directors feel it is even more representative to include first and second place winners of each league in the play-offs for the tournament championship.

To illustrate the advantages of the divisional breakdown of leagues, the following examples are given. If 16 teams enter a basketball tournament, it requires 120 games to complete a round robin: $(N \times N - 1) \div 2 = (16 \times 15) \div 2 = 120$. If time or facilities are not available to play this many games, the teams can be subdivided into two divisions of 8 teams. This breakdown results in the playing of 28 games in each league or a total of 56 games. It also means that each team plays a total of 7 league games whereas in a 16-team league, they each play 15 games.

The 16 teams can also be subdivided into four divisions of four teams each. This subdivision requires the playing of six games in each division or a total of 24 games for the four leagues. However, it also reduces the number of games played by each team to three.

Rotation Method

The basic method used in making up round robin schedules is the system of rotation. Letters (A, B, C—a, b, c) or numbers (I, II, III—1, 2, 3) are used to represent the teams, and after these symbols are properly rotated, team names are substituted for the symbols. The symbols are listed vertically or horizontally.

1 *vs.* 2
3 *vs.* 4
5 *vs.* 6

1	3	5
vs.	*vs.*	*vs.*
2	4	6

One number is held in the same position while all other numbers are rotated. The rotation is clockwise or counterclockwise, but the same direction must be used throughout the entire rotation process. After the numbers are listed, they must be rotated once for each round, namely, until each team plays every other team. In the following example of six teams, it is necessary for each team to play five games; consequently, there are five rounds. In this illustration the numeral 1 remains constant and all other numbers are rotated clockwise.

ROUND 1	ROUND 2	ROUND 3	ROUND 4	ROUND 5
1 *vs.* 2	1 *vs.* 3	1 *vs.* 5	1 *vs.* 6	1 *vs.* 4
3 *vs.* 4	5 *vs.* 2	6 *vs.* 3	4 *vs.* 5	2 *vs.* 6
5 *vs.* 6	6 *vs.* 4	4 *vs.* 2	2 *vs.* 3	3 *vs.* 5

For a double round robin, the rotation process is repeated. This might be desirable if there are too few teams in the league and time and facilities permit more games. If six teams are in the league, each team plays ten games in a double round robin.

Type I

SPORT ______________ LEAGUE ______________ DATE ________

TEAMS	WON	LOST	PLACE	POINTS	MANAGER'S NAME	TEL. NO.
1.____	__	__	__	__	______	____
2.____	__	__	__	__	______	____
3.____	__	__	__	__	______	____
4.____	__	__	__	__	______	____
5.____	__	__	__	__	______	____
6.____	__	__	__	__	______	____

	TEAM	SCORE		TEAM	DATE	PLACE	TIME
* 1		vs	2				
3		vs	4				
5		vs	6				

1		vs.	3				
5		vs	2				
6		vs	4				

1		vs	5				
6		vs	3				
4		vs	2				

1		vs	6				
4		vs	5				
2		vs	3				

1		vs	4				
2		vs	6				
3		vs	5				

* Record names of teams in spaces that correspond with the team number listed above.

Figure 16. Types of Six-

Type II

SPORT ______________ LEAGUE ______________ YEAR ______

DIVISION________

NO.	TEAMS	SCHEDULE			SCORES			WON	LOST	PLACE	POINTS
1	______	1x4	1x5	1x6	__	__	__	__	__	__	__
2	______	2x1	2x3	2x6	__	__	__	__	__	__	__
3	______	3x1	3x5	3x6	__	__	__	__	__	__	__
4	______	4x2	4x3	4x6	__	__	__	__	__	__	__
5	______	5x2	5x4	5x6	__	__	__	__	__	__	__
6	______							__	__	__	__

DIVISION________

NO.	TEAMS	SCHEDULE			SCORES			WON	LOST	PLACE	POINTS
1	______	1x4	1x5	1x6	__	__	__	__	__	__	__
2	______	2x1	2x3	2x6	__	__	__	__	__	__	__
3	______	3x1	3x5	3x6	__	__	__	__	__	__	__
4	______	4x2	4x3	4x6	__	__	__	__	__	__	__
5	______	5x2	5x4	5x6	__	__	__	__	__	__	__
6	______							__	__	__	__

DIVISION________

NO.	TEAMS	SCHEDULE			SCORES			WON	LOST	PLACE	POINTS
1	______	1x4	1x5	1x6	__	__	__	__	__	__	__
2	______	2x1	2x3	2x6	__	__	__	__	__	__	__
3	______	3x1	3x5	3x6	__	__	__	__	__	__	__
4	______	4x2	4x3	4x6	__	__	__	__	__	__	__
5	______	5x2	5x4	5x6	__	__	__	__	__	__	__
6	______							__	__	__	__

DIVISION________

NO.	TEAMS	SCHEDULE			SCORES			WON	LOST	PLACE	POINTS
1	______	1x4	1x5	1x6	__	__	__	__	__	__	__
2	______	2x1	2x3	2x6	__	__	__	__	__	__	__
3	______	3x1	3x5	3x6	__	__	__	__	__	__	__
4	______	4x2	4x3	4x6	__	__	__	__	__	__	__
5	______	5x2	5x4	5x6	__	__	__	__	__	__	__
6	______							__	__	__	__

Team Round Robin Forms.

In drawing up a round robin schedule for an uneven number of teams, the same rotation is followed but a "bye" replaces one of the numbers. This indicates that the team corresponding to the number opposite the bye does not play in that particular round. In the following plan, the bye replaces six and is held stationary while all other numbers are rotated clockwise.

ROUND 1	ROUND 2	ROUND 3	ROUND 4	ROUND 5
1 *vs.* 2	3 *vs.* 1	5 *vs.* 3	4 *vs.* 5	2 *vs.* 4
3 *vs.* 4	5 *vs.* 2	4 *vs.* 1	2 *vs.* 3	1 *vs.* 5
5–Bye	4–Bye	2–Bye	1–Bye	3–Bye

Schedule makers save considerable time and effort by using a tournament calculator and round robin charts or tables instead of working out a rotation plan each time a schedule is drawn. For the convenience of tournament directors a calculator for three to thirty-two teams and round robin schedules for three to sixteen teams are included in Chapter 16, Figures 59 and 64.

Another time saver is to make up schedule forms which permit substitution of team names for numbers. Two types are shown in Figure 16 for six-team leagues. Type I can be used as a worksheet from which a schedule is typed or mimeographed or it serves as a schedule as it is by merely substituting names for numbers. Though Type II is not as functional for scheduling, it does provide space for four six-team divisions whereas the other form requires an entire sheet for one division.

Graph Methods

There are several methods of setting up round robin schedules in graph form. Figures 17 and 18 are examples of the most common graph forms. To use these forms, the names of the teams or their symbols (numbers or letters) are listed both horizontally and vertically in the same order. Then the teams scheduled to meet in the round robin are indicated by the intersecting lines. Types I and II in Figure 17 can be used also as schedule sheets, recording the score

Type I Type II

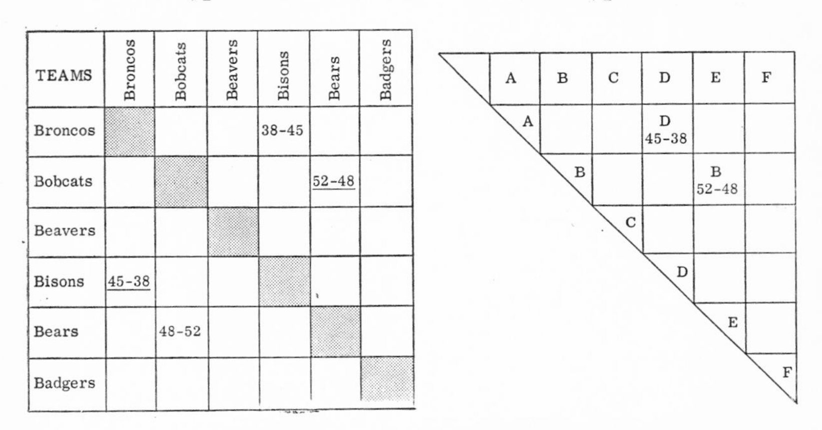

TEAMS	Broncos	Bobcats	Beavers	Bisons	Bears	Badgers
Broncos				38-45		
Bobcats					52-48	
Beavers						
Bisons	45-38					
Bears		48-52				
Badgers						

	A	B	C	D	E	F
	A			D 45-38		
		B			B 52-48	
			C			
				D		
					E	
						F

Figure 17. Two Types of Six-Team Graph Round Robin Schedules. Type I: Score Recorded Twice. Type II: Score Recorded Once.

in the appropriate intersecting spaces. In Type I, the scores are written across from the team names in two squares. The score is first listed and underlined in the winner's square (Bisons, 45–38) and then reversed in the loser's square (Bronchos, 38–45).

Type II, cut diagonally, shows scores recorded in only one space. With this type of graph, it is necessary to record the name of the winning team (D) and the score (45–38). If this kind of recording procedure is used on the Type I graph, it is possible to utilize Type I for a double round robin, recording the scores in the upper half for the first complete round and listing scores in the lower half for the second round robin. A survey of these graphs shows which teams have won and lost and also which games remain to be played. One of the disadvantages is that if daily schedules are not made carefully from the graphs, there is danger that teams will not play regularly or perhaps meet each other more than once.

A scheduling inconsistency of this nature will not occur as often if the kind of graph illustrated in Figure 18 is used.

Type I

	A	B	C	D	E	F
A		1	2	3	4	5
B			3	4	5	2
C				5	1	4
D					2	1
E						3
F						

Type II

	A	B	C	D	E	BYE
A		1	2	3	4	5
B			3	4	5	2
C				5	1	4
D					2	1
E						3
BYE						

Figure 18. Six- and Five-Team Graph Round Robin Schedules. *(Left)* Six Teams. *(Right)* Five Teams.

Usually, scores are not recorded on this type of graph (although it is possible to record them on the lower half of the squares). The letters in Figure 18 represent teams or other entrants and the numbers indicate games which can be scheduled on the same date (assuming that facilities are available). If this scheme is followed, teams are not scheduled to play more than one game on any date. As an example, in the six-team graph, number 2 signifies that A plays C, B plays F, and D plays E on the same day. In the five-team graph, which shows byes, 2 shows that A plays C, B draws a bye, and D plays E. It is not necessary for round 2 to follow 1 or to maintain any particular order as long as all rounds are played, but there is less chance for error if the schedule follows the logical progression of rounds: 1, 2, 3, 4, and 5.

The type of graph round robin illustrated in Figure 18 can be drawn up for any number of teams if the procedure described below is followed. For clarity, the description is for six and five teams, shown in graphs in Figure 18.

1. For six teams, begin under the second team (B) on the first row (A row), and write numbers consecutively from 1 through 5 (one number less than the number of teams to be

scheduled). For five teams record numbers from 1 through 5 (the number of teams playing) listing the highest number (5) in the bye column.

2. In the second row (B row) indent two squares. Start the horizontal numbering with a number which is one higher (3) than the number immediately above it (2). *Do not record any numbers in the F or bye column* (the last column to the right).
3. Continue the indentation and progression for subsequent rows. In carrying out the numerical progression, revert back to 1 after writing the highest number. (In the sample graphs, after recording 5, start with 1.)
4. For the F or bye column place the highest odd number (in this case, 5) in the first block. Proceeding vertically, place the smallest even number in the next block (in this case, 2), then the highest even number (which does not exceed the highest odd number) in the third block (4), the smallest odd number in the next block, and so on. With the exception of the top and bottom numbers in this F or bye column the numbers are always one less than the first number in the horizontal row.

Round Robin Variations

Several types of round robin variations which hold considerable interest for participants can be structured to run off abbreviated tournaments. Actually the basic principle of round robin play is altered very little and the difference is in scoring contests and determining league winners. It is possible to complete some of these tournaments in a few hours, or at the most, one or two days.

PLAY 'TIL YOU WIN METHOD. The "play 'til you win" method is a round robin variation which can be used for several sports. As an example, six players draw for positions in a round robin handball tournament. The round robin continues, into a double round robin if necessary, until one player wins five games or five points (one point is awarded for each game won). Only one 11-point game is played in a match instead of the usual two out of three 21-point games. This tournament could be won by a player if he scored a victory in each of his first five games which requires the playing of a single round robin. However, it might be necessary to play part of a second round robin before one player wins five points, as shown in the following table.

PLAYER	GAMES WON	GAMES LOST	POINTS
Art	5	2	5
Bob	4	3	4
Cal	4	3	4
Don	3	4	3
Jim	3	4	3
Tom	2	5	2

Art's won and lost record was 4–2 before winning his last game. The round robin can be continued to determine 2nd place, 3rd, 4th, or a play-off can be held to break any ties. It takes approximately one and a half hours to complete this tournament. In the illustration above, it is necessary for Art to play a maximum of 75 game points. This compares with 63 winning points in three regulation 21-point handball games. Depending on the condition and playing ability of the contestants, it might be necessary to complete the tournament on a succeeding day.

LOMBARD TOURNAMENT. Another variation of the round robin and similar to the "play 'til you win" method is called the "Lombard tournament method." This method can be modified for volleyball, touch football, softball, hockey, squash, handball, tennis, badminton, and table tennis. In basketball, this method can be used to great advantage in organizing a "quickie" tournament on a gymnasium floor where numerous students are shooting baskets and welcome the opportunity to play in a tournament. The length of the abbreviated games can be determined by dividing the regulation time for one complete game by the number of teams. If courts are available, a centralized timing device can be used to time games on a straight running time basis. Assuming the length of one game is forty minutes and there are eight teams competing, the length of each shortened game is five minutes. Each team plays every other team a five-minute game. After the round robin is completed, each team's points for seven games are totaled. Points scored by the opponents are also added and this sum is subtracted from the offensive point total. The team with the highest positive total wins. Another method of ranking teams is to count the won and lost record for the seven games played by each team. The playing time for all seven games is equivalent to the time required for one regulation game. Additional competition can be arranged by scheduling the first two or first four teams in a play-off of regulation games for the next day or succeeding days.

ELIMINATION TOURNAMENTS

This type of tournament competition is based on the elimination of all losing participants until the winner is named. Each game results in the elimination of the losing team or moving the loser to another bracket for another chance at the championship or the opportunity to win a less important championship. There are two basic kinds of elimination tournaments, the straight or single elimination and the double elimination. Each has variations in the form of consolations and combinations.

Single Elimination Tournament

The single elimination tournament is the simplest and quickest way of determining a winner. Each time a game is played the losing team is eliminated. This tournament is used to best advantage when there are numerous entries and time and facilities are limited. It is not an objective measure of ability because the best team or player might lose in an early round due to an "off-day." Similarly, the runner-up might not be the second best in the tourney because a better player or team might be eliminated by the winner in an earlier match. The most undesirable element is the fact that participants are eliminated when at the same time, participation is one of the important principles of intramural sports. Single elimination and other elimination tournaments are only recommended when it is not feasible to use round robin tournaments.

NUMBER OF GAMES. The number of games or matches in a single elimination tournament is determined by subtracting one from the number of entrants. The formula is N − 1, with N representing the number of entrants. For example, if there are 16 entries, 16 − 1 = 15 games. If there are 11 entries, 11 − 1 = 10 games to be played to complete the tourney.

The perfect power of the number 2 is an important factor in tournament construction. The perfect power of 2 is 2 multiplied by itself, that product multiplied by 2, that product multiplied by 2, and so forth. The number 2 raised to the third power (2 × 2 × 2) equals 8. In drawing up a tournament, it is necessary for the number of lines (on which team names or byes are placed) to equal the power of 2. Since two lines make up a bracket for one game, it also means that the number of brackets must be even in number. If this is not the case, teams are not eliminated equally in each round. The following table illustrates the powers of two with which tournament directors are most concerned. Generally, it is not necessary to use more than 128 lines (2 raised to the seventh power).

POWERS OF TWO

2^2 (raised to the second power)	2 × 2	= 4
2^3 (raised to the third power)	2 × 2 × 2	= 8
2^4 (raised to the fourth power)	2 × 2 × 2 × 2	= 16
2^5 (raised to the fifth power)	2 × 2 × 2 × 2 × 2	= 32
2^6 (raised to the sixth power)	2 × 2 × 2 × 2 × 2 × 2 ...	= 64
2^7 (raised to the seventh power)	2 × 2 × 2 × 2 × 2 × 2 × 2	=128

The number of rounds in a single elimination tournament is determined by the power of 2. If the number of entries is equivalent to a power of 2, the number of rounds is equal to that power of 2. For example, if the number of entries is 16 then 2 is raised to the fourth power and equals four rounds. When the number of entries is not equivalent to a power of 2, the number of rounds is equal to the next higher power of 2 which exceeds the number of entries. For ex-

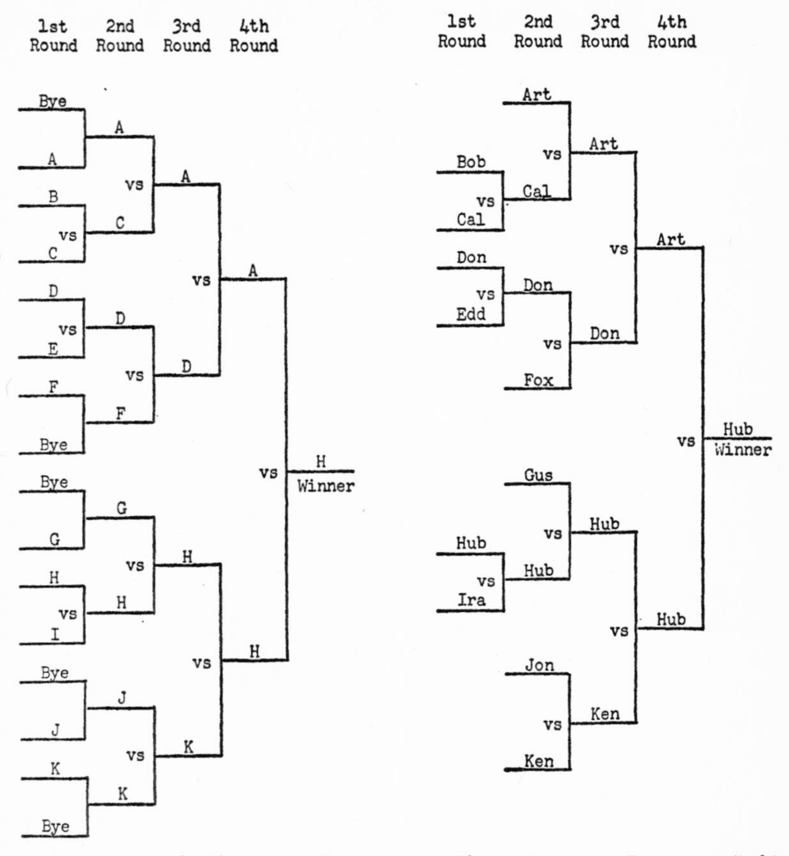

Figure 19. Single Elimination Tournaments: Eleven Teams or Entrants. *(Left)* Listed Byes (5). *(Right)* Implied Byes (5).

ample, if 28 teams are entered, there are five rounds because 2 must be raised to the fifth power ($2 \times 2 \times 2 \times 2 \times 2$), 32, which is the next higher power of 2 over the number 28.

PLACEMENT OF BYES. As previously indicated, the number of lines and brackets in a tournament must equal a power of 2. When entries are not sufficient to fill in all of the lines to reach this equivalent, it is necessary to place byes on the extra lines. This means that a team in the same bracket as a bye does not play a game in the first round.

All byes must appear in the first round. This is a fundamental of bye placement.

Byes are only necessary when the number of entries is not equal to a power of two. To determine the number of byes for a given tournament, the number of entries must be subtracted from the next higher perfect power of 2. For example, if eleven teams are entered in a tournament, the next higher power of 2 is 16. Sixteen minus 11 equals 5, the number of byes. Figure 19 shows a single elimination tournament for 11 teams or entrants, with four rounds and five byes.

In placing byes, the tournament draw sheet exhibits a neat appearance if the byes are positioned symmetrically. If there are two byes, one should be placed on the top line of the draw sheet and the other on the bottom line. When four byes are necessary, one should be on the top line of the draw, another on the bottom line of the upper half of the tournament and the other two in comparable positions in the bottom half of the tournament. When there is an uneven number of byes, the extra bye should be placed in the bottom half of the tournament. For the table showing the number and placement of byes on a tournament draw sheet, see Figure 60 in Chapter 16. From the information within this table it is easy to construct the draw sheet.

Figure 19 illustrates draw sheets with listed byes and with implied byes. With listed byes, names of entrants and the byes are written on the draw sheet for the first round. With implied byes, the names of those receiving byes are not listed in the first round. In this case the number of lines equals the number of entries; the byes are advanced to the second round. This procedure takes up less space but the draw sheet is more difficult to construct, particularly for inexperienced tournament directors. Additional single elimination tournament draw sheets (for 3 to 16 entries) appear in Chapter 16, Figure 61.

Assignment of positions. In making up the pairings or assigning tournament positions to entrants, several methods can be used: (1) drawing positions by lot; (2) assigning positions in the order in which entries are received; and (3) assigning teams on the basis of player ability or team strength. The first two methods should be used only when lack of information prevents assignment on the basis of team strength. If positions are determined by chance, there is a possibility that the best teams might meet in the first round. This further magnifies the disadvantage of elimination tourneys because teams winning the first four places are not always the best teams. Whenever possible, the best teams should be distributed equally throughout the tournament draw.

Double Elimination Tournament

The double elimination tournament is often called a "second chance" or "continuous consolation" tournament. A team or entrant which loses the first game in the winner's bracket is rescheduled to play games in the losers' bracket, with the possibility of eventually winning the tournament. The winner of the losers' bracket plays the winner of the winners' bracket. If the losers' bracket team loses this game, the tourney is completed. However, if the losers' bracket team wins, each team has one loss and an additional game must be played to select the champion. Thus, in a double elimination tournament no participant is eliminated until he loses twice and every entry plays a minimum of two games.

The double elimination tournament approaches the round robin in determining an adequate winner. It overcomes the disadvantage of one "bad game" or an unlucky draw in the tourney. It does violate the intramural principle of participation, however, but not to the same degree as the single elimination, in that some teams are eliminated as soon as they play and lose two games and other teams play numerous additional games. Double eliminations are cumbersome if there are more than 16 entries. Another possible disadvantage is found in individual and dual sports tourneys. An entrant who is overmatched, in handball for example, might lose his first match by one-sided scores. This player might lose interest, feeling that there is ultimate defeat even if he wins the losers' bracket. This same player might receive greater satisfaction in entering a consolation bracket with other losers, knowing that there is a winner of the consolation bracket who does not play an overmatched player from the winners' bracket.

The number of games or matches can be determined by applying the following formulas with N representing the number of entries.

Minimum number of games to play = 2 (N − 1)
Maximum number of games to play = 2 (N − 1) + 1

If there are ten entries (see Figure 20) the number of

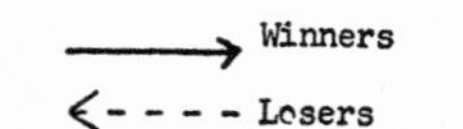

Cal
If neces-sary
Jon
Jon
Winner

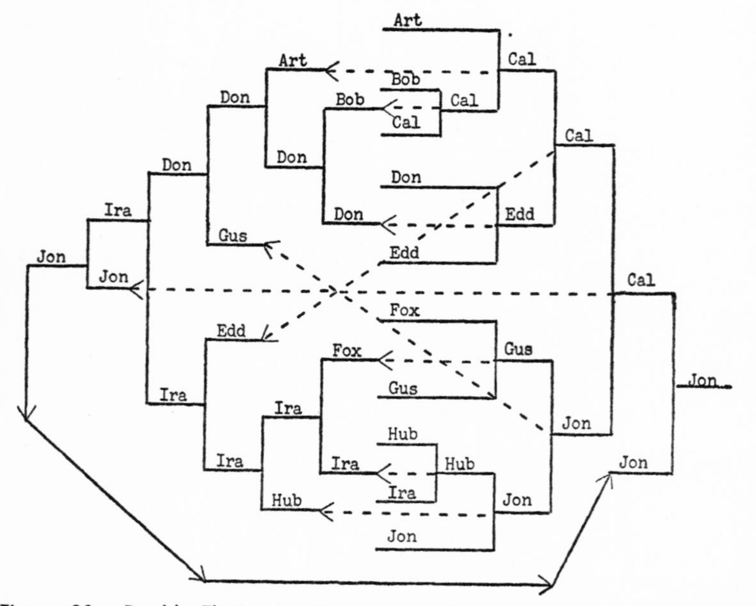

Figure 20. Double Elimination Tournaments: Ten Teams or Entrants, Eighteen

games is 18, figured $2\ (10 - 1) = 18$ games, if an additional game is unnecessary; or the number of games is 19, figured $2\ (10 - 1) + 1 = 19$ games, if an additional game is necessary.

Figure 20 shows two methods of arranging double elimi-

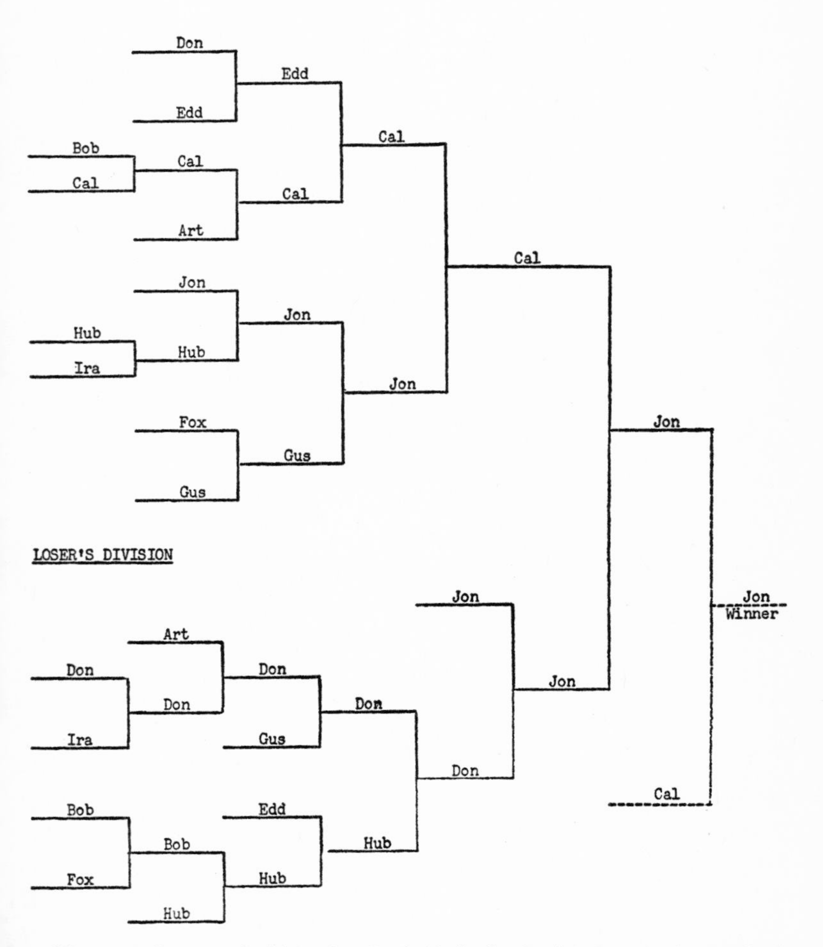

or Nineteen Games. *(Left)* Back-to-Back Method. *(Right)* Over-Under Method.

nation tournaments on draw sheets. In the back-to-back method, the winners' and losers' brackets are arranged back to back with the winners advancing to the right and losers following the broken lines and arrows to the left. The winner of the losers' bracket (Jon) follows the arrows around to the front to play the undefeated finalist (Cal). A second game is played if Jon, representing the losers' bracket, wins because this is the hitherto undefeated finalist's (Cal's) first loss. In the over-under method, the losers' bracket is arranged under the winners' bracket. As teams or entrants lose, they are transposed to the losers' bracket, with the winner and loser finalists (Cal and Jon) meeting for the championship.

The back-to-back method is less confusing in positioning losing teams because arrows indicate the route of play. However, the over-under method has an advantage in flexibility of crossing losing teams. Pairings in the losers' bracket should be arranged to prevent teams or entrants from playing each other a second time until absolutely necessary. This is done by crossing losers from the top and bottom half of the winners' bracket. If this matter is not taken into consideration, a team can be eliminated by the same team in the early rounds.

Placement of byes follows the same rules as for single elimination tournaments except that it is necessary to have byes beyond the first round of the losers' bracket. There is less confusion for participants and more conservation of space if byes are implied instead of listed in drawing up double elimination tournaments. Additional double elimination tournament draw sheets appear in Chapter 16, Figure 62.

SEMI-DOUBLE ELIMINATION TOURNAMENT. The semi-double elimination tournament is so named because competition starts on a double elimination basis and finishes with single elimination. Entries are paired in an elimination tournament with winners continuing in the winners' bracket and all first round losers and losers in the second round who drew first round byes continuing in a losers' bracket. From this point on, all games in both brackets are played on a single elimination basis. The winners of the losers' and winners' brackets play off for the championship. In this tournament, each team does not get two losses but does play a minimum of two games. After the first round, teams in the winners' division are eliminated with one defeat whereas losing teams are allowed an additional loss prior to the second round of the losers' division. This is a good tourney when there is a large number of entries and little time to determine a winner. It has the advantage of compensating for an "off-game" in the first round.

Consolation Tournaments

Consolation tournaments are arranged in conjunction with single and double elimination tournaments. They offer opportunities for additional games to losers of the main tournament who have the greatest need for this experience. Consolation rounds overcome the single elimination tourney objection of eliminating approximately half of the participants in the first round. When consolation eliminations are used, the minimum number of games for a straight elimination tourney is two and the minimum for a double elimination is three. Consolation draws can be structured using the over-under or back-to-back methods as shown in Figures 21 and 22. Some of the possible consolation combinations are discussed in the following paragraphs.

Simple elimination tournament. The most common type of consolation tournament is the one which includes all first round losers and also losers of the second round who received byes in the first round. The latter situation only exists when the number of entries is not a perfect power of 2. In this case it is necessary to wait until byed teams play their first games before the consolation draw is completed. If the byed teams win, losers of these games do not play in this type of consolation tourney because they played and won their first round games. In the example shown in Figure 21, Hub was given a bye in the first round, then lost

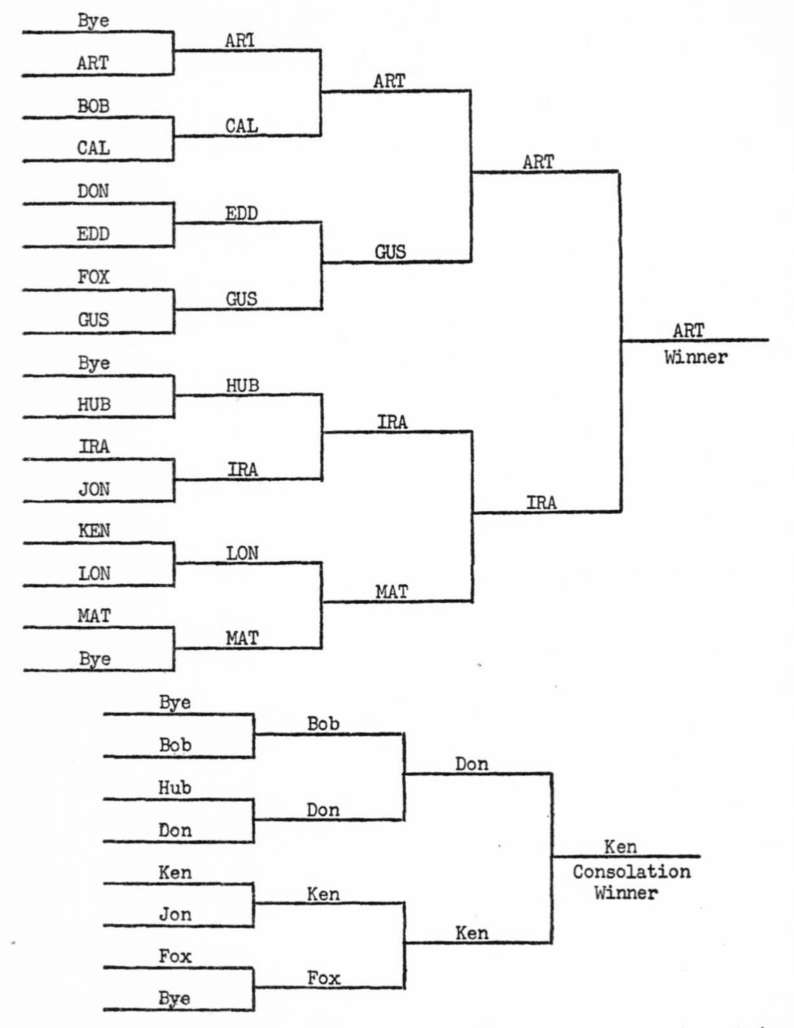

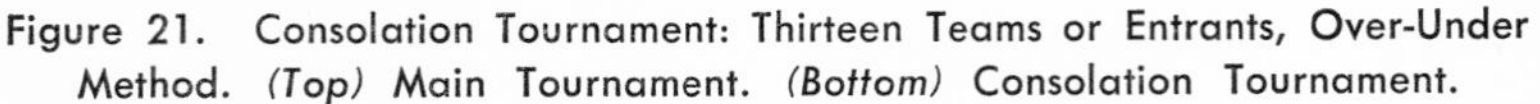

Figure 21. Consolation Tournament: Thirteen Teams or Entrants, Over-Under Method. *(Top)* Main Tournament. *(Bottom)* Consolation Tournament.

his first game, thus moving him to a position in the consolation division. However, Cal and Lon who lost to Mat and Art, two byed players, do not play in the consolation because they won their first games.

———— Winners

<---- Losers

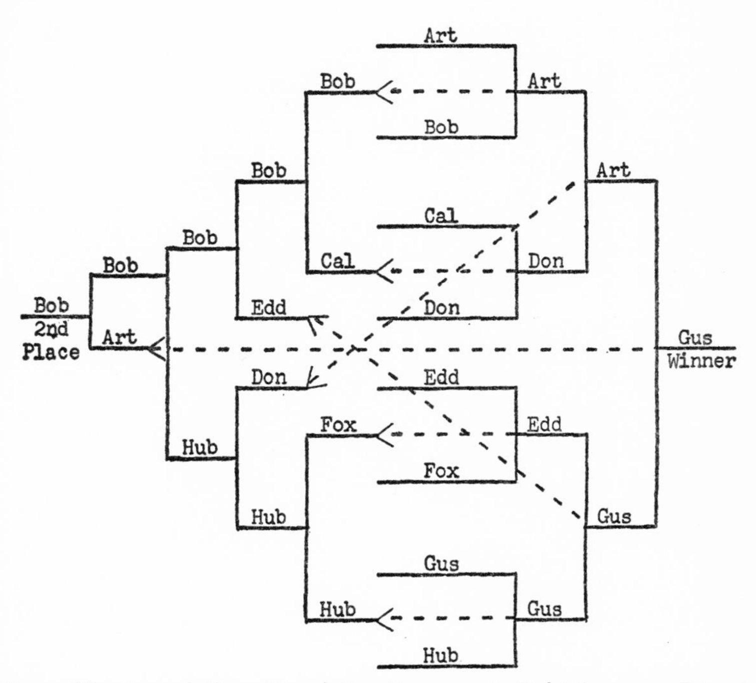

Figure 22. Second Place Consolation Tournament: Eight Teams or Entrants, Back-to-Back Method. (This would illustrate a Double Elimination Draw if second place Bob were to play Gus, the winner.)

Second place tournament. In the second type of consolation tournament, all players eliminated from the main tournament are eligible for additional competition. This type of consolation is sometimes called the "second place" tournament because it selects a second place winner in addition to the champion. This type of consolation is actually similar to a double elimination tournament with the exception that the winner of the losers' bracket does not meet the winner of the winners' bracket. In the illustration in Figure 22, winners advance to the right in the main tournament and losers follow the broken lines and arrows to the left. Gus won this tourney and Bob finished in second place. Art could be credited with third place and Hub with fourth place or the players could play off to determine third and fourth place positions. This second place tournament is arranged using the back-to-back method but as is the case with all other consolation tournament structures, it could be set up using the over-under method. It is also true that numerous consolation combinations are devised ranging from the first round losers to the inclusion of all losers. The method selected will be determined by the desired outcome, assuming time, facilities, and equipment are available.

BAGNALL-WILD TOURNAMENT. Another type of consolation tournament which selects second and third place winners with reasonable accuracy is referred to as the Bagnall-Wild. This method, or variations of it, is particularly popular in conference wrestling meets where considerable importance is given to team points awarded to second and third place winners of each weight division. All contestants who are defeated prior to the finals by the single elimination winner enter a consolation bracket. The winner of this bracket plays the loser of the main tournament final game for second place. It is possible that the tournament winner could eliminate a team that was better than the defeated finalist, and the consolation elimination should determine which team deserves second place.

In the main tournament in Figure 21, Cal and Gus were eliminated by the winner, Art. Cal and Gus are scheduled to play with the winner meeting Ira for second place. If Ira loses, he is automatically awarded third place because he played and defeated all others who are eligible for third place, namely, Mat, Hub, and Jon. If Ira wins, the winner of the Cal and Gus match plays the consolation elimination winner of Jon, Hub, and Mat for third place. The disadvantage of this kind of tournament is that the second and third consolation brackets cannot be arranged and played until the main tournament winner is named.

CONTINUOUS PLAYBACKS. Continuous consolations can be arranged for each round of the winners' and losers' divisions to determine the rank order of teams participating in a single-elimination consolation tournament. The consolations extend from the semifinals of the winners' division to the last play-off of the losers' division. Losers in the losers' bracket are continuously placed in consolation playbacks until all teams are ranked. In an eight-team tournament, rank order of teams is as follows:

1. winner of main tournament
2. runner-up in main tournament
3. winner of play-off between semifinal losers of main tournament
4. loser of play-off between semifinal losers of main tournament
5. winner of consolation tournament
6. runner-up in consolation tournament
7. winner of play-off between semifinal losers of consolation tournament
8. loser of play-off between semifinal losers of consolation tournament

This type of playback ranks any number of teams by setting up additional consolations for losing teams.

CHALLENGE TOURNAMENTS

Challenge or perpetual tournaments are usually conducted over an extended period of time. They are better suited for individual and dual sports such as tennis, golf, handball, paddleball, squash, and horseshoes, but they can be adapted for team competition. These tournaments require little supervision as most of the schedule arrangements are made by the participants. The biggest advantage is that no one is eliminated and when the tournament ends, players are objectively grouped according to ability. Every player is encouraged to work up to the highest possible position on the tournament chart. Challenge tournaments, the ladder tournament in particular, are often used to select and position players on individual sport varsity squads such as tennis, golf, or wrestling. This type of tournament is flexible in that play is terminated at any time but, in fairness to the contestants, a definite time limit should be set before the tournament begins.

Participants' names and telephone numbers are recorded on slips of cardboard or similar material and attached to the tournament boards or inserted in slots. Peg boards are most satisfactory to serve as backing for challenge tournaments. Players can be positioned on the tournament chart according to the order in which entries were received or according to positions drawn by lot; seeded according to past performance or known ability of the players (this can be with best players at the bottom, requiring them to work their way to the top); or positioned on the basis of a single elimination or other tournament. After players are in place, competition begins by players issuing challenges to other players. The challenge must be accepted and played within a specified period of time. Players are usually restricted to challenging players one row above or one or two positions above, although some tournament rules permit random challenging. If a challenger defeats a player in a higher position, the two players exchange places on the chart; if the defender wins, their positions remain the same. When a challenger loses, he must meet another contestant before reissuing a challenge to the player who defeated him. At the end of the tournament, the player in the top position is the winner. Another variation has the top four or five players continuing in a round robin or elimination play-off. As a matter of interest, some tournament directors find it advisable to post game scores on a supplemental sheet. A messenger board can also be located next to the tournament chart for the convenience of players who wish to register challenges by listing date, time, and court together with the name of the player being challenged.

The ladder, pyramid, funnel, king or crown, round-the-clock, spider web, and bump board tournaments are next discussed to present variations in challenge-type tournaments.

Ladder Tournament

The ladder tournament is the most popular type of challenge tournament. The tournament gets its name from the design of the chart which gives the appearance of rungs on a ladder. (See Fig. 23.) The advantage of this kind of tournament is that each player is ranked according to ability

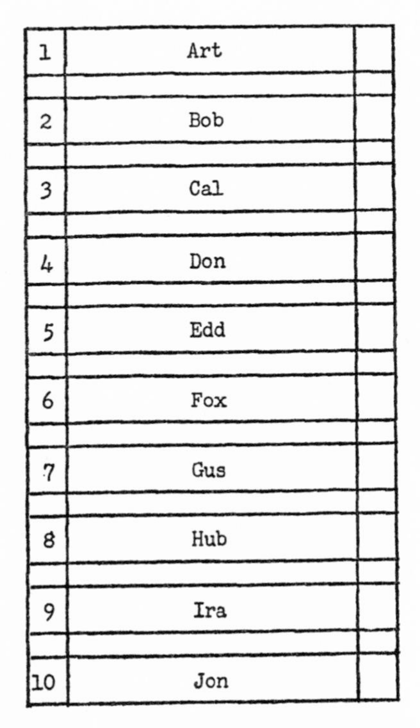

1
Art
2
Bob
3
Cal
4
Don
5
Edd
6
Fox
7
Gus
8
Hub
9
Ira
10
Jon

Figure 23. Ladder Tournament: Ten Entrants.

when the tourney is concluded. After entrants are placed on the ladder, players challenge other players as follows: (1) a player challenges only the player immediately above him; (2) a player challenges players on the two rungs immediately above him; (3) a player challenges the three players immediately above him; or (4) challenging takes place in any position and in either direction. One of the four methods must be chosen for any given ladder tournament. Each contestant should receive a copy of the tournament rules and the rules of the sport involved. When a challenger defeats a defender, the two players switch places. In Figure 23, if Don beats Bob, Don moves up to the second position and Bob goes to fourth place. New players enter the tournament by challenging and defeating the last place entry.

Ladders can be arranged in combination to handle additional entries or to group players with a wide range of ability. If ladders are arranged vertically, the top players of the lower ladder can challenge the bottom players of the upper ladder. If ladders are arranged horizontally, it permits horizontal challenging. When ladders are arranged side by side, the winners of each ladder can play off for the championship in a round robin or elimination tournament.

Pyramid Tournament

The pyramid tournament (see Fig. 24) differs from the ladder tournament in that, with the exception of the best

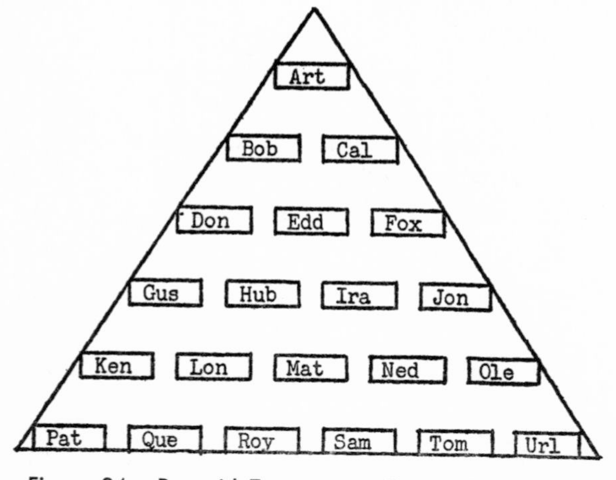

Figure 24. Pyramid Tournament: Twenty-One Entrants.

player or winner, players are ranked by groups instead of individual ability. The pyramid allows more participation and usually permits more flexibility in challenging. As in the ladder tournament, there are a number of variations used in arranging challenges: (1) a player must challenge someone in his horizontal row before challenging a player in the row immediately above; (2) a player challenges any player in the row immediately above; (3) a player challenges only the player to his immediate right or left before challenging someone in the row above; (4) a contestant challenges only the players to his immediate right or left in the row above; or (5) a player challenges anybody anywhere on the board. Players only change positions when a challenger from one row defeats a player from the row above. New players enter by challenging someone in the last row.

Another method of pyramiding winners is the *open pyramid.* No player is positioned on the pyramid chart at the beginning of the tournament. The number of places or positions in the bottom row of the pyramid must be equal to one-half the number of entries. Each player is free to challenge any other player in the tourney and winners are awarded positions on the bottom row of the pyramid. Contestants move to the row above by challenging and defeating a player on the same level, but this advancement is only possible when there is a vacant position in the row above. The first player to gain the top position is the winner. It is possible to extend the tournament by following one of the five challenge procedures listed in the preceding paragraph.

King or Crown Tournament

The king or crown tournament is a combination of several pyramid tournaments. (See Fig. 25.) The biggest advantage is that this type of tournament can handle a large number of entries. Pyramids are arranged at different levels; the number depends on the number of participants.

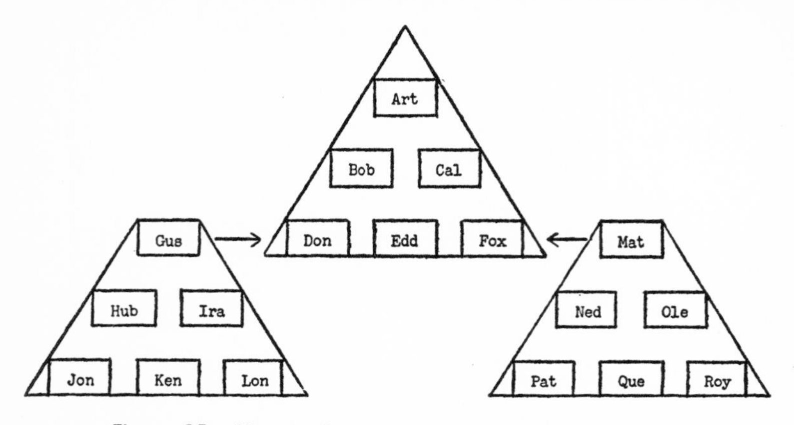

Figure 25. King or Crown Tournament: Eighteen Entrants.

After a player reaches the top in one of the lower pyramids, he can challenge horizontally, and, if he wins, he gains a position in the bottom row of the higher pyramid. The king or winner is the player who advances to or holds the top position in the uppermost pyramid at the end of the tournament. Original player positions are assigned by the methods previously discussed or the entire tournament is run on an open pyramid basis.

Funnel Tournament

The funnel tournament (Fig. 26) is a combination of the pyramid and ladder tournaments. Players in the bottom section follow pyramid rules for advancement and the top four players advance according to ladder tournament rules. This type of tournament provides greater participation and objectively selects the first four winners in order of ability. The chart could be designed to include more players in the ladder section, thus providing more than the first four place winners. The chart could be arranged in reverse order with the pyramid on the top and ladder on the bottom. In this case, players attempt to work to the lowest position on the ladder.

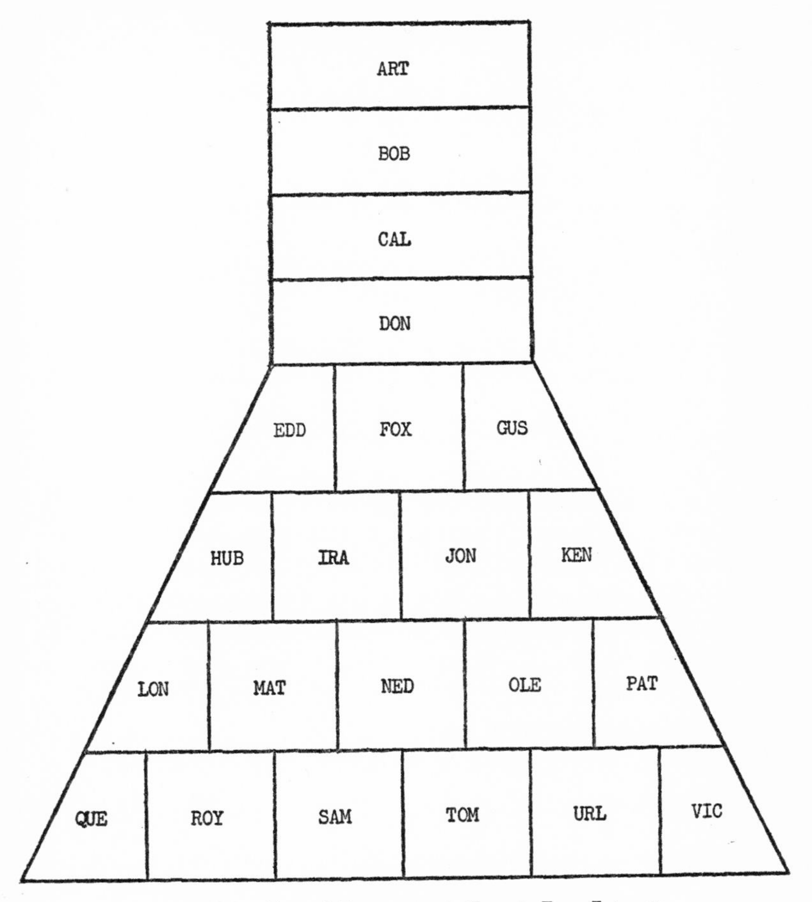

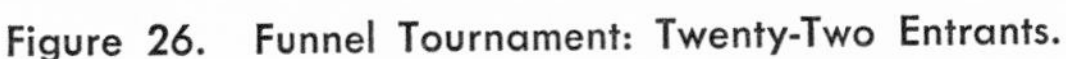
Figure 26. Funnel Tournament: Twenty-Two Entrants.

Round-the-Clock Tournament

The round-the-clock tournament is one in which players are positioned according to hours on the face of a clock. (See Fig. 27.) The rules can be set up with one of two objectives for the winner: (1) the winner is the player who advances in a clockwise direction to the twelve-o'clock position; or (2) the winner is the first player to make one complete revolution to his starting position. A player

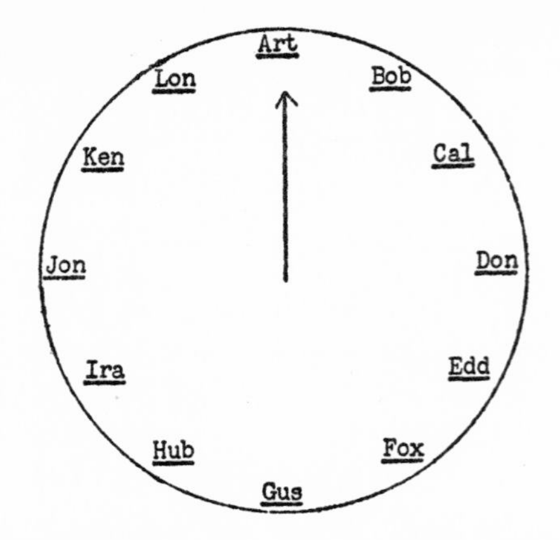

Figure 27. Round-the-Clock Tournament: Twelve Entrants.

challenges one, two, or three players in advance of his position. The arrow on the clock is set to indicate the winning hour position or to designate the player who advances the farthest. Variations can be arranged in which several revolutions are required and more than twelve entries are accommodated by using several clock faces.

Spider Web Tournament

The spider web tournament, sometimes called the hexagon, as illustrated in Figure 28, is conducted as is the

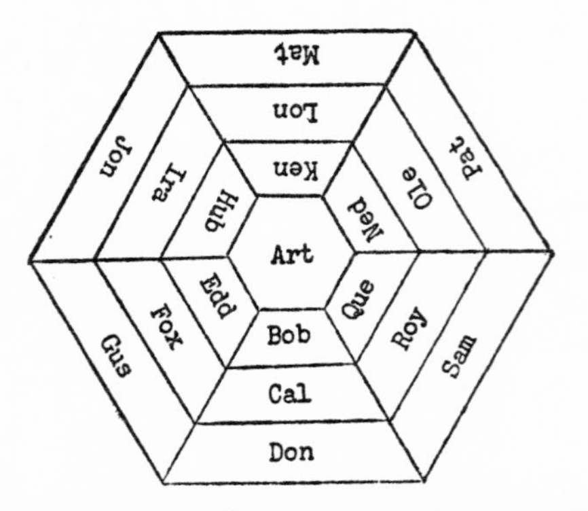

Figure 28. Spider Web Tournament: Nineteen Entrants.

pyramid tournament. The same procedures used for starting and advancing in the pyramid apply to the spider web. The greatest advantage is the large number of participants that can be included on the chart. The object of the spider web is to advance to the center and hold that position. A disadvantage is that the player in the center must accept numerous challenges from the six players in the inside center hexagon. Some of these players play challenge games with opponents in the next outer hexagon, but to eliminate some of the pressure on the player in the center, it might be wise to require a player to play someone in the inside center hexagon before permitting him to challenge the center player.

Bump Board Tournament

The bump board is actually a nonchallenge-type tournament in which players do not challenge and compete against each other but rather challenge a record or score which appears on the board in an attempt to bump or replace the player who holds that particular record or score.

Archery, bowling, rifle shooting, and golf are sports which are adaptable to bump board scoring. For example, names of the top ten bowlers and their scores are listed on the board. A bowler who bowls the fifth highest score moves into fifth place on the board and all bowlers below him are moved down one position with the last player being bumped from the board. Contestants bowl at any time in an attempt to gain a position on the board.

The bump board also provides excellent motivation for students to participate in track, swimming, Sigma Delta Psi, and other events which are graded on time and distance. Names of the top six record holders and their records can be listed for each event, such as the 100-yard dash, one-half mile run, broad jump, hurdles, shot put, etc. Contestants can challenge these records at any time and be tested by intramural staff members. Any competitor who breaks a record has his name and record placed in the appropriate position on the board and other names are adjusted accordingly with the last player removed from the board.

INFORMAL-TYPE TOURNAMENTS

The marker, ringer, rotation, and detour are informal-type tournaments. They are best suited to motivate student participation in corecreational and other less formal activities, but it is not advisable to use them when it is important to select a winner objectively.

Marker Tournament

The marker is also referred to as the tombstone or accumulative tournament. Teams or individuals compete to reach a predetermined objective or goal which is usually a certain score, time, or distance. Players total daily results over a period of time and the first one reaching the objective is the winner. Sports which lend themselves to this type of tournament are golf, archery, bowling, track, swimming, free throw shooting, horseshoes, and rifle shooting.

To stimulate interest in bowling, a goal of 10,000 pins could be set with restrictions on the number of lines which can be bowled each day and the number of days each week on which they can be bowled. For example, a contestant could not bowl more than three lines each day or bowl on more than four days each week. The first bowler to reach 10,000 pins is the winner.

In swimming, a goal of 25 miles can be set either with or without a limitation on the number of pool laps each day. The former restriction assures a closer finish and the latter undoubtedly produces a winner who is the best conditioned swimmer. In horseshoes, the player throwing the greatest number of ringers out of a designated number of rounds over a period of time is the winner. Similarly, the highest number of free throws made out of a specific number of tries over a two-week period could designate the winner of a free throw contest.

Ringer Tournament

The ringer tournament is a modification of the marker or tombstone, and results in totaling only the best scores made over a period of time with the highest accumulation determining the winner. In golf, each entrant posts his entire first round hole-by-hole score on the bulletin board or tournament chart. After the next round, he circles scores for holes which are better than the previous scores and substitutes the lower scores for those on the chart. At the end of the tournament, the hole scores are totaled for the best 18 holes of golf played by each player. The player with the lowest total is the winner. It is possible that many contestants have a final score which is considerably under par.

In bowling, the best weekly game of a three-game series is circled, and at the end of a five-week period the bowler with the highest total for the best five games is the winner.

Rotation Tournament

The rotation tournament is also known as the bridge tournament because it is frequently used for bridge and other card games. This tournament is played on the basis of time instead of the number of points necessary to complete a game or match. It is suitable for table tennis, volleyball, badminton, handball, squash, paddleball, tennis. For example, there are four volleyball courts, eight teams, and one hour of playing time. At the end of each ten-minute period, a whistle is blown and teams ahead at that time rotate clockwise to the next court while losers remain on the same court. At the end of the hour, six rounds have been played and the winner is the team which wins the most rounds or partial matches. The disadvantage of this tourney is that teams might meet each other more than once, depending on which teams win and which teams lose. The biggest advantage is that the tournament is played in a short period of time and provides an excellent opportunity for socializing.

Another variation is to select one court as king or head court and another court as "poison" court. Winners at the king court remain while losers go to the poison court. The tournament winner is the team which occupies the king court when the final whistle blows to end competition.

Still another variation results in changing partners. For example, in handball doubles, the winners not only advance to the next court but also pair up with the losers. This procedure means that players have new partners for each round. To determine a tournament winner, a record is kept of each player's wins. The winner is the player who accumulates the greatest number of wins. It is also possible for this type of tournament to be run on complete matches or games instead of time periods and to arrange for each player to play with every other player.

Detour Tournament

The basic purpose of the detour tournament is to provide practice games for losing teams and, therefore, give extra participation to teams that need it most. The detour is best suited for teams numbering 4, 8, 12, 16, and other multiples of 4 because uneven-numbered groups result in unmatched practice games, which is the major reason for this type of competition. One point is scored against a team for each loss. The undefeated team at the end of the tourney receives no points and is the winner.

Teams are paired for the first round with the winners waiting for the next round while the losers take time to play practice games. Winners of the first round are then scheduled for the next round and losers are scheduled for their regular tournament games. Opponents should be assigned to prevent teams from meeting more than once. This procedure is followed after each round. Practice games are scheduled even after the round in which the undefeated winner is named. Teams can be ranked in order with zero points representing first place; one point, second; two points, third; etc.

Telephone, Telegraph, and Postal Tournaments

Competition by telephone, telegraph, or mail is particularly suited for extramural sports in which teams from one or more schools compete against teams from one or more other schools. Numerous activities are utilized for this type of competition but the most popular are bowling, golf, archery, swimming, track, Sigma Delta Psi, horseshoes, and free throws.

Competition is usually conducted at the same time at each of the participating schools according to prearranged regulations. After the contests are completed, each team sends in the results at a designated time via telephone, telegraph, or mail. If competition involves just two teams, the results are interchanged. If several schools are entered, the results are sent to a central location where they are tabulated and winners announced.

EQUALIZATION AND CLASSIFICATION

One of the most important considerations in setting up a league, meet, or tournament is to use classification and other methods to equalize competition among the participants. Student interest and enthusiasm in the intramural program are proportional to reasonable opportunities for success in competition. If the participant loses consistently or loses by one-sided scores, he might turn from the intramural program to some other form of recreation in which he can succeed to a satisfactory degree. Various methods of equalizing competition for teams and individuals are discussed in this section.

Seeding

One of the disadvantages of making up elimination tournament pairings by lot or other random methods is the possibility that the best players might meet in the first round, thereby eliminating good players and allowing mediocre players to rank second or third in the final standings.

In league play, it is also desirable to have the best teams compete against each other in the final round. To prevent elimination of the best players in the early rounds and to assure the best competition for the final rounds, it is advisable at times to seed the most skillful players or teams. Seeding is accomplished by positioning players so their early matches are with players of lesser ability. The object, barring any upsets, is to have the finals between the two best players, the semifinals between the four best players, and so on. An objection to this plan is that it permits players who are dissatisfied with their arbitrary placing to be critical of tournament officials; whereas in the ordinary draw by lot, the player has no one to blame if he is paired with a champion opponent. The secret of successful seeding is in the accurate judgment of the player's ability. This judgment is usually based on previous tournament results together with opinions of coaches, teachers, or other experts in the field.

In general, not more than one out of every four entries should be seeded. In large tournaments, only one out of every eight entries is satisfactory. However, for the purpose of flexibility in arranging seeded players, the following plan can be used as a guide:

1. Four entries—seed not more than 2 players.
2. Five to 8 entries—seed not more than 4 players.
3. Nine to 16 entries—seed not more than 8 players.
4. Seventeen to 32 entries—seed not more than 16 players.
5. Thirty-three to 64 entries—seed not more than 32 players.

One of the most effective methods of seeding is to place the best player at the top of the tournament draw sheet, second-seeded player at the bottom of the draw sheet, third best player at the bottom of the upper half of the tournament, fourth-seeded player at the top of the lower half of the tournament, fifth-seeded in upper half, sixth in lower half, and so on, with odd numbers appearing in the top and even numbers in the bottom half of the tournament. If players are correctly rated and they play according to their ability, the number 1 seeded player meets 3, and 2 meets 4 in the semifinals, with 1 defeating 2 in the finals for the championship. Obviously, this is not always the case. If it were, it would not be necessary to play the tournament. The objective is to seed the players to conduct the fairest possible tournament. When information is insufficient to determine which player should be seeded first, second, third, and fourth, it is advisable to have the four players draw for number 1 seed, numbers 2, 3, and 4.

Some tournament directors follow a slightly different pattern and give the number 1 seeded player a greater advantage by reversing the placement of the third- and fourth-seeded players. Number 4 is positioned in the upper half of the tournament and 3 in the lower half. This means that 1 should meet 4, and 2 should meet 3 in the semifinals. In the interest of fair competition, it is desirable to seed 1 and 3 in the same half and 2 and 4 in the other half of the tournament.

When there are byes in a tournament, they should be assigned to the seeded players. The seedings then coincide with the byes and give the draw sheet an appearance of balance and symmetry. It also advances the best players to the second round and gives weaker players an opportunity to play in at least one match against players with less ability than the seeded players.

In positioning seeded players on the tournament draw sheet, it is not absolutely essential to have the names appear at the top and bottom of the various quarter, eighth, 16th and 32nd brackets. As mentioned previously, proportional distribution of seedings does provide neatness which always reflects credit to those in charge of the tournament. It is necessary to place seeded players so they do not meet other seeded players until the latest possible match. The table which follows indicates which seeded players should meet first, therefore necessitating their placement in the same quarter, eighth, 16th and 32nd brackets. For example, when eight players are seeded, the number 1 seeded player is positioned in the same eighth or 16th bracket as the number 5 seeded player. Refer to Chapter 16, Fig. 63 for placement of seedings for four, eight, sixteen, and thirty-two entry draw sheets.

SEEDING PLACES

UPPER BRACKET		LOWER BRACKET
	2 Seedings	
No. 1 seed		No. 2 seed
	4 Seedings	
No. 1 *vs.* No. 3		No. 2 *vs.* No. 4
	8 Seedings	
No. 1 *vs.* No. 5		No. 2 *vs.* No. 6
No. 3 *vs.* No. 7		No. 4 *vs.* No. 8
	16 Seedings	
No. 1 *vs.* No. 9		No. 2 *vs.* No. 10
No. 5 *vs.* No. 13		No. 6 *vs.* No. 14
No. 3 *vs.* No. 11		No. 4 *vs.* No. 12
No. 7 *vs.* No. 15		No. 8 *vs.* No. 16
	32 Seedings	
No. 1 *vs.* No. 17		No. 2 *vs.* No. 18
No. 9 *vs.* No. 25		No. 10 *vs.* No. 26
No. 5 *vs.* No. 21		No. 6 *vs.* No. 22
No. 13 *vs.* No. 29		No. 14 *vs.* No. 30
No. 3 *vs.* No. 19		No. 4 *vs.* No. 20
No. 11 *vs.* No. 27		No. 12 *vs.* No. 28
No. 7 *vs.* No. 23		No. 8 *vs.* No. 24
No. 15 *vs.* No. 31		No. 16 *vs.* No. 32

Classes or Flights

Competition in intramural sports is frequently equalized by placing teams or players in separate classes or flights. Entrants are assigned to classes through some objective measure, such as their performance in preliminary competition or according to the class selection made by the participants. In case of the latter, teams decide which class, such as Class A, B, C, or D, they prefer to enter on the basis of judgment of their own ability. This procedure is not as accurate as having them play off for class positions and, occasionally, teams choose to play in a lower classification than their ability warrants with the idea that they want to be assured of winning a class championship. Some programs refer to these classifications by other names such as actives and pledges, major and minor leagues and old pros, novices, and rookies.

COMBINATION TOURNAMENTS. The round robin, elimination play-off is an excellent method for classifying teams, equalizing competition, and determining sport champions when there are numerous teams participating. In this plan, teams are divided into leagues with a convenient number of teams in each league. After a round robin is played in each league, teams are assigned to classes for a single elimination play-off to determine the respective class champions. The number of classes is determined by the number of teams in each league. If four teams are in each league, there are four classes: A, B, C, and D. Five-team leagues result in five classes, six-team leagues provide six classes, and so on. The illustration in Figure 29 shows eight four-team leagues. At the completion of the round robin, the undefeated teams from each league are placed in the Class A play-offs. Second place teams in each league are assigned to Class B play-offs, third place teams to Class C play-offs, and fourth place teams to Class D play-offs. Under this league and elimination plan, teams compete against teams of their own relative ability. For example, it is possible for a team to lose all of its round robin games, enter the Class D play-offs with all other winless teams, and then win the all-school Class D play-offs by winning all of its play-off games. Too often these last place teams are not included in the play-offs when they perhaps have the greatest need for participation. This method adds considerable interest for players of lesser ability and also helps eliminate forfeits. Play-off games between all-school Class A, B, C, and D champions are not recommended because a good team might intentionally lose to be assigned to a lesser class with the aim of winning the all-school championship. It usually results in unfair competition, particularly between Class A and Class D.

The elimination round robin is a reverse procedure in

CLASS A PLAY-OFFS (First place teams from each league)

Figure 29. Round Robin Elimination Tournament: Playoffs. (The Class A won-lost record of 2 and 1; third place teams,

CLASS C PLAY-OFFS (Third place teams from each league)

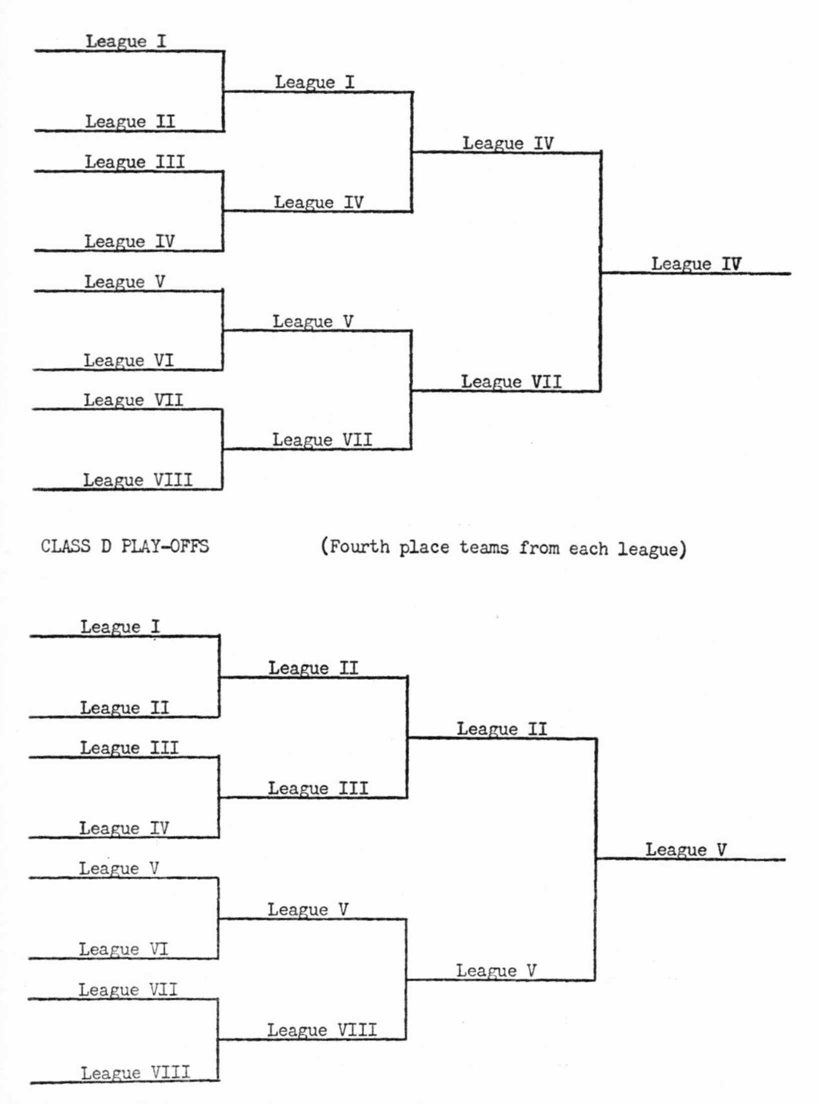

winner is the Intramural Champion. Second place teams usually have a 1 and 2; and fourth place teams, 0 and 3.)

which teams play a partial double elimination tournament to determine to which league they are assigned. After completing two rounds of a double round robin tournament, the teams are placed in four leagues. League I consists of the undefeated teams, League II of the teams that won the first game and lost the second, League III of the teams that lost the first game and won the second, and League IV of teams that lost both games (see Fig. 30). A round robin is played in each league after which it is possible to have a single elimination play-off, similar to the one described in the previous paragraph.

QUALIFYING ROUNDS OR HEATS. Occasionally, time and space are too limited to permit an elimination tournament for a large number of entries. When this occurs in sports which allow rating contestants according to time and distance, as in track and swimming, or a score made, as in golf,

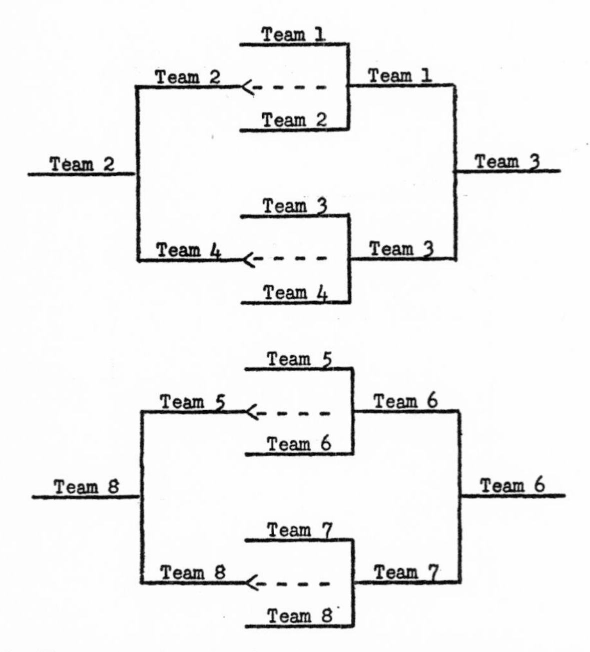

Figure 30. Elimination Round Robin Tournament: Sixteen Teams. League I
III (lost-won): Teams 2, 8, 9, 16; League

bowling, archery, and a free throw contest, the number of participants can be quickly reduced by holding one or more qualifying rounds. In this type of competition, each player is given the same number of chances to participate in the preliminary rounds, and a limited number of players, preferably a perfect power of 2, who make the best scores, continue in the tournament.

The most familiar use of qualifying heats is found in track and swimming where only the best performers advance to the finals. In golf, numerous players play in the qualifying rounds but only the top 32 players continue in the elimination tourney. Another method of using the qualifying plan in golf is to place golfers in different flights on the basis of scores made in the qualifying rounds.

WEIGHT CLASSES. One of the simplest methods of classifying teams is to establish weight categories. In colleges, a

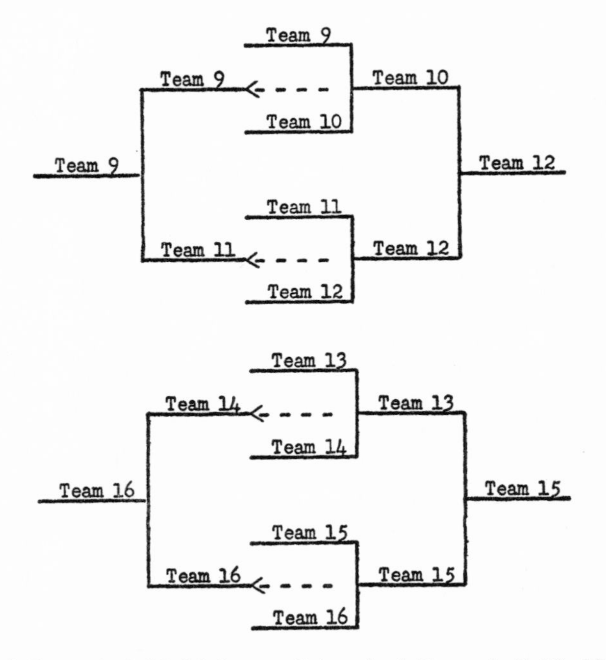

(two wins): Teams 3, 6, 12, 15; League II (won-lost): Teams 1, 7, 10, 13; League IV (two losses): Teams 4, 5, 11, 14.

weight classification frequently used is lightweight, under 150 pounds, and heavyweight, over 150 pounds. Additional weight classes can be included if desirable. For high schools, a practical three-weight classification is 100 pounds, 125 pounds, and unlimited. A good five-weight division is 80 pounds, 95 pounds, 110 pounds, 125 pounds, and unlimited.

In sports such as wrestling, the weight classes for the participants are established by wrestling rules. Players can also be assigned to leagues, teams, or divisions by age, height, and weight or lined up according to height and counted off by numbers.

Handicapping

The procedure of handicapping is used to equalize competition between opponents of unequal ability. Bowling (see Fig. 68 in Chap. 16) and golf are examples of activities which are suitable for handicapping. In competition, there is usually a wide range of player ability. For this reason, it is important to utilize handicap systems, and, if possible, use them in conjunction with classification methods. In bowling, teams with lesser ability do not enter competition if they do not have a reasonable chance to defeat some other teams in the league. The handicap system provides an equalizer by giving points to the weaker team on the basis of a percentage of the difference in team averages. One hundred per cent of the difference should not be given because a smaller percentage encourages every member of the league to bowl his best at all times. The handicap enables weaker team B to add points to its score so it is within striking distance of stronger team A. If team A has an average or below average performance and team B has a better than average total, team B has an opportunity to defeat stronger team A. (See pages 108 and 124 for detailed information on bowling and golf handicap methods.)

There are numerous forms of handicapping, particularly

in informal competition. In racket games such as squash and badminton, the good player can receive a minus six handicap which means he must score six points before he starts to score from zero. The poorer player could start the game with a plus handicap of six. The size of the handicap depends on the difference in the two players' ability. In tennis singles, the better player could cover the entire doubles court while his opponent plays within the singles' boundaries. In badminton doubles, the good players are allowed only one serve to every two serves by the poorer players. In handball, the better player cannot have any of his shots touch one or both side walls.

A nonhandicapped contest is usually considered to be "played from scratch." Generally, basketball, baseball, football, and similar games are not handicapped. Handicap procedures are usually not in effect when important championships are decided. They are undoubtedly used more on an informal basis, but they do have a place in certain intramural sports such as bowling, archery, golf, horseshoes, and rifle shooting.

SUMMARY

1. One of the most strategic elements in a successful intramural program is proper selection of the meet, league, or tournament method to use in conducting a particular sport activity.
2. Meets, leagues, and tournaments are well-developed plans for providing organized and impartially scheduled competitive participation in a sport usually designed to select one or more winners.
3. In selecting the type of competitive method, it is necessary to consider what the activity is; why it is conducted; the age, interests, and abilities of the participants; time, facilities, and equipment available; number of winners desired; accuracy with which players rank in order of finishing, and personnel available to supervise and officiate the competition.
4. Meets are used for contests which include a number of separate events and which must be completed within a

day or so, possibly within an afternoon or evening. Meets are especially suitable for track and field, swimming, gymnastics, ice skating, and field days or sports festivals.

5. Such team games as basketball, softball, touch football, baseball, volleyball, and hockey, and individualistic sports such as tennis, handball, and squash cannot be conducted on the meet plan. Leagues are a better method.
6. Leagues refer to grouping individuals or teams for competitive purposes. Leagues are generally arranged with games scheduled on a round robin or partial round robin basis.
7. The round robin tournament or percentage plan, which allows each contestant to play every other contestant and the winner to be selected according to won and lost records or the percentage of victories, provides the most participation although it is time consuming.
8. League standings are listed on a percentage or nonpercentage basis. If teams do not play the same number of games, the nonpercentage plan should be used.
9. Before drawing up a round robin, it is necessary to determine the total number of games and number of rounds needed to complete a schedule in which all competitors meet each other.
10. To determine the number of games necessary to complete a round robin, the number of teams should be multiplied by the number of teams minus one and the result divided by two. The final result equals the number of necessary games.
11. The "time" disadvantage of full round robins can be partially offset by playing a partial round robin or dividing the large number of teams into smaller leagues or divisions and having the respective league winners play off for the championship.
12. The basic method used in making up round robin schedules is the system of rotation in which letters or numbers are used to represent teams and are rotated either clockwise or counterclockwise.
13. In drawing up a round robin schedule for an uneven number of teams, the same rotation described above is followed but a "bye" replaces one of the numbers.
14. Round robin variations which can be structured to run off abbreviated tournaments and which hold considerable in-

terest for participants include the "play 'til you win" method and the Lombard tournament.

15. Elimination tournaments are based on the elimination of all losing participants until the winner is named.
16. The two basic elimination tournaments are the straight or single elimination and the double elimination. Each has several variations in the form of consolations and combinations.
17. The single elimination tournament is the simplest and quickest method of determining a winner and is used to best advantage when there are numerous entries and time and facilities are limited.
18. Each time a game is played in a single elimination tournament, the losing team is eliminated.
19. The number of games or matches in a single elimination tournament is determined by subtracting one from the number of entrants.
20. In drawing up a tournament, it is necessary for the number of lines on which team names or byes are placed to equal the power of 2, which is 2 multiplied by itself.
21. Byes should be used when entries are insufficient to fill in all of the lines to reach the power of 2.
22. Double elimination tournaments are also referred to as "second chance" or "continuous consolation" tournaments.
23. A team or entrant which loses the first game in a double elimination tournament winners' bracket is rescheduled to play games in the losers' bracket with the possibility of eventually winning the tournament.
24. Every entrant in a double elimination tournament plays a minimum of two games.
25. The minimum number of games or matches for the double elimination tournament is determined by multiplying the number of entrants minus one by two. The maximum number is obtained by multiplying the number of entrants minus one by two and adding one to that total.
26. Placement of byes in double elimination tournaments follows the same rules as for single elimination tournaments except it is necessary to have byes beyond the first round of the losers' bracket.
27. The semi-double elimination tournament starts competition on a double elimination basis and finishes with single elimination.

28. Consolation tournaments offer opportunities to the losers of the main tournament for additional competition and to overcome some of the criticism of single elimination tournaments.
29. Types of consolation tournaments include simple elimination, second place, Bagnall-Wild, and continuous playbacks.
30. Challenge or perpetual tournaments, usually conducted over an extended period of time, are best suited for individual and dual sports such as tennis, golf, handball, paddleball, squash, horseshoes, etc., because they do not eliminate any participant and require very little supervision.
31. Participants entering a challenge or perpetual tournament are positioned on a chart in order of entry, according to positions drawn by lot, seeded on the basis of past performance or known ability, or positioned on the basis of single elimination or other tournament results.
32. Types of challenge or perpetual tournaments include ladder, pyramid, funnel, king or crown, round-the-clock, spider web, and bump board.
33. The ladder tournament is the most popular type of challenge tournament because each player is ranked according to ability when the tourney is concluded.
34. The pyramid tournament is arranged in the form of a pyramid and differs from the ladder tournament in that, with the exception of the best player or winner, players are ranked by groups instead of individual ability. The pyramid tournament allows more participation and usually permits more flexibility in challenging.
35. The king or crown tournament is a combination of several pyramid tournaments and can handle a large number of entries.
36. The funnel tournament is a combination of the pyramid and ladder tournaments.
37. The round-the-clock tournament is one in which players are positioned according to hours on the face of a clock.
38. The spider web tournament is similar to the pyramid tournament with the object to advance to the center and hold that position.
39. The bump board tournament is actually a nonchallenge-type tournament in that players do not challenge and compete against each other but rather challenge a record or

score which appears on a board to bump or replace the player who holds that particular record or score.

40. The marker, ringer, rotation, and detour tournaments are informal types which are designed to motivate student participation in corecreational or other less formal activities.
41. One of the most important considerations in setting up a league, meet, or tournament is to use classification and other methods to equalize competition among the participants.
42. Seeding above-average ability players by positioning them so their early matches are with players of lesser ability prevents elimination of the best players or teams in early rounds and assures the best competition for the final rounds.
43. In general, not more than one out of every four entries should be seeded; in some large tournaments one out of every eight is satisfactory.
44. The byes in a tournament should be assigned to the seeded players.
45. Intramural competition can be equalized by placing teams or players in separate classes or flights according to class selection made by the participants, performance in preliminary competition, or some other objective method.
46. The round robin elimination play-off, in which teams are divided into leagues and round robin and single elimination play-offs are conducted, is an excellent method to classify teams and equalize competition.
47. When time and space are too limited to permit an elimination tournament for a large number of entries in sports such as track and swimming, the number of participants can be quickly reduced by holding one or more qualifying rounds.
48. The handicap system provides an equalizer by giving points to the weaker team on the basis of a percentage of the difference in team averages.
49. Handicap systems are used primarily in such sports as golf, archery, bowling, horseshoes, and rifle shooting.

10

Point Systems for Groups and Individuals

Intramural point systems for groups and individuals are used almost as extensively as awards by intramural directors to motivate interest in the over-all program, to encourage student participation in a wide variety of activities, and to serve as a basis for making awards. Point systems are sometimes classified as a type of award because points are awarded on the basis of participation and achievement for the various sports and an all-year I-M sports trophy is presented to the group that accumulates the greatest number of points during the school year. Teams must take part in most of the tournaments or they cannot be in the contest for the all-year award. Valid point systems are considered to be measurements of athletic progress just as school grades are an indication of scholastic standing.

There is a close relationship between point systems and awards; arguments for and against are comparable. Those in favor insist not only that the point system adds interest but also that the over-all competitiveness encourages participation in new as well as in regular sports in the program. Some intramural directors contend that initiation of a point system results in double the amount of participation during the first few years. While the enthusiastic student participates if a point plan is not in operation, many additional students are included in the program with a little added incentive. Not everyone has a wholesome attitude toward the necessity of physical recreation and, therefore, a slight inducement is necessary. Proponents further point out that if students gain worthwhile values from intramural participation, a motivating device such as the point system does not detract from these values but instead provides encouragement for additional students to share the values of participation. This argument implies that if a point system is helpful, it is necessary.

Opponents of point systems argue that students cease to enter activities for the fun of participation and that the major objective is to enter and win at any cost for the sake of earning points. To a degree, participation is forced, is not voluntary, violating a primary objective of intramurals. They contend that undue emphasis is placed on some sports because of the large number of points given, while others are neglected if they are low in point value, are not adaptable, or do not fit the pattern of the system. Opponents also argue that motivation is artificial and breeds the notion that a student must be recognized for everything he accomplishes. They also object to the amount of time required to keep the office point records up-to-date, particularly with an individual point system. It is their firm belief (1) that much time and effort is saved if the point system is eliminated, and (2) that such elimination does not lower the percentage of participation.

Point systems for groups and individuals are beneficial or detrimental to the intramural program in direct proportion to the adequacy with which they are selected and administered. Some of the watchwords are simplicity, equality, participation, achievement, fairness, uniformity, adaptability, and conformity. The intramural director must constantly evaluate point systems to keep them in balance with the total program.

Whether point plans are imperative to the success of intramurals or unnecessary, they are consistently used. The question of their usefulness needs further study. As is the case with awards, point systems must be selected or constructed to coincide with the objectives of intramurals. If an inequitable point system is adopted, it creates many administrative problems which an intramural director wants to avoid.

TYPES OF SYSTEMS AND DISTRIBUTION METHODS

Although point systems have the same objectives, there are perhaps as many variations as there are schools using them. Many systems have the same basic elements but the items for which points are awarded produce many combinations. This is necessary in many instances because the point system must be adapted to the local intramural program.

However, there are two general types of point systems: (1) one which includes only intramural sports activities, and (2) one which is all-encompassing to the extent that it covers all intramural sports activities and other student activities such as band, organization membership, committee work, debate, and scholarship. A review of the following areas for which points are awarded gives an indication of the possible combinations of the two general types mentioned above.

1. Scholarship: awarded for good grades and deducted for low grades
2. Publications: additional points for editor, business manager, staff members
3. Organizational membership: fraternities, clubs—additional points for officers, committee members, and committee chairmen
4. Honorary societies
5. Debate and other speech activities
6. Band and other instrumental groups
7. Choir and glee club
8. Theater groups: actors, stage crew, publicity staff
9. Varsity sports squad members: additional points for letter winners, captain
10. Selection to varsity all-conference, district, and regional teams
11. Intramural sports participants: additional points to winners of intramural contests
12. Attendance at I-M council meetings

13. Sportsmanship and reliability
14. Physical fitness test: awarded for passing
15. Hygienic habits: posture and cleanliness

The most important element in establishing a good point system is to make sure participants have an equal opportunity to earn points and that points are equally distributed. It is difficult to justify the all-encompassing point system because there is too much subjective judgment involved in assigning points for such items as sportsmanship, reliability, posture, and cleanliness. Whether bonus points attained by only one or two students (e.g., the captain of a varsity team or a newspaper editor) should be awarded is also questionable. These are undoubtedly more justifiable for individual than for group point systems.

In addition to the numerous items which receive points, the combinations are further complicated by the different methods of distributing points. Some of these procedures are briefly surveyed to indicate the types of plans that are used in intramural programs.

Comparative order—high total wins. After a sport is concluded, each participating group is rated according to its respective order of finish. The last place team receives one point; second from last, two points, and so on; and the first place team is awarded points equal to the number of participating teams. When several sports are promoted throughout the year and some of them are considered more important than others from the standpoint of interest and number of players on a team, the sports are classified into major, intermediate, and minor divisions. Under this plan, the last place team gets one point for a minor division sport, two points for an intermediate sport, and three points for a major sport. All rankings are multiplied by two for intermediate sports and by three for major sports. The group with the highest total for all sports at the end of the school year is the all-year champion.

Another method used to equate sports and to assign points for comparative rankings is to multiply the number of games played by each team by the number of players required for a team and divide this product by an arbitrary number such as ten. This factor is multiplied by the ranking of each team to give the number of points earned. As an example, there are eight volleyball teams in a league, six players to a team, and each team plays seven games in the round robin. Six times seven divided by ten equals 4.2. This number multiplied by the inverse ranking of each team results in 33.6 points for the first place team, 29.4 for the second place team, 25.2 for third, and so on.

COMPARATIVE ORDER—LOW TOTAL WINS. This procedure is the reverse of the high total plan and is similar to cross-country scoring wherein the team with the low total wins. The first place team receives one point and the last place team is awarded the number of points equal to the number of participating teams. There are two disadvantages to this plan: (1) there is a psychological preference for having a team with the high total win, and (2) groups that do not enter have to be assigned more points than the last place team or it is more advantageous not to enter any sport. If this fact were not taken into consideration, groups not entering receive no points and the winner is given one point.

COMPARATIVE ORDER PLUS ENTRANCE POINTS. Teams receive points according to place of finish, as previously described, and in addition, earn points for entering the tournament. Each team gets 10 points for entering each sport, or if a major sport, 30 points; intermediate, 20 points; and minor, 10 points. One point can also be given to each individual who enters a sport such as track and swimming. In using the comparative order-low total method, it is necessary to subtract points instead of adding them for entry. The winner could easily end the year with a negative point total.

COMPARATIVE ORDER PLUS POINTS PER GAME. With this method, points are assigned for winning each game in addition to the points that are awarded for the order of finish in the league. Any arbitrary number of points can be established for winning games such as 2, 5, 10, and so on, per game.

AWARDING WINNERS, RUNNERS-UP, THIRD, AND FOURTH PLACES. When competition is completed, points are assigned to the first four places. The number of points may be 4, 3, 2, 1; 8, 6, 4, 2; 40, 30, 20, 10; 100, 80, 60, 40; or any other four-number combination. This procedure is good for a large number of teams which cannot be ranked for comparative scoring with a reasonable degree of accuracy. Objections that it places too much emphasis on superior teams are offset by giving points for entering and for winning games.

COMBINATION PLANS. Point systems can be devised to include any part or all of the following distribution methods:

1. Comparative order of team rankings from first to last place.
2. Distribution of points to first, second, third, and fourth place teams. More places can be included; however, points are not usually assigned to more than the first few teams.
3. Entrance points for teams and/or individuals.
4. Points for winning games.
5. Bonus points; for example, winning an all-school championship.
6. Division of points into Groups I, II, and III (Major, Intermediate, and Minor categories) according to interest, number of members on a team, and number of games played.
7. Separate point plans for each sport or distinct plans for individual, dual, and team sports.
8. Different point plans for each type of competition such as round robin, double elimination, meet, single elimination, and so on.

SELECTION OF A POINT PLAN

Since there are numerous point systems, perhaps no two exactly alike, it is necessary for an intramural director to give careful consideration to some of the positive and negative aspects before devising or adapting a point system. It should definitely fit the local situation and not be selected because someone else found it to be completely successful. Every effort should be made to adapt a point plan that upgrades and maintains proper balance in the intramural program. It should not detract from satisfactory student experiences in the program. Much ill will is generated among participants through an inequitable point system.

Major consideration in any point system should be the equality of student opportunities to earn points and the fairness with which points are distributed. Small or large organizations and groups should have a chance to accumulate the highest point total. At the same time, the number of entries or teams from a large group should not be restricted. One of the purposes of the point plan is to encourage, not discourage, participation. An adjustment for more than one team from the same organization can be made, such as allowing any number of teams to enter but only assigning points to the team that advances the farthest in the tournament.

Insofar as possible, a point system should supplement the intramural program to the extent that it adds interest and encourages participation, but it should not be emphasized to the degree that it is the most important aspect of a student's life. Occasionally a program becomes overbalanced because of exaggerated efforts to reach the entire student body with quantity programing and little or no attention is paid to the program's quality elements. To this extent, a point system should be, in a sense, incidental to the over-all program. When a point system gets out of focus, students are often encouraged to use any means, fair or foul, to earn points for their organization.

A point system should take into consideration participation or entering and achievement or winning, with proper balance between these two essentials. If too much credit is given for entering, such as awarding points for more than one team or for each individual entering a track meet or wrestling tournament, there is a danger of forced participation and the possibility of endangering the student's health. An organization can penalize its members to the extent of paying a fine if they do not enter a wrestling tournament or track or swimming meet in which points are awarded for every person entering. Some students are forced into competition and endanger their health because they are not properly conditioned.

Points should not be assigned for negative participation such as forfeits and the use of ineligible players. If points were awarded for forfeits, groups might resort to bargaining for points on the telephone, particularly if the emphasis is on entrance points. One group might call another and suggest that they forfeit to their opponents in handball this week if their opponents forfeit to them in badminton next week. This results in telephone victories, participation points, and no participation. Methods vary in handling forfeit points. For each forfeit, some directors subtract a set number of points, perhaps ten, from the total number of points earned to that time; or they eliminate the number of points the team would win had they played the game; or they do not assign any points for the sport in which the forfeit occurred. These same procedures are followed when a team uses an ineligible player.

A point system should not be so complicated that it is difficult for students to understand and time-consuming to administer. It should simply record an up-to-date ranking of teams after each sport is completed. When records are not kept up-to-date, the system loses its effectiveness. Some opponents of point programs feel time spent in calculating points is better spent on other more important phases of the intramural program. Often student managers are responsible for recording points as well as maintaining other office records. It is advisable to strike a reasonable medium in determining the size of point figures to be used. It is doubtful if fractions, ¼ or ½, and large numbers, 1,000 and 10,000, should be used because they are difficult to handle. On the other hand, because points do not cost anything, it seems logical to use 10 or 100 points instead of 1.

When devising or selecting distribution methods, consideration should be given to assigning different point values to the various sports. These values are determined on the basis of whether the sport is individual, dual, or team; the number of players required for a team; the number of games played; and the number of teams or entries competing. Many of these factors vary with the local situation. Sports with different point values can be divided into groups or classes. The name used to distinguish these groups is unimportant but if they are referred to as major, intermediate, and minor sports, it should be understood that these classifications do not mean one sport is more important than another. They are classified strictly on the basis of the above factors. Distribution methods should also be adaptable to the various types of competition. If possible, they should apply to round robin, single elimination, double elimination, and combination tournaments as well as to meets.

It is questionable if bonus points should be assigned for such things as winning games outside the regular competing unit, entering every event, or having every member of an organization enter a certain number of activities. If there are units of competition resembling dormitories, fraternities, and independents, these teams should earn points for winning within their own unit but they should not receive bonus points for winning games outside their unit as is the case when unit winners compete for an all-school championship. It is also doubtful if points should be awarded for items such as sportsmanship and reliability, which cannot be measured objectively. These elements are extremely important and are emphasized through sportsmanship programs. The inclusion of subjective items and bonus points tends to reduce the validity of the point system. Awarding points in the same sport more than once during the school year, without making an adjustment in point values, also reduces the system's fairness and validity. In intramurals, attention must always be given to fair competition and this especially applies to point distribution methods.

A point system should be so designed that it is unnecessary either to enter every sport or to win every championship. Obviously, teams are required to enter most activities but it should be possible to win first place in a few sports, finish reasonably high in several more, finish low in a few sports, and perhaps not enter one or two sports. Ideally, year-end point totals should be relatively close and the all-year winner should not be decided until intramural activities for the school year are almost concluded. If a team is far in advance of other teams and a winner is determined early or if there is a wide range of point distribution, it is highly possible the point system contains some inequitable elements.

All-year awards are usually based on point totals. Thus, it is essential that winners are objectively determined. There are several methods used for awarding all-year winners. The winning organization usually receives a permanent plaque or trophy with its name engraved on it and the opportunity for permanent possession if it is won any three years or three out of five years. In case of the rotating trophy, a group holding the large trophy in its possession for one year receives a smaller trophy as a memento of its achievement.

Occasionally, a successful point system encourages the intramural director to add new sports or too many sports to the program. This sometimes produces forced participation and "overactivitied" students. Certainly, the addition of new sports should not be discouraged but it is questionable if they should be thrown into the point system immediately, if at all. The mere fact that a sport is not included in the point system does not mean it is less important than those sports which are included. To be effective, a point system must be constantly evaluated to make sure it is not out of balance and detrimental instead of an asset to the program.

PARTICIPATION—ACHIEVEMENT POINT SYSTEM

A point system is presented here to serve as a guide for those who have the responsibility for selecting or devising a

	SPORT	MINIMUM POINTS	MAXIMUM POINTS
1.	ARCHERY	25	75
2.	BADMINTON	25	75
3.	BASEBALL	50	150
4.	BASKETBALL (A)	50	150
5.	BASKETBALL (B)	25	75
6.	BOWLING	50	150
7.	CROSS COUNTRY	25	75
8.	FENCING	25	75
9.	FREE THROW CONTEST	25	75
10.	GOLF	35	100
11.	HANDBALL	25	75
12.	HORSESHOES	25	75
13.	ICE HOCKEY	50	150
14.	PADDLEBALL	25	75
15.	RELAYS	25	75
16.	RIFLE SHOOTING	35	100
17.	SIGMA DELTA PSI	35	100
18.	SPEED SKATING	35	100
19.	SOCCER	50	150
20.	SOFTBALL (Fast Pitch)	50	150
21.	SOFTBALL (Slow Pitch)	50	150
22.	SQUASH	25	75
23.	SWIMMING	35	100
24.	TABLE TENNIS	25	75
25.	TENNIS	35	100
26.	TOUCH FOOTBALL	50	150
27.	TRACK	35	100
28.	VOLLEYBALL	50	150
29.	WATER POLO	25	75
30.	WRESTLING	35	100

Figure 31. Participation-Achievement Point System: Minimum and Maximum Scale.

plan. This suggested participation-achievement point system incorporates many of the basic considerations previously discussed.

Minimum-Maximum Scale

The minimum-maximum scale (see Fig. 31) groups the various sports according to the amount of time and effort necessary to participate and achieve in these sports. This scale is arranged on the basis of three divisions: (1) 25 minimum points and 75 maximum points (minor division); (2) 35 minimum points and 100 maximum points (intermediate division); and (3) 50 minimum points and 150 maximum points (major division). In grouping sports within a division, consideration is given to the number of players required for a team, the tournament method used to determine a winner in each sport, the number of games played in each sport, and the number of teams that usually enter the various sports. A team that plays an entire round robin schedule deserves more points than a team that competes in a one- or two-day meet. Also a nine-player softball team that plays in a league should be credited with more points than a four-player tennis team that competes in a single elimination tournament. A large number of teams entered in a round robin tournament requires more games to be played by more teams than a large number of teams entered in a single elimination tournament.

Although some of these factors are stable, it might be necessary to revise the scale because of varying conditions in local situations. If points are given in one sport more than once during the school year, the minimum and maximum points should be adjusted. As an example, if there are separate bowling leagues in the first and second semesters and points are assigned in both leagues, the minimum and maximum points could be set at 25–75, which equals half of the 50–150 scale established for bowling points assigned only once during the year. Similarly, local conditions might result in selecting different tournaments which affect the point scale. The time, facilities, equipment, and number of participants vary with existing situations and might necessitate a change in some sports' point values.

Point Distribution

In the participation-achievement point plan, the first place team in each sport receives the maximum number of points and the last place team receives the minimum number of points. Teams finishing between first and last place are assigned points proportional to their place of finish. The number of teams entered determines the size of the point interval. In the 50 minimum-150 maximum scale, the interval for 11 teams is 10: 50, 60, 70, 80, 90, 100, 110, 120, 130, 140, 150. For 21 teams the interval is 5. The number of teams entered does not always result in equal intervals of whole numbers but often involves use of fractions or decimals. To eliminate fractions and decimals, it is possible to use two whole-number intervals such as 5 and 4. With 12 teams in a 25–75 scale, the interval between first and second place is 5, second and third is 4, fourth and fifth is 5, and so on, or 75, 70, 66, 61, 57, 52, 48, 43, 39, 34, 30, 25. If the number of teams produces more of one size interval than the other, such as more five's than four's, the smaller number of intervals can be equally positioned throughout the distribution.

Another procedure involves the use of one interval from the last place team up through as many places as there are equal intervals and then dividing the remaining points among some of the top place teams. This, however, detracts from the fairness of the system because it favors the superior teams. Equal distribution of intervals throughout the range of teams adds validity to the point system.

The point distribution for a bowling league (round robin) and a track meet is shown in Figure 32. The distribution is comparable for leagues and meets, but, in this example, bowling is in the 50–150 major division and track is in the 35–100 intermediate division. This participation-

TEAMS IN BOWLING LEAGUE	WON	LOST	PERCENT	POINTS
1. PSI OMEGA	45	15	750	150
2. PHI BETA PI	41	19	683	143
3. PHI EPSILON KAPPA	38	22	633	137
4. NU SIGMA NU	35	25	583	130
5. ALPHA GAMMA RHO	33	27	550	123
6. ALPHA MU SIGMA	32	28	533	117
7. DELTA SIGMA PI	30	30	500	110
8. PHI CHI WHITE	29	31	483 } Tie	100
9. DELTA SIGMA DELTA	29	31	483 } Tie	100
10. PHI RHO SIGMA	28	32	467	90
11. THETA TAU	27	33	450	83
12. XI PSI PHI	26	34	433	77
13. PHI CHI BLUE	24	36	400	70
14. PHI DELTA CHI	23	37	383	63
15. KAPPA ETA KAPPA	21	39	350	57
16. ALPHA RHO CHI	19	41	317	50

TRACK MEET

TEAMS IN TRACK MEET	PLACE	POINTS
1. ZETA PSI	1	100
2. KAPPA SIGMA	2	96
3. PHI EPSILON PI	3 } Tie	90
4. SIGMA CHI	3 } Tie	90
5. TAU KAPPA EPSILON	5	85
6. TRIANGLE	6	81
7. SIGMA NU	7	77
8. BETA THETA PI	8	73
9. PSI UPSILON	9	69
10. SIGMA ALPHA EPSILON	10	66
11. PHI DELTA THETA	11	62
12. THETA CHI	12	58
13. CHI PSI	13	54
14. THETA XI	14	50
15. ACACIA	15 } Tie	45
16. THETA DELTA CHI	15 } Tie	45
17. DELTA UPSILON	17	39
18. ALPHA TAU OMEGA	18	35

Figure 32. Participation-Achievement Point Distribution. *(Top)* Bowling League. *(Bottom)* Track Meet.

achievement plan permits an organization to enter any number of teams but only the team which advances the farthest earns points. The only advantage of entering more than one team is that the extra teams serve as a defensive mechanism to prevent other teams from earning points. Extra teams also reduce the size of the interval. In bowling, Phi Chi White received 100 points for finishing in a tie for eighth place. The Phi Chi Blue team finished in thirteenth place and received no points although they are listed for 70 points. In the accumulative point tables, the Phi Chi organization is credited with only 100 points. However, to establish the correct interval, it is necessary to list all teams including those which represent the same organization. In this illustration, the Phi Chi Blue team did not provide much of a defense to prevent other teams from getting points. While they were winning 24 points and thus preventing others from earning points, they also lost 36 games which might have assisted some teams in gaining a higher position in the standings. However, the Blue team's effectiveness in preventing advancement of other teams depends on whether its victories were against some of the top teams in the league and organizations which accumulated high point totals in sports that were played previous to the completion of the bowling league.

In case of ties in the standings, the number of points assigned to those positions are added and the total divided by the number of teams tied. In the track meet (Fig. 32), Phi Epsilon Pi and Sigma Chi are tied for third place. The points assigned to third and fourth place are 92 and 88. The sum of these numbers is 180, which, divided by two, equals 90. Each of the tied teams receives 90 points. Some teams do not earn meet points in a track or swimming meet. In this instance, places can be determined by the number of participants each organization entered or a tie can be declared among the teams and the participation-achievement points divided according to the foregoing tie procedure.

It is not necessary to have all team competition with this

suggested point system. In tennis, golf, horseshoes, or handball, for example, if three- or four-man teams are not used, points can be given to the individual who advances the farthest. As is the case with teams, any number of individuals can enter but only one player may earn points for his organization.

The touch football Class A, B, C, D play-offs in Figure 33 illustrate how the participation-achievement point system applies to a single elimination tournament. This system is just as suitable for double elimination tournaments or any other tournament in which there is a complete ranking or partial ranking of teams. In the touch football play-offs, teams are classified on the basis of the round robin-elimination method described on page 203. First place teams in each league are grouped in Class A, second place teams in Class B, third in Class C, and fourth in Class D. Losers of the first round in Class D get the minimum number of points, 50. The winner gets the maximum points, 150, with other teams earning points proportional to their final position in the play-offs. It should be noted that the winners of one class are awarded as many points as the losers in the first round of the class immediately above. Phi Gamma Delta earns 100 points for winning Class C as do the losers in the first round of Class B. It seems fair to have a winning team in one class earn as many points as the teams losing their first game in the next higher class. Note also that Kappa Sigma has two entries, the Green team in Class B and the White team in Class C. The White team did not receive 84 points but prevented Sigma Alpha Mu from advancing to the 84-point bracket. Since the Green team advanced farthest, it was given 116 points in the Class B play-offs.

For single elimination tournaments which are not divided into classes, the points are listed across the bottom or top of each round and teams losing in that round receive the listed number of points. In a sport such as table tennis, which is in the 25–75 minimum-maximum scale, there are five rounds in a 32-team tournament draw. Table tennis teams losing in the first round earn 25 points, second round losers receive

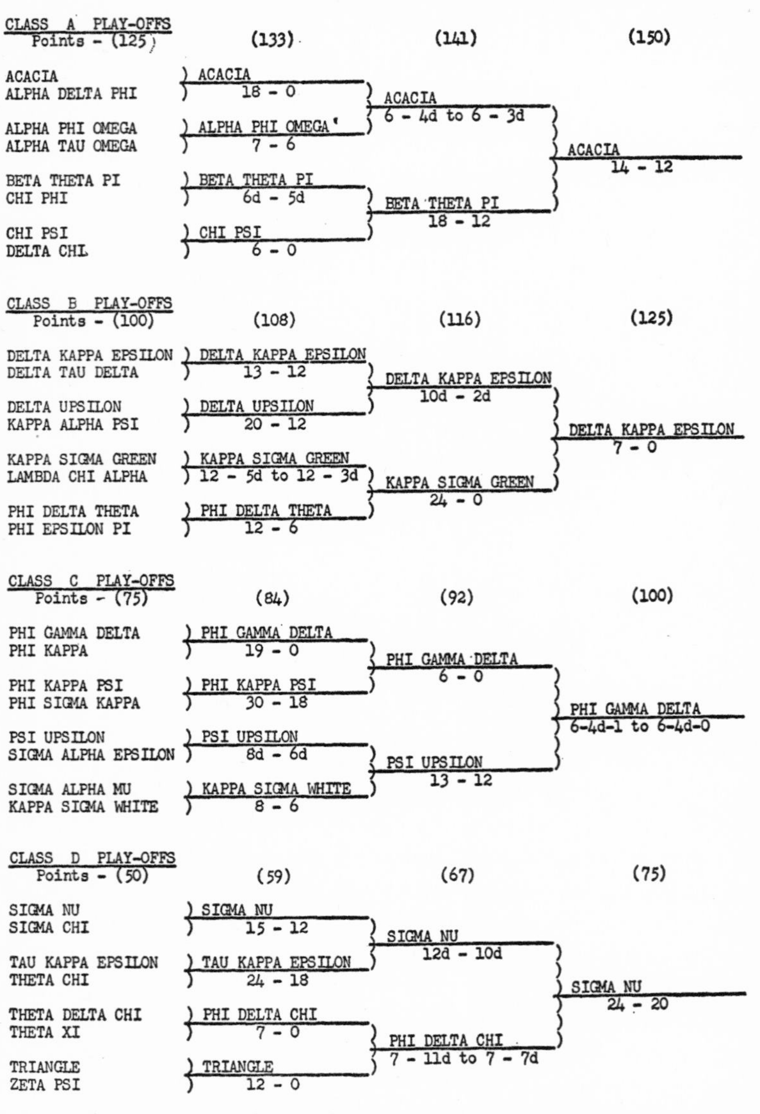

Figure 33. Point Distribution for Touch Football Elimination Play-offs.

38, third round losers 50, the fourth round loser 62, and the winner 75.

Point Totals

A sample of the all-year point totals is shown in Figure 34. Under the participation-achievement point system, points are not awarded to teams which forfeit or use ineligible players. However, it is necessary to include these teams in the number of teams entered to determine the proper interval. In this illustration, there are 21 sports with a total of 2,250 possible points, a minimum total of 760 possible points (if every sport is entered) and an average total of 1,505 possible points.

Phi Epsilon Kappa won the all-year championship with 1,602 total points. They won championships in touch football and golf and finished last in table tennis and the free throw contest. The second place organization, Phi Delta Chi, won three sport championships but failed to compile enough points in other sports to overtake the first place unit. Theta Tau won third place despite not entering a team in track. It is interesting to note that Delta Theta Phi did not win a championship and still finished in fourth place. The last place organization ended the year with 1,358 total points, just 244 points behind the first place total.

Point Tables

When using the participation-achievement point system, it is time-consuming and it increases the chance for error if point intervals are refigured each time a tournament is conducted. There is also the possibility they are figured slightly different each time. So, for these reasons, it is advisable to make up point tables which list point intervals for various numbers of teams. Participation-achievement point tables for major, intermediate, and minor sport divisions are available in Chapter 16, Figures 65, 66, and 67. When the number of teams or places for which points are to be assigned in the tournament is determined, selection of the

PARTICIPATION - ACHIEVEMENT POINT TOTALS

Legend

■ - Winners
D - Dropped
O - No Entry
F - Forfeit
I - Ineligible Player

	CROSS COUNTRY	TOUCH FOOTBALL	TABLE TENNIS	HANDBALL	HORSESHOES	RIFLE SHOOTING	PADDLEBALL	BASKETBALL (A)	BASKETBALL (B)	BOWLING	ICE HOCKEY	FREE THROWS	SQUASH	VOLLEYBALL	WRESTLING	SWIMMING	BASEBALL	SOFTBALL	GOLF	TENNIS	TRACK	TOTAL POINTS	PLACE
ALPHA GAMMA RHO	44	112	50	0	31	57	25	88	46	119	94	38	25	131	55	67	106	100	35	87	65	1375	15
ALPHA MU SIGMA	56	144	28	31	25	61	28	81	43	100	112	35	65	100	59	44	119	94	76	0	**100**	1401	13
ALPHA RHO CHI	60	106	44	42	28	96	0	138	25	69	138	0	**75**	106	51	63	112	69	88	83	52	1445	8
DELTA SIGMA DELTA	25	138	47	28	0	65	52	50	71	112	106	52	48	56	96	90	**150**	50	84	D	92	1412	11
DELTA SIGMA PI	66	50	72	45	62	48	69	131	0	106	56	65	52	144	47	0	50	**150**	72	43	96	1424	10
DELTA THETA PHI	63	131	69	38	35	52	62	56	68	138	62	69	45	94	43	86	69	112	80	92	61	1525	4
KAPPA ETA KAPPA	28	56	**75**	72	55	**100**	65	125	39	I	131	31	55	75	67	40	131	56	96	52	83	1432	9
MU BETA CHI	53	119	31	35	38	0	55	144	0	62	88	45	38	125	39	95	56	144	47	57	87	1358	17
NU SIGMA NU	50	62	56	48	58	74	**75**	119	36	56	119	42	69	62	88	49	144	62	92	39	74	1474	7
PHI BETA PI	47	125	53	25	69	70	31	62	50	144	50	62	35	69	84	58	125	106	43	61	35	1404	12
PHI CHI	31	81	60	55	52	92	42	112	61	88	100	58	31	119	**100**	35	62	138	39	**100**	39	1495	5
PHI DELTA CHI	**75**	75	63	52	65	87	58	100	64	81	**150**	28	62	50	72	**100**	100	75	67	78	70	1572	2
PHI EPSILON KAPPA	40	**150**	25	69	48	78	45	106	54	94	144	25	58	112	92	54	94	88	**100**	48	78	**1602**	**1**
PHI RHO SIGMA	37	100	F	65	42	35	72	69	32	125	81	**75**	28	138	35	81	88	81	63	96	57	1400	14
PSI OMEGA	34	94	37	58	72	83	35	75	57	**150**	75	55	F	88	80	0	81	125	55	70	48	1372	16
THETA TAU	72	69	66	62	**75**	43	48	**150**	29	50	125	48	72	81	76	77	138	131	59	65	0	1536	3
XI PSI PHI	69	88	40	**75**	45	39	38	94	**75**	131	69	72	0	**150**	63	72	75	119	51	74	43	1482	6

Figure 34. Participation-Achievement Point Totals.

correct category in the table reveals the number of points for each team. Point tables greatly facilitate the administration of a point system.

Four simple steps to keep in mind in utilizing the participation-achievement point system follow:

1. Refer to the minimum-maximum scale to determine in which division (major, intermediate, or minor) the sport is located.
2. Determine the number of teams or places which receive points.
3. Refer to the point tables for the actual point distribution.
4. Record accumulated point totals throughout the school year.

INDIVIDUAL POINT SYSTEMS

Individual point systems are similar to group point systems and in many instances the methods of distributing points are used interchangeably. Under this plan, individuals receive participation points as members of teams and for taking part in nonteam activities, and they also receive achievement points if their team wins or if they win in individual competition. Individual systems are better suited for junior and senior high schools and small colleges although some large universities use them to great advantage. However, the individual systems are less popular and are not used as extensively as group systems. Group plans have greater continuity from year to year than individual plans. It is easier to compare organization standings to determine if they improved over the past several years. Organizations such as fraternities, dormitories, and clubs maintain their identity over an extended period of time and carry on traditions whereas individuals leave the institution after a few years.

A carefully planned and administered individual point system is helpful in creating interest and encouraging participation in intramurals. Students are interested in seeing where they stand in intramural participation and competition, just as they are in knowing where they rank in a classroom examination. A well-devised individual point plan serves as a stimulus for participation in the following ways:

1. It encourages students to belong to a team. This results in the formation of more teams and a greater number of players for each team.
2. It is an excellent method to create interest in noncompetitive activities and furnishes an incentive for the student who seeks physical recreation apart from the group.
3. Individuals are encouraged to obtain an over-all knowledge of sports rather than specializing in a few.
4. Students enroll in physical education classes or join sport clubs to secure basic skills which enhance their opportunities for success in intramurals.
5. Interest is aroused by making an award at the end of the school year to students earning the most points.
6. Some all-encompassing plans encourage participation in all school activities and not just sports activities, thus broadening the learning experiences of each participating student.
7. All students are individually recognized to a degree whereas only a few students gain recognition playing on a championship team.

The individual point system serves as a basis for making awards to one student or several of the top ranking students. Presenting awards only to first place team members overlooks the good athlete who belongs to an organization which is weak athletically. Although he competes faithfully with his unit throughout his school career, there is little opportunity for recognition because of his team's lack of success. The individual plan enables a deserving student to gain recognition regardless of team success. Trophies, plaques, medals, blankets, numerals, and letters are types of awards given to all-year individual winners. These are presented to the first-ranking student, the first five or top ten students.

The record keeping for the individual system is more detailed than it is for group plans, and many intramural directors do not use it for this reason. Student managers or assistants frequently take charge of this detail. The problem of recording individual points is reduced by setting up a routine system which requires a minimum of supervision by the program director. The intramural office furnishes individuals as well as group scoring charts for organizations to post on their bulletin boards. Unit managers keep the records up-to-date so each member knows the ranking of his organization and his own participation-achievement record. The intramural office clerical staff keeps a similar record which is available to every unit manager for checking purposes.

In establishing an individual point system, it is necessary to observe precautions to assure effective administration and desirable outcome. The basic considerations discussed earlier in this chapter apply to individual as well as group plans. Each student must have equal opportunity to earn points. Uniform programs of activities and even standards of competition must be provided or students belonging to one group have an unfair advantage in accumulating points. Excessive participation must be controlled. Careful scheduling of activities controls participation and helps eliminate any negative effect on students' studies, health, or home life. Loose standards in the individual point system usually have greater consequences than laxity in group point systems.

INDIVIDUAL SCORING PLANS

A study of individual scoring plans shows they are used for sports only or are all-encompassing to the extent that any or all student activities are included. All of the plans are either based on team participation only, individual participation only, or a combination of team and individual participation.

Team Basis

Under the team plan, points are assigned to individuals on the basis of their team's performance. However, if a student does not participate in all games, he receives points in proportion to the number of games in which he played. As an example, if his team earned 100 participation-achievement points in softball and he only played in one of ten games, he receives 10 points or one tenth of the total, 100. This procedure could apply to any comparative order group point system.

Another plan does not consider the number of games played by each team member but gives blanket point coverage to all team members. The first four teams receive five, four, three, and two points, respectively, and all others receive one point. Individuals are assigned the same number of points as earned by their team. This avoids excessive record keeping with the same totals transferred from the group chart to individual records. If major and minor sport classifications are used, the number of points is doubled for sports in the major category.

Individual Basis

This plan does not take into account final results of team play. Consideration is given only to the individual's participation and performance. Points are awarded for individual performance in track, swimming, wrestling, handball, paddleball, squash, tennis, table tennis, horseshoes, badminton, archery, bowling, free throws, golf, fencing, and rifle shooting and any other activity in which a student competes individually. The participation-achievement point system or any other previously discussed method of distribution can be used to award points. In addition, entrance points can be assigned for participation, but not achievement, on teams and for participation in noncompetitive activities. The individual plan frequently includes noncompetitive activities which are measured subjectively, such as sportsmanship, reliability, dependability, posture, health habits, hiking, and cycling.

Combination Plans

Combination team and individual plans recognize and encourage participation in team games as well as individual competitive and noncompetitive activities. Student participation and success are measured in both individual and team activities. A combination plan is more effective than either plan by itself in determining the individual's over-all rating of participation and achievement in the intramural program. While the team plan is commendable for promoting strong group spirit, it is open to the criticism that for sports such as track, swimming, and wrestling, it gives a team member who does not contribute meet-points to the team total the same rating as the individual who wins place-points in one or more events.

Not only is it possible to rank students through individual point systems based on team and individual plans, but it is also possible to have these same results serve as rankings for organizations. For example, points for students are individually awarded and recorded. Group rankings are then determined by adding together the total points earned by individual members of each group. Numerous combinations involving group and individual point systems are devised to credit students and teams for intramural participation and achievement.

Another type of point system designed for self-testing activities is used in the Sigma Delta Psi tests. In these tests, certain standards are established which the student tries to attain. He earns points not only for trying to pass the test and for passing the test but also for successful performance beyond the minimum requirement. The Sigma Delta Psi point system does not measure the student's performance against an opponent, his success as a member of a team, or the number of times he participates; rather, it measures his ability to compete against predetermined standards. A maximum of 100 points is awarded for achievement at the top of the scale in each activity and a minimum of 1 point at the bottom of the scale. Test results which fall between these limitations are assigned proportional points. If the student is tested in 12 activities, the maximum total possible points is 1,200. The Sigma Delta Psi activity tests, requirements, and scoring tables appear in the Appendix.

For individual competition, a student accumulates points

by performing his best in each self-testing activity or event. The participant with the highest total for all activities is the winner. For group competition, each organization enters as many members as it wishes but only the top ten individual totals apply toward the team championship. The organization accumulating the highest total for the top ten individuals is the winner. It is possible to name all-around individual and group winners as well as individual winners for each activity or event.

SUMMARY

1. Intramural point systems for groups and individuals are used almost as extensively as awards by intramural directors to motivate interest in the over-all program, to encourage student participation in a wide variety of activities, and to serve as a basis for making awards.
2. Arguments for point systems include heightened interest, increased participation in new as well as regular sports, and an inducement for participation by disinterested or reticent students.
3. Arguments against point systems include the elimination of the fun of participation as students enter an activity merely to win points, discrepancies in point totals awarded different sports, artificial motivation, and undue time necessary to keep records.
4. As is the case with awards, point systems must be selected or constructed to coincide with the objectives of intramurals.
5. There are two general types of point systems: (1) one which includes only intramural sports activities, and (2) one which is all-encompassing to the extent that it covers all intramural sports activities and other student activities such as band, organization membership, committee work, debate, and scholarship.
6. The most important element in establishing a good point system is to make sure participants have an equal opportunity to earn points and that points are equally distributed.
7. Methods of distributing points in a point system include Comparative Order—High Total Wins; Comparative Order

–Low Total Wins; Comparative Order Plus Entrance Points; Comparative Order Plus Points Per Game; Awarding Winners, Runners-Up, Third, and Fourth Places, and other combination plans.

8. Point systems should be selected to fit the local situation, upgrade and maintain proper balance in the intramural program, and not detract from satisfactory student experiences in the program.
9. Small or large organizations and groups should have a chance to accumulate the highest point total and the number of entries or teams from a large group should not be restricted.
10. An adjustment for more than one team from the same organization can be made, such as allowing any number of teams to enter but only assigning points to the team that advances the farthest in the tournament.
11. Insofar as possible, a point system should supplement the intramural program to the extent that it adds interest and encourages participation, but it should not be emphasized to the degree that it is the most important aspect of a student's life.
12. A point system should take into consideration participation or entering and achievement or winning, with proper balance between these two essentials.
13. Points should not be assigned for negative participation such as for forfeits and use of ineligible players.
14. Forfeits are usually handled by subtracting a set number of points for each forfeit from the total number of points earned up to that time, by eliminating the number of points the team would have won had they played the game, or by not assigning any points for the sport in which the forfeit occurred.
15. A point system should not be so complicated that it is difficult for students to understand and too time consuming to administer.
16. It is advisable to strike a reasonable medium in determining the size of the point figures to be used, i.e., no fractions or large numbers.
17. Consideration should be given to assigning different point values to the various sports based on whether the sport is individual, dual, or team; the number of players required

for a team; the number of games played; and the number of teams or entries competing.

18. Sports with different point values can be divided into groups or classes such as major, intermediate, and minor although none is more important than another.
19. Distribution methods should be adaptable to various types of competition—round robin, single elimination, double elimination, and combination tournaments, as well as meets.
20. The inclusion of bonus points and subjective items tends to reduce the validity of the point system.
21. A point system should be so designed that it is not necessary to enter every sport or win every championship.
22. All-year awards are usually based on point totals and, thus, winners should be objectively determined.
23. Successful point systems should not encourage intramural directors to add too many new sports to the program.
24. Individual point systems are quite similar to group point systems and in many instances the methods of distributing points are used interchangeably.
25. In the individual point system, individuals receive participation points as members of teams and for taking part in nonteam activities and they also receive achievement points if their team wins or if they win in individual competition.
26. Individual point systems are better suited for junior and senior high schools and small colleges although some large universities use them to great advantage.
27. A carefully planned and administered individual point system is helpful in creating interest and encouraging participation in intramurals.
28. A well-devised individual point plan serves as stimulus for participation and as a basis for making awards to one student or several of the top ranking students, and enables a deserving student to gain recognition regardless of team success.
29. Precautions observed in setting up a group point system apply to setting up an individual point system.
30. Individual scoring plans are based on team participation only, individual participation only, or a combination of team and individual participation.

31. Another type of point system measures the student's ability to compete against predetermined standards such as in Sigma Delta Psi tests.
32. Point systems for groups and individuals are beneficial or detrimental to the intramural program in direct proportion to the adequacy with which they are selected and administered.
33. Only to the extent that point systems result in desirable outcomes and conform to intramural objectives are they justified.

11

Intramural Rules and Regulations

Rules and regulations are as necessary to govern intramural competition as they are for successfully handling varsity competition. Basically, rules for both types of competition are standardized, but because of varying situations and changing times, there are different applications and occasional rule changes. Present rules and regulations evolved over a period of years. When unusual situations arose, a new rule was introduced to prevent reoccurrence of the situation and bring about the most satisfactory intramural play. It is not practical to set up rules which regulate every minor aspect of the intramural program. Because intramural staffs are usually limited in the amount of time they have to perform numerous details, it is advisable to educate students as to the spirit of the rules and place the major responsibility for adhering to them on the team captains and players.

The first need for rules centers about the general conditions which hold for all sports, such as eligibility of players, special conditions under which leagues are organized, protests, forfeits, and enforcement of rules. These matters are discussed in this chapter. In general, this type of rule is administered by the intramural office.

A second category of rules involves those which apply to each sport individually. Frequently, the rules of a particular sport have to be modified for intramural competition. Such changes usually are aimed at expediting the playing of games and making play less strenuous and complicated. Special rulings of this nature are not discussed here; they were treated in Chapter 7.

GENERAL ELIGIBILITY RULES AND PROBLEMS

Some rules apply to all players, regardless of league or unit classification. Other rules, special rules, apply to particular leagues. Both kinds of rules will be presented here.

Scholarship Requirements

The tendency with respect to scholastic requirements for intramural eligibility is to make the rules as simple as possible. Earlier intramural programs were strict with regard to the scholarship requirement; in fact, candidates had to fulfill requirements similar to those for the varsity men. Before a candidate could participate he had to be certified by the proper school authorities. The secretarial work involved in preparing candidate lists and checking scholarship proved burdensome to both intramural staffs and school officials. Even from the start, the number of teams was small, the difficulties and annoyances confronted were numerous.

The next step, therefore, was to make the scholastic rules more elastic by stating that no student on "probation" (remaining in school conditionally) was eligible for intramural contests, a ruling fairly satisfactory in small systems. In large systems, however, where the attendance mounted into thousands, it required too much time and trouble to check the status of all players, and pressure of duties frequently prevented the intramural staff from doing this effectively. The result, therefore, was that many protests were made on games played because it was afterwards found that ineligible persons participated.

As a result of experiences such as those described above, most schools follow the rule that any student enrolled in the school is eligible scholastically to take part in intramural work. This amounts to saying that there is *no* scholastic requirement insofar as the intramural authorities are concerned. The burden of deciding whether a student shall participate is left with school authorities.

Simplification of the scholarship rule has lessened much of the department's office work. This is a much needed help, for the intramural staff is usually hard pressed to meet all demands of a rapidly expanding program. The efforts of the director and his assistants should be centered on promotion of the program rather than on inconsequential office details.

Furthermore, there is a very logical argument against barring all scholastically deficient students. Intramural directors argue that students are able to study better if they take part in wholesome physical recreation programs. It is undoubtedly wiser for school authorities to follow the positive approach of promoting a counseling program which orients students in correct relationships and proper budgeting of time and talents to develop the intellectual, social, spiritual, and physical phases of their lives.

From the intramural standpoint, there is no logic in depriving students of needed exercise and recreation when faculty authorities themselves do not place a check on the choice of student amusement. Nor can it be said that the intramural type of sport encroaches upon the student's time and proves detrimental to his studies. In this connection, it is interesting to note that some states do not have a scholarship rule in high-school interscholastic sports. Certainly, a scholastic ruling is not fitting for intramural participation where there is no rule applicable to varsity competition.

Participation by Professionals

Intramural directors do not agree on a proper rule regarding professionalism. Some schools permit the professional player to participate; others bar a professional athlete from all intramural sports; and others bar an individual only from the sport in which he is a professional. The last viewpoint is the most widely accepted one. It overcomes objections to the other two methods. While the first plan of ignoring the problem does simplify things, it carries with it the practical objection that a star player in an important position, like a pitcher on the baseball team, or a key man on a basketball team, can make it possible for his team to win games so easily that interest is lost. On the other hand, the rule which bars a former professional from all sports is not in harmony with the principles of intramurals; for it prevents a person who is a professional in baseball, for instance, from participating in sports such as soccer, handball, and volleyball—games entirely unlike that of baseball.

Participation by Varsity, Reserve, and Freshman Members

The overlapping of varsity, reserve, and freshman squads with intramural squads is one of the most difficult questions of eligibility.

VARSITY LETTER WINNERS. Most schools prohibit lettermen from competing in sports in which they won their varsity award. This restriction also applies to transfer students who earned letters at other institutions. The problem is more complex in large schools, and there is a difference of opinion as to how it should be handled. In the small school, there is a wide range and reasonably clear-cut line of ability between the intramural player and varsity player. However, in some of the larger universities, the range is as wide but the line of ability between these players is not as clearly defined. There are numerous students participating in intramurals who have the ability to make the varsity but who do not go out for varsity teams because they must work, are too busy pursuing a degree in engineering, law, medicine, or dentistry, honestly believe they are not good enough to make the squad, or were not recruited and consequently do not feel they should report.

Similarly, there are transfer students who earned varsity awards at other schools who are not eligible to play on intramural teams, because of the aforementioned rule, but yet are not as good as some of the players who are playing in the intramural program. It seems unjust to prohibit a player of lesser ability from participating just because he won a letter at a small school. There is a great deal of controversy as to whether directors should strictly adhere to the principle that the program must be geared to the average student and bar all letter winners or whether rules should be liberalized to make them equitable for all students.

Some directors feel the use of lettermen in the sport in which the award was earned is legitimate, particularly if intramural competition is organized on a class basis such as Class A, B, C, and D. Class structuring gives opportunities to above average, average, and below average ability students to participate with reasonable success at various levels of competition. Several ideas are suggested and can be utilized to overcome the letterman problem:

1. Allow only one letterman to be a member of an intramural team or permit only one letterman to actually play at any one time.
2. Require lettermen to wait one year, or other stated period of time, after varsity competition before being eligible for intramurals.
3. Arrange special leagues composed of lettermen (however, these students might prefer to play with their own fraternity or dormitory team).
4. Permit lettermen to play in graduate and faculty leagues.
5. Bar lettermen that come from institutions of comparable size and athletic prowess.

Since it is humanly impossible for an intramural staff to categorize student ability just by watching the players in action, it is necessary for each director to evaluate his situation and establish eligibility rules which result in the greatest benefits for the greatest number of students.

VARSITY SQUADS. Members of varsity squads are barred from the sport for which they are practicing and usually from other intramural sports unless the coach registers his consent with the intramural office. Procedures on this rule vary with the school and coach. Some coaches do not want

their candidates to participate in any I-M spor
the chance of injury or because they feel these of
get enough exercise and should spend any extra tes
ing. Others do not object to participation in lesy-
activities such as bowling, table tennis, or ts
contests.

One of the major problems with this rule is determining the status of players dropped from the varsity squad. Early in the season, the squad is usually very large and it is customary for the coach to make a number of cuts until only a limited and select number of candidates remain. If the varsity and intramural seasons are conducted simultaneously, enforcement of the eligibility rule under discussion works a hardship on candidates who were clearly not of varsity caliber and yet whose enthusiasm led them to try out for a major team. This difficulty can be partially avoided by scheduling intramural activities to start later than varsity practices. In this way, the rule does not go into effect until the varsity squad is well reduced. This delay is not always possible when playing facilities are limited, and, often, another expedient must be found.

The following plan solves this particular problem reasonably well: bar all players who are retained on the varsity squad after the first varsity game is played. The reasons for choosing this particular time are twofold. First, the varsity coach, in fairness to the players, may try out many men in the first game (which is often of a practice nature) and then make a radical cut. Inasmuch as the season is just beginning, the dropped candidate should have a chance to play elsewhere. Second, from the standpoint of intramural success, it is not advisable to prolong the time limit because players retained on the varsity any longer than the time above specified cannot be demoted and transferred to intramural teams without having a disrupting influence on the latter's competition. These players are apt to be superior to the general run of intramural participants. The appearance of newcomers on a team after it is organized usually causes resentment on the part of the members who apparently won and then are set aside. The introduction of such into intramural leagues after they are well under roduces unfairness in competition because a certain might not have played against one team (A) and yet his presence is used against a second team (B) which loses because of his particular ability.

There are some who stay on the varsity squad in a sport and lose out both ways: that is, they neither receive a varsity award nor have a chance to compete in intramurals. This is a choice which the individual must make. The success of the whole intramural program should not be upset by favoring one or two individuals who are on the borderline.

Some varsity sports cause more trouble than others. For example, in track there is no set number of men to a team and many varsity track coaches do not cut their squads but allow all who are interested to remain under their direction. Under these circumstances, the best thing to do is to wait until the first varsity track meet is concluded and then bar all men who are retained on the varsity squad after that time. The varsity coach should co-operate at this juncture by giving a list of the men whom he considers of varsity caliber and possible letter winners. The posting or distribution of such a list gives each man a definite status of varsity or nonvarsity rank and stifles many complaints which otherwise might arise.

Reserves and freshmen. The Reserve team, or Junior Varsity, is common to practically all schools, and both Reserve and Freshman teams are found in larger collegiate institutions. These teams are of the varsity type, receive special coaching and, in many instances, play outside schedules; therefore, the players must be distinguished from the intramural players. From the standpoint of causing eligibility troubles, these teams cause more trouble than the varsity. The varsity men are so well known that any attempt on their part to participate in an intramural game is quickly discovered. The players on the secondary squads, however, are not as well known by the student body and are sometimes successful in playing an entire game before their ineligibility is discovered.

Two methods can be used to overcome this difficulty. The first is used by smaller schools which conduct intramural leagues before selecting material for these other squads. This plan helps to uncover material. There is, however, the objection that intramural competition is through at a time when the intense interest in a particular sport is just beginning. In some cases, coaches even bar freshmen and reserve players with exceptional ability. The fairer method from the intramural standpoint is to conduct its schedules so that they last throughout the customary season and thus parallel the varsity schedule in time and length. This second method necessitates close co-operation with the coaches who are handling freshman and reserve squads. Names of ineligibles are posted on the bulletin board or distributed through athletic councils with the statement that the men in question are ineligible for intramural competition in a particular sport.

Another problem is that of the exceptional athlete, who, before he wins the school letter, becomes scholastically ineligible for the varsity. If the intramural department simply excludes lettermen and varsity squad men, this individual is eligible for intramural competition and becomes a source of trouble. Although the reserve team is open to him, this inducement (especially where the reserve team does not play outside games) is not as strong as intramural participation. The picture is then presented of an athlete capable of being a star on the varsity team winning everything in sight in the intramural leagues. The difficulty is often doubled in individual sports, such as track and swimming, wherein there is no reserve team to take care of such ineligibles. Certainly there should be some check on the inclinations of such an individual, for it seems absurd that at a time when the varsity needs his services, he is using his talent in inferior competition and thereby depriving *bona fide* intramural participants of a chance for fun and recognition.

Two methods handle this particular problem. The first bars the winner of a freshman or reserve award from intramural competition thereafter in the sport in which he won the honor. This is workable, but most authorities maintain it is unfair, their arguments being that there are some freshman lettermen who are never able to win a place on the varsity squad and that such a rule bars them from both varsity and intramural activities even though they did keep themselves scholastically eligible.

Another rule, and one that usually satisfies the objections mentioned above, bars any player from a sport in which he won his freshman (or reserve) numerals and has since become scholastically ineligible for the varsity. If such a player is scholastically eligible, this signifies that the varsity coach does not consider him of varsity ability. If, on the other hand, he is scholastically ineligible, then he should be barred on the grounds that he is of varsity caliber. It often happens that an exceptional freshman athlete decides later not to go out for the varsity, but instead to try intramural competition which takes less time. This raises the point whether such a skilled athlete should be permitted to participate in intramurals. If the decision is to bar him, then the last mentioned rule does not cover his case; it has to be slightly altered to state that any winner of the freshman letter is barred from intramural competition in that sport unless the varsity coach's consent can be obtained on the ground that the athlete is not of sufficient ability to make the varsity squad. To cover scholastic ineligibility, transfer lettermen, and athletes of varsity caliber, the following rule is sometimes used: "The intramural office in co-operation with varsity coaches can exercise authority to bar from intramural leagues any student of varsity caliber who is not out for varsity competition."

SPECIAL ELIGIBILITY RULES FOR GROUPS

In addition to the rules of eligibility already stated, there are special rules which must also be set up to satisfy the requirements for different leagues, such as class or fraternity.

Interclass and Intercollege

Certain restrictions are necessary for class leagues. Some students, for instance, fail in certain studies and occupy a borderline position between two classes—between freshman and sophomore, for example. The best way to solve this is to accept the registrar's basis for considering an individual as a freshman, sophomore, junior, or senior. The ruling usually found in high schools which requires 16 units to graduate is 3 units for sophomore rating, 7 for junior, and 11 for senior. A study of these factors shows that, while the intramural department needs a ruling to cover such cases, this ruling is governed by the local situation.

In general, it seems that the interclass basis for teams is giving way to more equitable classifications. Is it not reasonable to assume that a senior team is better than a freshman team because of the additional years of experience? This is especially true in high-school intramurals.

Graduate

The larger universities usually offer graduate work and there is often a demand for graduate teams. This demand usually arises only in the popular sports that require few players and are easily organized, for graduate students usually have little time for extracurricular activities. Questions concerning graduate eligibility can be very troublesome, particularly in connection with lettermen and open campus tournaments in tennis, handball, and similar sports. Some schools bar graduate or professional students from representing undergraduate groups. Professional students in law or medicine, for example, should be permitted to compete with students of similar status or with teams in the graduate divisions of the intramural sports program.

Competition in universities is often based on college units instead of interclass. There is little difficulty in framing an eligibility rule for these conditions. A problem may arise if, for example, a person is taking a combined course in two departments, that is, Liberal Arts and Law, and rates both as senior literary student and freshman law student. The best rule is to stipulate that the last college in which he enrolled governs his status.

Schools that have part-time students in day school, night school, or extension classes require registration for a minimum number of credits before they are eligible for intramurals. Otherwise such students might register for one night-school class just to be eligible for intramural sports. The limitation depends on the school and type of credit offered for different classifications.

Fraternity

Some institutions do not allow a pledge to represent a fraternity. This is a matter of personal opinion on the part of the intramural authorities, and yet there are practical reasons for barring pledges. Sometimes a pledge never becomes a member of the particular fraternity; another and more common occurrence is that a fraternity in the midst of a close championship race pledges an individual of athletic ability to assist its chances of winning; others pledge a good player only while the sport is in season. The latter difficulty is surmounted by inserting a rule that no student pledged after the first game is played in any sport is eligible for that particular sport.

Some schools do not allow freshmen to compete in fraternity competition. The rule is necessitated by the tendency of upper classmen to shirk participation in the more strenuous sports and yet insist that the freshmen take part, in order that participation points for the group-scoring chart be obtained even though there is little chance of winning. This tendency, if abused, means that certain freshmen during this critical period of adjustment to college life take part in too many athletic activities and fail in their studies. Another argument for barring freshmen is that often first-year men are the only ones required to take physical education classes, and, therefore, the upper classmen need exercise the most.

People who argue that freshmen should be encouraged to go into intramural activities base their claims primarily on two points: first, that interest for the following years is aroused in the first year; also, that freshmen have fewer campus activities than the upper classmen and therefore it is more urgent that they should be supplied with proper recreation.

It is not uncommon in larger universities to find a student belonging to two fraternities, both a social and a professional. This is because a certain number of years of general academic training is required before a student specializes in medicine, law, dentistry, or other fields. This situation can be covered by requiring the player in question to represent his professional fraternity; with this exception, however, that if the professional fraternity does not have a team (quite common because professional students do not have the free time that general students do, especially in the afternoons), then the player is eligible to play with the social fraternity to which he belongs. Another more liberal rule permits the student to establish his loyalty with whichever team he so desires but he cannot change during the school year or before some specified period of time. With the recent development of graduate leagues, however, some schools have adopted a rigid rule which prevents a graduate student from competing in any undergraduate activity.

Dormitory

Dormitory competition is usually based on floor, house, block, or precinct units. There is a problem of students moving within the dorms from one house or floor to another. A rule must guide eligibility in this case and a possible solution is to require students to play with the house or floor team from which they moved until the end of the quarter, semester, or school year.

Another conflict arises when members of fraternities, professional or social, reside in the dormitory. Some rule must establish eligibility. The student can be given the privilege of declaring his loyalty to the fraternity or dormitory and once his decision is reached, he cannot switch in the middle of the season; he may switch, however, after a specified period of time—at the end of a quarter or semester.

Independent and Other Groups

The most important rule pertaining to independent groups and other units classed as miscellaneous is that eligibility lists be presented before the season starts. In this way, there is no overlapping of players, each group preserves an identity, and each team knows who comprises the opposing team's personnel. Some systems do not allow a team to add any new names after the original list is turned in; on the other hand, some systems permit a team to keep adding players.

Each of these plans has a disadvantage: the first does not allow the captain of a team sufficient time to try out his men and replace those who fail to show proper interest; while the second is distinctly at fault in permitting teams that have a chance for the championship to scour around late in the season and bring in a few star players who might turn the decision in their favor—a practice that is objectionable, for the players secured in this way usually supplant other players who were regular members throughout the entire season. The best rule, therefore, is a compromise. This is effected by requiring the original list but by allowing names to be added to it before the second game of the season is played. For instance, in softball, the original list might contain fifteen names and the lineup for the first game has to be chosen from these names; following the first game, however, and before the second game is played, new names can be added.

Unless the campus is zoned, it might be necessary to have a rule restricting use of fraternity and dormitory students by independent teams. These teams are able to secure players from the entire campus whereas fraternities and dormitories are restricted to players in their own group and it violates the principle of group loyalty to allow independents to "raid" organized groups. This is particularly unfair if teams play off for an all-school championship. Some schools allow dormitory and fraternity students to play with independent teams if their groups do not sponsor teams or if they agree to release their players to the independents.

Class B Leagues

Class B leagues are sometimes formed when there is considerable enthusiasm in a certain sport and more than one team can be entered from a single organization. When A and B teams are entered, a rule is necessary to prevent free interchanging of players between leagues. Eligibility lists containing the names of Class A and Class B players must be submitted. The rule found most successful permits the interchange of Class B players to the Class A League at any time, on the assumption that they have a right to graduate to a higher league, but does not permit the transfer of a Class A man to Class B. The restriction in the second case is aimed at preventing the dropping of good players to the subordinate league in case the Class A team proves to be out of the running and the Class B team is a championship contender. Any transfer is final; a player cannot have this opportunity more than once.

Other Classifications

In some junior and senior high schools, additional classifications are formed by the more scientific methods of classification of players into more equalized groups. In the schools in which classification scales are used, the sponsors feel that many difficulties of classifying players are eliminated and also that more players are brought into the program. Instead of only Class A and B leagues, it is not uncommon to find at least five or six leagues according to the various classifications.

Some colleges and universities have established different levels of competition, using one of two methods: (1) teams arbitrarily enter the class level they feel is best suited for them; or (2) after completing round robin play, teams are placed in Class A, B, C, or D on the basis of their league standing.

LIMITATIONS ON PARTICIPATION

In addition to the general and special rules of eligibility certain other restrictions must be placed upon the activities of each intramural player. The purpose of these additional restrictions is primarily to safeguard the participant's welfare.

Number of Teams

The question of whether a player should be eligible for more than one team in a particular sport is an important one. Many intramural departments favor the idea of limiting a player to participation on but one team. These department heads argue that (1) more participants are thereby secured than when duplication is allowed, and (2) this limitation on participation safeguards the student from overexertion or overattention to athletics.

The above rule is probably the one most generally followed, but in the larger universities, where there is considerable competition based on social units, special permission to play on two teams in the same sport is sometimes granted. The contention is that fraternities have such a hold upon their members that almost invariably they cause sufficient pressure to keep all their good players in the fraternity league. This means that these players are ineligible for the class (or college) league, which is a democratic unit that ordinarily attracts both fraternity and independent men and enables them to mingle on common footing. Furthermore, it is maintained that a man representing his fraternity should have a chance to win his class numerals while in college, and the same holds true for a man representing an independent organization. If, however, an individual point system is in effect to acquire numeral awards, this objection to apparent discrimination between fraternity and nonfraternity men does not hold.

The following rule alleviates such objections: a student can play on two teams in the same sport, provided the teams are in opposite units such as fraternity and dormitory. Allowing players to play on two teams could cause scheduling difficulties because the teams involved might be scheduled to play at the same hour. This is a problem if Team A is scheduled to play against Team B and several of their players also play on other teams. Theoretically, there could be 36 scheduling conflicts if Teams A and B were scheduled to play each other in softball and each of their players also played on other teams.

Another drawback to permitting one player to be a member of two different teams is that it might be impossible to play off a championship series between the winners of different leagues if a player is a member of the two teams scheduled to meet each other in the final game. Requiring players, when entering, to designate which team they will play with, in case their two teams meet for the championship, eliminates this conflict.

In general, local authorities are the best judges of whether players should play on more than one team. The decision rests on the number of games to be played and whether playing periods are regulation or reduced. Considering that most intramural teams do not devote much time to practice, it is not likely that playing on two teams overworks an individual. A player should not be permitted to participate in more than two leagues.

Currently, there is a definite trend toward permitting a player to participate on only one team in the same sport. This came about because of increased enrollments and wider programs of sports which are offered by most intramural departments. In the past, with a much more limited variety of activities, it was more common (and more justifiable) to grant permission to a player to represent two teams in the same sport.

Number of Sports

There is always the argument that players should be limited to a certain degree in the number of intramural sports in which they can participate. Many circumstances act automatically to prevent a player from overexerting and from spending too much time in intramural activities: (1) different sports often overlap, so that the player cannot be present for all of them and must make a selection; (2) sports which demand considerable endurance are restricted through training regulations; (3) sports fairly strenuous in nature have reduced playing spaces and shortened playing periods; and (4) many of the activities are more or less a matter of skill than of physical strength or speed.

If it is kept in mind that the regimen of intramural athletes in no way compares to that of varsity athletes, then it becomes clear that there is little danger of overparticipation on the part of intramural players. This is especially true in smaller institutions which do not offer as large a choice of sports. In larger institutions, restrictions can be introduced gradually as it becomes possible to place the sports on a higher level. There is evidence to show that intramural authorities are taking care of such limitations as the need arises, for individual scoring charts have rules governing the amount of participation any one individual can attempt.

Medical Restrictions

Although the student is responsible for his own physical well-being, the intramural department, in conjunction with the health service, is interested in helping the student understand this responsibility and in supervising the physical welfare of all intramural participants. A *must* rule in all departments should be that students have a medical examination before taking part in intramural sports. Most schools, particularly colleges and universities, require medical examinations of all incoming students. The examination is given at school, if there is a health service, or by the family doctor or a staff of local physicians co-operating with the school. Some intramural departments require only the entrance medical examination, others an examination every year, and still others a medical exam every two years. Those requiring an initial exam only usually insist on special exams for more strenuous sports such as cross country and wrestling.

After the medical exam is analyzed, a student is classified for athletic competition as follows: (1) no restriction; (2) no swimming, due to sinus and other respiratory conditions; (3) no strenuous sports such as boxing, wrestling, track, basketball, football; (4) adapted activities only; (5) no activities. The classification is noted on a health permit card which is carried by the student at all times. Some departments require that these cards be shown to supervisors or referees before students participate in meets or games. Another method is to publish a list of students with classifications of two or below so all team managers can check the health eligibility of their players.

To make participants aware of their health responsibility, it is helpful to have all team members fill in and sign a health card supplied by the intramural sports department (see Fig. 35) each year before they take part in any intramural activity. The card indicates that on the basis of a recent medical examination, they consider themselves physically fit to participate in intramural sports.

It has already been explained that certain sports which require considerable endurance and in some cases personal contact should not be promoted for general student participation, but rather for a selected group of players who have superior athletic ability and who undergo a conditioning program which helps reduce chances for injury or overstrain. Football, cross country, weight lifting, boxing, and wrestling

No.__________

HEALTH CARD

This certifies that I had a medical examination within the past year by one of the following:

☐ Health Service Physician
☐ Personal Physician ☐ Other Physician
☐ Insurance Physician ____________________

On the basis of this examination I consider myself physically fit to take part in a vigorous sports program and hereby request permission to participate in Intramural Sports.

____________________ ____________________
Organization or team Print name—Last First

Date__________ ____________________
—OVER— Signature

HEALTH CARD

It is the wish of the Intramural Sports Department to help each individual safeguard his health. Accordingly, any student who desires to take part in intramural sports must have had a medical examination within the past year.

Each student is responsible for such examination and for having a signed health card on file in the intramural office.

Students with paid fee statements can receive a medical examination at the Health Service without additional charge.

—OVER—

Figure 35. Sample Intramural Health Card.

come under this category. The separate discussion given to each of these events in the chapter on "Program of Activities" includes special rules that should be observed in each case before individuals compete.

Transfer Restrictions

It is important that there be a ruling which prevents a player from transferring from one organization to another after the season begins. This, if allowed, might be a common occurrence, for players on losing teams would attempt to transfer to teams that have the best chance for the championship. Therefore, most schools have a rule which attaches a player for the whole season to the organization with which he first participates. In some instances, in schools where players are limited to participation on but one team in a sport, there is a provision that a player who is not used in the lineup for the first two games can appeal his case to the intramural office, and, if successful, transfer to a team where he has more chance of playing regularly.

The above rule applies to teams in the same sport and does not in any way conflict with the right of an individual to represent one organization in a certain sport and another organization (for which he is eligible) in another sport that is going on at the same time. For membership transfer in special groups, the reader should refer to the eligibility rules for fraternities and dormitories.

In certain sports, where players are ranked according to ability, no transfer of membership within a team is possible after play begins. For example, lineups submitted for number one and number two players in handball, horseshoes, table tennis, squash, paddleball, and tennis must be retained during tournament play. There should be no shifting of the original players and their positions, although new players can be substituted for them.

Rules for Violations and Infractions

One of the most important phases of conducting a quality intramural program is the enforcement of rules and regulations. If regulations are loosely followed or numerous exceptions are made to the rules, it implies that the program is poorly administered or there is no need for established rules and regulations. One principle stated by a few intramural directors is that once an exception is made to a rule, there is no longer any need for that rule.

Violations occur through forfeits and protests involving eligibility of players and noneligibility situations. Rule infractions in large schools are usually more frequent and difficult to handle than in small schools because of the large number of activities and number of participating students. In some metropolitan areas, there might be a problem of nonstudents playing on teams through the invitation of an irresponsible student friend. To control violations and violators, it is necessary for the office staff to have the complete co-operation of team managers, players, and intramural officials.

Forfeits

One measure of the effectiveness of a particular program is the number of scheduled games or matches which are forfeited. In examining some intramural programs, it may not be unusual to find 25 per cent of the contests forfeited and a few leagues or tournaments in which only 50 per cent of the games are played.

Absence of forfeits usually means efficiently administered intramural programs which result in satisfied participants; and, satisfied participants are the best program advertisers. Responsibility cannot be taught if students are permitted to participate in a haphazard manner. This principle applies to the violation of any intramural regulation and to eligibility rules, in particular. Forfeits discourage the necessary *esprit de corps* which is so essential for good intramural programs.

Frequently, negative techniques are used to prevent forfeits. A forfeit fee is required when entering a tournament. This recourse provides an "out" or alternative to participating, namely, paying instead of playing. Teams must forfeit if they do not have a full team or are not ready to play at the scheduled game time or if they are five or ten minutes late. Certainly, tardiness cannot be condoned and managers must be encouraged to have their teams ready to play at the appointed time. Keeping in mind the basic intramural principle of participation, it seems logical to invoke rules which encourage participation in these situations. For example, a team should be permitted (if necessary) to begin a game with less than the required number of players. If a team arrives late, the team that was on time should be given advantage points such as one goal in hockey for every five minutes or portion thereof the opposing team is late, two points per minute in basketball, one run in baseball, one run in softball for every five minutes or portion thereof, in addition to having their choice of field or at bat. When both teams are late, the teams should play a shortened game. Other examples of negative emphasis are (1) failure to give or even subtract participation points for forfeits, and (2) charging a forfeit to a team if it does not list first and last names on score cards.

Although it is practically impossible to reach this goal, no intramural director should be satisfied until all forfeits are eliminated. A positive approach to the problem must be utilized in an effort to attain this objective. First, the intramural director must evaluate all office procedures to make sure there is no administrative reason for forfeits. Schedules must be carefully arranged with proper notification to the contestants. Rules and regulations must include the possibility of postponing games in case of an emergency.

Second, after eliminating customary reasons for forfeiting, the director must promote a positive educational campaign against forfeitures. This is done through athletic council meetings, mimeographed material, and other publicity media. Students must be made aware that forfeits are not only demoralizing to their team but have a detrimental effect on the entire intramural program. Intramural participants look forward with anticipation to playing their scheduled games and are greatly disappointed when their opponents fail to appear. Repeated disappointment results in decreased participation.

It should be pointed out that, in essence, an entry blank is a contract. When the entry is submitted, the team requests participation and agrees to be present for all scheduled games. The director fulfills his part of the contract by providing opposition, play space, equipment, and officials. If teams fail to live up to their part of the agreement, it is impossible for the director to fulfill the opposition clause of the contract. It should be made very clear that the participants are the only ones who can eliminate forfeits and such elimination results in a better program for them.

When a forfeit occurs, the team should be contacted immediately to determine the cause. This aids in preventing future forfeits by this team and also provides an additional opportunity to carry the "campaign" to the students. They appreciate the personal attention of the intramural staff and are pleased to know that an effort is being made to understand the participant's problems.

In large institutions, the amount of personal attention possible is related to the size of the intramural staff and number of forfeits. To aid in controlling forfeits in large departments where personal contact is not feasible, a letter similar to the one in Figure 36 can be used. Every director confronted with this problem should use a realistic, positive approach in the prevention and elimination of forfeits.

Protests

Protests should be avoided whenever possible. Therefore, the grounds on which protests are permitted to be made must be very definite and deserving. For instance, a protest based on the eligibility of some player on the opposing team is considered sufficient grounds for an appeal to intramural authorities; also a protest is justified when an interpretation of a playing rule is considered to be at fault. Never should a case of appeal be allowed on points that con-

TO: INTRAMURAL TEAM CAPTAINS

FROM: INTRAMURAL DIRECTOR

SUBJECT: FORFEITED GAMES

YOUR ____Touch Football____ TEAM, ____Tiger A. C.____,
FORFEITED ITS LAST SCHEDULED GAME. PLEASE KEEP IN MIND THAT FORFEITS ARE NOT ONLY DETRIMENTAL TO YOUR TEAM BUT HAVE A DEMORALIZING EFFECT ON YOUR OPPONENTS AS WELL. ELIMINATION OF FORFEITS RESULTS IN A BETTER INTRAMURAL PROGRAM FOR YOU.

WE SOLICIT YOUR COMPLETE COOPERATION AND REQUEST THAT YOU CHECK (X) YOUR INTENTIONS BELOW.

________ DROP OUR TEAM FROM THE SCHEDULE. WE WILL BE MORE CAREFUL WHEN ENTERING TEAMS IN THE FUTURE.

________ PLEASE CONTINUE TO SCHEDULE OUR TEAM. WE WILL DEFINITELY BE PRESENT FOR ALL FUTURE CONTESTS.

SIGNED________________________
TEAM CAPTAIN

RETURN THIS LETTER IN THE ENCLOSED SELF-ADDRESSED, STAMPED ENVELOPE. YOUR COOPERATION IS SINCERELY APPRECIATED.

Figure 36. Sample Intramural Forfeit Letter.

cern the judgment of an official, such as fair or foul ball, ball or strike. Even though the decision is considered wrong, it cannot be changed on such a basis without entirely destroying the official's authority. Only when the official alters the playing rules in an unauthorized manner should an appeal be granted. Teams must notify the official that the game is being played under protest as soon as this type of discrepancy occurs. In some of the larger institutions, protests other than those concerning eligibility are made on the field of play. Many protests are avoided by using a mature, well-trained, and experienced field supervisor to whom protests are made immediately and often settled quickly while a game is in progress. Protests so made and overruled by a field supervisor can be appealed to the intramural director.

If the two captains of the teams mutually agree on a change in some rule, they should abide by their agreement and not be permitted to change their minds later. This privilege of the captains is often exercised in the regulation of time of playing periods and resubstitution of players, but it should never be extended to sanction using ineligible players. Frequently a team, from the standpoint of sportsmanship, permits an opposing team which is one or two men short to recruit from the spectators. This works out satisfactorily if the first team wins, but if the team with the ineligible players wins, the result invariably is one of dissatisfaction and ill-feeling. It is best to avoid such aftermaths by refusing to recognize the use of ineligible players in any official game.

In sports such as tennis or handball, where players participate without officials, there sometimes arises an occasion in which the two opponents cannot agree on the results of their match. In this case, the department should furnish a member of its staff to act as an official while the disputed match is played off.

Protests should be made promptly, otherwise the entire schedule is disrupted even after it is apparently completed. Therefore, it is well to file protests within 24 hours after the game in question is played. This gives time for a defeated team, if it thinks there was an incorrect ruling by the official or that an ineligible man was competing, to look up the facts and present its case.

Occasionally, one team knows beforehand that an ineligible man is present in the opposing lineup, but withholds the protest until after the game is played; then, if the game was won they do not bring up the matter, but if it is lost, they claim the game on a protest. This type of action makes doubly certain of winning and is poor sportsmanship.

Appeals are usually settled by the intramural director. Many departments have a student committee to work with the director in handling appeals and such a representation does have some effect in making the student body feel it has a voice in the department's policies. As a general rule, however, responsibility is shifted to the director and he can expect to make most of the decisions.

There are various methods for selecting representatives for a student board of appeals. One method is to have a committee of three, consisting of the intramural director, intramural manager, and sport manager of the particular sport in which the appeal is made. With larger departments, the assistant director or field supervisor can be substituted and there also can be two intramural managers instead of one. Some schools elect a representative-at-large to represent the unit interests on this council. The number on the board varies; some schools have five or more. In case a manager's or other student representative's own class or fraternity is involved, it is best to provide for a substitute and the two teams in the controversy should agree on a person to fill the vacancy. Usually, a member of the varsity coaching staff is satisfactory as a neutral party. Testimony is secured from the game officials and from the manager of each of the groups involved.

Some schools require a monetary deposit on every protest as evidence of good faith. If the protest is upheld, the money is returned; if it is not, the intramural department keeps the money. This tends to discourage unnecessary protests. There are some people who object to the principle of this expedient. These objectors hold that some protests are made in good faith and in a sportsman-like way and should be accorded dignified treatment, without penalty, regardless of whether the protest is upheld or rejected.

The intramural department should follow a strict course of action in regard to its decisions on cases of ineligibility and other rule infractions. Laxity in rendering and administering decisions encourages players to follow a path of least concern. As mentioned earlier in this chapter, it is impossible to teach responsibility to participants if rules are not adequately enforced. Some directors have expressed the opposite view based on the argument that the primary objective is to get students to participate and, therefore, rules and regulations should be lenient. If rules are going to be treated in this manner, it is questionable if there is need for any rules.

The same type of positive approach advocated in the discussion on forfeits is necessary in controlling eligibility of intramural players. One of the most negative procedures is for the director to do nothing, unless a protest is registered, even though he knows of illegal participation in the program. The department officials should not only take action but also encourage managers, officials, and players to report inconsistencies to the office in an effort to equalize competition and "clean up" the program. This should not be construed as "tattling" on someone but rather as a cooperative effort to make the intramural program beneficial and enjoyable for everyone. The director's goal should be to conduct the program on such a high level that the student's pride in his program does not permit him to violate eligibility rules or other regulations. Students must be made aware of the effect of rule infractions on themselves and the program and the vital role the student plays in eliminating violations. Students must be made to realize that anyone who violates rules and wins really has not won at all.

The type of punishment used varies with schools. The following list gives an indication of a few methods of reprimanding players and teams for use of ineligibles:

1. Forfeit of the game or games in which the player played
2. Removal of participation points for the sport in which the player was involved

3. Disqualification of player from intramural sports participation for a specified period of time, such as one year or the remainder of the school year
4. Barring of teams or organizations from competition for a specified period of time
5. Indefinite suspension from the program, if violations are repeated
6. Recording of violations on the student's permanent school record
7. Disciplinary action by school authorities

Infractions that sometimes occur and are subject to the above methods of disciplining are being a letter winner and withholding the fact, playing under an assumed name, playing on more than one team in the same sport, and illegally transferring team membership.

Punishment for violators eliminates the violation but it is doubtful if it prohibits future violations or is of any positive good to the violator. Unfortunately, most intramural staffs are not adequate to counsel students who ineligibly participate in intramurals. A good counseling program not only reduces future eligibility inconsistencies but also is of inestimable value to the violator, which is most important. In some of the larger schools, cases are referred to the school's counseling division. When dealing with ineligibles, it is important for the director to be certain he does not hold resentment toward the student or team. If he does, it tends to establish prejudices, either consciously or unconsciously, in future relationships with these individuals.

Managers

There are two types of intramural student managers: the over-all program manager such as sophomore, junior, and senior manager and the individual unit or team manager. This discussion is primarily concerned with the unit or team manager and his responsibility in observing intramural rules and regulations.

Every participating team or unit such as fraternity, dormitory house, or independent club must appoint or elect an athletic manager. Managers serve in a liaison capacity between the intramural office and team players. They are the contact through which information such as schedules and rules is relayed to the players. It is through the manager that many comments and suggestions are communicated to the intramural office. Many present intramural procedures come from ideas presented by athletic managers.

Organizations in competition for top intramural honors are usually ones that have alert, efficient managers. Each manager should visit the intramural office frequently to meet personnel in charge of activities. He should also be thoroughly familiar with rules and regulations of the intramural program as outlined in the intramural handbook and the manager's manual. Managers should be selected after due consideration of individual qualifications. They must be interested in sports and the welfare of their groups. When they accept responsibility, it must be carried through with fidelity and loyalty to their organizations. Managers must be conscientious and willing to do more work than asked of them.

Good managers are one of the keys to a successful and smooth operating program. They play an extremely important role in eliminating ineligibility situations and avoiding other rule infractions. They must accept responsibility for having their teams present for all scheduled contests. They must also accept responsibility for using only eligible players on their teams. It is a good idea to require them to sign a statement similar to the one shown in Figure 11, page 140, to the effect that they know the eligibility rules, understand them, have checked the eligibility of all their players, and accept full responsibility if any discrepancies are found. Unless a procedure such as this is followed, managers might say they did not know or understand a rule when questioned about the eligibility of one of their players.

Some team members are dishonest with their team captains or managers and sometimes withhold eligibility information. To aid the team manager and place responsibility on the individual player it is advisable to require each player to sign an eligibility card once each year. This card includes the player's name, team name, campus address, telephone number, statement of eligibility, and signature. The statement reads:

> This certifies that I know and understand the Intramural Eligibility Rules and agree to abide by them without exception. On the basis of this pledge, I request permission to participate in the Intramural Sports Program. It is my understanding that failure to comply with these rules will suspend me from I-M competition and a record of this negligent conduct will be placed in my permanent school file.

Before a player signs this card he is asked to read the summary of intramural rules on the reverse side of the card. A sample of the type of information from the back of an eligibility card follows:

I-M Points of Reference

1. I have had a medical examination within the past two years and consider myself physically fit for participation in a vigorous sports program.
2. I am an undergraduate student taking at least six credits.
3. I am a graduate student taking at least three credits.
4. I am a faculty member taking at least three credits.
5. I shall play for only one team in the same sport.
6. I am a bona fide member of the fraternity, dormitory house, or other organization which my team represents.
7. I have clearance for participating on a team outside of my fraternity, dormitory house, or other campus organization.
8. I am a collegiate letter winner and/or professional athlete and have special certification for intramural sports participation.
9. I am a varsity or freshman squad member and my coach has granted permission for participation in intramural sports other than intercollegiate sports for which I am a candidate.
10. I was a varsity or freshman squad member but quit or was dropped before the fourth week of practice.
11. I am a varsity candidate but am not on the squad this year due to scholastic deficiencies or the transfer rule.
12. I shall read the Intramural Sports Handbook for additional information about eligibility rules.

Requiring managers to fill out complete rosters when submitting entries also aids in controlling eligibility and helps them organize their teams early. If they make an entry by just submitting a team name and manager's name, they might not organize their actual team until a day or two before the first game.

The following is a summary of manager's duties. This list should be helpful in understanding what the manager does in the intramural program.

1. Enter team in desired sports before the closing date.
2. Notify team members of place, time, and date of the game and see that all players are ready to play at the scheduled time.
3. Complete all arrangements if postponements are necessary.
4. Familiarize team members with playing rules of each sport and especially intramural rules and regulations.
5. Print on the playing card first and last names of all participating team members to aid office records and publicity accounts.
6. Contact the intramural department frequently and check individual and team records of your organization.
7. Maintain a high standard of sportsmanship for your group. Intramural sports are conducted for the good of the student body and for the friendly contacts that are made through participation. Players should insist on an honorable victory or none at all.
8. Make arrangements for facilities and equipment for practice or "grudge" games.
9. Represent your team or delegate a representative in all protests and other negotiations.
10. Attend athletic council meetings scheduled by the intramural office.
11. Keep team rosters up to date and notify intramural office of address changes throughout the school year.
12. Return correct score sheets, official ratings, and other reports to the intramural office.

Student Officials

One of the most important groups in controlling eligibility and preventing infractions of other intramural rules is the corps of student officials who serve as referees, umpires, scorekeepers, and timers for meets and games. Student officials not only administer events and games according to prescribed rules but also are in an excellent position to notice if a player participates on more than one team in the same sport and other eligibility inconsistencies. They should report any possible clues of illegal participation to the intramural office for further investigation.

Good officiating is perhaps one of the most crucial phases of an intramural program. Most participants have their only contact with the intramural staff through student officials. Many unnecessary protests are prevented through good officiating. Often it is possible to keep protests from reaching the intramural office by having them solved on the playing field or court by the officials and supervisor. Officials can be selected from physical education students, varsity athletes, or other students. Because of the importance of officiating, candidates should be properly trained in rules and officiating techniques. This is accomplished through interpretation meetings, written and practical tests, and clinics. Some schools have an intramural official's association to carry out this educational training program. An intramural staff member should advise and direct activities of such an association to assure adequately trained officials.

In high schools and some colleges, intramural departments customarily rely on volunteer officials. Coaches are generally co-operative in assigning varsity players to officiate. The coach considers this a valuable experience for his varsity players. It enables them to learn the rules and regulations of the sport and to become acquainted with their application in game situations. Some intramural departments require each participating team to furnish an extra player who can serve as referee. Rather than have these extra players work the games involving their friends, they can be sent to an adjoining field or court to officiate and, in turn, two extra players from another field or court can be assigned to work the game.

The most satisfactory arrangement, however, is to have a corps of student officials trained and assigned by the intramural office. They should be paid for their work, if at all possible. Paying officials at a rate a little above standard student wages enables the intramural office to secure better officials and to demand better than average performance from officials. If students are not paid or are paid a meager wage, they often accept their assignment with the idea that they are doing the intramural office a favor by officiating instead of realizing that officials are employees of the department and are accountable for efficient service. Officials can be assigned to work several games in one day because intramural games are usually played under time limits or with shortened periods. Although the amount of money per hour or per game seems insignificant, weekly total income is considerable and aids the student in defraying his school expenses. Officiating budgets of large intramural departments run as high as several thousands of dollars.

Student officials should wear distinguishing uniforms such as regular referee shirts or T-shirts with "Intramural Official" stamped or lettered on the back. Some departments use an official's bib made of black and white striped material which slips over the head and is tied around the waist with two apron strings. Bibs are inexpensive when compared to the cost of a complete referee's shirt. Bibs can be worn over jackets or sweaters on cool days and over T-shirts on warm days or for working indoors.

It is advisable to rate student officials and assign those giving the best performance. A student should be permitted to work as frequently as he desires if his name is at or near the top of the list. Since intramural directors are interested in obtaining the best possible officiating, a rating list provides competition within the group of officials and encourages each member to do his best. Team captains, intramural supervisors, and other intramural staff members should co-operate in rating officials. If the department has a form similar to the one shown in Figure 37, it can be filled out by each team captain at the end of each game

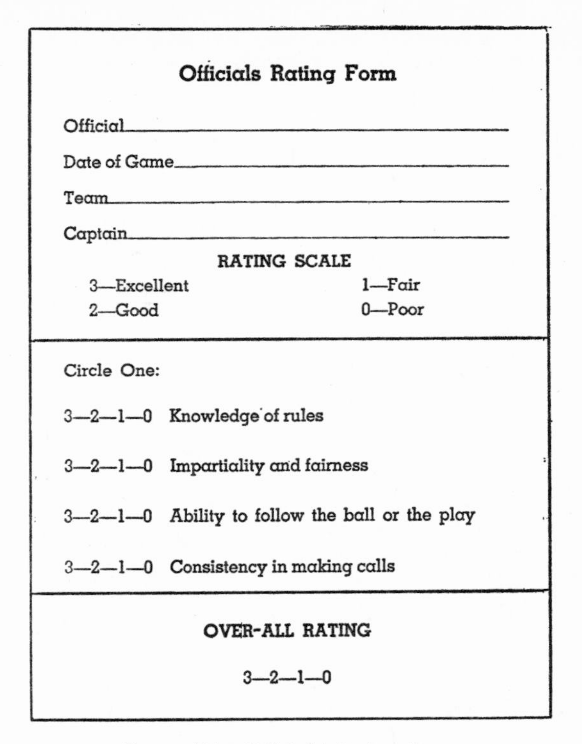

Officials Rating Form

Official______________________________

Date of Game__________________________

Team________________________________

Captain______________________________

RATING SCALE

3—Excellent 1—Fair
2—Good 0—Poor

Circle One:

3—2—1—0 Knowledge of rules

3—2—1—0 Impartiality and fairness

3—2—1—0 Ability to follow the ball or the play

3—2—1—0 Consistency in making calls

OVER-ALL RATING

3—2—1—0

Figure 37. Officials' Rating Form.

and submitted to the intramural department. Although it is logical to assume that losing team captains may rate officials lower than winning team captains and, therefore, the validity of these ratings might be questioned, over a period of a few games weak traits on the part of some officials usually will show up. Ratings, minus team designations, should be made available to the student officials so they can follow their own progress.

To make the rating system more effective, it is a good idea to have the student officials rate teams on sportsmanship. The philosophy behind sportsmanship is that each player should treat officials and his opponents with the same respect and consideration he likes to receive from them. Unsportsman-like conduct is usually a sign of emotional immaturity, and one of the desirable and hoped for outcomes of participation in athletic contests is that players learn to control their emotions.

In rating teams on sportsmanship, officials should consider organization of the team, attitude toward officials, knowledge of intramural rules and regulations, and sportsmanship toward opponents. After formulating a general opinion of the team's attitude, the official should give the respective group of players an over-all rating based on the following scale:

3—no difficulty
2—occasional verbal disagreement
1—unreasonable comments: complaining, arguing
0—abusive language, chronic complaining, violent protesting

Officials should place the rating immediately following the team name on the score card. Under this plan, teams with a "0" rating or several "1" ratings are called into the intramural office to explain their actions and show cause why they should not be dropped from the program.

Critics of this two-way rating system argue the validity of the ratings. The real value of the system comes from the fact that poor officiating and unsportsman-like conduct are constantly brought to the attention of officials and players. An official is more concerned about doing a good job if he knows he is being rated on his performance and he has less tendency to loaf and talk back to the players. Similarly, a team thinks twice before reacting in such a manner that eliminates them from the program. Rating teams on their sportsmanship in each game is more effective than telling them now and then in meetings or through other channels that they should demonstrate good sportsmanship.

Intramural rules and regulations are a necessity and must be adequately enforced to be effective. The intramural department must enlist the co-operation of staff, student officials, team managers, and players in maintaining rule enforcement which results in an equitable and better program for all concerned.

SUMMARY

1. Rules and regulations are as necessary to intramural sports as they are to varsity competition.
2. General rules include those which govern all sports, such as eligibility of players, special conditions under which leagues are organized, protests, forfeits, and enforcement of rules.
3. There are also rules which apply to individual sports which help expedite play and make play less strenuous and complicated.
4. Most schools follow the rule that any person who is permitted to be a student in the school is eligible scholastically to take part in intramural work.
5. Intramural directors do not agree on a proper rule regarding professionalism.
6. Most schools prohibit lettermen from competing in sports in which they won their varsity award or awards. This also applies to transfer students who won varsity awards at other institutions.
7. Members of varsity squads are barred from the sport for which they are practicing and usually from other intramural sports unless the coach registers his consent with the intramural office.
8. The fairest method to handle "reserve," "junior varsity," or freshmen athletes' eligibility for intramurals is to conduct intramural schedules so they parallel varsity schedules in time and length.
9. Exceptional athletes, ineligible for the varsity, are usually barred from competing in the sports in which they won freshmen numerals.
10. The best method to determine class eligibility is to accept the registrar's basis whether an individual is a freshman, sophomore, junior, or senior.
11. Intramural departments should have definite rules regarding participation by graduate students, especially those that are varsity lettermen, and part-time students enrolled in night classes, day classes, or extension classes.
12. Fraternity participation should be closely watched. Some schools bar freshmen or pledges. If a student belongs to

two fraternities, social and professional, he should decide at registration time with which team he wants to play.

13. Dormitory competition is complicated if students move from one house or floor to another; or, if students who are living in dormitories are also members of fraternities.
14. The most important rule pertaining to independent groups and other miscellaneous units is that eligibility lists be presented before the season starts.
15. The best rule for Class A and B league players allows Class B players to move up to Class A teams but not vice-versa.
16. There is a definite trend toward permitting a player to participate on only one team in the same sport.
17. There is little danger of overparticipation on the part of intramural participants.
18. A must rule in all intramural programs should be that students must have a medical examination before taking part in intramural sports.
19. To make participants aware of their responsibility, it is helpful to have them sign a health card declaring themselves physically fit before they take part in any intramural activity.
20. Normally, schools have a rule which attaches a man for the whole season to the organization with which he first participates in a certain sport.
21. One of the most important phases of conducting a quality intramural program is the enforcement of rules and regulations.
22. A positive approach should be adopted regarding all forfeits. The intramural department should check all reasons for forfeits and, through an educational campaign, point out the bad effects of forfeits.
23. Protests should be avoided whenever possible. Rule interpretations and player eligibility are justified reasons for protests; official's judgment is not. Protests should be made promptly following completion of a game or match.
24. Protest appeals are usually handled by the intramural director, sometimes with the aid of a student Board of Appeal.
25. A positive approach, similar to that used in handling for-

feits, should be used in controlling eligibility of intramural players.

26. Students must be made aware of the effect of eligibility rule infractions on themselves and the entire program.
27. Unit or team managers are vitally important to the proper functioning of intramural rules and regulations.
28. Team managers must accept responsibility for having their teams arrive at the game or match area on time, for eligibility requirements, and for briefing their team members on the rules of each sport.
29. Good officiating is one of the most important elements in an intramural program. Officials are in the best position to check ineligible players.
30. Student officials should be paid, if funds are available, and trained through clinics, meetings, and practice officiating.
31. Officials should rate teams on sportsmanship, and team managers should rate officials on general all-around ability and handling of the game or match.
32. The intramural department must enlist the co-operation of staff, student officials, team or unit managers, and players in maintaining rule enforcement. A more equitable and better program for all is the result of this co-operation.

12

Publicity and Recognition

PUBLICITY

Publicity is a basic essential in promoting an intramural program. The objective is to put the program across to the students and staff. Obviously, no one takes part in activities unless he knows something about them. Students must not only know what the activities are but also should understand that it is their program and is conducted for their benefit. Getting this point across in a large school system is sometimes a very real communications problem. Numerous average or "shy type" students, after learning an intramural program exists, are surprised and amazed to find the program is designed for them. Although the primary purpose of the publicity program is to inform the student of sport opportunities available to him, every opportunity should be utilized to interpret intramural sports to individuals outside the school.

For publicity purposes, an intramural director must use the best principles of advertising and use them repeatedly. It cannot be assumed that one method is sufficient to tell the intramural story. In the business world, a good product tends to sell itself through customer word-of-mouth advertising. The intramural director should be constantly aware that an efficiently administered program results in satisfied participants and satisfied participants are the best method of publicizing the program. The following paragraphs discuss some of the media to use for disseminating intramural information.

Student Newspaper

This can be the most important source of intramural publicity in schools where daily newspapers are published. This is particularly true in colleges that offer courses in journalism and publish weekly or daily student newspapers as a laboratory requirement of the classes. If properly circulated, the paper reaches all students and parts of it are usually read by all students.

Continuity is an extremely important element in newspaper publicity. If schedules and game results appear regularly every day, students soon rely on this source of information. In some cases, it is impossible to report all games in story form. As a minimum, facts of some of the games should be reported and final scores of all games should be listed. Scoring rules can be modified to reveal more information about the listed games. For example, in touch football the score can be listed as Bulldogs 12–5d–1, Bearcats 12–5d–0. This tabulation indicates both teams scored two touchdowns, each had five first downs, and the Bulldogs won the game on the penetration rule during overtime.

In addition to schedules, scores, and game stories, advance stories for future activities, entry deadlines, feature stories, and weekly columns are helpful in promoting interest in intramurals. Whenever possible, intramural stories should include names of the participants. Students much prefer to read about themselves than other students.

Some intramural directors find it difficult to get information published in the student newspaper. The sports editor is not interested in intramural sports and argues that varsity coverage is more important, there isn't enough space, reporters refuse to cover intramurals, etc. Games are played during the late afternoons and evenings; student reporters prefer to cover daytime stories which leave their evenings free. Some student reporters prefer to cover varsity practice and games because they are more spectacular and they get a vicarious thrill from associating with star players on the varsity teams.

Some directors feel newspaper publicity is important enough to pay reporters to cover intramurals. Others place student managers or graduate assistants in charge of program publicity. After the news is reported, there is an additional problem of getting it printed. Some student papers try to compete with the local newspapers to the extent of running news wire releases. They forget their original responsibility of printing the news of the local school community. Personal conferences with the editors are often necessary to understand the mutual problems involved. Student letters to the editor help bring the problem into proper focus. If editors are encouraged to conduct a readership survey, they soon learn that students usually prefer to read about themselves.

Local Radio and Television

In some or the larger school systems, student radio stations and educational television units are in operation. These can be used to great advantage in telling students as well as the local community about the intramural program. "Spot" announcements about entry deadlines or special events are very helpful. Film clips of intramural action can be used on television programs. Some student radio stations broadcast the entire intramural championship games in such games as basketball, touch football, or softball. Occasionally, local nonstudent press, radio, and television are interested in carrying intramural sports information. Intramural directors should be alert to furnish them appropriate news which tell the intramural story.

Intramural Handbook

Most departments find publication of an annual intramural handbook a valuable publicity aid. They can be distributed to each of the team captains, other members of the school staff, to each participant or every member of the student body. Some departments print intramural information in a section of the physical education handbook or the student activities handbook.

A few of the large departments publish handbook information separately for dormitories, fraternities, independents, and faculty groups. Still others have developed unique calendars which have rules, regulations, and additional program material printed on the back of each monthly page.

Intramural directors have established an "exchange of ideas" program through the exchange of I-M Handbooks. It is standard operating procedure for a director to send a copy of his handbook in return for a handbook received from another school. Other persons interested in obtaining handbooks need only address the request to the Intramural Director in care of the particular school.

The average size of a handbook is five inches by seven inches. Some directors prefer this size or smaller because the team captain or manager can carry it in his pocket as a ready reference. In general, handbooks contain most of the following items:

1. Philosophy and objectives of the program
2. Activities in the program
3. Activities calendar with starting dates
4. Yearly calendar
5. Messages from the college president, school superintendent, dean of students, athletic director, intramural director, and student chairman of intramurals
6. Departmental organization
7. Departmental personnel, building schedules, office room, and telephone number
8. Constitution and by-laws of the intramural councils or associations
9. Rules and regulations covering eligibility, protests, forfeits, entry fees, and postponements
10. Locker and equipment privileges
11. Indoor and outdoor facilities and facilities map
12. Health and safety information
13. Description and distribution of awards

14. Intramural officials association
15. Point tables and explanation of the point system
16. Pictures of intramural staff, winning teams, and game action
17. Publicity—how students are informed about intramurals
18. Corecreation and extramural sports
19. Tournament draw sheets depicting winners in certain sports
20. Summary of team captain's or manager's responsibilities
21. Participation records—number of teams, games, forfeits, participants, and participations
22. All-star or all-school team selections
23. Faculty program
24. Summer session program
25. Winners' list from previous year including names of team members; also list of team champions from previous years
26. Comparison tables of team point totals indicating previous year's place and previous year's finish
27. History of the intramural program and unusual happenings
28. Special events, such as open house, faculty-student night, and sports festivals
29. Requirements of Sigma Delta Psi, national honorary athletic fraternity
30. Information about practices, informal workouts, and challenge games

Bulletin Board

A well-organized, properly maintained bulletin board is a must for comprehensive intramural publicity. Schedules, notices, charts, diagrams, tournament draw sheets, posters, and other attention getters should be displayed on the bulletin board. No one item should remain on the board for an extended period of time and game results and league standings must be kept up to date. Neat, easily read materials and individual headings for the various activities are a necessity. All items should be attractively arranged and tacked down at the four corners to keep the paper flat against the board. This type of orderliness casts a good reflection on the intramural department. Disorganized bulletin boards usually indicate the program is run in a similar manner.

The bulletin board should be placed in a conspicuous and convenient place in the building. The location should be determined by its ready visibility upon entrance into the building or intramural areas. Whenever possible, the board should be lighted.

Portable bulletin boards are helpful for displaying information in the activity area. Rules, running team scores, and other specifics for wrestling tournaments, swimming meets, track meets, free throw contests, etc., can be posted in the area where the competition takes place.

Commercial concerns make tournament charts and activity posters which are eye catching and can be used on the bulletin board or posted in an area by themselves. The items include single and double elimination tournament charts; ladder, funnel, and pyramid tournament charts; league standings and all purpose charts; yearly, monthly, and biweekly calendars; activity posters for each sport; and other posters headed with such words as announcement, notice, intramurals, meeting, or practice. Activity posters may have drawings of players performing the specific activities with additional room for writing in information about the tournament. If a write-on, wipe-off grease pencil is used, these materials can be reused more than 100 times. In some schools, the print shop or art department assists in designing and making attractive bulletin board materials.

New Student Orientation Program

The fall season opens in many schools with an orientation program designed to welcome freshmen and transfer students and acquaint them with the facilities and program of the intramural department. It not only provides a good publicity medium but also helps facilitate the difficult transition from high school to college. Skits, films, and talks by members of the intramural staff will encourage students to take advantage of intramural opportunities. After a brief introductory program, students might be divided into groups for actual participation in one or more sports. The intramural department should furnish playing equipment such as tennis rackets, basketballs, handball gloves, and table tennis materials. Most of the events should be carried on informally for immediate enjoyment, but in some of the sports, first match winners might continue in a short-term tournament if they so desire.

A four- or six-page intramural folder can be distributed to all new students together with other information from the registrar's office. This folder could briefly describe the purpose of the intramural program, tell how to participate, list activities in the program, and give dates when activities begin as well as telling where additional information can be secured. It is less expensive to circularize all students with this abbreviated information than to provide every student with an I-M handbook. Those who are interested in intramurals can secure a copy of the handbook later on. This folder method is used particularly by intramural departments in large colleges and universities.

Announcements and Notices

Elementary schools, high schools, and some colleges do not have daily student newspapers, so it is necessary to use other methods of communication. In schools with public address systems, intramural announcements are made from the principals' or superintendents' offices. Announcements are also made in homerooms, study halls, and student assemblies via teacher notices sent from the main offices. Since it is customary for public school students to enroll in physical education classes, gymnasium classes furnish a good chance to reach them effectively. Frequently, in colleges and universities, only freshmen or underclassmen are required to take physical education, so only a portion of the student body is reached through class announcements.

One practical system of organizing leagues is to send

notices to organization presidents or athletic representatives announcing that entries are being accepted for future activities. These notices should be followed with reminders in the student newspaper that entries are due on a certain date. When the deadline is reached, the list of entries can be compared with the list of total organizations, and nonentrants can be telephoned or personally contacted to see if they wish to enter the tournament. This method cannot be used in organizing miscellaneous groups that have no permanency or in organizing nonteam, individual, and dual sport tournaments. For independent or nonpermanent groups, it is wise to establish athletic clubs which lend permanency and a degree of loyalty to the teams during the entire school year.

Some departments circularize all student organizations with mimeographed or dittoed intramural information. Bulletins, schedules, and notices can be made more attractive with sport figures and unique letter arrangements. Organizations can easily be encouraged to post this type of material on their bulletin boards. More detailed information can be reported in a mimeographed, weekly intramural bulletin. Complete game results of the previous week, league standings, outstanding individual performances, and information about future activities are of interest to the intramural participant. A few directors find it helpful to send out postal cards to players when the tournament is completed, thanking them for participating, expressing the hope that the experience was enjoyable, and asking them for comments to improve future tournaments.

News Release

The intramural director, school news service, or public relations department can send a form letter to the hometown newspaper of each member of the championship team, giving pertinent information about the performance of the team. Points of interest such as team name, scores of games, number of teams, and students participating should be included. Local hometown newspapers often appreciate receiving this information and print it.

School Yearbook

Each school yearbook or annual has a section on athletics. Editors should be encouraged to include an intramural section which contains the names of sport winners and pictures of some of the representative teams. When annuals follow the custom of printing individual records of senior students covering their school career, membership on intramural teams should be included among the various activities and honors.

Manager's Manual

The manager's manual or workbook, popularly referred to by students as the "man-man", is a very direct publicity method for communicating with team managers or captains. The manager's manual differs from the intramural handbook in that it has more specific information for groups such as fraternities, dormitories, or independent athletic clubs.

Material in the manager's manual should be arranged chronologically to aid the team captain in entering and managing his intramural teams for the entire year. Manuals should be looseleaf folders or notebooks to permit addition of tournament schedules. The introduction should contain the philosophy of a good manager, emphasizing qualifications, responsibilities, and tips on how to have more effective intramural participation from the student's viewpoint. There should also be an explanation of the student's role in eliminating forfeits, preventing ineligibility situations, and promoting good sportsmanship. In addition the following items should be included in a manager's manual:

1. How to submit entries
2. How to rate officials
3. How to register protests and postpone games
4. Complete explanation of the point system with point tables
5. Dated entry blanks for each sport

6. Summary forms for recording individual and team participation
7. Rules and regulations for each sport arranged chronologically

Manager's manuals can be checked out to team representatives at the beginning of the school year and returned when the last intramural activity is finished. After bringing the material up-to-date, the same manuals can be used the following year.

Although the manual contains information similar to that in the handbook, it is more detailed and directed toward understanding the participation problems of the student. This material is particularly helpful to the new athletic manager and it is also convenient for any manager who enters a team. The systematic arrangement of entry blanks and activity regulations enables him to follow the program by checking the date and turning to the proper page in the manual.

Film

Intramural departments in larger schools find it advantageous to make a film describing the intramural program. The 15–20-minute film usually shows the purpose of intramurals, how students enter the activities, available facilities, and action shots of students participating in intramural games. If a local sports commentator or sports personality can narrate the film, it adds considerably to its effectiveness. The film can be shown to campus groups to encourage participation and to off-campus organizations for better school-community public relations.

Other Media

There are a number of other, perhaps less direct, methods of creating interest among students and of getting the intramural story before the general public. Scheduling an intramural game as a preliminary to a varsity game, conducting an I-M cross-country meet between halves of a varsity football game, or running the relay championships during a track-meet intermission—all have publicity value. In a very real sense, awards advertise the program. This is especially true of those which can be worn by a student, such as a championship sweater, jacket, T-shirt, belt buckle, or a medal attached to a tie clasp or watch chain. Trophy exhibits in building lobbies are helpful, as are cups, plaques, banners, ribbons, and trophies displayed in student living units. Open houses and sports clinics appeal to the general public and student body. Information can be spread among schoolmen by writing articles for professional journals, setting up exhibits at school conventions, and displaying materials on nondepartmental bulletin boards.

Regardless of what publicity aids are used, it is still necessary to maintain some personal solicitation. This applies particularly to faculty groups and independents or nonorganized groups on the campus. However, the amount of personal solicitation depends on how effectively the publicity program is conducted, established traditions in the program, and the efficiency with which the entire intramural program is administered.

RECOGNITION THROUGH AWARDS

Life consists of varying degrees of success and failure. Certainly, success is important to the creative development of and developing creativity within individuals; and in everyday life individuals fail as often as they succeed.

The old adage of "success breeds success" is trite but true. Recognition of individual achievement, a "pat on the back," encourages additional attempts to gain success. As an individual grows and succeeds, the forms of recognition change but the need is still present. In the intramural program, there are numerous opportunities for success on the part of the participant. He can succeed by performing well during a game, even if his team loses, or he can share in the success of his team's victory. This performance could involve scoring the most points or just a few points, depending on the player's ability and previous success. When a team wins, success is shared by all members of the team. For some, the success element continues in subsequent games until they are eliminated from the tournament; for a few, intramural success terminates with the winning of the championship game.

While the success factor is in operation during participation, failure elements are also present. Players frequently fail or make mistakes during the contests. The participant that keeps the number of mistakes to a minimum usually wins the game. It is important for individuals to understand failure and its relationship with success. Before one can succeed he must be willing to take the risk of failing. Often, students do not attempt certain things because they are afraid to fail—afraid to make mistakes. All human beings make mistakes; to "err is human." There is nothing wrong with making a mistake, provided the individual admits a mistake was made, corrects it, and moves ahead. An unrealistic approach to failure can result in refusal to take chances or cause a student to project blame for his mistake onto someone else.

Recognition of success by intramural participants is accomplished through awards, all-star teams, performance records, and publicity accounts of student achievement. A few educators regard these measures as "promotional" and superfluous. Frequently, however, adults evaluate youth programs by adult standards. They forget the little things that had an important impact on their own lives. Obviously, a person's sense of values changes as he develops and progresses in every phase of life. Many of the ingredients of success are abstract and immeasurable, but certainly encouragement in the form of recognition causes the student to try something a little bigger and more important. Every intramural director must evaluate success and failure elements in the program and establish balanced standards for recognition of intramural participants.

Although the use of awards in an intramural program is a very controversial subject, most intramural directors follow the practice of presenting some type of award to the winners or participants in the program. There are numerous arguments pro and con. Some people argue that awards are unnecessary and students should participate for the mere love of the sport. Opponents of this feel that achievement is recognized in all other phases of life. Life from earliest childhood is a succession of awards for doing things well. Parents give special favors such as ice cream or tickets to the movies for good behavior. In education, valedictorians are selected and much attention is given to scholarship, fellowships, research grants, and memberships in honor societies. Employees are given promotions, salary increases, and bonuses for performing work efficiently and effectively. In these respects, awards are not far removed from actual life situations but rather are actual life experiences.

Proponents believe awards induce greater participation through added incentive and interest. Others argue that this interest is negative and artificial and that participation is just as great if awards are discontinued. A third segment feels that participation is as great if awards are not given because students become accustomed to the program and establish habits of participation. Students often appreciate receiving a token or symbol of their achievement. Usually, students enter the tournaments for the fun of playing and are pleasantly surprised when they are presented with an award denoting a level of success.

Another argument against awards is that a good publicity program often eliminates the need for awards. The affirmative side looks at this viewpoint with a positive approach by saying that displaying trophies, cups, plaques, banners, and shields and wearing medals, belt buckles, jackets, and sweaters are excellent methods of publicizing the intramural program.

Opponents of awards present another argument. They claim all importance and meaning of awards are lost once the student graduates from school. Those in favor of awards view this reasoning with a different emphasis. They point out that athletes have only a comparatively few years to enjoy athletic interests on a high level of organized play and honors should be forthcoming to them when deserved. Other fields, i.e., music, art, writing, and dramatics, present long-term achievement opportunities. Therefore, the school athlete should receive recognition for the few years he competes on a team basis.

Undoubtedly, the many arguments for and against awards will continue. It is possible that awards are inherently wrong. If this is true, there is a great deal of falsity in intramural programs because the practice of giving awards is almost universal. At the same time, it is possible that giving awards is a legitimate procedure and educationally sound, for if it is not, it may be necessary to change our complete emphasis on education. Certainly this is an area which needs much study.

Some considerations must be noted if awards are to be used judiciously and intelligently. Award procedures should be designed to promote the objectives of the intramural program. A distinction is made between awards and rewards. An award should be a symbol of the individual's achievement and not a reward for participating or an inducement to participate in healthful forms of recreation. The fun of playing should be the greatest incentive to take part in intramurals.

Awards should not be expensive or extravagant. This is particularly true if limited funds are available for equipment and other program needs. The award should always remain a symbol of achievement rather than a prize in which the merit is based on its monetary value.

Much of the value of awards is lost if they are not promptly distributed after having been won. There is no time when recognition means more to winning participants than immediately following the victory. An individual naturally wants to wear his award and the group is eager to display its trophy. Some delay is usually caused by engraving the trophy with the name of the team or names of individual team members. If given their choice between a slight delay for engraving or prompt delivery, students usually accept the delay in exchange for a more personalized award. However, undue delay results in indifference not only to awards but also to the program in general. Many intramural departments fail in this respect. Bestowing of awards is a matter of detail and intramural work is largely dependent upon successful attention to details.

Classification of Recipients

In general, there are three policies that are followed in making awards: (1) to award the group as a whole; (2) to award individual members of a group; and (3) to award certain individuals who do not have a group connection. Whichever plan is followed is determined largely by the permanence of the group, as the succeeding discussion shows.

GROUP AWARDS. Group awards are discussed from the standpoint of their suitability to (1) permanent groups, (2) semipermanent groups, and (3) temporary groups.

Permanent groups. A unit that has strong and permanent organization can be presented with a team award such as a trophy, pennant, cup, plaque, or shield. The fact that a group has a common and frequent meeting place means that the award can be displayed in such a way that all members share a mutual interest in it. In high schools, the homeroom or class, whichever unit is used, possesses this advantage for both members and supporters of the winning team to enjoy a common award. In colleges, the same advantage is possessed by dormitories, fraternities, and athletic clubs.

Groups from such units not only keep their identity intact throughout school days but also offer a chance to their members to retain their attachment after they become alumni. For these reasons, the team award is a significant and enduring bond. In some cases, individual awards are presented to team members.

Group all-year point-scoring implies a certain amount of permanence. The group as a whole remains the same even though each sport claims a different personnel of players. Hence, a group award is proper. It should be distinct from awards given to the various champions of each sport. The distinction can be made by giving a shield instead of a trophy or by giving a larger trophy. Some schools give unusually large trophies to their group all-year winners.

Semipermanent groups. To a lesser degree, units such as religious organizations, eating co-ops, and military companies can be interested in a trophy or other team award, but these units offer only a casual and temporary affiliation. Group spirit is usually not so strong. Therefore, the team trophy, if one is given, should be less important and supplemented by individual awards (charms or medals) to the various team members. If the individual awards are not granted, the team trophy should have the names of the team members displayed in some way; if not on the trophy itself, on a list posted beside it. A rotating trophy or plaque is well adapted for competition among groups of this type.

Temporary groups. Last, there is the type of group which affiliates for one seasonal activity and does not have members other than the players themselves. The independent unit and the arbitrary unit furnish examples. Here, a common trophy may not be suitable, for the team disbands when the particular league or tournament is finished and a trophy is meaningless, as there is no significant place to display it permanently. For teams of such nature, individual awards such as ribbons, charms, or medals are proper.

INDIVIDUAL AWARDS. Provision must be made for awarding individuals when they compete without group affiliation. This is true in individual sports such as track, swimming, tennis, handball, wrestling, table tennis, paddleball, golf, and badminton, conducted as open tournaments or meets for all eligible persons in school. This type of award can also be presented to the "athlete of the year." When there are only a few awards to make, small trophies are sometimes given, but in general, the type of award follows the same description as those used for individual members of winning teams: numerals, belt buckles, medals, charms, jackets, T-shirts, blankets, hanging or standing shields, sweaters, wall or desk plaques, small cups, ribbons, and certificates.

In addition to awarding a team trophy, some intramural departments present individual awards to members of the winning team. The team trophy is sometimes purchased through funds established by participating groups, such as fraternities, and individual awards are purchased by the department. Some directors feel there is greater recognition value in presenting individual awards as opposed to one team award. When selecting individual awards, it is preferable to choose awards which can be worn or displayed rather than those which are hidden in a pocket or left in a desk or bureau drawer.

Kinds of Awards

There is great variance in the kinds of awards presented to winners. Local customs and prevailing varsity awards and other factors should be taken into consideration in making the selection.

CLASS INSIGNIA. Numeral awards, monogram letters, and various other designs of wearing insignia often represent the highest honor that is possible for the intramural department to confer. The award, therefore, should be one which is open to every student in school. Numeral awards are sometimes granted with sweaters, jackets, blankets, or jerseys but this procedure could prove too costly. It is customary to grant numeral awards separately. This practice is especially true in high schools because, in many states, interscholastic rules place a limit on the amount that can be expended on awards. The department could present the winning team with numeral monograms only and winning individuals then must furnish the sweaters or jerseys, if desired.

There is also wide variance in class numeral awards. Some schools give an intramural school letter which is a modification of the varsity letter (an English "M" instead of a block "M" or some other distinction); others give the letter of the respective department or college (for example, "E" for Engineering); and still others award class numerals (for example, 1965). When the combination of the class and department is used as a unit of competition, a combination of the department letter is made such as 19 E 65.

The different class-winners can wear numeral jerseys corresponding in color to their class colors. Some institutions have freshmen, sophomores, juniors, and seniors wear distinctive caps or toques, and when such a custom prevails the intramural department can follow a similar color design. This scheme helps promote class spirit. The other scheme is to have the jerseys similar in color and use varied numeral colors to distinguish between major and minor sports. Another method, sometimes used to denote major and minor sports, follows the varsity plan of having letters of varying sizes. Letter sizes commonly used are as follows: (1) department or college letters, 7 inches high for major sports and 5 inches high for minor sports; (2) class numerals, 4 inches high and 2¾ inches wide for major sports and 3¼ inches by 2 inches for minor sports. In general, the trend is to make no distinction of sports as major or minor except that some receive more points toward a point-system total.

The prestige of numerals remains higher, however, if they are granted only for sports recognized as requiring all-around prowess. From this standpoint, sports requiring special and co-ordinated skill, such as horseshoe pitching and basketball free-throwing, should not be awarded by school numerals but rather by ribbons, medals, small cups, or points toward the monogram.

MONOGRAM LETTERS. Intramural monograms usually represent a combination of the intramural departmental letter and the class numerals of the year in which the award is won. They fit well into the individual-point system plan for granting awards. The school colors can also be used; or class colors; or distinctive colors for the intramural department alone. When an individual wins this award in two or more years, the distinction can be noted by having two or more stars or bars or chevrons included in the monogram. Another point in favor of the monogram is that it can be used with any unit, whereas numerals are used primarily for class teams.

The monogram is given on the basis of winning a certain total of points scored on the individual point system. Another procedure is to give the monogram to a certain number of individuals (for example, fifty students) who earn the highest point totals during the year. (See Chapter 10 for an explanation of such programs.) One difficulty is that there may be no incentive to maintain the interest of the individual who has won the monogram early in his school career. Another question in this connection is whether points should be carried over from one year to the next for each individual or whether he should start each school year with a clean slate. In the latter case, individuals who spend considerable time in intramural activities yet fail to win their monogram by a small margin of points are discouraged by the prospect of starting over again.

TROPHIES AND CUPS. In a wide range of style and design, trophies are made of wood, plastic, bakelite, and metals with silver, gold, and bronze plating. In general, trophies and cups should not be too ornate. In purchasing these awards, care must be taken to select durable materials which do not break easily and plating which does not easily tarnish.

Most trophies have emblematic figures attached to depict the sport for which the award was won: for example, a bowler in position to roll the ball; a tennis player set to make a serve; a swimmer set for a take-off; and others in typical poses. There is usually ample plate area for inscription of team and player names. Some companies are making purposeful trophies such as penholders, desk sets, clocks, calendars, ash trays, or lighters.

Cups are made of metal with silver, gold, and bronze plating and can be purchased with or without the bakelite base. If a school has a seal of its own, it can be placed on the front of the cup and adds considerably to the general appearance.

A few firms produce inexpensive plastic cups and trophies which are less costly than some medals. These are popular for "on-the-spot" presentation. Some of them have sport figures; others have space for imprinted bands. Sport, date, team and player name, and level of award won can be recorded on the bands. Some of these awards are very attractive in silver, gold, or bronze and from a display standpoint, are better than medals for individual awards.

When sports are grouped into major and minor divisions, or major, intermediate, and minor, or teams compete at different class levels of competition such as class A, B, C, and D, it is advisable to grade the size of the cup or trophy to correspond with the importance of the particular sport or level of competition. A team winning the all-school championship in basketball after playing sixteen games deserves a larger trophy than a team winning a one-day bowling tournament. If attention is not given to graded sizes, it is possible for a team to receive a larger trophy for a class D championship than for a class A championship. An exact guide cannot be included here because styles and quality vary considerably but as an example, the all-year trophy may be 25 inches high, the all-school class B basketball trophy 16 inches high, the all-school class C basketball trophy 14 inches high, and the all-school class D trophy 12 inches high.

An important question pertaining to team trophies is whether to give them out permanently or to pass them around from year to year to the new winners. Of course, if one trophy changes hands in succeeding years, it means a big saving to the department. A rotating cup or trophy is often allowed to be retained permanently if it is won twice in succession. Another ruling states that if one team wins the cup three times (not necessarily consecutively), it has the right to full ownership. Many schools present sport trophies or cups permanently but rotate the larger all-year scoring trophies. Each year the name of the new winner is engraved on the rotating trophy. As a general rule, fraternities and dormitories that have an exclusive place to display a cup prefer the idea of owning it permanently; but units whose teams possess a common meeting place, such as a gymnasium, class, and military unit, are content to use one cup over and over again.

MEDALS. The three most popular types of awards under this category are the small solid ball, shaped like a football, basketball, or baseball (in track a winged shoe is used in the same manner); large flat medals with sport designs standing out in strong relief, with or without suspended ribbon; and small flat medals which are worn as charms. The first style is the one commonly given to varsity champions in the various team sports. The second style is favored in meets such as track or swimming, and a design in relief can represent a particular event—dash, jump, relay, etc. Many intramural departments prefer the third style because small charms are inexpensive. Some departments have designed medals which are used exclusively at their school.

Standard design means a big saving because medal firms cut one die which is used by many schools. Size and shape then remain the same for all sports, with a figure inserted in the center space in a pose representing a particular sport. This medal can have an enamel border around the edge in the colors of a school. Raised letters at the bottom of the medal give the name of the school. It is customary to engrave the name of the league, division, year, winning team, and player on the back of the medal.

Medals and charms come in gold-filled, gold plate, silver, and bronze finishes. Usually, gold medals are presented to first place winners, silver to second, and bronze to third.

TROPHY BOARDS. A very good custom used to permanently recognize group or individual merit is to display trophy boards or framed placards on gymnasium, office, or lobby walls or along hallways. The names of the sports are painted or burned on these boards and names of various winners are inserted later. Separate boards are needed for team and individual sports. The school's industrial arts department could be encouraged to help design and make trophy boards to minimize expense.

PLAQUES. A team award which can be substituted for the cup or trophy is the wall shield or plaque. A medallion, with an emblematic figure, is attached to the shield or plaque. These figures signify the sport in which the plaque was earned. It is possible to buy medallions and have the plaque made locally, with the lettering added by proficient students or professionals. These awards are more durable than some cups and trophies.

CERTIFICATES AND RIBBONS. Another method of award recognition is to issue certificates to winning teams and honor participants. Examples of a junior high-school team award and a university honor award are shown in Figures 38 and 39. Awards such as these are dignified and will be

Wynn Seale Junior High School

Intramural Department

19_____

__________Homeroom __________Grade

Softball Champions

NAME OF TEAM MEMBERS

__________ Principal

__________ Assistant Principal

__________ Intramural Director

Figure 38. Junior High School Intramural Award Certificate. (Courtesy of Wynn Seale Junior High School, Corpus Christi, Texas.)

Figure 39. University Intramural Honor Award Certificate. (Courtesy of University of Michigan Intramural Sports Department.)

treasured by recipients even in adulthood. Often the significance of a numeral or medal is minimal after a winner's schooldays are over. The certificate is also desirable as an award to individuals selected for All-Star teams.

Comic or other unique certificates are sometimes presented to participants in the intramural program. An example of the content of such a certificate presented to members of a last place team is the following:

> This is to certify that John Olson, a member in good standing of the Alley Cats bowling team, is entitled to every privilege of a last place team. Your team was considered the strongest in the league because it held up everyone else. The only reason you didn't go up was that everyone knocked you down! BUT WAIT 'TIL NEXT YEAR! ! ! !

The practice of giving ribbons, particularly in high-school intramurals, works out very well. Ribbons are secured in different colors to correspond to the rank (1st, 2nd, 3rd) of the winning teams or individuals. The name of the sport and school are printed on the ribbons. Gold or black are two colors well suited for lettering purposes. Some schools use their school colors for all their ribbons; for example, a white ribbon and purple lettering for school colors purple and white.

There is an economic consideration in giving ribbon awards. The ribbons can be purchased in large quantities and kept for several years. Instead of having the events and dates printed on the ribbon at the time of purchase, a standard form can be procured, and dates, names, events, and other pertinent information typed on the ribbon.

Ribbons can also be pasted in scrapbooks and kept for reminiscing much more easily than other types of awards. Cloth banners and pennants in colors of the schools are sometimes given and can be made with the aid of school home-economics personnel.

Other Awards

There are a few other awards which are used less frequently but should be mentioned as possible methods for student recognition. Awarding of jackets, sweaters, jerseys, T-shirts, and blankets, although costly, is very worthwhile and practical. These items are usually presented for more important honors which the department wishes to bestow. Such honors include all-school and all-year championships or possibly the highest or five highest individual point winners during the school year. The school insignia, emblem, monogram, or numerals can be presented with this type of award. Students wearing this award have the advantage of advertising the intramural program throughout the school and community.

Other awards which are worn, but less noticeably so, are the small emblems or keys, belt buckles, and tie clasps. Each of these awards can display the figure of the sport in which the student distinguished himself, the school insignia or distinctive design of the intramural department. Small emblems or keys are worn on the coat lapel and are comparable to the varsity lettermen's pins or fraternal organization pins.

In girls' and women's intramural programs, awards are sometimes made in the form of blazer jackets, usually in school colors, with a distinctive emblem over the upper left pocket. Only a few awards of this type are made yearly and, in some cases, only to seniors who have participated for four years. The fewer the number of awards thus given, the more the awards are coveted. In addition to the previously discussed awards, scarfs, pins, necklaces, and bracelets are also suitable for girls' and women's programs.

Limitations to Number of Awards

In intramural competition, where many awards must necessarily be given, some definite limitation is necessary, not only from the standpoint of expense, but also to prevent awards from becoming so common as to lose much of their value in the student's estimation. This problem is not complicated when a single trophy is given to a team as a whole but when individuals must be given separate awards, then prearranged limitations must be followed.

Sports on a team basis. It is necessary to limit a team in any sport to a certain number of individual awards: for instance, football, 15; soccer, 13; baseball, 12; basketball, 8; or to one more player than the required number for a team, such as basketball, 6; softball, 10. This is usually necessary from the standpoint of a limited budget. If, however, a winning team has used so many substitutes that awards are desired for a larger number, the privilege can be granted on the condition the winning organization bears the extra expense.

In team sports, it is usually only in the more important divisions, such as the class or college unit, that more than first place is awarded. Generally, not more than one group trophy is ever awarded in these leagues but individuals of more than one team can be honored. The reason is that competition is highest in these units and chances of making the team are more difficult.

The department must draw a line in the privilege of wearing numerals so they are not worn so casually that their values become meaningless. In smaller schools, the custom is to award only the first place team, but in larger institutions, where there are many candidates trying out, or where there is a great increase in the number of teams, a more liberal provision is often made, which includes not only the highest two but sometimes the highest three teams. If the department wishes to award the three high teams, it could be necessary to devise a practical solution to provide for the increased expense. Occasionally, where the class league is very strong, the department can arrange to provide complete numeral jerseys for the winning team; to provide numerals separately to the second team, so that jerseys are paid for by the class treasury or team members themselves; and to make no material grant to the third team, but merely permits its members the privilege of wearing the class honors, if they pay for them.

The intramural director should be willing to co-operate in buying awards (for players who have the privilege of buying an award), for he frequently can obtain them at a much lower price. In such cases, however, the money should be raised beforehand, because in actual practice intramural personnel find it difficult to make collections after awards are made.

In some sports, such as track or swimming, the team basis is not strong enough to justify giving awards to all members who competed for the winning team. If this were done, some athletes making very few points would win numerals or comparable awards because their team won the championship, whereas other athletes, who had made a considerably high total, would lose out because their team was not a winner. The best way to handle this situation is to follow the procedure used in open meets, as next explained, and award numerals or other prizes to individuals winning a first place or a certain number of points, regardless of the showing of the team.

SPORTS ON AN INDIVIDUAL BASIS. In the event that sports of an individualistic nature are not conducted on a team basis, but rather as open tournaments or meets, there is the same necessity for limitation.

Tournaments. In tournaments, an award can be given to the first and possibly second and third places. The number of total awards to be granted is best figured by a comparison with the number of individual awards made in the team sports and also by a comparison of the number of participants attracted by the respective sports. It is not wise to award as many places in doubles events as in singles because the elimination series is naturally only half as large and because twice as many awards are necessary.

Some of the tournaments, however, are conducted by weight classifications where from three to ten separate class tournaments are staged in each sport. This makes it difficult to limit the sport to a proper equivalent of awards in comparison with other sports conducted without weight divisions. The winners of each weight division are usually recognized and awarded, and possibly second and third places to some extent by giving less expensive awards. If the school uses a system of individual scoring charts, then second place, etc., can find a certain amount of recognition through the granting of points, without further consideration.

Meets. Some of the individual sports, such as track and swimming, are conducted on a meet-plan wherein there are as many as ten or more events. Each event is compared to one division of a tournament conducted according to weight classifications. There is a difference in the case of meets, however, in that an individual can take part in a number of events, whereas in a wrestling or boxing tournament he is limited to one weight division. In meets with several events, it is customary to give medals, ribbons, or other awards for first, second, and third places. Where group spirit is not a factor, some participants drop out of competition as soon as an award is earned. One way to offset this practice is to present a small cup to the highest individual point-winner in the meet. The winning of more than one medal in a meet is generally admissible, but for other sports, only one award is usually given to an individual in the same sport for one season.

TWO-SEASON SPORTS. A sport that covers two seasons, such as track, raises the question whether the same individual should be awarded twice, both for his winning performance indoors and outdoors. Certainly, he should not be awarded two sets of numerals. Various plans can be adopted. One is to use a point system and count points in both meets toward the required total. Still another way is to award numerals the first time an award is won. Then those who have already won numerals in the indoor meet are given medals if they again become winners in the outdoor meet.

Financing Awards

The custom of soliciting business people in a particular community for trophies is one that should be discouraged. Business people are already pressed with many demands of this nature and it puts the intramural department on a less dignified and stable basis. The intramural department should find some method of financing its awards rather than be placed in a situation of having to depend upon philanthropic support.

This general attitude toward indiscriminate solicitation does not mean that help should never be secured in this particular way. Sometimes, a certain individual in a community is interested in this field of work and is glad to offer a trophy. Again, high schools that are starting intramural sports for the first time can find a way out of initial financial difficulties by getting the backing of leading civic organizations and encouraging each of them to offer a rotating trophy. It is customary, as a token of appreciation, to have trophies secured in this way carry the name of the doner. The point to be remembered is that while such help can be given enthusiastically to help set up a new intramural program, it should not be sought to the point where it brings prejudice against the intramural idea itself.

Some intramural departments use an entrance fee or forfeit fee to cover the cost of awards. Charging participating organizations yearly dues is another source of award income. Others use revenue from sports nights, carnivals, concessions, or similar school promotions.

Ideally, awards should be financed through the general school budget. If it is assumed that awards are an important and justifiable phase of the intramural program, then they should be financed through the same funds as all other phases of the intramural school educational program. Every effort should be made to use inexpensive awards.

Presentation of Awards

The degree to which intramural student recognition is effective is often determined by the manner in which the honors are bestowed. Presenting awards at an auspicious occasion instead of in the intramural office provides additional student recognition over and above the award which symbolizes achievement. For this reason, annual intramural award banquets are very popular at some schools. In addition to recognizing students for intramural achievement through presentation of awards and other honors, the program usually includes speeches by local sports notables and school dignitaries. Sometimes, sport films or other outstanding entertainment are featured.

An annual award picnic attended by all intramural winners of the school year has proved equally effective. With the outdoor atmosphere, it is possible to arrange recreational activities such as foot races, relays, stunts, games, and novelty contests. A program similar to the indoor banquet can be arranged but generally the emphasis is on a more informal gathering with presentation of awards, fun, and food. If banquets and picnics are not utilized, arrangements should be made to present awards at school assemblies or convocations.

Selection of All-Star Teams

Another form of recognition is the selection of all-star teams, a procedure which is followed in many intramural systems. It tends to stimulate interest in intramurals and also brings some of the better athletes to the attention of the varsity coaches. Selections of this nature are easier to handle in a small system where the director personally supervises the games and can give reasonable assurance that selections will be made equitably. In larger schools, however, where a great number of teams participate, and several games are played at the same time, it is difficult to draw a distinction except in the case of an outstanding star, and the selections then become largely a matter of guesswork.

If such a team is to be selected, it is advisable to have a large selection group. The intramural staff, officials, and sports writers of the school paper should be consulted. When selections are determined by such a large number of votes coming from different sources, there is less chance of a good player being overlooked or for any suspicion of favoritism. Usually, those players who are selected for this honor receive a special certificate, signed by the director, indicating their achievement.

There is no general approval of the all-star idea. Some people think it adds a great stimulus to competition; but, on the other hand, there are others who think it resembles professionalism, and, also, that any gain which results is offset by the disappointment of players who do not receive recognition.

Other Forms of Recognition

There are several other, perhaps less obvious, methods of recognizing intramural achievement. Photographs of each championship team can be given to the respective members. Cameras which take and develop pictures in one process are useful for this type of recognition as well as other phases of intramural publicity. Including pictures and names of the various winners in the intramural handbook and the school annual also helps give credit to outstanding players.

Publicity accounts of intramural games in the student newspaper provide daily recognition for individual performances. Printed programs for championship games listing player's names, positions, season records, and past winners give added "glamor" to final games. Still another method of denoting achievement is the establishment of all-time, yearly, and seasonal records for each sport. These can be published in the handbook and student newspaper and recorded on bulletin boards or special record boards in the gymnasium.

Recognition of student achievement in the intramural program can take the form of presenting an award as a symbol of success or giving credit for success through banquets, all-star teams, and publicity media. Although the exact value of success-recognition is difficult to measure, it does help offset the ill-effects of failure. Every intramural director must be constantly aware of presenting success-opportunities for participants in the program.

SUMMARY

1. The main purpose of intramural publicity is to sell the program to the students, staff, and faculty.
2. Student newspapers are usually the most important publicity vehicle for intramural departments. Radio and television, when available, are also helpful.
3. Other important publicity possibilities include handbooks, bulletin boards, a new student orientation program, announcements and notices, news releases to student's home town newspapers, sections in school yearbooks or annuals, manager's manuals, and films.
4. Personal solicitation is also important, especially in selling faculty and independent, nonorganized groups.
5. Recognition of success by intramural participants can be accomplished through awards, all-star teams, performance records, and publicity accounts of student achievement.
6. Although the use of awards in an intramural program is a very controversial subject, most intramural directors follow the practice of presenting some type of award to the winners or participants in the program.
7. Award procedures should always be designed to promote the objectives of the intramural program. Awards are not rewards; nor should they be expensive.
8. Recipients of awards include the group as a whole, individual members of a group, and individuals without group affiliation.
9. Group awards are given to permanent, semipermanent, and temporary groups. Trophies, pennants, cups, plaques, or shields are suitable for permanent groups but individual awards are better for semipermanent and temporary groups.
10. Individuals competing without group affiliation in individual sports, such as track, swimming, and tennis, conducted as open tournaments or meets must be given individual awards.
11. Local customs, prevailing varsity awards, quantity of awards needed, and available budget are all important considerations to determine the types of awards.
12. Numeral awards, monogram letters, and various other designs of wearing insignia often represent the highest honor

that it is possible for the intramural department to confer. These awards should be open to every student in school.

13. Intramural monograms usually represent a combination of the intramural departmental letter and the class numerals of the year in which the award is won.
14. Sizes of trophies and cups should be proportionate to the importance of the particular sport or level of competition.
15. Other awards include medals, charms, trophy boards, certificates and ribbons, jackets, sweaters, jerseys, T-shirts, blankets, keys, tie clasps, belt buckles, and blazer jackets.
16. Limitations must be placed on individual awards because of expense and the loss of value that results from indiscriminate use.
17. Awards should be financed through the general school budget and should be inexpensive.
18. Awards are often made more effective by presenting them at an annual intramural award banquet.
19. All-star teams help increase student interest in intramurals but there is no general approval of them.
20. Although the exact value of success recognition is difficult to measure, it does help offset the ill-effects of failure.

13

Extramural and Other Programs

Certain kinds of programs and special events of concern to every intramural director do not appear in all intramural programs. These include extramural, corecreation and faculty programs, and special events such as open houses, aquatic shows, and sports clinics. In some schools these events may be so well integrated with the total intramural program that it is incorrect to consider them special. In other schools, these special programs may not be integrated with the intramural activities; they may be nonexistent for reasons ranging from disagreement with the basic philosophy of the intramural program to lack of staff, facilities, and equipment. These types of programs are an extension of the usual intramural department's activities. Their effect on the over-all program concerns motivation and a slightly different emphasis on student participation.

EXTRAMURAL PROGRAM

Extramural sports involve competition between teams or individuals representing different institutions, or, in the case of playdays, teams coming from different schools but not participating with their own school unit. (In this chapter the extramural program is not interpreted to include varsity competition.) Physical educators generally accept the idea that extramural activities are an extension of intramural activities, although there are some who argue that extramurals are in the same category as interinstitutional sports and the difference lies in who has the responsibility to administer them. Intramural directors usually assume administrative responsibility for extramural programs. This type of activity, in some respects, seems to fill the gap between the varsity athletic and the intramural program. This may be an indication that intramural and varsity programs are inadequate to meet student needs and that a total re-evaluation is desirable. If intramural and interschool programs were expanded properly, it is possible that extramural competition, in its present state, would disappear.

With the exception of noncompetitive-type extramural events, such as playdays, schools are represented by teams of lesser ability than the varsity. Procedures associated with varsity team competition such as travel, practices, eligibility, and supervision are minimized from the standpoint that extramural participation takes place less frequently and is less specialized. If competitive extramural activities are administered properly, it is reasonable to assume that students taking part in them receive benefits comparable to those received through varsity competition.

Types of Extramural Activities

In extramural activities, games are either played at the site of one of the opponents or competition takes place at each of the participating schools and results are compared to determine the winner. The former method seems to be more desirable because it affords greater opportunities for sociability, leadership, and other realistic experiences which come from meeting opponents face to face. Postal, telephone, and telegraphic meets are used in case of the latter.

Sports days. Sports days, a popular form of extramurals, are conducted with the emphasis on teams maintaining their identity with their own schools. In terms of competitiveness, greater importance may be attached to some sports days than others, depending on the method and purpose of organization. In some situations, teams play as representatives of their own schools, but the purpose of the sports day is sociability and not determining a champion, although scores may be recorded for added interest. Other sports days are organized for the specific purpose of deciding a winner. In either case, sports participation is usually followed by a party, picnic, or banquet for the students.

The competitive-type sports day or sports festival frequently involves intramural champions from one school playing intramural champions from another school or the champions from several schools meeting at a central location to determine winners of the various sports. Schools taking part in the sports festival usually correspond to schools which make up the interscholastic or intercollegiate conference for that particular area. Sports consist of basketball, softball, touch football, bowling, volleyball, handball, table tennis, golf, wrestling, tennis, and any other sport which can be organized on a team basis. A point system is used to determine the sports festival winner. As an example, five points are awarded to the first place winner in each sport, four points to the second place winner, three to third, two to one, and one to last place. Sports festivals may be scheduled for each season or only once during the school year. The site of the festival may be rotated each year. Expenses for awards, officials, and equipment may be shared each year by participating schools, or when the festival is rotated from school to school, the host school may assume financial responsibility.

Rules of some sports festivals allow schools to send all-star teams in each sport instead of intramural champions. This practice is questionable because it may result in divided loyalty within organizations and affect the units of competition in the intramural program. When all-star teams are chosen to represent various schools, students are often encouraged to further their own selfish interests rather than the interests of the intramural team they play with during the school year. As an example, a basketball player may concentrate on becoming high-point man in every game he plays and overlook the importance of team play in an effort to make the all-star squad. Selection of intramural champions to participate in sports festivals has the advantage of providing an added incentive for intramural participation and achievement because team members know they will represent their school if they are winners. If this objective or goal is to be reached, it is necessary for every member of the team to overcome personal motives and put forth a concentrated effort for the good of the entire group.

CHALLENGE GAMES. Another type of extramural activity consists of challenge games between organizations from different schools. Dormitories, clubs, classes, fraternities, and other student groups challenge their counterparts at other schools. In some colleges, fraternities invite chapters from other schools to compete in a regional tournament. Athletic clubs such as judo, rowing, sailing, archery, fencing, soccer, and volleyball organize practice and compete with the objective of some day attaining varsity status in their school. One of their best means of competition is to schedule games, meets, or matches with similar groups outside their own school. In larger cities, their schedule may include contests with other schools, in and out of their city, and with the local YMCA, athletic clubs, and industrial groups. When competition is arranged with other schools, particularly out-of-town schools, these teams may have their schedule correspond with the varsity schedule. This permits them to play their contests prior to the varsity game and later attend the game and lend their support to the varsity team. Some schools provide transportation for their sports clubs by taking them along with the varsity team.

PLAYDAYS. The most popular extramural activity in elementary, junior, and senior high schools is the playday or field day. This plan is similar to sport days except that teams are organized at the playday site and the major objectives are participation, fun, and sociability. Teams are designated by colors, names, or other symbols and members of each team may represent all schools in attendance. Playdays have the advantage of including all students regardless of ability. Those in charge of sports days may have a tendency to encourage only the best players because each school wants to be represented by its best team for competition. If students of lesser ability are assigned to the team, they usually spend most of their time sitting on the bench or sidelines as substitutes. Playdays also afford excellent opportunities for leadership planning and administering the program with faculty members.

Arguments Against an Extramural Program

There is considerable disagreement among intramural directors on the acceptance of extramural sports, particularly highly competitive types, as a part of the total intramural program. Although extramurals are gaining support in some areas, especially in colleges and universities, some surveys and intramural conferences show opposition to extramurals. For example, in 1957, assembled intramural directors of the National Intramural Association voted two to one against extramurals in colleges and universities. The Western Conference Intramural Directors in 1955 subscribed in principle to extramurals in the form of special interest clubs, but opposed intramural champions or other selected groups competing with similar units from other schools. Ellis J. Mendelsohn [1] surveyed 107 intramural directors and found 63 were against and 44 were in favor of extramural programs.

One of the major arguments against extramural activities is that development of intramural potential is reduced and, in the opinion of some directors, extramural programs may eventually destroy intramural programs. They fear that some programs will lose their balance and the intramural director might become an extramural coach. Time, facilities, staff, equipment, and money are put to better use when they are applied to participation for the many, rather than the few. Many feel a good intramural program eliminates any need for extramural programs. On the other hand, some intramural educators think extramural activities

[1] Ellis J. Mendelsohn, "Recent Trends and Developments of Extramural Activities in Colleges and Universities," *Proceedings, College Physical Education Association* (1956), p. 155.

would be justified if intramural programs were completely developed to handle the intramural needs of all students. Because there are few perfect programs, objectors also say extramurals are a deterrent to achieving intramural objectives.

Others opposed to extramurals insist they are intercollegiate or interscholastic in nature and should be administered through varsity programs rather than through the intramural program. If extramural activities are the responsibility of I-M directors, they conflict with varsity activities and cause resentment between the two groups. In some conferences, players who are not out for varsity sports lose a year of eligibility for competing in extramural games. If this happens to a star varsity player who is not playing for the varsity team because he is scholastically deficient for that particular year, relationships between the coaches and the intramural staff are apt to be strained. Another negative consideration arises because extramural sports are varsity in nature and some of the inconsistencies in varsity sports may infiltrate extramurals and eventually intramurals.

Opponents further say that extramural games are thrust onto an already overburdened staff and the result is inadequate administration of both intramural and extramural programs. Consequently, extramural items such as travel, liability, and supervision are frequently left to participating students. They furnish their own transportation to and from contests and assume liability for injuries which occur during extramural competition. Another drawback is that competition is frequently unequal when student-arranged. Opponents say extramural activities should be discontinued when they harm participants through inadequate transportation and supervision of playing conditions. Extramural programs cannot be justified unless precautions are taken which are customary for varsity programs.

Arguments for an Extramural Program

Proponents of extramural sports agree that proper administration is paramount to success and benefits to the participants. Their major argument is that many students with varying degrees of ability, who cannot make the varsity, are afforded experiences similar to those received by varsity squad members. They also say that an extramural program includes more activities than the interscholastic and intercollegiate programs, thus providing an even greater range of opportunity for more students. Some feel extramural sports are an excellent answer to those who object to interscholastic competition at the junior high-school level. They point out that the same benefits result and the fact that extramural meets are held less frequently and do not involve extensive practices and league championships reduces criticism of harmful participation.

Many intramural directors feel that extramural programs provide the same type of incentives as awards and point systems. The one or two extramural meets each year are highpoints of the intramural program and encourage players to work hard so their team represents their school for these events. This type of stimulation adds interest to the intramural program and more students want to participate. Advocates of extramurals say that if intramural participation is increased by added incentives, then this alone is justification for promoting extramural activities.

Important Considerations of Extramurals

There is considerable difference of opinion among intramural directors as to whether an extramural program has a place in the total program or if extramural activities are to be viewed as an unwanted "step child." Apparently, there are more schools who do not have extramural programs than schools who have them. It is possible that some who oppose extramural activities reached their decision prematurely without objectively appraising the over-all program. Extramural activities may have been prejudged because of student pressure to include this type of activity in a program where staff and facilities are already overloaded with no prospect of increased funds to alleviate the situation.

Obviously, there is a definite need for further study in this area to determine the relationship of the extramural program to intramural and varsity programs. If the relationship is found to be positive, it is necessary to formulate extramural philosophy and objectives which lead to establishment of sound policies and procedures to assure adequate standards of participation.

When extramural programs are conducted, some limitations should be noted to insure worthwhile experiences for the participants. In the main these limitations involve institutional control. The distance of travel to the extramural site should be restricted. Long distances take students away from their studies for an extended period of time and have a fatiguing effect on students which limits their performance and fun of participation. Extramural activities are more effective if participating units come from a reasonably close geographic area. Transportation should be furnished by the school and not by the students. Accident insurance should be carried to protect the participants while they are traveling and competing. Adequate facilities, competent officiating, and equipment should be provided for all games. The entire operation should be supervised by members of the intramural staff with the aid of students. It is unrealistic if the students are required to furnish their own transportation and assume responsibility in case of accident or injury. If extramural activities are worthy of student participation, school administrators must finance and supervise the total extramural program.

CORECREATION PROGRAM

At one time women were not allowed to attend educational institutions of higher learning. Not too long ago men seldom witnessed a women's gymnasium class even though class members were conservatively costumed in long black stockings, full sleeve middies, and full length bloomers. Today, traditions have been dissolved to a point where many physical education classes are taught on a coeducational basis. Community groups, such as churches, camps, and social service centers, are also placing greater emphasis on recreation for mixed groups. One of the most encouraging trends is the inclusion of corecreation activities in intramural programs. Unfortunately, staff, facilities, and equipment are frequently inadequate to fully develop this type of program.

Corecreation activities, popularly known as "corec," involve both men and women and truly fulfill the principle of "sports for all." In properly conducted, "corec" programs, all members of the school participate—upper grades, lower grades, and faculty. In schools for men or women, participation is extramural because guests must be brought in from other schools to carry out the program.

Two phases of the intramural program apply equally to corecreation programs: (1) organized or scheduled competition, and (2) informal, free-play participation. However, in corecreation programs there is much more emphasis on the informal aspect than on leagues, tournaments, and championships, although some schools successfully promote organized competition. When men and women compete, considerable attention must be given to equating teams and modifying rules. Women's teams should not play against men's teams as most men are superior in performing physical skills. The program is usually designed to stress less strenuous and less highly organized activities which contribute to the fun, spirit, and fellowship of mixed play.

Although there is a natural desire for students to know and understand the opposite sex, they are often afraid to take part in activities together. Frequently, through application of adult standards, it is assumed that youths develop these associations naturally, when in reality there is lack of opportunity to establish wholesome relationships. Fears and misinformation during adolescent years widen the area of confusion. Students need programs which encourage mutual understanding between boys' and girls' groups.

Much of an individual's life consists of sharing responsibilities, socializing, and working with members of the opposite sex. One of the major functions of education is to provide experiences which aid in solving personal problems and making social adjustments whether these situations arise at home or in the business world. A corecreation program makes a very positive contribution to this educational process.

The corecreation program is a type of laboratory in which students have opportunities to develop an appreciation for commonality and differences of interests, limitations, and skills. The degree of social adjustment, or lack of it, varies considerably with each student. A well-integrated and -administered program benefits all students, regardless of their stage of personal adjustment.

Through corecreation activities, participants are encouraged to overcome shyness and hesitancy in meeting the opposite sex. They gain in poise and confidence in social relationships. They usually give more attention to their personal conduct and other mannerisms when in the presence of their counterparts. This reaction may be somewhat automatic. Men, for example, frequently refine their language and conduct when in the company of women.

Corecreation sessions reach students who may not otherwise participate. Some of them may not take part in competitive or informal activities with their own sex by themselves but, when given the chance to participate with their girl friends or boy friends, they enter the program enthusiastically. These programs also bring together students of like interests, thus establishing many new friendships with each sex and between sexes.

Types of Activities

Corecreation activities must be carefully selected to encourage the desired benefits of coparticipation. Activities which involve bodily contact and are highly competitive and strenuous should be avoided. Activities should be selected to coincide with skills taught in the men's and women's physical education classes and the sports activities of the men's and women's intramural programs. Special emphasis should be given to activities which can be utilized after the student graduates. A well-balanced program includes competitive and noncompetitive team, individual, and dual sports activities and informal, outing, and social activities.

When both sexes participate in sports of a moderately competitive nature, it is necessary to alter or modify the playing rules. For team play, the membership of each team is usually divided equally between men and women, with the men playing under various restrictions. In swimming events such as the relay, men may be required to swim in sweat suits or night shirts. For bowling, handicap systems are used which give the girls more pins proportionally than the boys. A method sometimes used for corecreation basketball requires each boy to wear boxing gloves.

Through creative imagination members of the intramural staff can devise numerous rules' modifications for all corecreation activities. Some examples of rules' modifications follow:

SOFTBALL

1. Teams consist of five girls and five boys.
2. A special extrasoft and extralarge ball is used which travels farther with an easy swing of the bat than a power swing.
3. The pitcher must be a girl and the catcher must be a boy.
4. Girls and boys must bat in alternate order.
5. Boys must bat opposite their regular way, i.e., righthanders bat left handed and vice versa.
6. Boys cannot steal bases or bunt at any time.
7. A run can score from third base only on a hit ball.

VOLLEYBALL

1. Teams are made up of four girls and four boys.
2. All serves must be underhand.
3. Boys cannot spike or drive the ball across the net.
4. Each ball must be returned with a slight arch.
5. Each girl is allowed one assist to get the ball over the net on the serve.

6. Each team is permitted three volleys, but for girls one volley is defined as either one or two successive hits by the same girl.
7. Girls are required to handle the ball at least once in each series of volleys before the ball is returned to the other side.

Selection of corecreation activities for a particular school depends on over-all campus recreation programs. Some schools have a student union or other organization which conducts programs emphasizing social recreation activities. Students have daily opportunities to participate in activities such as folk and social dancing, chess, checkers, billiards, bowling, bridge, singing, outings, shuffleboard, table tennis, and record-listening sessions.

Although some of these activities, such as bowling, shuffleboard, and table tennis, may also be included in corecreation sessions sponsored by the intramural office, there is generally less emphasis placed on activities offered by other campus groups. Duplication of opportunities should be limited. Lack of attention in this respect may weaken one or both programs and cause dissension among campus sponsoring organizations. The following is a list of activities for corecreation programs:

archery
badminton
billiards
bowling
box hockey
bridge
canoeing
checkers
chess
croquet
curling
darts
fencing
folk dancing
golf
ice skating
outings
paddle-tennis
riding
rifle shooting
record-listening sessions
roller skating
sailing
shuffleboard
singing
skiing
slow-pitch softball
sleigh rides
social dancing
swimming
table tennis
tennis
tobogganing
trampoline
volleyball

Administrative Suggestions

In developing a corecreation program, it is advisable to have all interested groups involved in the planning. Representatives of the men's and women's intramural departments, student organizations, and any other campus units which sponsor activities of a corecreation nature should be invited to attend planning sessions. Co-operation of these groups promotes understanding in selecting program activities, modifying game rules, establishing policies and regulations, arranging facilities and equipment, and providing supervision of playing areas.

Co-operative planning by students and faculty aids in avoiding conflicts with other campus functions. In scheduling corecreation sessions, it is advisable to set them up consistently and at regular intervals so students establish habits of participation. Sessions should be planned for the same days each week, such as Fridays and/or Saturdays, rather than on an irregular basis. Weekend programs encourage students to remain on campus for their recreation and aids in promoting greater loyalty toward their school. The most desirable arrangement provides daily corecreation opportunities. If facilities are available, students should have the chance to recreate informally and corecreationally throughout all periods of the day. This is particularly true on large campuses where students have a varied class and work schedule.

The corecreation program is usually financed through the intramural budget. When students voluntarily assist in supervising and planning activities, there may be little need for additional corecreation funds. Publicity can be handled through the normal channels which disseminate information about the intramural and other campus recreation programs. Intramural facilities and equipment can be used, involving a small additional expenditure of funds. When off-campus facilities are used, it is sometimes necessary to pay rental and transportation costs. If the department budget cannot cover these expenses, each participating student can be charged a nominal fee. However, this frequently is a nuisance fee from the administrative standpoint. It is much better if the entire corecreation program is financed by the same sources as other phases of the school's educational program.

Corecreation activities are often held in either a men's or women's gymnasium. Since many older buildings do not have locker and shower facilities which accommodate both sexes, some special dressing room arrangements must be made for indoor participation. If locker and shower rooms are available, attention must be given to obstructing the view at exits and entrances. Most newer structures are designed to permit both sexes easy access to the various playing areas and their respective locker rooms. When students play in a strange facility, men in a women's gym, or vice versa, signs must be appropriately displayed to designate areas and direct traffic from one place to another. This procedure is particularly helpful when rotating groups at specified intervals to assure each participant an equal opportunity to use the various play areas.

All facilities can be opened for informal mixed play, competitive tournaments, or a combination of these two plans. Competitive tournaments are usually more effective when scheduled during one or two evenings rather than several weeks. Tournaments which are arranged "on the spot" are extremely successful because all forfeits are eliminated. Competition is encouraged by extending special invitations to campus organizations such as fraternities, sororities, dormitories, special interest clubs, and class groups. Whether the session consists of informal play or tournaments, it is helpful to provide a congenial host and hostess to greet students and remind them that the program is arranged for their benefit. A first impression of an overcautious guard at the door often leaves participants with an unwelcome feeling and may cause them to seek recreation elsewhere.

Exhibitions in the pool or gymnasium are excellent means of exposing students to new skills. Fencing, judo, archery, badminton, tennis, gymnastic, and aquatic clubs have opportunities to exhibit bodily prowess and sports skills with the objective of entertaining students and possibly gaining new members. Interest is also added when members of varsity teams attend corecreation programs, not for purposes of exhibition but to actively participate with their classmates. Dancing and coke sessions can follow sports activities.

Creative thinking by student and faculty planners produces numerous ideas for effective corecreation programs. The potential, as is the case in all phases of the intramural program, is practically unlimited. However, the usual precautions must be exercised to prevent overactivated students and maintain adequate program balance in terms of the objectives of intramural sports.

FACULTY PROGRAM

Although not all students might agree, members of the faculty have the same needs and likings for physical recreation as students. Unfortunately, facilities and intramural staff members are not always available to conduct programs for the faculty and when these limitations exist, it is reasonable to give major attention to the students. However, the determined I-M director should find some time and place to schedule faculty activities, even if it is necessary to use off-campus facilities such as bowling alleys, public golf courses, local parks, and playgrounds. In small schools, the faculty may not be large enough to field sufficient teams for a league and instead may play challenge games with student groups or local off-campus men's teams. Larger faculties have sufficient personnel to organize their own teams and leagues. Whether the school is large or small, there are enough faculty members to participate in individual and dual sports.

Scheduling faculty activities sometimes presents a problem due to the unpredictability of staff members' schedules. They often have to attend local or out-of-town meetings on short notice and occasionally they are assigned to help with additional school functions. For these reasons, it is necessary to develop a flexible scheduling system for faculty competition. As an example, substitution rules for bowling and golf teams must be lenient to allow for unexpected changes in team membership and, similarly, handicap systems must be altered to provide handicaps for new substitutes.

In some schools, faculty members are encouraged to play with student teams because the social contacts narrow the degree of unfamiliarity between the student body and the faculty. This is particularly helpful in large schools. Other schools do not permit faculty members to play on student teams because they eliminate needed student participation and recognition opportunities. Another reason for disallowing faculty participation on student teams is that a staff member's work load may not permit him to follow a rigid league or tournament schedule. Consequently, matches or games designed to benefit the student may be excessively delayed or forfeited. It is difficult to set up hard and fast rules covering faculty participation on student teams but a note of caution should be sounded so that intramural policymakers make wise decisions on this matter.

Types of Activities

The response for team, individual, and dual sports and informal participation varies with the numerical size of the faculty. The most popular sports in these categories are volleyball, bowling, slow-pitch softball, basketball, rifle shooting, water polo, tennis, golf, handball, squash, paddleball, badminton, swimming, and horseshoes. Basketball is too strenuous for older men and may only be successful where faculties include young instructors and teaching and research assistants.

The most effective means for faculty physical recreation is the informal participation in which faculty members "drop in" at their leisure and engage in individual and dual sports in an atmosphere of sociability. However, some departments are extremely successful in conducting team competition on a league and tournament basis between the various colleges, classes, and departments. Point systems are also useful in creating friendly rivalries between departments or other faculty groups. This type of competition is very helpful in establishing rapport among faculty members, particularly in a large school system where opportunities for faculty interaction are limited.

Whenever possible, special dressing or locker room facilities should be provided for faculty members. They can share showers and steam rooms with students but a separate dressing and lounging area for relaxation before and after participation is greatly appreciated. Another procedure which meets with faculty approval is the reservation of the swimming pool for their exclusive use at times such as the noon hour. Although it is argued that students and faculty should be encouraged to participate together, other opportunities are provided for this purpose, such as faculty-student nights. Special pool privileges are inviting to teachers who hesitate to participate when students are present. They often feel embarrassment in attempting skills which students perform in an exceptional manner.

Faculty-Family Sessions

Faculty-family sessions are the most popular phase of the entire faculty intramural program. All sports facilities are reserved at a specified time for use by faculty members and their wives and children. The selected time should be when students are least likely to use the facilities, such as Friday evening, Saturday evening, or Sunday afternoon. The swimming pool, trampoline, and gymnasium, where parents and their children play badminton, volleyball, tennis, and basketball, are favorite areas. When weather permits, outdoor areas are utilized for play activities. Family picnics often precede or terminate the day's outdoor activities.

The only expense involved is the cost of supervision and depreciation of equipment and facilities. Frequently, members are not charged for joining these sessions and gain admittance by registering themselves and members of their family. If a fee is assessed, it can be dues, an initiation fee, or a nominal charge for each attendance. Campus facilities for physical recreation should be open and free of nuisance fees just as the school library is open and free to members of the student body and faculty.

One regulation which should be strictly enforced is that children not be admitted unless accompanied by their parents. These sessions are designed for the entire family and parents are encouraged to play with their children. If children are brought or sent to the session the program loses its basic purpose and becomes a "baby sitting" organization. In addition to promoting family play, requiring parents to attend aids the problem of supervision because they assume responsibility for their own children. Only additional supervision needed is at the entrance, in the pool, and the trampoline area.

Some departments permit parents and children to bring a limited number of guests, perhaps three or four. A boy may invite members of his Boy Scout patrol. Parents may celebrate their child's birthday by inviting neighborhood friends to a gymnasium play session followed by a birthday party at home. One danger of this procedure is that guests and friends soon outnumber faculty members and their children. Children become so numerous that a supervision problem is created. Where this practice is followed, a rule should be made to limit the number of children so that parents provide one adult supervisor for every four children.

Faculty-Student Sports Nights

A faculty-student sports event is promoted successfully in some schools. These programs are designed to promote sports fun, fellowship, and competition between faculty and student players. In this setting, students and teachers are able to better know and understand each other. Mutual respect is often generated which provides for a better climate for learning in the classroom. This is particularly true in large school systems where classes are so big there is little opportunity for students and teachers to know each other, much less understand one another.

Students usually welcome the challenge to play against and try to defeat one or several of their instructors. They appreciate the teacher's willingness to "come down" to the student level. Occasionally, they are shocked to hear their instructors complain about referee's decisions. They also note that many faculty members are as much concerned about awards and recognition as students. Soon they reach the conclusion that their teachers are really quite human despite false impressions received in the classroom.

Team, dual, and individual sports competition can be arranged once each year or during fall, winter, and spring seasons. Contests are scheduled for the afternoon and evening but usually not for more than one day. If events are scheduled over several days, times and dates of the matches are often arranged by the contestants. Regular intramural activities are selected with emphasis on those which appear in the faculty program. It is not absolutely necessary to restrict activities to those of the faculty program, but it is advantageous from the standpoint of maintaining relatively equal competition. If other activities are selected or the school does not have faculty intramural activities, it is usually possible to find some members of the staff who are reasonably proficient in performing the necessary competitive skills.

In addition to offering a variety of sports, it is advisable to schedule more than one game or match involving several teams or players. Three or four bowling matches, four or five volleyball games, several handball games, and some squash matches, all composed of different teams and players, can be arranged. Championship I-M faculty teams can play student champions but little emphasis should be placed on determining which team is better. Primary purpose of faculty-student programs is to expose as many students and faculty as possible to these social experiences, regardless of player ability. Participants' abilities should be taken into consideration only in scheduling individual matches and games to provide equal competition.

For added interest, a simple point system can be utilized.

One point is awarded to the faculty or student winner of each match or game. Three volleyball games equal three points, four handball games four points, five bowling matches five points, etc. A progressive point total is maintained with the final total determining the faculty or student winner. If there are 20 contests scheduled for the faculty-student sports night, the faculty or students could win by such scores as 11 to 9, 12 to 8, or 13 to 7.

A printed program listing team captains, players, officials, time, and courts serves as a cherished student souvenir as well as an effective method of administering and publicizing the faculty-students sports night. The printed schedule instructs team captains to introduce their members to the opposition prior to the start of play. It also suggests the losers treat the winners to coffee or milk. Regardless of which group wins, the experience of participating in a faculty-student sports night is enjoyable and meaningful.

SPECIAL EVENTS

Special events vary in name and content but have the same major objectives of orientation, education, and entertainment. Sports exhibitions, festivals, circuses, carnivals, fairs, and open houses attract large numbers of participants and spectators. Such functions stimulate interest in sports and publicize intramural activities to the campus and community. In some schools, limited intramural budgets are supplemented by charging small admission fees to these events.

Special events are usually more popular during winter because there is a much wider choice of indoor activities. Separate exhibitions are held in track, gymnastics, wrestling, fencing, diving, and weight lifting, or all are combined in one large demonstration. If feasible, the championship games in basketball, volleyball, and other indoor sports are played during these occasions. Novelty track and swimming events are sometimes included to add a humorous note.

Open House

The open house is an annual feature of many school intramural programs. For this occasion, all sport facilities are used at the same time and spectators can watch many activities. This type of program involves numerous minute details and must be very carefully planned and administered. Student managers are extremely helpful in assisting with supervision and co-ordination of activities.

The annual open house offers an opportunity to play championship games before a large audience, with the players gaining recognition for their participation and success. It is an excellent means of publicizing the intramural program to student and faculty groups, parents, participants' friends, and members of the community. The open house also serves as an educational opportunity to explain rules and sports techniques to the students and sports public. A reproduction of the program for an Open House appears as Appendix A.

Winter Sports Carnival

Outdoor winter sports carnivals are popular where ice and snow are consistently available each winter. They are usually the most outstanding features of the entire athletic program. Activities include cross-country skiing, cross-country snowshoeing, ski relays, snowshoe dashes, ski jumping for distance, speed skating, and sled races. The meet plan is followed for awarding points.

These events can be combined with school "snow weeks." A student king and queen reign the entire week and are honored guests at the ice show and snow-week ball. When extensive carnivals are planned, they should provide activities for the highly skilled performers such as ice hockey, figure skating, and skiing for form and distance as well as humorous events such as barrel stave races, broom ball hockey with no skates, and dog sled races in which students serve as the dogs.

Aquatic Festival

Aquatic festivals or shows are staged indoors or outdoors, depending on available water facilities. Indoor productions are usually quite elaborate water pageants which portray a central theme. Many hours of practice are required to perform the synchronized swimming movements. An admission charge covers the cost of background material and costumes. These events are sometimes sponsored by the girls or boys but are usually more appealing if promoted on a corecreational basis.

For the nonpageant-type festival, there is a wide variety of regulation and unusual aquatic events and contests from which to make a selection. Swimming and diving events and canoe and boat races interest spectators. For indoor and outdoor water exhibitions, life saving and boat safety are not only interesting but educational.

Sports Clinic

The sports clinic is staged at the beginning of the school year to acquaint students and faculty members with activities in which they can participate. At these sessions, beginners are given special instruction and the more experienced players have an opportunity to analyze and improve their game. Instruction is given by the varsity coaches and physical education teachers who are experts in the various skills. Demonstrations are given by varsity athletes and other skilled performers from the student body and faculty. Commercial establishments sometimes provide special services in the form of equipment loans and displays and instruction by experts. The clinic can be conducted over a period of one afternoon or evening with each session emphasizing several different sports activities. Another method is to schedule several clinics throughout the school year, prior to the time various sports are offered in the intramural program. This type of clinic publicizes the intramural program and encourages students to participate who may not have previously because of lack of ability and knowledge.

SUMMARY

1. Extramurals, corecreational, and faculty programs and special events such as open houses, aquatic shows, and sports clinics are either part of the total intramural program, are added features of the program, or are nonexistent for reasons ranging from disagreement with basic philosophy to lack of staff, facilities, and equipment.
2. Extramural sports involve competition between teams or individuals representing different institutions, or in the case of play-days, coming from different schools but not participating with their own school unit.
3. Intramural directors usually assume administrative responsibility for extramural programs.
4. In extramurals, games are either played at the site of one of the opponents or competition takes place at each of the participating schools and results are compared to determine the winner.
5. Sports days are a popular form of extramurals and are conducted with the emphasis on teams maintaining their identity with their own schools although the primary purpose is sociability.
6. The competitive-type sports day or sports festival involves intramural champions from two or more schools meeting at a central location to determine winners of the various sports.
7. Sports festivals consist of sports such as basketball, softball, touch football, and bowling, and frequently use a point system to determine the winners.
8. Another type of extramural sports consists of challenge games between organizations from different schools, such as fraternities, sororities, clubs, dormitories, classes, etc.
9. The most popular extramural method in elementary, junior, and senior high schools is the play- or field-day at which teams are organized at the play-day site and the major objectives are fun, participation, and sociability.
10. There is considerable disagreement among intramural directors on the acceptance of extramural sports as a part of the total intramural program.
11. Arguments against extramurals include the following: (1) development of intramural potential is reduced and extramurals may eventually destroy intramural programs;

(2) extramurals are intercollegiate or interscholastic in nature and should be administered through varsity programs; (3) some of the inconsistencies of varsity sports may infiltrate extramurals and, eventually, intramurals; and (4) extramurals are thrust onto an already overburdened staff and the result is inadequate administration of the intramural and extramural programs.

12. Arguments for extramurals include the following: (1) many students with varying degrees of ability, who cannot make the varsity, are afforded experiences similar to those received by varsity squad members; (2) extramurals include more activities than the intercollegiate and interscholastic programs, thus providing an even greater range of opportunity for more students; (3) extramurals provide the same types of incentives as awards and point systems; and (4) if intramural participation is increased by added incentives, then this alone is justification for promoting extramurals.
13. There are more schools who do not have extramurals than those who have them.
14. Certain institutional controls, including restricted travel, competent officiating, adequate equipment, accident insurance, and supervised facilities, should be a part of all extramurals.
15. Corecreation activities, popularly known as "corec," involve both girls and boys and truly fulfill the principle of "sports for all."
16. Corec activities are either organized or informal, with more emphasis on the latter.
17. Corec sessions help individuals overcome shyness and provide an opportunity to meet the opposite sex.
18. Corec activities should be carefully selected to avoid activities which have bodily contact and are highly competitive and strenuous.
19. Playing rules have to be modified in corec activities and teams must contain an equal number of boys and girls.
20. Corec activities include archery, badminton, billiards, bowling, box hockey, dancing, darts, golf, ice skating, roller skating, skiing, swimming, tennis, etc.
21. All interested groups should help plan corec activities, including men's and women's intramural departments, student organizations, and other campus units.

22. The corec program is usually financed through the intramural budget and held in a men's or women's gymnasium.
23. Faculty members need recreation as much as students, although students should be of first concern to the intramural director if facilities, budget, and staff are limited.
24. Scheduling faculty activities sometimes presents a problem because of the unpredictability of the members' schedules.
25. Popular faculty sports include volleyball, slow-pitch softball, squash, bowling, badminton, swimming, horseshoes, etc.
26. The most effective means for faculty physical recreation is the informal participation in which faculty members "drop in" at their leisure and engage in individual and dual sports in an atmosphere of sociability.
27. The faculty-family session is one of the most popular phases of the entire faculty intramural program.
28. All sports facilities are reserved at a specified time such as Friday and/or Saturday evenings and Sunday afternoon for use by faculty members, their families, and perhaps a limited number of guests.
29. Children should not be admitted to faculty-family sessions unless accompanied by their parents.
30. Faculty-student sports nights feature team, dual, and individual competition between students and faculty members.
31. Special events include open houses, winter sports carnivals, aquatic festivals, sports clinics, sports exhibitions, circuses, and fairs.
32. All special events have the same major objectives of orientation, education, and entertainment.

14

Adapting and Evaluating Intramural Programs

Although not always specifically emphasized, most of the material presented in previous chapters applies to or can be adapted to all levels of student education—colleges and secondary and elementary schools. However, there are some comments and considerations which concern secondary and elementary school intramural participation and the girls' and women's intramural program. This discussion points out some of the guiding principals for these intramural programs.

Elementary School Programs

Intramural participation in the primary grades consists mostly of "free play" activities during recess, noon hours, and physical education class periods. There is little need for highly organized competition at this early age. Skills of running, jumping, throwing, climbing, and balancing are learned through games of low organization, rhythms, stunts, and relays.

In the upper elementary grades, from grade five and up, it is desirable to conduct intramural activities within and between grades. The need for this type of program is reflected in the tremendous growth and interest in activities sponsored by Little League Baseball, Biddy Basketball, and Pee Wee Football organizations. All program activities should emphasize skills learned in physical education instructional classes. For elementary school intramurals, it is possible to involve numerous students in leadership and management opportunities. Adequate teacher supervision is important to make this leadership educational and effective.

Courts, fields, and rules for games should be consistently modified for this age group. Care should be taken to eliminate excessively strenuous and overtiring activities. It is essential constantly to maintain equalization of competition because elementary students might be adversely affected by repeated failures. At this period in life, individual growth patterns vary considerably. Therefore, it is wise to classify students for competition according to age, weight, and height instead of any one of these criteria.

An excellent guide for conducting competitive sports in elementary school intramural programs is presented in the following recommendations of The National Conference on Physical Education for Children of Elementary School Age:

> The kind of competitive sports planned for children in the elementary school must be based on what is best for the growth and development of boys and girls at this level of maturity.
>
> In the elementary school, children grow at variable rates, and at the same chronological age there are many differences in maturity. In children who are growing rapidly, growth demands much of their energy. Emotional pressures may drive the child past the stage of healthful participation. Bone ossification and development is incomplete.
>
> In consideration of these factors, the kind of competition indicated in the following program outline are recommended as best meeting the physical activity needs of elementary school boys and girls:
>
> 1. First, as a foundation, all children should have broad, varied, and graded physical education under competent instruction through all grades. In many of the activities in this program, the competitive element is an important factor. The element of competition provides enjoyment and, under good leadership, leads to desirable social and emotional as well as physical growth.
>
> 2. Based upon a sound, comprehensive instructional program in grades five through eight, children should have opportunity to play in supervised intramural games and contests with others who are of corresponding maturity and ability within their own school. In grades below the fifth, the competitive elements found in the usual activities will satisfy the needs of the children.
>
> 3. As a further opportunity to play with others, beyond the confines of their own school or neighborhood, play or sports day programs may

be planned with emphasis on constructive social, emotional, and health outcomes. Teams may be formed of participants coming from more than a single school or agency, thus making playing together important.

Tackle football and boxing should not be included in the program because of common agreement among educational and medical authorities that these activities are undesirable for children of elementary school age.

Schools should plan with parents and community agencies to insure the kind of program outlined above as part of the educational experiences of every child.

It should be kept in mind that the child is important in this setting and not the teacher, parent, school, or agency.[1]

Secondary School Programs

Unfortunately, the intramural program in most secondary schools is the weakest phase of the physical education program. The physical education staff is frequently understaffed and primary attention is usually given to instructional and varsity athletic programs. If the varsity coach is assigned to supervise the intramural program, he often conducts only a skeleton program and spends most of his time coaching and developing the varsity team. This is understandable from the coach's viewpoint. When a person is assigned more duties than time permits, it is natural to follow one's greatest interest; in this case, coaching the varsity team. In some schools, the coach not only coaches and teaches but supervises the intramural program as well. In other situations, a faculty supervisor is responsible for intramurals. This staff member might be interested in sports and in working with intramural students but is not always qualified to conduct an adequate program. He might not have any physical education background and is associated with the physical education program only through his job of running the intramural program.

Another reason for ineffective programs at the secondary school level is that teacher education institutions frequently

[1] National Conference on Physical Education for Children of Elementary School Age, *Physical Education for Children of Elementary School Age* (Chicago: Athletic Institute, 1951), p. 22.

fail to prepare physical education teachers adequately in the intramural area. Perhaps one unit of a physical education course on administration is devoted to intramurals, or perhaps the maximum attention, in all but a few colleges and universities, is one course on the administration of intramural sports. When poorly prepared graduates start teaching they are not anxious to institute programs or carry on existing intramural programs if they do not have "intramural know-how." Many graduates accept the theory and philosophy of intramurals but they are not adequately trained in the mechanics of conducting a successful intramural program. A program is only as good as its leadership. Things which are not regarded as important are not important to persons holding this conception but this does not preclude the possibility that they are of basic importance. Intramurals in the secondary schools tend to be as important as the emphasis placed on them by teacher education institutions.

The arguments for and against interscholastic competition at the junior high-school level give considerable impetus to intramurals. Several professional groups, including the American Association for Health, Physical Education, and Recreation, recommend intramural and extramural competition in place of varsity athletic programs in junior high schools. They indicate there are very few values from interscholastic competition which cannot be obtained from well-administered intramural, extramural, and physical education instruction programs. Some school authorities feel it is much more advisable to conduct activities with educational values in an educational setting than organize sports programs which lean toward community commercialization and undue pressures to win. Those who favor the latter to the exclusion of intramurals might never have reaped the benefits of a truly well-organized and -administered junior high-school intramural program.

In some communities, elementary- and secondary-school recreation programs are jointly sponsored by the municipal recreation and intramural departments. The school usually has good indoor and outdoor facilities and, when supplemented by park playgrounds and other municipal areas, provides an excellent foundation for a comprehensive recreation program. Community school programs of recreation and adult education are conducted in school buildings in the late afternoons and evenings. Combined use of school and community facilities is a sound economic policy. The intramural program is easily adjusted to community school programs and it makes a meaningful contribution to the total recreation of the community.

There is a wealth of untapped intramural sports potential lying dormant in most schools. Many school administrators are convinced or can be easily convinced that intramurals are educationally sound and have a legitimate place in the school curriculum. There is a great source of student leadership available just waiting for guidance and direction from intramurally trained physical education teachers. The cost of programing is amazingly low, often as little as a few cents per student. The tremendous student participation in a well-run intramural program results in an excellent return on each dollar invested by the school. Certainly intramurals should receive greater attention in the nation's schools than they do.

The following account of a junior high-school program is an example of how intramurals are adapted to fit a local situation. The account illustrates organization, supervision, participation, units of competition, rule modification, activities, officiating, tournament methods, scheduling, time periods, publicity, finances, equipment, recognition, and imagination. It is an excellent example of what some elementary, junior, and senior high schools can do with a little initiative and very little expense to uncover some of the dormant potential of intramural sports programs.

The usually noisy spectators were silent—all 280 of them who had jammed into the gym balcony. The score in the intramural volleyball game was 19–20 with 15 seconds to play, and the losing team had the serve. The 16 players on the court were tense as the ball was served. It hit the net and fell to the floor. The game was over. The score was unusual, but the crowded stands and eager participants were not unusual at our intramurals. The count of spectators has ranged from 105 to 410 depending on the intramural sport and the stage of the tournament. By now, someone has probably glanced back to the statement of 15 seconds left to play in the volleyball game. He realizes that volleyball is a game which is won by the team that scores 15 points first, provided it has at least a two point lead.

Our intramural program in Wynn Seale Junior High School, Corpus Christi, Texas, is a little unusual, but it fits our school needs. An explanation of it might give some new ideas or help solve a few problems. A few years ago our school had an intramural program that was run by one of the coaches. When he was transferred, the program was dropped for a semester. Then I was drafted by the principal. He was instrumental in having the school board set up the position of director of intramurals with a salary schedule comparable to that of junior high-school coaches but with no varsity coaching involved. This gave me more time to concentrate on solving intramural problems.

The first two years the intramurals were carried on after school. The sports offered were football, basketball, volleyball, track, and softball. The results were discouraging to me as we were plagued with too many forfeited games and poor spectator attendance. During the second year, the answer to one of my problems occurred during a ping-pong tournament. Owing to the large number of entries, part of the games were scheduled for the mornings. None of these games was forfeited, and we had to fight the spectators off.

The following year we switched to having the basketball games in the mornings. That was the answer! The students came to school early; but when school was out, they wanted to go home. We noticed that during this time the usual early morning playground scuffles and problems were almost nonexistent.

Now our intramurals are run exclusively in the mornings. This has necessitated a few changes in the standard rules which will be explained as each sport is taken up separately.

Flag Football

Time: 7:55 A.M. to 8:20 A.M. with 3 games played at the same time.
Field Size: 20 by 60 yards
Team Size: 7 boys on a team
Major Rules: Each player wears a 2-foot flag tucked in the back of his shorts. The ball is down when the flag is pulled off the ball carrier. No tying of tails, stiff arming, or down-field blocking is allowed. Defense of your tail with your hands is illegal, but you

may spin around and around. Three completed forward passes in 4 downs makes a first down. Points after touchdowns are tried.

Basketball

Time: 7:55 A.M. to 8:20 A.M.—2 ten-minute halves

Volleyball

Time: 8:00 A.M. to 8:20 A.M.—20 minute time limit
Team Size: Coeducational with 8 on a team

Softball

Time: 7:45 A.M. to 8:20 A.M.
Rules: Regulation rules are used. Score is counted to end of nearest full inning of time limit (usually 5 innings).

Track

Time: 7:45 A.M. field events—8:00 A.M. track events.

Wynn Seale's being a three-grade level junior high school, we have three divisions in all sports. The teams are homeroom teams. Officiating on the ninth grade level is done by myself and on the seventh and eighth grade levels by ninth grade pupils except for championship games which I call.

There are 1,150 students in our school and 35 homerooms. In volleyball alone this year, we had 31 homeroom teams entered for a total of 248 players and an average of 192 spectators per game for the 37 mornings of the tournament. Last year, during the ninth-grade high-jump event where the competition was very keen, over 600 students crowded the field and the jumping lanes to see the finish.

We use several types of tournaments, depending upon the number of teams entered and the sport. The most popular is the consolation type. No dates are set in the schedules posted in the main hall as bad weather often causes long delays, so announcements are made over the public address system the morning before the team plays.

The last important part of our intramural program is the cost—just my salary. As I am also a physical education teacher all physical education equipment is used. No trophies are awarded; the students are happy just to play. The winners get their pictures in the school paper and yearbook. The homeroom teacher usually gives a coke party to the class. One of my regrets in the past has been that not too many teachers showed up to watch their teams play. This year even the light is shining brighter there as more have already been to the games than ever before in the past.[2]

[2] Peter H. Curran, "Intramural Program at Corpus Christi, Texas," *The Bulletin of the National Association of Secondary-School Principals,* XXXXII, No. 241 (November, 1958).

Girls' and Women's Programs

A cursory review of girls' and women's programs might lead one to believe there are many major differences in providing recreational opportunities for men and women students. However, a more exhaustive study shows the underlying program philosophy, aims, and objectives are basically the same. Men and women and boys and girls have many of the same basic needs for integrated living—intellectual, social, spiritual, and physical well-being.

When directors of men's and women's intramural programs compare notes, they frequently find their problems are similar. These problems include forfeits, finances, facilities, equipment, staff, awards, rules and regulations, health and safety, officiating, scheduling, and equalization of competition. Certain aspects are slightly different, but in most respects they are comparable. Some schools conduct intramural programs on a corecreational basis, with men and women sharing the same facilities. In this situation, numerous activities are sponsored in which men and women play together and other tournaments are also arranged in which they compete separately.

It seems highly desirable for men and women intramural directors to co-operate in planning, organizing, and administering joint programs. Occasionally, this co-operation does not advance beyond the thought stage because of personality conflicts among the personnel in charge of the program. It is unfortunate when this stands in the way of program progress, particularly when it has such a restrictive effect on wholesome recreation opportunities for men and women students. Each intramural director must utilize introspection or reflection to determine whether personal considerations impede program developments. In making any administrative decision, the needs of the students must be the basic determinant.

Associations. Intramural programs for girls and women are often conducted by the various athletic, sports, and recreation associations. The word "girls" is used in elementary and secondary schools and the word "women" applies in colleges and universities. These associations have various names. The GAA or WAA is the Girls' or Women's Athletic Association; the GRA or WRA is the Girls' or Women's Recreation Association; and the GSA or WSA is the Girls' or Women's Sports Association. Names are also found in combination, such as the Girls' or Women's Sports and Recreation Association (GSRA or WSRA) and the Girls' or Women's Athletic and Recreation Association (GARA or WARA). These associations promote intramural and extramural activities through special interest clubs, special events, tournaments, and informal play (see Fig. 4).

ATHLETIC AND RECREATION FEDERATION OF COLLEGE WOMEN. The Athletic and Recreation Federation of College Women (ARFCW), which replaced the Athletic Conference of American College Women, is a national organization of women's collegiate athletic and recreation associations in the United States. The ARFCW aids local associations in promoting activities which meet present and future student needs. National and state conventions are held in alternate years for coordinating ideas and evaluating programs.

In 1955 the ARFCW adopted this platform to implement programs of collegiate athletic and recreation associations:

1. To improve skills through interest and enjoyment, and to increase the number of women participating in WAA or WRA activities
2. To promote those activities which will meet the present and future needs of college women
3. To accept as far as possible only women instructors to advise WAA or WRA activities
4. To stress as far as possible the requirement of a yearly medical examination, by a physician, of all participants in the WAA or WRA programs as established by the individual school or organization
5. To offer assistance in the promotion of a constructive program of athletics and recreational activities for high school girls and the community
6. To de-emphasize competitive commercial women's sports

7. To promote good sportsmanship, fair play, and respect for the individual skill of others at all times
8. To promote a recreational program in which men and women may participate together
9. To promote a WAA or WRA program without overemphasizing a system of awards
10. To stimulate interest in ARFCW by publicity through WAA or WRA programs
11. To encourage participation of college women in officiating WAA or WRA activities, and to urge them to take rating examinations
12. To uphold the Standards of Athletics for Girls and Women, as set forth by the Division for Girls and Women's Sports

DIVISION FOR GIRLS AND WOMEN'S SPORTS (DGWS). The efficient Division for Girls and Women's Sports of the American Association for Health, Physical Education, and Recreation is the guiding influence for promoting wholesome sports programs for girls and women. The desirable practices advocated by this organization are not restricted to school programs but include out-of-school programs. This group recognizes that competition alone does not guarantee desired outcomes. It is possible for evils to exist regardless of whether the competition is in intramurals, extramurals, or intermurals. Competition is completely affected by the manner in which programs are conducted, and quality participation results only to the extent that quality programs are conducted.

The DGWS believes that "for the welfare of the girls and women who participate in sports, certain practices should be followed." The recommended practices which can be used as guides in conducting sports programs follow.

STANDARDS FOR DESIRABLE PRACTICES

The program of sports activities for girls and women should:

1. Be based upon the recognition of individual differences in age; body build; interests; ability; experience; health; and the stages of physiological, emotional, and social maturity of the participants

2. Be organized to provide opportunity for groupings at all skill levels, development from simple to complex skills, development of

leadership and group achievement, and evaluation of the suitability of each activity

3. Encourage the development of skill and sportsmanship by a variety of sound methods and practices
4. Be scheduled at regular periods of limited length at frequent intervals and at a time of day when energy is at a high level
5. Provide for the selection of members of all teams so that they play against those of approximately the same ability and maturity
6. Be taught, coached, and officiated by qualified women *whenever* and *wherever* possible
7. Be officiated by officials whose decisions are sound, consistent, and impartial
8. Include the use of official rules authorized by the Division for Girls and Women's Sports of the American Association for Health, Physical Education, and Recreation
9. Stimulate the participants to play for the enjoyment of playing and not for tangible rewards or because of artificial incentives
10. Include a variety of sports, both team and individual, and provide opportunity for all girls wishing to participate to be a member of a team in those sports for which teams are organized
11. Include informal social events in connection with competition
12. Require written parental permission for minors engaging in any extramural competition
13. Include guidance for girls and women concerning appropriate costume for sports
14. Limit extramural competition to a small geographic area
15. Furnish safe transportation in bonded carriers
16. Be financed by the promoting agency and not be dependent on gate receipts for its existence
17. Include competition for girls independent from that arranged for boys (eliminating such events as double-header games or "curtain raisers") except in those activities in which boys and girls are encouraged to play together on mixed teams
18. Be limited as to the total length of sports seasons and the maximum number of practice periods and games to be played in a day or a week.

LEADERSHIP

Administrators, teachers or coaches, and players should be primarily concerned with the outcomes of the program.

1. The Administrator is directly responsible for:
   a. selecting qualified women to direct the program
   b. providing facilities, equipment, and finances to carry on the program

c. providing equal use of facilities and equipment for boys and girls
d. providing health safeguards
e. guiding publicity to emphasize the educational and recreational values of the program

2. The teacher or coach is responsible for:
a. having a thorough knowledge of the games and their rules and strategy
b. providing opportunity for all girls to play
c. encouraging skillful play for full enjoyment of the game
d. emphasizing the importance of health examinations
e. developing intelligent leadership and wise followership among the players
f. conducting activities on a sound competitive basis
g. exemplifying those traits which she tries to develop in others

3. The player is responsible for her own conduct as shown through:
a. intelligent health practices
b. courtesy, fair play, and good sportsmanship
c. high quality leadership within her own group
d. emotional control in all game situations
e. playing to the best of her ability

HEALTH

Provision must be made for careful supervision of the health of all players.

1. Participants must have periodic health examinations.
2. After serious illness or injury, written permission from a physician should be required to resume participation.
3. First aid supplies should be available at practices and games.
4. Participation during the menstrual period should be determined on the basis of individual differences.
5. Equipment and facilities should be hygienic and safe.
6. Players should be removed from activity if they are injured or overfatigued or show evidence of emotional instability.

PUBLICITY

A planned program of publicity should present interesting information on the program, its standards, aims, and outcomes. The publicity should be carefully interpreted to newswriters, parents, community leaders, the players, and their associates. Publicity should stress:

1. The recreational and social values of sports rather than the winning of championships

2. Achievements of the groups and teams rather than those of individuals

TYPES OF COMPETITION

The method of organizing competition must be determined in terms of desirable outcomes. The guides to constructive competition are that the program of sports shall offer equal opportunity to all in terms of individual ability, be wide in range, be adapted to the needs and interests of the participants, and be honestly and expertly led.

Intramural. Competition of groups playing one another within their school, industrial group, or organization. Intramural competition should have priority for facilities, time, and leadership because it serves the greatest number of players.

Extramural. Competition involving a group or team from one school, recreational center, industrial group, or organization playing with a group or team from another school, industrial group, or organization. Types of extramural competition are:

1. Sports Days. An event, frequently including more than one activity, to which several schools, playgrounds, industrial groups, or organizations may bring two or more groups of players. Each group participates as a unit.

2. Playdays. An informal type of competition in which color teams are selected from the players of the participating schools or clubs.

3. Telegraphic Meets. Teams compete with each other by establishing records against time or for score while performing in their own locations. Such records are sent to a central committee for comparison. Archery, pistol and rifle, swimming events, bowling, and track and field are adaptable to this plan.

4. Invitational Events. Such as a symposium, jamboree, game, or match other than a league game.

5. Interscholastic or Intercollegiate Games. Players for selected games trained and coached to play a series of scheduled games and tournaments with similar teams from other schools, playgrounds, cities, or institutions within a limited geographical area. To be offered only as a supplement to adequate intramural and extramural programs.

No one type of competitive organization can be designated as the approved form. The method of organizing competition must be determined by the desirable possibilities it provides, not by the type into which it can be classified.

The One Purpose of Sports for Girls and Women Is the Good of Those Who Play.[3]

[3] An adaptation of *Standards in Sports for Girls and Women* (rev. ed.; Washington, D.C.: American Association for Health, Physical Education, and Recreation, Division for Girls and Women's Sports, 1957). Specific standards for guiding competition for girls and women in the various team and individual sports appear in the respective sport guides of the Association.

Evaluation of Intramural Programs

Evaluation of an intramural program is a continuous process and is as important to program progress as self-analysis is to the growth and development of an individual. Good program-analysis not only determines the progress which is made but also indicates what future progress is necessary. It aids in establishing goals which the intramural director must keep in mind as he plans and organizes for future program development. The game of golf presents an analogy in that the golfer constantly tries to achieve par. Scores kept during the season, and perhaps from year to year, indicate progress being made and progress to be made. The golfer's goal is attained or partially attained through careful self-analysis and studying and mastering correct techniques.

In intramural evaluation, it is necessary to determine if the program accomplishes what it intends to accomplish. To what degree does the program meet the predetermined aims and objectives? To what degree are the needs and interests of the students met? To answer these questions and to improve the situation which exists as a result of these answers, standards of reference must be utilized. These standards are usually for an ideal program, but they can be for one which is better than the existing program. The evaluative process not only measures progress but also frequently provides ideas and suggestions for program improvement and methods of implementation. Several suggestions for intramural program evaluation are discussed in the following sections.

EVALUATION THROUGH RECORDS. Statistics on intramural sports participation can be misleading. Figures are sometimes interpreted to mean what the interpreter wants them to mean. Perhaps no two schools keep participation records exactly the same. Each director demands a greater or lesser degree of accuracy in maintaining records. Consequently, a "participation" in one program does not have the same meaning as it has in another program. One of the evils in intramurals is the rivalry that sometimes develops from comparing participation records between schools. In the first place, there are too many variables, and second, in an attempt to "get ahead" of another school, major emphasis might be placed on quantity participation at the expense of quality participation. The practice of designing activities solely to increase participation is questionable.

Some directors do not keep records because they are understaffed and feel the time is better spent in other program phases. In other programs, record keeping is the only method of evaluation used. Still others suggest their program is good enough or is as good as it can be. Evaluation exists only to the extent that excuses are made as to why the program is the way it is and why it cannot be better. This state of complacency is completely unfair to the students in the school system.

The basic reason for keeping records is that they can be compared with departmental records of previous years to show progress and perhaps indicate the necessity for program modification and improvement. The following items of information aid the evaluative process:

1. Participants. This is the number of different students taking part in the program. The figure is particularly meaningful when compared with the number of students enrolled in school. This comparison shows what percentage of the total student body takes part in intramural activities. If these records are kept accurately, avoiding duplication, they also show how many times each student participated. In larger schools, records of this type are cumbersome. Often, the number of players per team is multiplied by the number of teams. This is not a valid figure and does not account for duplicate participation when the totals of several sports are added.
2. Participations. A participation is counted *each time* a player plays in a match or game. If 12 team members from 2 teams play in 6 basketball games, there are 72 participations. However, 2 players who play 5 games in a squash match account for 2 participations. This figure, which often exceeds several thousand, is found by totaling

the number of players' names on all score cards. Year-to-year comparisons show increases or decreases in over-all program participation. A slight modification in tournament methods results in increased participations. Adding a consolation tournament to a single elimination tournament or substituting a round robin for a double elimination tournament increases the number of participations.

3. Number of teams. The number of teams in each sport is a valid figure to use in comparing year-to-year progress, particularly if tournament and other program procedures remain constant. It does not account for individual and dual sport competition, however, unless these activities are conducted on a team basis.
4. Number of games. The number of games played is another valid figure for comparison, if they are counted in the same manner each year. For example, a bowling match consists of three games and a volleyball match can involve five games. One match should not be counted one year and the number of games per match the following year. A good principle to follow is to count all games no matter how much time is required to play them. All games in matches for individual and dual sports, such as handball and squash, should be included.
5. Forfeits, drop outs, protests, and eligibility cases. The number of forfeits, team drop outs, game protests, and player eligibility cases is an indication of student interest and responsibility and the effectiveness with which the program is administered. To a certain degree, it provides a measure for the quality aspect of participation.
6. Team sportsmanship and officials' ratings. The number of low sportsmanship ratings for teams is another measure of student co-operation and quality participation. Low officials' ratings show the general over-all level of officiating. One or two isolated ratings are not always valid, but the percentage of high, average, and low ratings is meaningful.

Evaluation through appraisal forms. Checklists, rating scales, score cards, surveys, and other appraisal devices are designed to evaluate intramural programs. Standards of reference are found in professional literature, such as masters and doctors theses, textbooks on intramural sports, and journalistic accounts of existing programs. Questions or statements of the recommended standards can be written out in checklist form. Those questions answered or statements checked in terms of the director's own program serve as a basis for evaluation. Individual items can be rated excellent, good, average, fair, and poor, according to the degree of compliance with recommended standards.

Three examples of evaluation forms are those of the Washington Conference on Intramural Sports,[4] the LaPorte Health and Physical Education Score Card No. II,[5] and the Educational Policies Commission Check List.[6] The Washington Conference Evaluation Form is a checklist of criteria for appraising college intramural programs. Ratings are given each individual standard on the basis of completely, to a great degree, to a moderate degree, very little, and not at all. The LaPorte Score Card has one section, Number X, devoted to intramural and interschool athletics for junior and senior high schools. Ratings are made on a point basis with a possible score of 30 points. The Educational Policies Commission's checklist on school athletics consists of 100 questions related to: (1) purposes of school athletics; (2) health and welfare of athletic participants; (3) organization and administration of school athletics; (4) facilities for school athletics; (5) personnel for the athletic program; (6) intramural programs; (7) elementary-school policies and programs; (8) junior high-school policies and programs; (9) interscholastic athletics for boys in senior high school; (10) athletics for girls; (11) financing athletic programs; and (12) community relations.

EVALUATION BY STUDY GROUPS. Outside intramural sports experts can be brought in to evaluate the intramural pro-

[4] American Association for Health, Physical Education and Recreation, *ibid.*, pp. 29–33.

[5] William Ralph LaPorte, *The Physical Education Curriculum* (6th ed.; Los Angeles: College Book Store, 1955), pp. 66–86.

[6] Educational Policies Commission, *School Athletics: Problems and Policies* (Washington, D.C.: National Education Association of the United States and the American Association of School Administrators, 1954), pp. 89–97.

gram. The observers should be both expert and impartial. This procedure is extremely effective, but it involves expenses which most intramural departments cannot afford.

Another effective procedure is to select a small group from the school or community to visit outstanding intramural programs in schools of comparable size. This group then compares other programs with the local program and makes suggestions for improvement. It is important to include nonphysical education personnel to reduce partiality. A distinguished business man in the community is a valuable asset to the study group.

EVALUATION BY STUDENTS. Student evaluation is not comprehensive but is of value in determining participants' satisfaction. Methods consist of surveys, conferences, interviews, suggestion boxes, and brainstorming sessions. Information obtained reveals popularity of activities, effectiveness with which the program is administered, and suggestions for improvement.

Brainstorming or ideation sessions are not directly evaluative but presented ideas often point up the many possibilities which are not yet realized in the intramural program. This serves as a basis for comparison, namely, what the program is and what it might be. In brainstorming, a group of students meet to present solutions for a particular problem. The objective is to solicit as many ideas as possible. The number of usable ideas is small but they are usually very good. Presence of faculty members sometimes inhibits student participation. These sessions are most effective when they take place in a relaxed, friendly atmosphere. Many ideas are waiting to be developed; and students, given the right set of circumstances, contribute many good suggestions for improving intramural programs.

SUMMARY

1. Most of the material in this book can be adapted to all levels of student education—colleges and secondary and elementary schools.

2. Intramural participation in the primary grades consists mostly of "free play" activities during recess, noon hours, and physical education class periods.
3. Skills of running, jumping, throwing, climbing, and balancing are learned through games of low organization, rhythms, stunts, and relays in the primary grades.
4. In the upper elementary grades, from grade five and up, it is desirable to conduct intramural activities within and between grades.
5. It is wise to classify students for competition in the upper elementary grades according to age, weight, and height instead of any *one* of these criteria.
6. The intramural program in most secondary schools is the weakest phase of the physical education program.
7. Reasons for such a poor intramural program in secondary schools include an understaffed physical education staff which spends most of its time on instructional and physical education programs and failure of teacher-education institutions to prepare physical education teachers adequately in the intramural area.
8. Several professional groups, including the American Association for Health, Physical Education, and Recreation, recommend intramural and extramural competition in place of varsity athletic programs in junior high schools. They say there are very few values from interscholastic competition which cannot be obtained from well-administered intramural, extramural, and physical education instruction programs at this age level.
9. In some communities, elementary and secondary school recreation programs are jointly sponsored by the municipal recreation and intramural departments.
10. There is a wealth of untapped intramural sports potential lying dormant in most schools—student leadership, low cost of programing, tremendous participation potential, etc.
11. Underlying program philosophy, aims, and objectives of girls' and women's and boys' and men's intramural programs are basically similar.
12. Men and women and boys and girls have many of the same basic needs for integrated living—intellectual, social, spiritual, and physical well-being.

13. Mutual problems for both sexes' intramural programs include forfeits, finances, facilities, equipment, staff, awards, rules and regulations, health and safety, officiating, scheduling, and equalization of competition.
14. It is desirable although not always workable for men and women intramural directors to co-operate in planning, organizing, and administering joint programs for students in their respective departments.
15. Most popular methods of promoting intramural programs for girls and women are the various athletic, sports, and recreation associations, such as the Girls' or Women's Athletic Association (GAA or WAA), the Girls' or Women's Sports Association (GSA or WSA), and the Girls' or Women's Recreation Associations (GRA or WRA).
16. The Athletic and Recreation Federation of College Women (ARFCW) is a national organization of women's collegiate athletic and recreation associations in the United States which aids local associations in promoting activities which meet present and future student needs.
17. The Division for Girls and Women's Sports (DGWS) of the American Association for Health, Physical Education, and Recreation is the guiding influence for promoting wholesome sports programs for girls and women.
18. Evaluation of an intramural program is a continuous process.
19. Good program analysis determines the progress which is made, indicates what future progress is necessary, aids in establishing goals for future program development, and determines if the intramural program accomplishes what it intends to accomplish.
20. Evaluation methods include statistics and records on number of participants, number of participations, number of teams, number of games, number of forfeits, drop outs, protests and eligibility cases, and team sportsmanship and officials' ratings; appraisal forms such as checklists, rating scales, score cards, surveys, etc.; evaluation by study groups of outside experts, students, businessmen, etc.; and student evaluations, including surveys, conferences, interviews, suggestion boxes, and brainstorming sessions.

15

Aids for Conducting Programs

The promotion of a truly attractive and successful intramural sports program requires more than accepting entries, arranging schedules, notifying teams as to playing time, assigning officials, and recording results.

An intramural sports program is greatly improved by the use of certain mechanical devices which require little time, a minimum of expense, and practically no effort to use. Various seemingly trivial devices add much to efficient promotion, make supervision easier, and give much more satisfaction and enjoyment to participants.

The different departments of most institutions are usually willing to co-operate in the completion of practical projects. For example, the industrial arts department might make equipment and the art department might make posters. Such co-operation provides interesting and worthwhile activities and minimizes the cost of desirable equipment.

Following are descriptions of a few successful practical aids that are common to a number of sports. However, similar aids can be devised for almost every sport. Archery enthusiasts are interested in having devices for trimming and gluing feathers or a portable backstop that can be stored when not in use; fencing instructors find an equipment rack conducive to better service from the weapons; and a locked field equipment cart is useful for sports where playing areas are far-removed from the gymnasium, intramural building, or intramural office. The ones described may be adapted to any program or possibly will suggest others that facilitate the promotion of an intramural sports program.

VOLLEYBALL FLASH SCORING DEVICE. Participants should be kept informed at all times as to the score of their game. A flash scoring device similar to the one shown in Figure 40 gives this information and requires little effort to use on the part of the official in charge. The rod part of the flash scoring device is inserted in the hollow pipe of the volleyball standards and the official calls the points and at the same time turns over the score cards to the proper numbers. The scores that show in large figures on the cards face the players' side; duplicate numbers appear in small figures on the officials' side of the cards. This arrangement indicates to the official the game score shown without his having to look over the top of the device. A more expensive and durable device can be made by using thin aluminum or galvanized iron instead of placards for the numbers.

Figure 40. Volleyball Scoring Device.

VOLLEYBALL OFFICIALS' PLATFORM. A home-made ladder standard and officials' platform combined, as shown in Figure 41, raises the official above the top of the volleyball net where he can easily see all parts of the court. From this position, he is assisted in rendering accurate decisions on whether balls are out of bounds. If the platform is made sufficiently large, two officials can work one game on parallel courts, using the same platform. The illustrated ladder

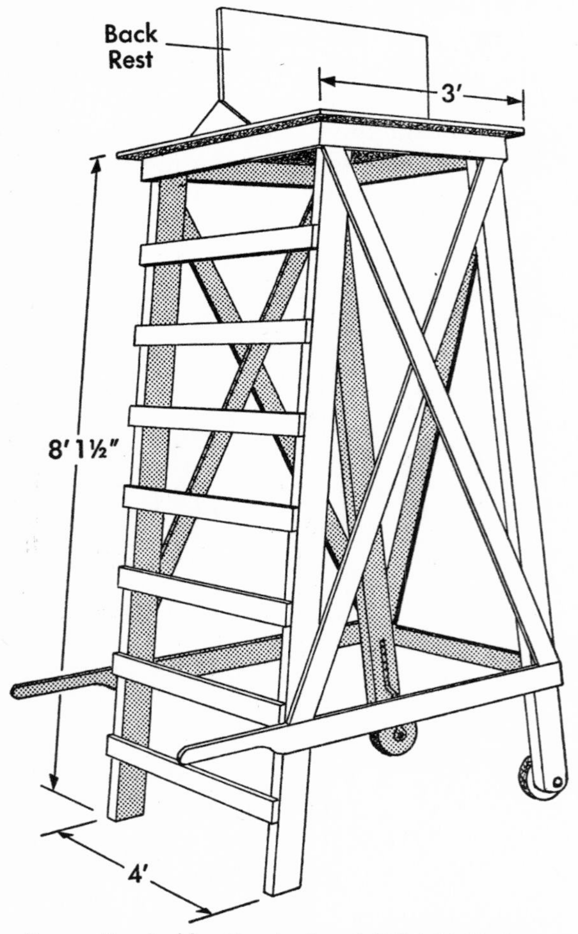

Figure 41. Ladder Standard and Officials' Platform.

standard and officials' platform has two rubber casters or rollers. Four casters or rollers with step down locks can be used for greater mobility. After the platform is moved into position, the locks are secured by stepping on them.

Basketball scoring device and timer. The flash scoring device for basketball illustrated in Figure 42 is operated similarly to the one described for volleyball. The basketball device, however, is constructed so that it can be placed upon a table. Also it contains a securely fastened timer and rules instructions in brief. On the base of this basketball device there is room for a pencil for the scorekeeper, a horn for the timekeeper, additional flash scoring cards, and other instructions for the game. These units are assigned to the various courts for the session or sessions, and, if desired, officials can be changed from one court to another without transfering all of the scorer's equipment.

Figure 42. Basketball Scoring Device and Timer.

DIVING FLASH CARDS. Instead of the cumbersome type of flash cards often given to judges to use in swimming meets, a very simple, easily handled, and inexpensive container with a set of flash score cards can be made. (See Fig. 43.) The container for the cards is of lightweight material, open at the top and one side. The score cards, with tabs, are distinctly marked with numbers from 1 to 10, punched and fastened in the corner of the container by a small bolt. The cards are also marked on the back. When the referee calls "scores" the judges use the numbered tab to pull the card from the container.

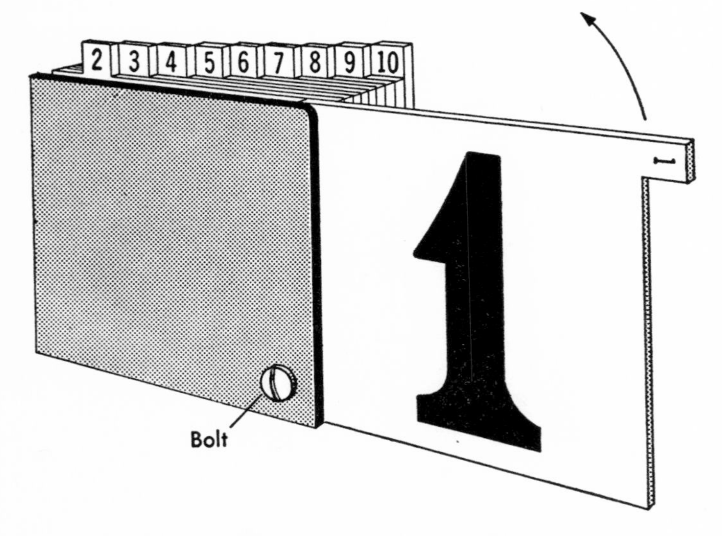

Figure 43. Diving Flash Cards.

BASKETBALL AND FOOTBALL CENTRAL TIMER. Basketball and football games of straight running-time can be centrally timed when played on adjacent courts or fields by using an interval timer or housewife's "kitchen minder." All games begin and end at the same time with no timeouts or time stoppage for any reasons. This system enables one person, in addition to officials, to supervise an entire day's or evening's basketball or football schedule in the same area.

PLAYING-FIELD CORNER FLAGS. For marking out fields for such sports as touch football, soccer, and speedball, it helps to have small flags at the corners of end-lines and goal lines (see Fig. 44).

For such markers, sink short, ½ inch gas pipes, capped at one end, into the ground at the desired points. Make a shallow recessed area around the top of each stake so the top of the pipe is a little below the level of the ground. Insert an ordinary screendoor spring, to the top of which is fastened a small piece of colored cloth, into each pipe.

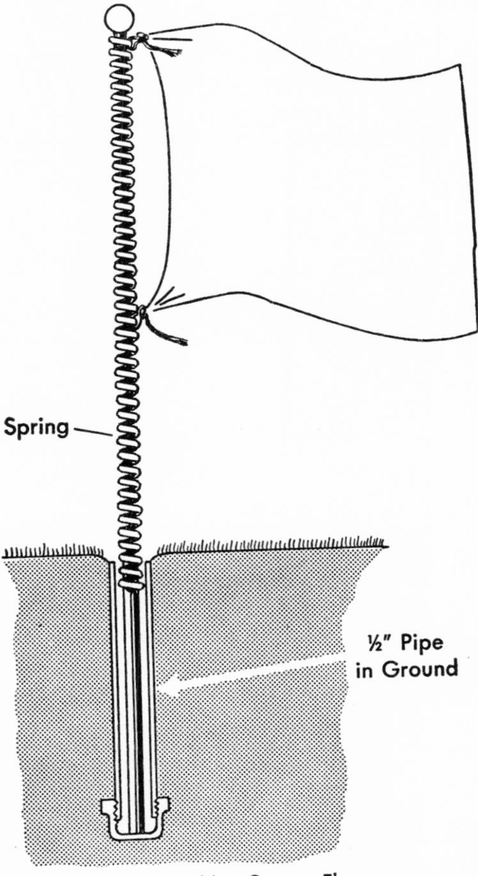

Figure 44. Corner Flag.

These improvised colored markers can be easily placed in position before, and quickly removed after, each contest. By using various color combinations, it is easy for players and officials to distinguish corners of specific lines. This type of flag is particularly helpful on grassy fields where lime lines are hard to follow. Being flexible, a flag of this type will not injure a player if he trips or falls on it.

Softball bases. Where finances do not permit purchase of canvas bases for softball, cement ones prove a very satisfactory substitute. If properly finished, cement bases are not dangerous. Cement bases should be official in size and shape, about 4 inches thick, and made of reinforced concrete. Bevel the edges and finish the top with white sand and cement so the base is more easily seen. Set the bases in the ground with the bottom of the beveled edge flush with the ground. Some schools have bases such as these made in their school shop class.

Official-size wooden bases with rings or hinge drawer handles flush with the top of the base are also easy to make. If these are several inches thick they will remain fixed when set in the ground. Canvas base straps are hooked on the rings or handles of the wooden bases. After games are finished, canvas bases can be removed and stored. Students who want to practice when diamonds are not scheduled for use and when they cannot get the canvas bases still have the wooden bases to use.

Playing area assignment board. When games are scheduled on several fields, and since players on the several teams do not arrive at the playing field at the same time, officials in charge are constantly answering questions as to where various teams play. An assignment board, as diagramed in Figure 45, if placed in an appropriate spot, perhaps at the main entrance of the playing area, assists in minimizing this confusion and in getting games started on time.

Identifying cards are prepared, as shown in Figure 46, for each team entered in the activity. Immediately upon arriving at the field, the supervisor in charge places the

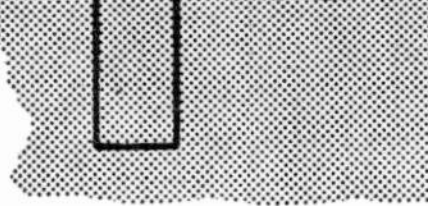

Figure 45. Assignment Board.

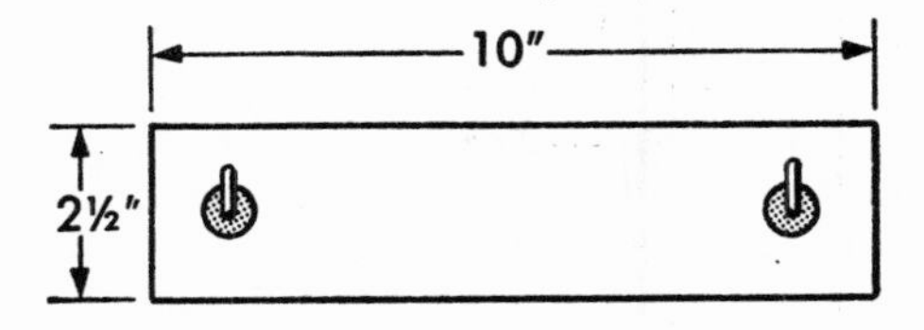

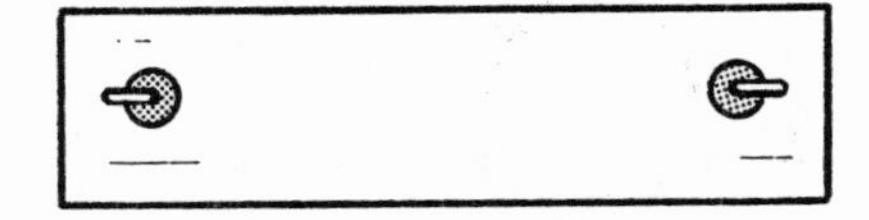

Figure 46. Identifying Cards.

cards on the assignment-board screw-hooks opposite the playing-field numbers assigned to the various teams. On windy days, some difficulty might be encountered with the cards blowing off the screw hooks, but this can be remedied by turning the hooks outward, as shown in Figure 46, or by using thin boards for the name tabs.

NET STANDARDS. For such games as badminton, paddle tennis, and deck tennis, standards for nets that are light in weight and do not require a long span or a great deal of tension can be made. To construct one similar to that illustrated in Figure 47, use salvaged automobile fly-wheels

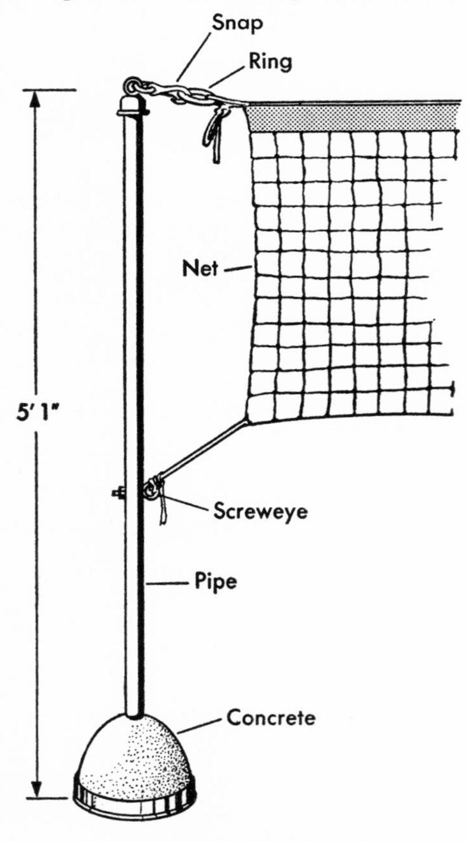

Figure 47. Net Standard.

with the cog removed, or a specially constructed form, for the base and an ordinary ¾-inch iron pipe of proper length for the upright. Place the pipe in the center of the form or thread it at one end and insert it in a threaded bushing placed in the center of the fly-wheel. Then pour wet cement inside the fly-wheel or form, reinforced with wire and molded quite high up and around the pipe, thus providing the necessary weight for the base. Insert eye bolts into drilled holes at game regulation points in the upright so that the nets can be hooked thereto with ordinary small harness snaps. After the cement is thoroughly set, paint the entire standard with some practical color, such as black.

This type of standard eliminates the necessity of floor plates, and, if the edges of the bottom are rounded, can be easily rolled about without damaging the floor. These standards are especially useful when temporary courts are needed for exhibitions.

Markers for equipment. Those who wish to mark their equipment plainly can do so by using an electric needle, an electric pen, and paint. An electric needle readily burns into wood or leather. Initials or monograms can easily be burned into baseball bats, paddles, gloves, and other wooden and leather equipment. Markings with an electric needle are fairly permanent; to remove them requires considerable sanding.

An electric pen can be used for writing, marking, etching, or engraving on tools and metal. The pen requires a small transformer; however the entire cost of the pen, ground terminal, writing points, connecting wires, clips, and transformer is comparatively small. The pen works on the same principle as an electric welding outfit, producing a hot spark or arc that actually writes on metal. Horseshoes, horns, tools, whistles, and watches can be marked with a pen. To eliminate any possibility of damaging the delicate works of a watch, it is advisable to remove the back while it is being marked. In addition to an intramural department mark, it is practical to place a number and the date purchased on such items as watches. This gives an assignment number for checking out the equipment; also some information as to the amount of service being obtained from various makes.

BAT RACK. A bat rack made of wood, similar to the one in Figure 48, will keep bats clean, dry, and in order. This kind of bat rack can be attached to the end of the dugout or to small posts driven in the ground.

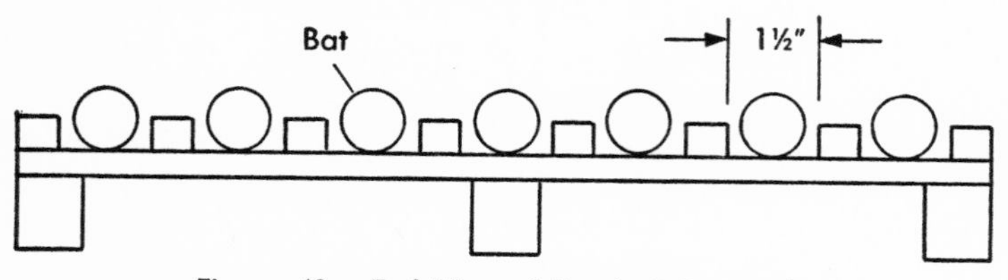

Figure 48. End View of Baseball Bat Rack.

CLIP BOARD. Clip boards, made preferably of long-wearing aluminum, with a pencil attached by a string, are handy to use to hold score cards at intramural games. The boards can be checked out from the supervisor or attached to post, screen, or other area near the field of play and are effective for such outdoor sports as softball, baseball, and touch football. Clip boards keep score cards clean, dry, and in good order and serve as a writing surface for officials and supervisors. Softball and baseball umpires mark scores between innings and, when working several games during the same day or evening, have a convenient place to keep score cards from previous games.

COURT RESERVATION BOARD. A reservation board with rules, as shown in Figure 49, can be placed at the corner of each court for sports such as handball, squash, badminton, and tennis. A summary of the rules for the respective game is glued to the top of the board and covered with a piece of glass or other transparent material.

Immediately below the rules are four or more spaces with slots into which a reservation card for a certain hour can be inserted. The number of spaces for reservations is determined by the maximum number of matches which can be scheduled on one court for one day.

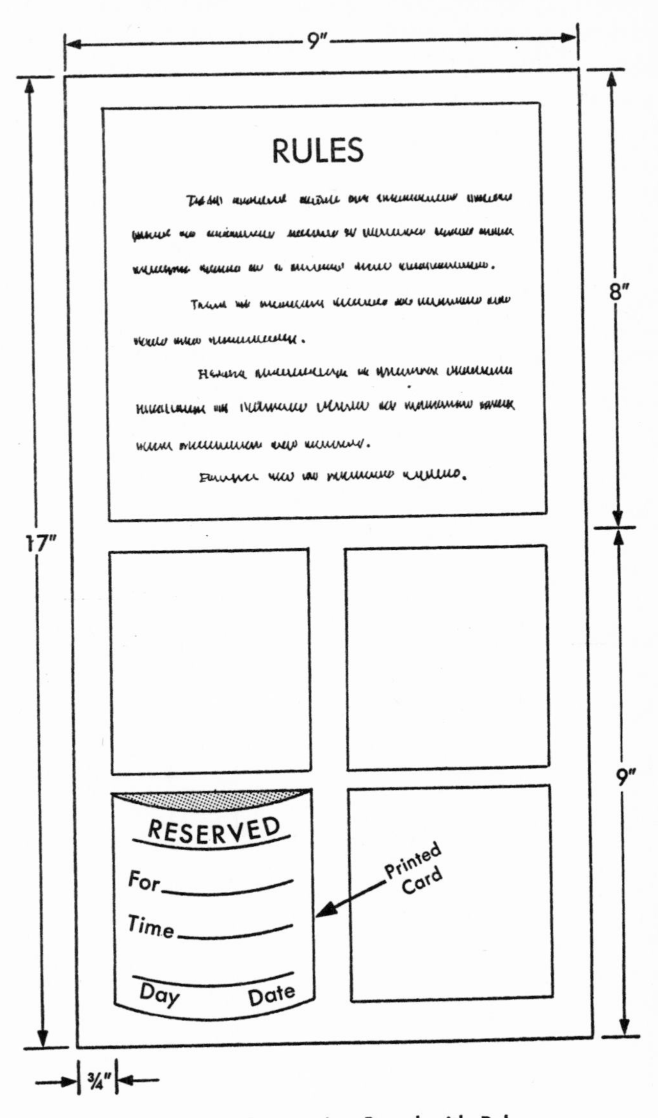

Figure 49. Reservation Board with Rules.

SOFTBALL BATTER'S BOX FRAME. Since softball diamonds must be frequently re-marked, much time can be saved by using a lightweight batter's box frame similar to the one diagramed in Figure 50 to assist the marking. Make the frame in the proper dimensions so it fits correctly to produce a regulation batter's box. The frame covers half of the batter's box. With a roller-type limer or wet-and-dry line marker, roll it around the outside of the frame because not all limers or markers make the same width line. The suggested frame makes a correct batter's box measured to the inside of the batter's box line. Measure the 6 inches between the base and frame to the inside of the line. After using the frame on both sides of home plate, connect two 8½ inch lines on each side of the plate which the frame covered.

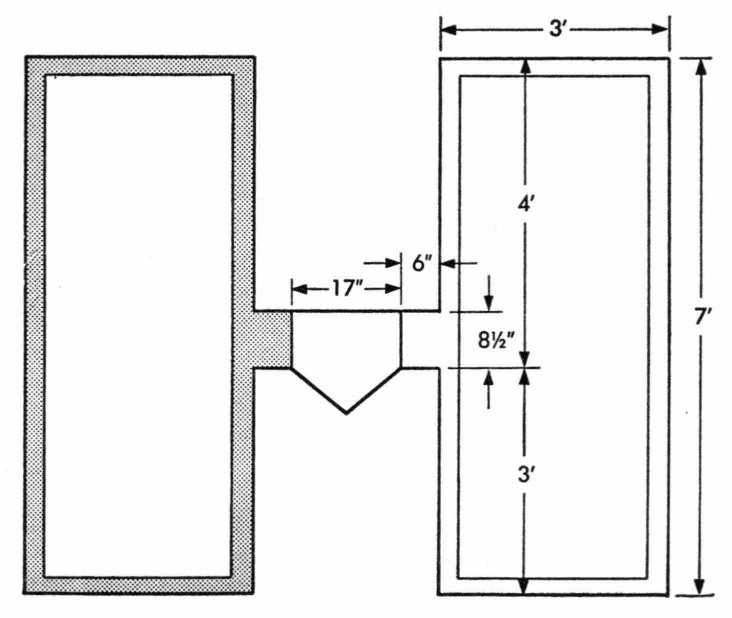

Figure 50. Softball Batter's Box Frame.

CIRCLE-O-GRAPH. Target faces for archery can be made very inexpensively of heavy wrapping paper and are satisfactory for practical use. A device called a circle-o-graph (see Fig. 51) is a valuable aid in describing the concentric circles for the target on the paper. To make a circle-o-graph, secure a strip of metal, celluloid, light wood, or cardboard about 25 inches long. Bore a hole in one end; this is the center point. From this point make five additional holes, all 4⅘ inches apart. Place the center hole in the middle of a piece of wrapping paper 50″ × 50″. Insert the point of a pencil through the center hole to hold the strip to the paper. Take another pencil and, in turn, place the point in the remaining five holes and, moving the strip, describe five complete circles. If desirable, paint the circles the colors marked on Figure 51. Oilcloth or muslin faces are more satisfactory for permanent use.

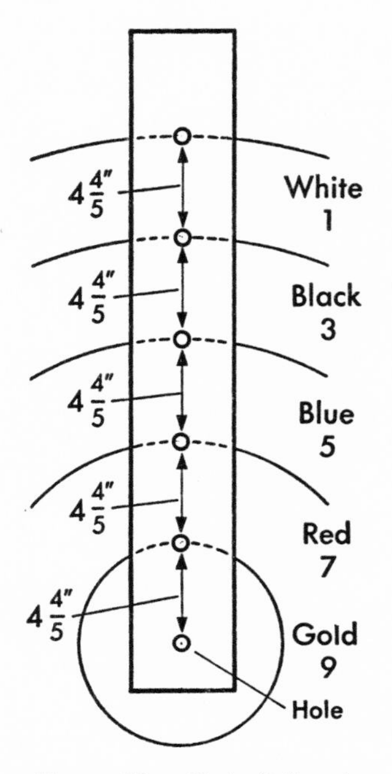

Figure 51. Circle-O-Graph.

SHOT AND DISCUS MARKER. The combination shot and discus circle marker illustrated in Figure 52 aids in marking and re-marking circles, once the board is laid out according to official measurements. The device is made of lightweight wood about 4′ 3″ long. Three ordinary large nails, used for pins, are driven in the board—one at one end of the piece of

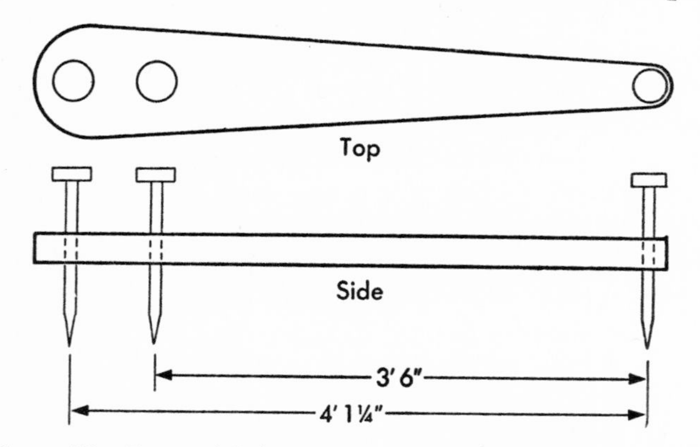

Figure 52. Top and Side View of Shot and Discus Circle Marker.

wood, a second nail 3′ 6″ from the end nail (the shot circle radius), and a third nail 4′ 1¼″ from the end nail (the discus radius). To re-mark either circle, the end pin must be held in place as the circles are scribed.

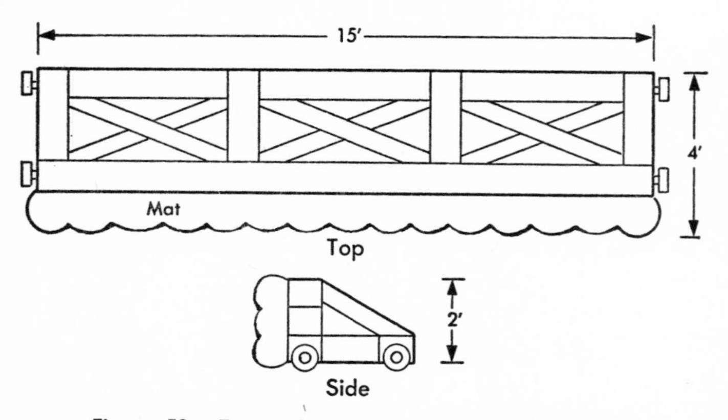

Figure 53. Top and Side View of Shot Put Guard.

SHOT PUT GUARD. A shot put guard (see Figure 53) prevents the shot from rolling after striking the ground. Such a unit can be made from rough lumber 10′ to 15′ long and 4′ wide, the front portion being covered with an old gymnasium mat or similar padding. Wheels on the ends make it portable.

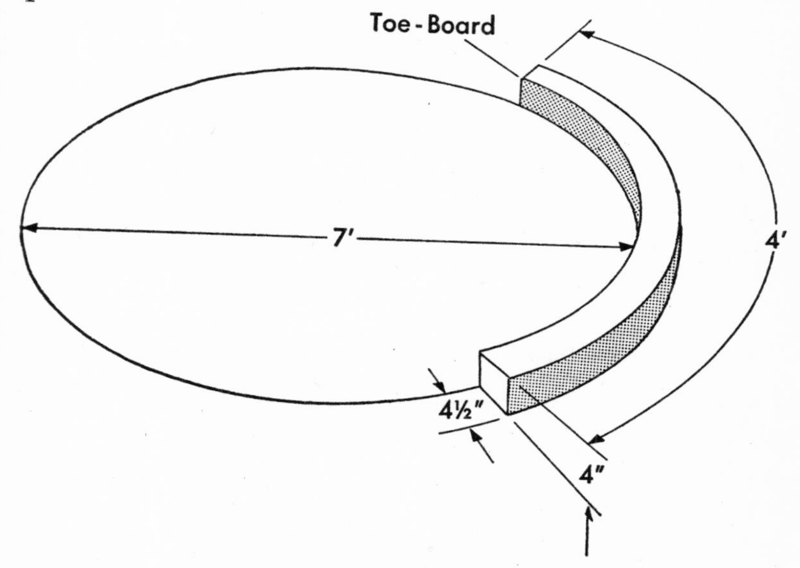

Figure 54. Toe-Board.

SHOT PUT TOE-BOARD AND PROTECTOR. A toe-board is an expensive piece of circular equipment which fits around a 4 foot segment of the circumference of the shot circle (see Fig. 54). A simple and inexpensive protector can be made from rough lumber heavy enough to withstand the bumps from the shot. The protector should be 10 to 15 feet long, 6 inches high, and 2 feet wide (see Fig. 55). This protector can be placed in front of and a short distance away from the toe-board.

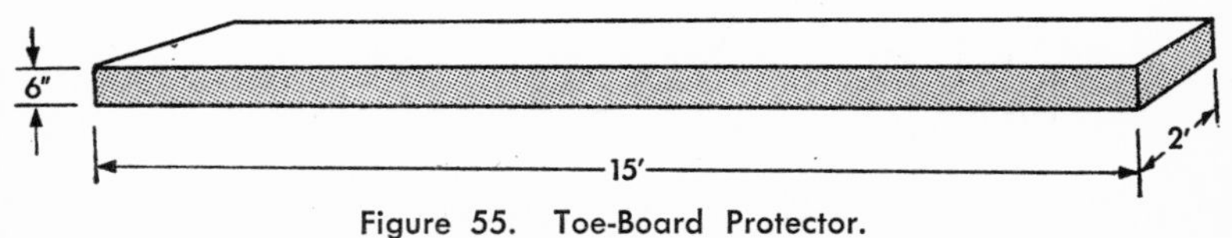

Figure 55. Toe-Board Protector.

TRACK JUDGES' STAND. A series of steps such as those shown in Figure 56 permits judges of finishes at track meets a clear view in determining places at the race's finish. Station those picking the winner on the first step, second place selectors on the second step, and so on.

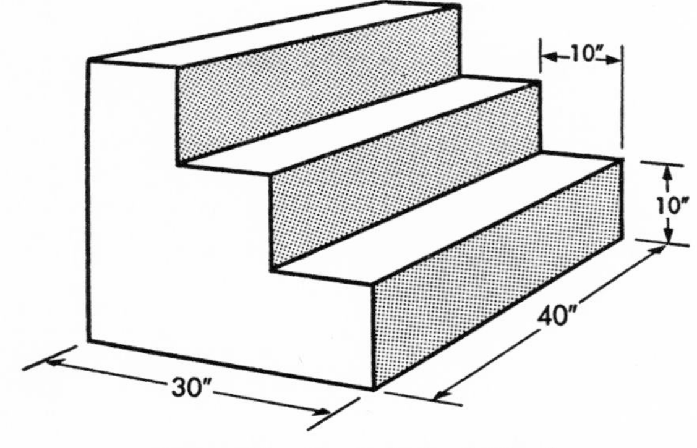

Figure 56. Track Judges' Stand.

STARTER'S PISTOL SUBSTITUTE. As a substitute for a starter's pistol a device such as that illustrated in Figure 57 is easily made and very practical. Two pieces of smooth wood about 10 inches long are hinged at one end and handles are fastened on the outside of each piece of wood. When quickly closed, this device makes a sharp, distinct noise quite similar to the report of gun and is very satisfactory for starting races.

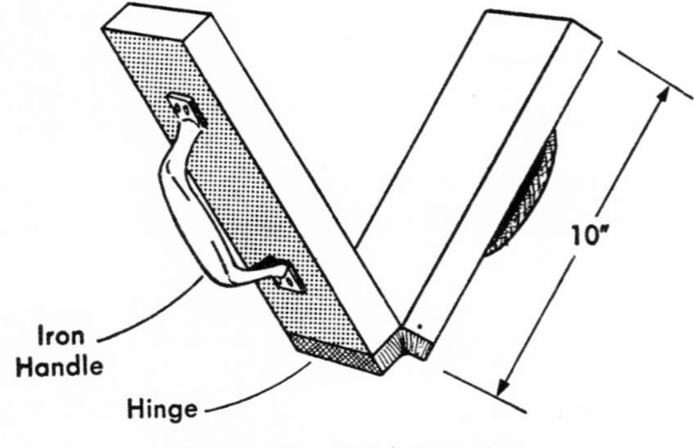

Figure 57. Pistol Substitute.

RULES CONTAINER. Some beginning instructors experience difficulty in keeping in mind the rules for the many games promoted during the year. For these persons and for students a rules container similar to the one shown in Figure 58 is a valuable aid. This can be made of metal or wood and hung on the wall or some other convenient spot. In this container, rules cards of fairly heavy cardboard can be kept. A brief summary of the rules should be typed up and pasted on the cardboards. When playing a particular game, the rules card for this sport can be pulled from the group and placed at the front. Then, if questions arise, referrals can be made to the rules placard.

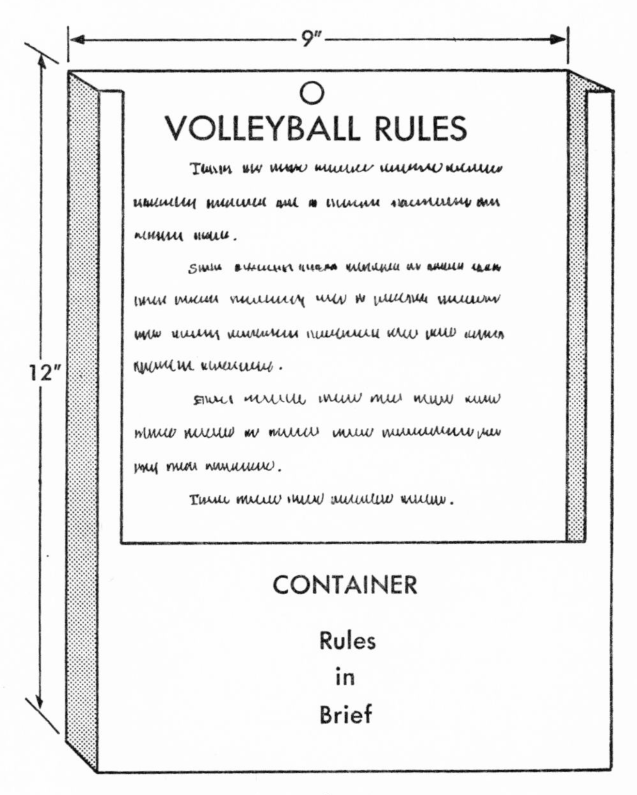

Figure 58. Rules Container.

Some intramural departments print a summary of rules on game score cards and keep them in a rules container. A similar set of brief rules might be attached to the respective standards or placed on walls near the respective playing courts.

PUBLIC ADDRESS SYSTEM. Some intramural and physical education buildings have built-in public address systems. Others have battery powered, portable systems. The latter are very practical; they can be strapped around a person's neck and carried in front or at the side of the body. A handle trigger is squeezed to operate the public address. Portable PA's are useful for calling heats at swimming and track meets, for informing contestants at wrestling and other matches, and for making announcements at corecreation sessions or other functions where large numbers of students and faculty are gathered.

TAPE RECORDER. Tape recorders, although not too "practical" because of their cost, can be utilized for protest hearings, championship intramural games, reviewing of activities, and facilities inspections.

A recorder placed in a protest hearing room records the entire discussion. The protest board can replay the tape several times before making its decision, and the I-M office has a permanent record of each protest presentation for future reference.

Play-by-play accounts of intramural championship games can be taped by radio, television, or journalism students or varsity coaches and presented to the winning team. Copies can also be kept by the I-M office for future publicity purposes.

Portable tape recorders, carried in the pocket or on a strap over the shoulder, are useful devices for a supervisor to have when reviewing activities or inspecting facilities. As a supervisor observes games, meets, and tournaments or inspects facilities for possible repairs and changes, he makes verbal note of what he sees into a small mouthpiece. Upon the supervisor's return to the I-M office, a secretary or the supervisor can make a written transcript of the recording.

VARIATIONS. A number of the suggestions for practical aids that have been given are capable of modification under varying circumstances. As one instance, the volleyball judge's stand may be occupied by two judges, sitting back to back, where two volleyball courts are laid out end-to-end and are in use at the same time. Each official then has a set of number signs which rest between his knees. When two or more volleyball courts are adjacent to each other, another modification is favored; it is then more feasible to string two or more nets on one rope (or wire) which is stretched from the walls of the gymnasium across the floor at the official playing height. With a large number of courts, this arrangement simplifies the preparation of the courts for play as the moving of many upright stands with heavy bases is a laborious job. Still another idea is to use plastic signs for numbers. These signs are neater and more durable than the heavy cardboard signs.

Under necessity, many improvisations of equipment are possible. Also, successful modifications can be made in the actual play of the game itself, examples being one-court basketball, sideline basketball, and one-goal soccer.

SUMMARY

1. An intramural sports program is greatly improved by the adoption of certain mechanical devices which demand little time, practically no effort, and a minimum of expense.
2. The different departments of most institutions, such as industrial arts and art, are usually willing to co-operate in the completion of practical projects.
3. These devices include a volleyball flash-scoring device and officials' platform, a basketball flash-scoring device, basketball central timer, diving flash-score scards, playing area assignment board, court reservation board, clip boards, corner flags for playing fields, net standards, marking equipment, rules container, frame for marking softball batter's box, bat rack, circle-o-graph for marking targets, track judges' stand, starter's pistol substitute, shot and discus circle marker, shot put guard, shot put toe-board protector, public address system, and tape recorder.

4. Typed or printed rules on index cards or on game score cards, and placed in a container, attached to standards, or taped to a wall are helpful for beginning instructors, coaches, umpires, and players. Every intramural department should have summaries readily available for each sport sponsored by the department.
5. Public address systems are useful for functions where large numbers are present and at meets, such as swimming, track, and wrestling, in order to inform both spectators and participants of the results of the activities.

16

Tournament Charts and Tables

The materials in this chapter will assist intramural, tournament, and other recreation directors in figuring points, percentages, time periods, seedings, byes, and handicaps. Many of the forms, charts, and tables are standard and can be utilized in all programs.

A study of these materials, together with the information in Chapter 9, will help the student understand many of the details involved in organizing leagues, meets, and tournaments, all of which are essential to successful intramural competition. The intramural director or any other person conducting competition is greatly assisted by these ready references. In many instances, a quick referral provides the answer or presents a guide to tournament construction and other competitive program operations.

The experienced intramural director or other recreation supervisor knows that convenient forms, charts, and tables speed up program administration. These media are shortcuts for repetitive office routines. If the director must refigure points, percentages, time periods, seedings, byes, or handicaps each time competition is arranged, he is endlessly wasting time and increasing the margin for errors.

In some of the larger programs, student assistants, student managers, or secretaries can effectively arrange tournament and other competitive procedures with the use of these office aids. The director of intramural sports can then spend his time on important matters such as program expansion, research, evaluation, and supervision.

Tournament calculator. The tournament calculator (Fig. 59) can be used to determine the number of rounds, byes, and games required for single elimination, double elimination, and round robin tournaments, of from 3 to 32 entries. (Formulas for determining this type of information are given in Chapter 9, but since these formulas are frequently forgotten or misunderstood, this calculator offers a ready reference and its use will minimize errors in the construction of tournaments.) A quick survey of this chart indicates which type of competition is best suited for the specific situation in terms of available time and facilities and number of entries to be organized. If there are 32 teams for a tournament and the intramural director plans to use a round robin, the calculator shows that a 32-team round robin requires 496 games.

Since it is highly impractical to play this many games, reference to the chart serves as a guide to the number of round robin games to be played when 32 teams are subdivided into eight 4-team leagues, four 8-team leagues, or two 16-team leagues. Four-team round robins require 6 games for each league; therefore, eight 4-team leagues total 48 games, considerably fewer than 496 games for a 32-team round robin.

If these 32 entries are arranged in four 8-team leagues, the total number of games is 112. The tournament calculator indicates that 28 games must be played to complete each 8-team round robin. Four (no. of leagues) times 28 games (no. per league) equals 112 games. The tournament director determines how many games can be played on the basis of available time, facilities, and equipment; and, then, with the aid of the calculator, he selects eight 4-team leagues, four 8-team leagues, or another tournament plan.

If there are 13 entries for a tennis tournament and it seems best to run a single elimination tournament, the calculator shows that 13 entries require 4 rounds and 12 games; for a 10-entry double elimination tournament, 8 or 9 rounds and 18 or 19 games.

NUMBER OF ENTRIES	SINGLE ELIMINATION				DOUBLE ELIMINATION				ROUND ROBIN		
	No. of Rounds	No. of Byes		No. of Games	No. of Rounds	No. of Byes		No. of Games	No. of Rounds	No. of Byes	No. of Games
		Top	Bottom			Top	Bottom				
3	2	0	1	2	4 or 5	0	1	4 or 5	3	3	3
4	2	0	0	3	4 or 5	0	0	6 or 7	3	0	6
5	3	1	2	4	6 or 7	1	2	8 or 9	5	5	10
6	3	1	1	5	6 or 7	1	1	10 or 11	5	0	15
7	3	0	1	6	6 or 7	0	1	12 or 13	7	7	21
8	3	0	0	7	6 or 7	0	0	14 or 15	7	0	28
9	4	3	4	8	8 or 9	3	4	16 or 17	9	9	36
10	4	3	3	9	8 or 9	3	3	18 or 19	9	0	45
11	4	2	3	10	8 or 9	2	3	20 or 21	11	11	55
12	4	2	2	11	8 or 9	2	2	22 or 23	11	0	66
13	4	1	2	12	8 or 9	1	2	24 or 25	13	13	78
14	4	1	1	13	8 or 9	1	1	26 or 27	13	0	91
15	4	0	1	14	8 or 9	0	1	28 or 29	15	15	105
16	4	0	0	15	8 or 9	0	0	30 or 31	15	0	120
17	5	7	8	16	10 or 11	7	8	32 or 33	17	17	136
18	5	7	7	17	10 or 11	7	7	34 or 35	17	0	153
19	5	6	7	18	10 or 11	6	7	36 or 37	19	19	171
20	5	6	6	19	10 or 11	6	6	38 or 39	19	0	190
21	5	5	6	20	10 or 11	5	6	40 or 41	21	21	210
22	5	5	5	21	10 or 11	5	5	42 or 43	21	0	231
23	5	4	5	22	10 or 11	4	5	44 or 45	23	23	253
24	5	4	4	23	10 or 11	4	4	46 or 47	23	0	276
25	5	3	4	24	10 or 11	3	4	48 or 49	25	25	300
26	5	3	3	25	10 or 11	3	3	50 or 51	25	0	325
27	5	2	3	26	10 or 11	2	3	52 or 53	27	27	351
28	5	2	2	27	10 or 11	2	2	54 or 55	27	0	378
29	5	1	2	28	10 or 11	1	2	56 or 57	29	29	406
30	5	1	1	29	10 or 11	1	1	58 or 59	29	0	435
31	5	0	1	30	10 or 11	0	1	60 or 61	31	31	465
32	5	0	0	31	10 or 11	0	0	62 or 63	31	0	496

Figure 59. Tournament Calculator for Single and Double Elimination and Round Robin Tournaments.

Number of Entries	Number of Byes	LINES		Number of Entries	Number of Byes
3	1	4	Use 4-Line Draw Sheets	33	31
4	0	None		34	30
5	3	1,5,8		35	29
6	2	1,8	Use 8-Line Draw Sheets	36	28
7	1	8		37	27
8	0	None		38	26
9	7	1,4,8,9,12,13,16		39	25
10	6	1,4,8,9,13,16		40	24
11	5	1,8,9,13,16		41	23
12	4	1,8,9,16	Use 16-Line Draw Sheets	42	22
13	3	1,9,16		43	21
14	2	1,16		44	20
15	1	16		45	19
16	0	None		46	18
17	15	1,4,5,8,9,13,16,17,20,21,24,25,28,29,32		47	17
18	14	1,4,5,8,9,13,16,17,20,24,25,28,29,32		48	16
19	13	1,4,8,9,13,16,17,20,24,25,28,29,32		49	15
20	12	1,4,8,9,13,16,17,20,24,25,29,32		50	14
21	11	1,4,8,9,16,17,20,24,25,29,32		51	13
22	10	1,4,8,9,16,17,24,25,29,32		52	12
23	9	1,8,9,16,17,24,25,29,32		53	11
24	8	1,8,9,16,17,24,25,32		54	10
25	7	1,8,16,17,24,25,32		55	9
26	6	1,8,16,17,25,32		56	8
27	5	1,16,17,25,32	Use 32-Line Draw Sheets	57	7
28	4	1,16,17,32		58	6
29	3	1,17,32		59	5
30	2	1,32		60	4
31	1	32		61	3
32	0	None		62	2
				63	1
				64	0

Figure 60. Number and Placement of Byes on

PLACEMENT OF BYES CHART. Positioning of byes on a tournament draw sheet is a difficult task for many confronted with tournament construction. The chart shown in Figure 60 will help immeasurably to expedite this task. This chart follows the "listed byes" technique of tournament structuring, but the "implied byes" method is possible by eliminating the word bye and advancing a team to the second round in a bracket corresponding to a bye position.

From a study of this table, the intramural director can readily determine how many lines his draw sheet should have, since the number depends upon the number of entries and byes. For example, the table shows that if there are 14 entries he will need a 16-line draw sheet and should

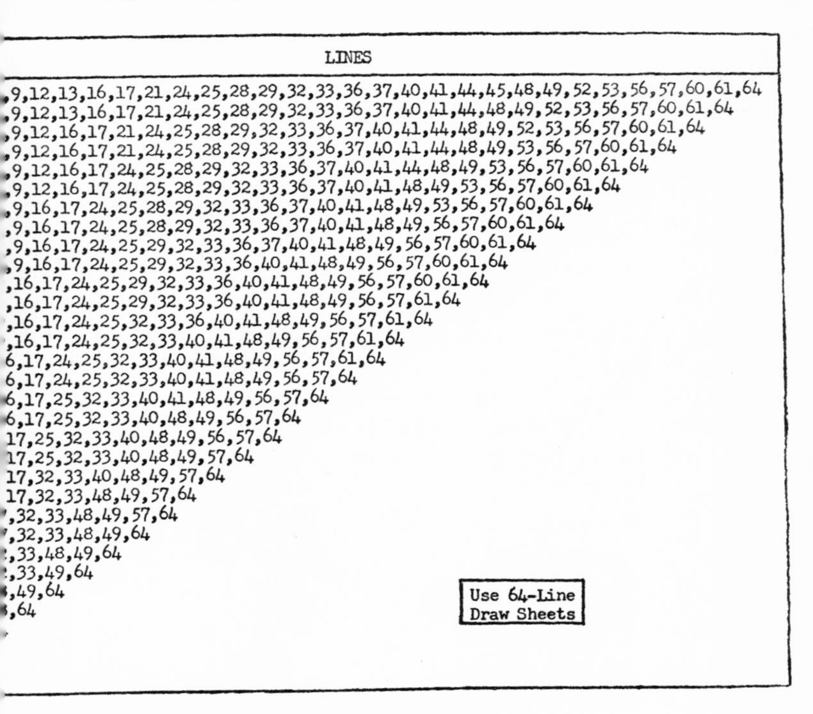

LINES
,9,12,13,16,17,21,24,25,28,29,32,33,36,37,40,41,44,45,48,49,52,53,56,57,60,61,64
,9,12,13,16,17,21,24,25,28,29,32,33,36,37,40,41,44,48,49,52,53,56,57,60,61,64
,9,12,16,17,21,24,25,28,29,32,33,36,37,40,41,44,48,49,52,53,56,57,60,61,64
,9,12,16,17,21,24,25,28,29,32,33,36,37,40,41,44,48,49,53,56,57,60,61,64
,9,12,16,17,24,25,28,29,32,33,36,37,40,41,44,48,49,53,56,57,60,61,64
,9,12,16,17,24,25,28,29,32,33,36,37,40,41,48,49,53,56,57,60,61,64
,9,16,17,24,25,28,29,32,33,36,37,40,41,48,49,53,56,57,60,61,64
,9,16,17,24,25,28,29,32,33,36,37,40,41,48,49,56,57,60,61,64
,9,16,17,24,25,29,32,33,36,37,40,41,48,49,56,57,60,61,64
,9,16,17,24,25,29,32,33,36,40,41,48,49,56,57,60,61,64
,16,17,24,25,29,32,33,36,40,41,48,49,56,57,60,61,64
,16,17,24,25,29,32,33,36,40,41,48,49,56,57,61,64
,16,17,24,25,32,33,36,40,41,48,49,56,57,61,64
,16,17,24,25,32,33,40,41,48,49,56,57,61,64
6,17,24,25,32,33,40,41,48,49,56,57,61,64
6,17,24,25,32,33,40,41,48,49,56,57,64
6,17,25,32,33,40,41,48,49,56,57,64
6,17,25,32,33,40,48,49,56,57,64
17,25,32,33,40,48,49,56,57,64
17,25,32,33,40,48,49,57,64
17,32,33,40,48,49,57,64
17,32,33,48,49,57,64
,32,33,48,49,57,64
,32,33,48,49,64
,33,48,49,64
,33,49,64
,49,64
,64

Use 64-Line Draw Sheets

ment Draw Sheet: Three to Sixty-Four Entrants.

place the 2 byes on lines 1 and 16. For eleven entries there must be 5 byes; on a 16-line draw sheet he places these byes on lines 1, 8, 9, 13, and 16. For 8 entries he needs an 8-line draw sheet, no byes to consider.

This placement of byes chart conforms to the principles of establishing byes as described in Chapter 9. All byes appear in the first round, and they are positioned symmetrically to give each tournament draw sheet a neat appearance. The extra bye is placed in the bottom half of the tournament when the number of byes is uneven. It is possible to obtain prepared draw sheets from a commercial concern should the intramural director not wish to make up his own.

SINGLE ELIMINATION TOURNAMENT DRAW SHEETS. For ready reference, single elimination tournament draw sheets are worked out in Figure 61a, b, and c, for 3 to 16 teams. These draw sheets indicate teams or entrants by letters (A, B, and so on), and show whether or not byes are necessary. (The byes on the draw sheets are placed in accordance with the placement of byes chart, Fig. 60.) For three and four teams or entrants, the tournament requires two rounds before a winner is decided; for from five to eight teams or entrants, 3 rounds and nine to sixteen teams or entrants, 4 rounds. In using these draw sheets the tournament supervisor merely substitutes team names or player names for the letters and his tournament is immediately set up. Copies can be mimeographed, then, for distribution among teams and participants.

How to construct draw sheets such as these has been explained in Chapter 9.

DOUBLE ELIMINATION TOURNAMENT DRAW SHEETS. Double elimination tournament draw sheets are more complicated in their construction than single elimination tournament draw sheets mainly because of the second tournament which evolves for the players who lose their first game and also because of the placement of byes. Though how to construct this kind of draw sheet is explained in Chapter 9, draw sheets are worked out in this book for from 3 to 16 entrants (see Fig. 62, a-h) for tournament supervisors.

The double elimination tournament draw sheets are arranged according to the back-to-back method and with implied byes. First names of individuals have been used so that winners and losers can be readily identified. Those who plan to run a double elimination tournament for teams can substitute the names of the teams for the names of individuals noted in the first round. In these draw sheets the winners of the first round advance to the right; the losers follow the broken lines and arrows to the left. At the completion of both tournaments the winners play. The block in the upper right hand corner shows a final play-off if it is necessary to have one (see page 392 for explanation).

THREE

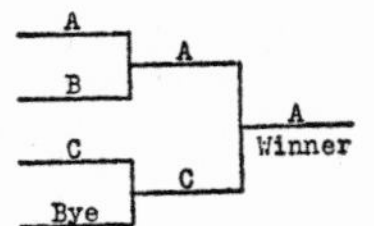

FOUR

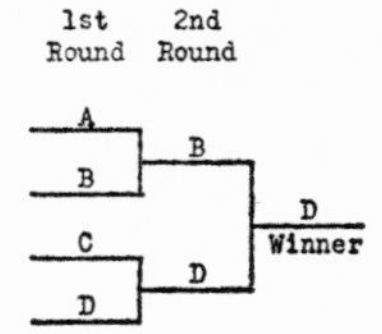

FIVE

SIX

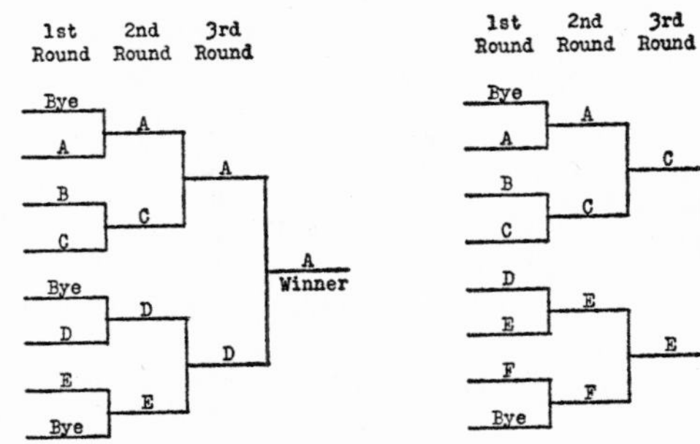

SEVEN

EIGHT

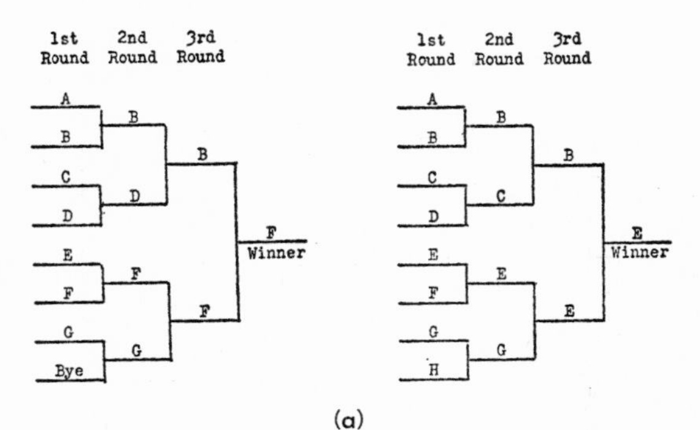

(a)

Figure 61. Single Elimination Tournament Draw Sheets: Three to Sixteen Teams or Entrants.

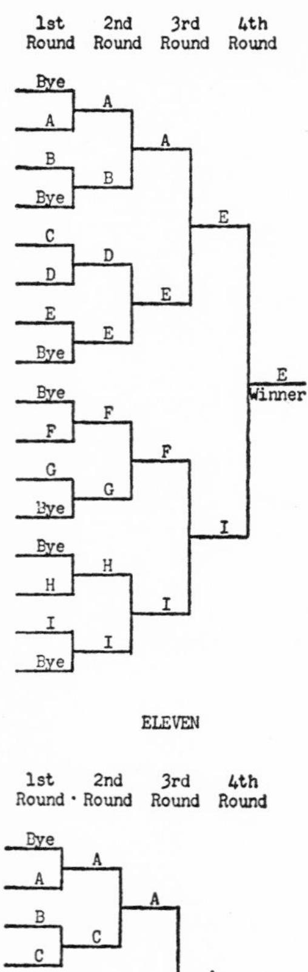

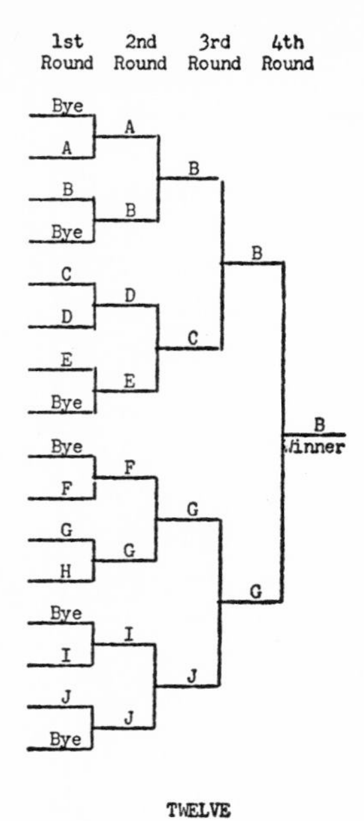

ELEVEN

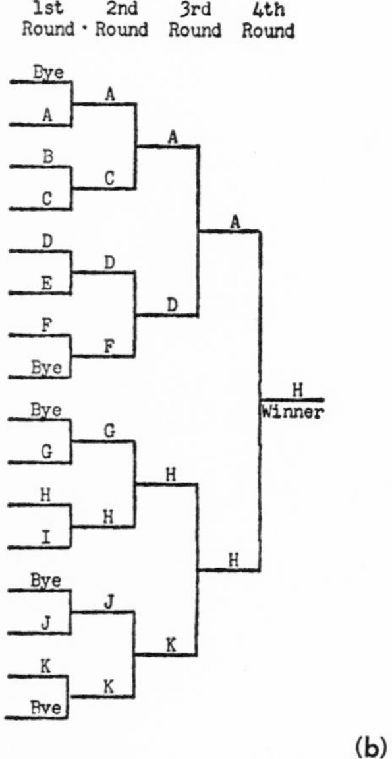

TWELVE

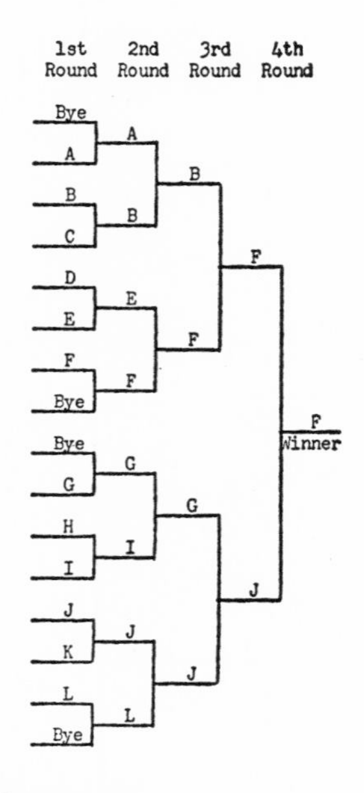

(b)

Figure 61. (Continued.)

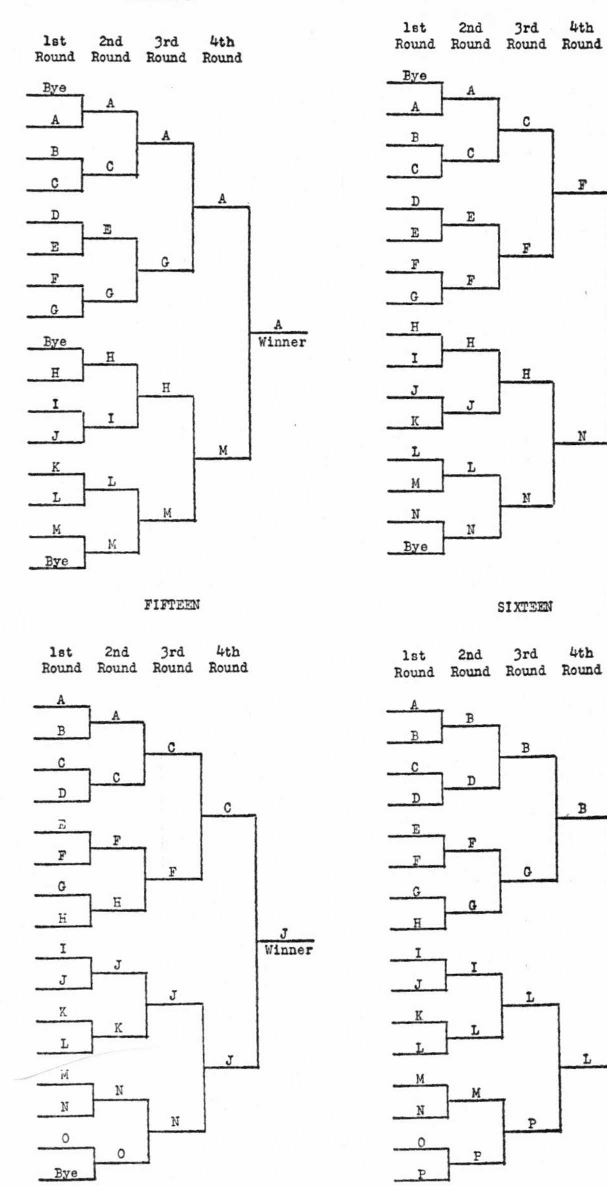

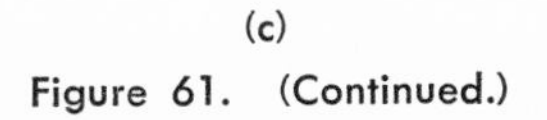

(c)

Figure 61. (Continued.)

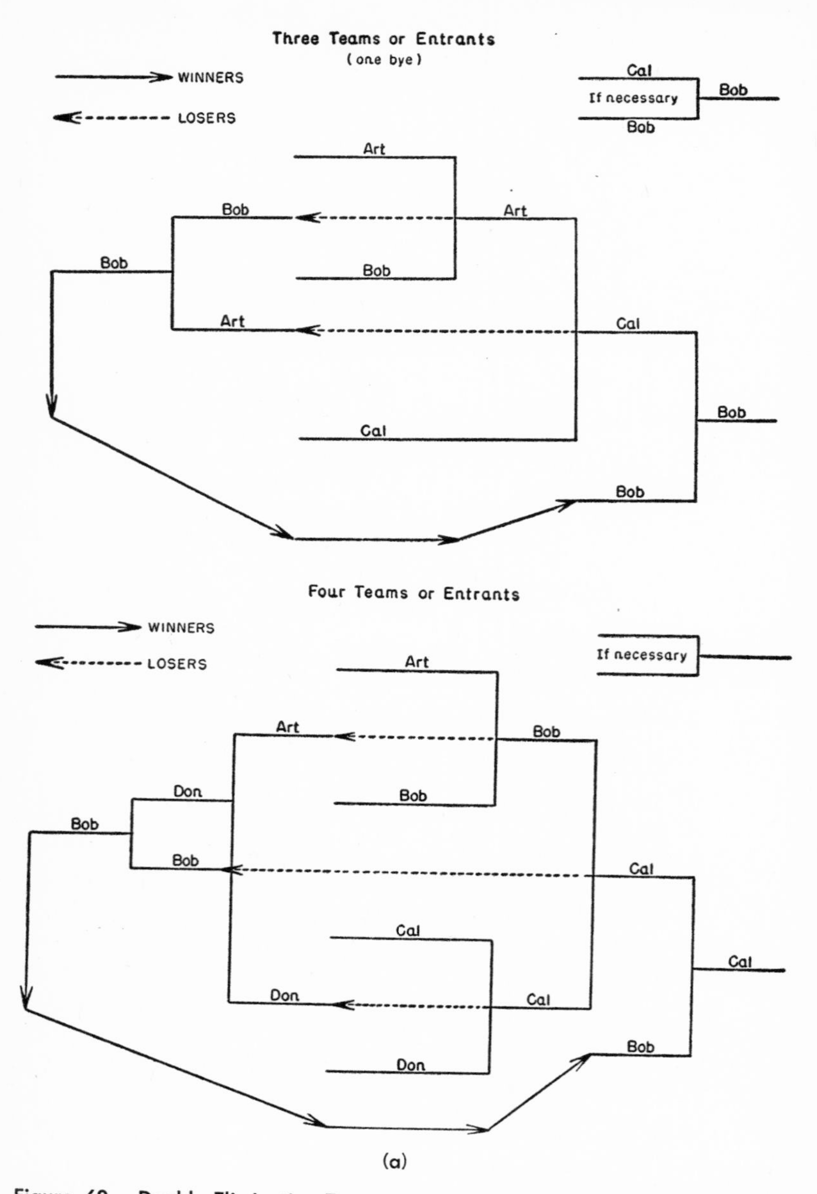

(a)

Figure 62. Double Elimination Tournament Draw Sheets, Back-to-Back Method with Implied Byes: Three to Sixteen Teams or Entrants.

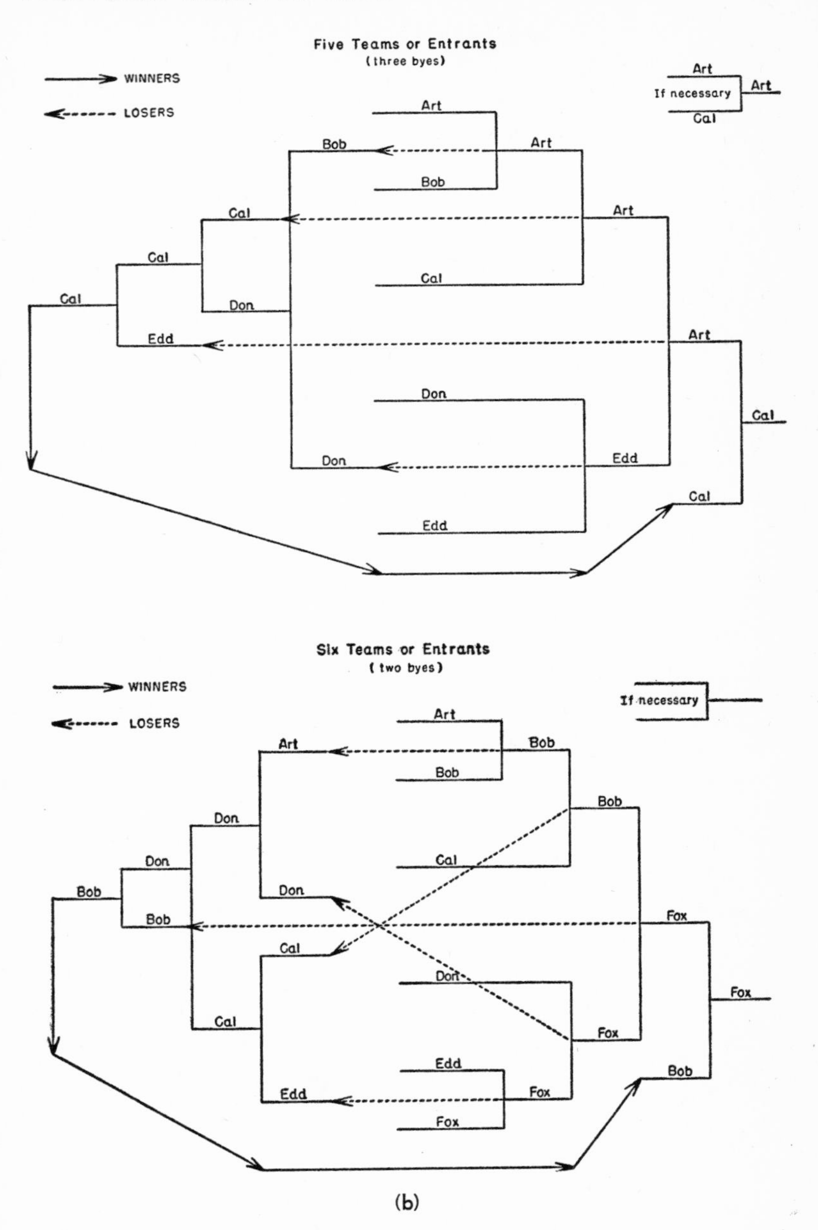

(b)

Figure 62. (Continued.)

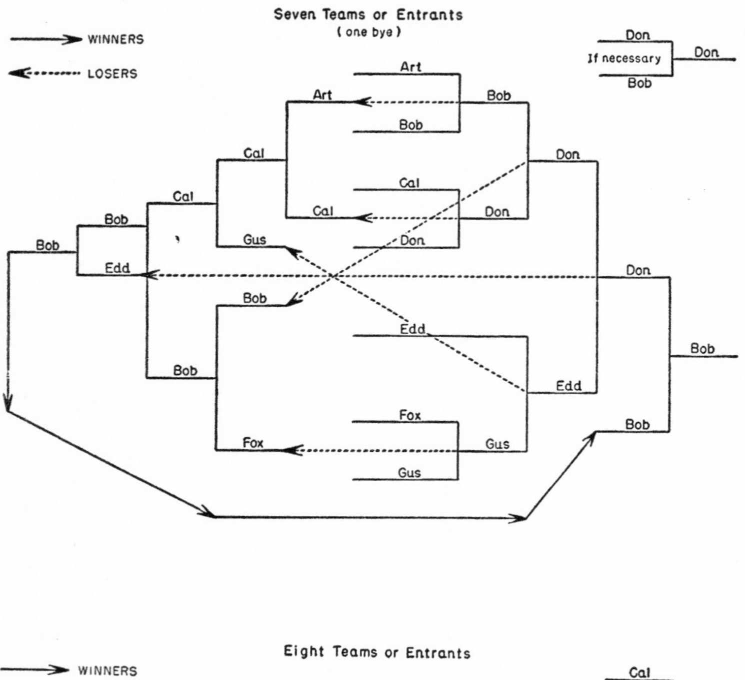

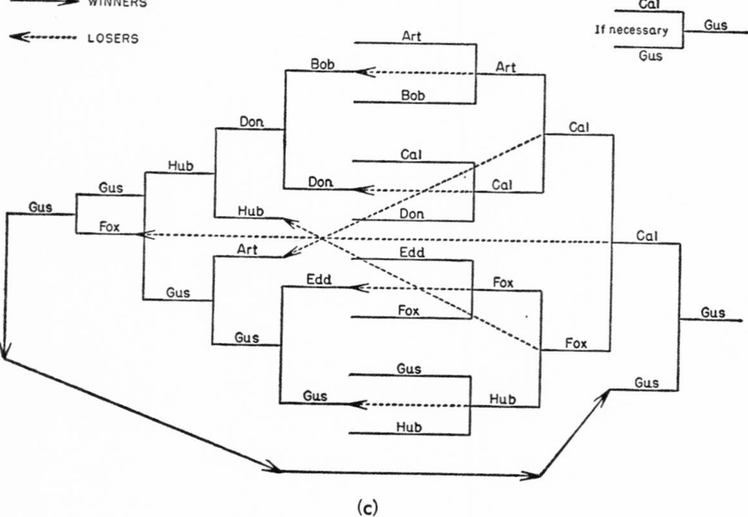

(c)

Figure 62. (Continued.)

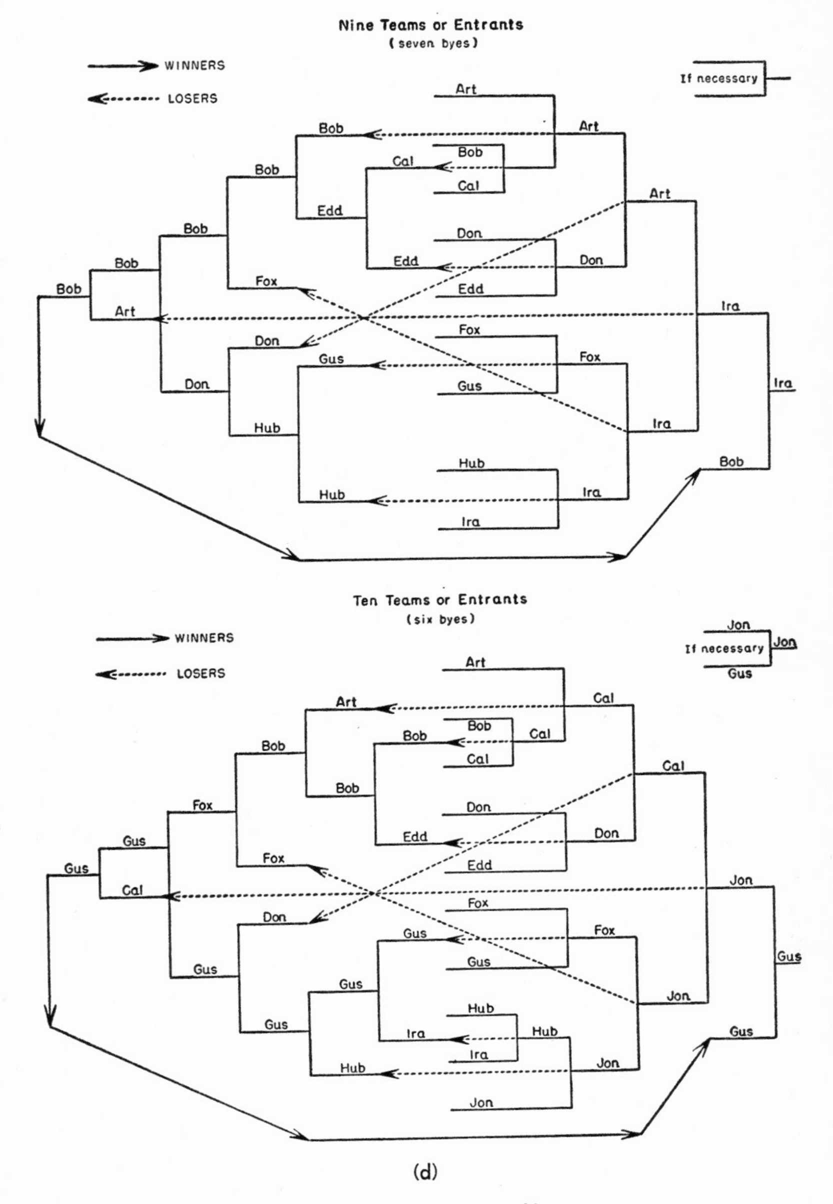

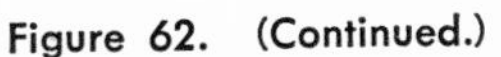
(d)

Figure 62. (Continued.)

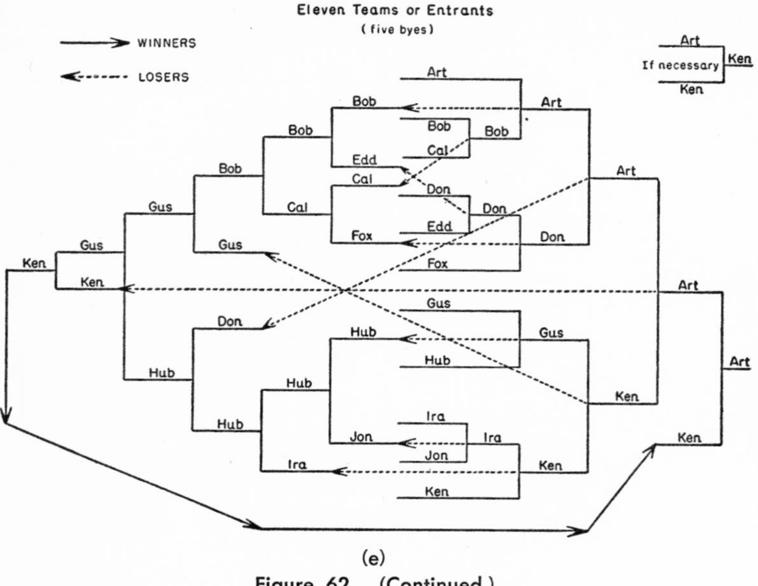

(e)

Figure 62. (Continued.)

A detailed explanation of this draw sheet may be helpful since this tournament and the succeeding double elimination tournaments are more complicated than the preceding ones. With a double elimination tournament of eleven games or entrants, there are five byes—Art, Fox, Gus, Hub, and Ken. These do not play in the first round. In the first round Bob plays Cal; Bob wins and advances to the right and *Cal* follows the broken line to the left. Don plays Edd; *Edd* loses and moves to the left. Ira plays Jon; *Jon* loses and moves to the left. In the second round, Art plays Bob and wins; therefore moves to the right. *Bob* follows the broken line to the left to find Edd his partner for the first round of the "losers" tournament. Don plays *Fox* who loses and moves to the left to meet Cal. Gus and Hub meet; *Hub* loses and moves to the left to play Jon. *Ira* plays Ken and loses. Ira waits until the second round of the losers before he plays.

In the third round, Art and Don—Gus and Ken meet. *Don* and *Gus* lose and follow the broken line to the left to meet Hub and Bob respectively (winners of the second round of the losers tournament) in the third round of the losers. In the fourth round of the winners *Ken* loses and moves to the left to play Gus who has won his contest with Hub. Art wins the main tournament; Ken wins the second tournament. Now Ken advances to the right to meet Art for the play-off, which Art wins. (Should Ken win, an additional contest is necessary because this would be Art's first loss. The bracket in the upper right would obtain then—this shows Ken the winner of the over-all.)

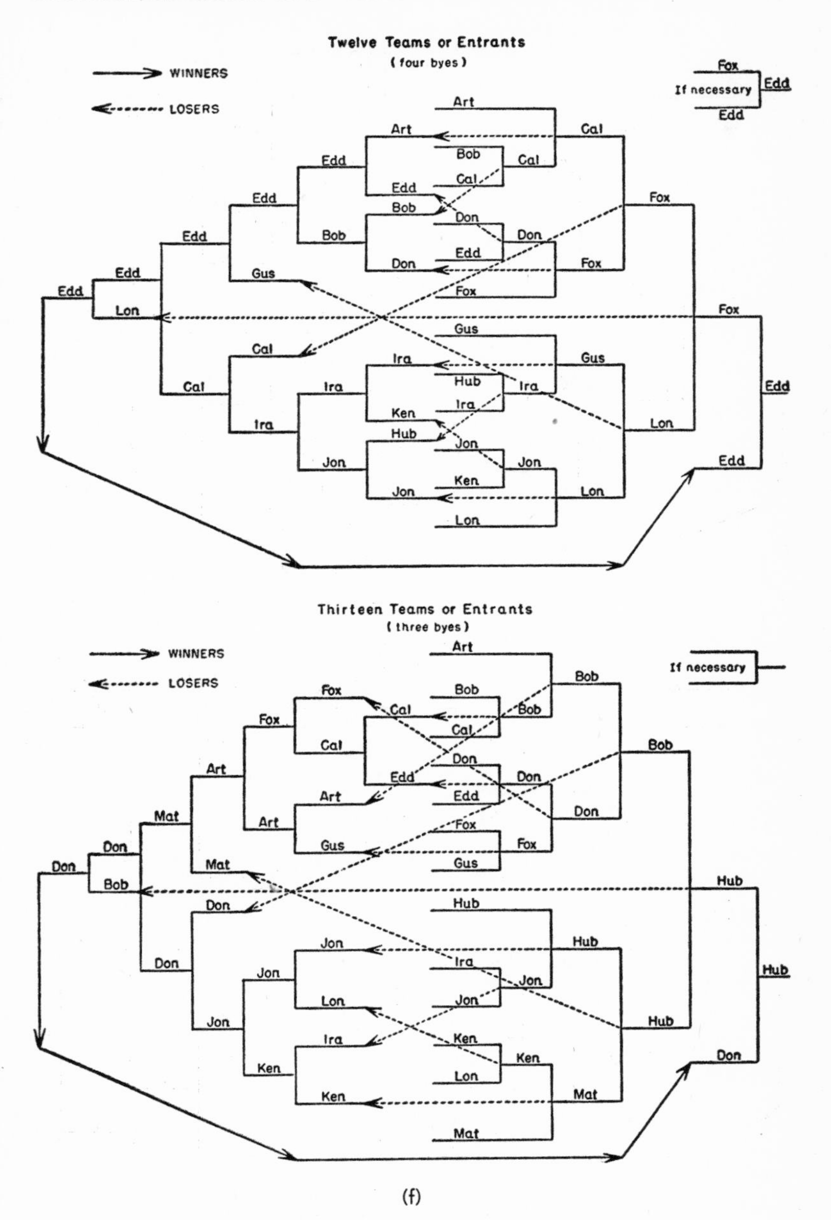

(f)

Figure 62. (Continued.)

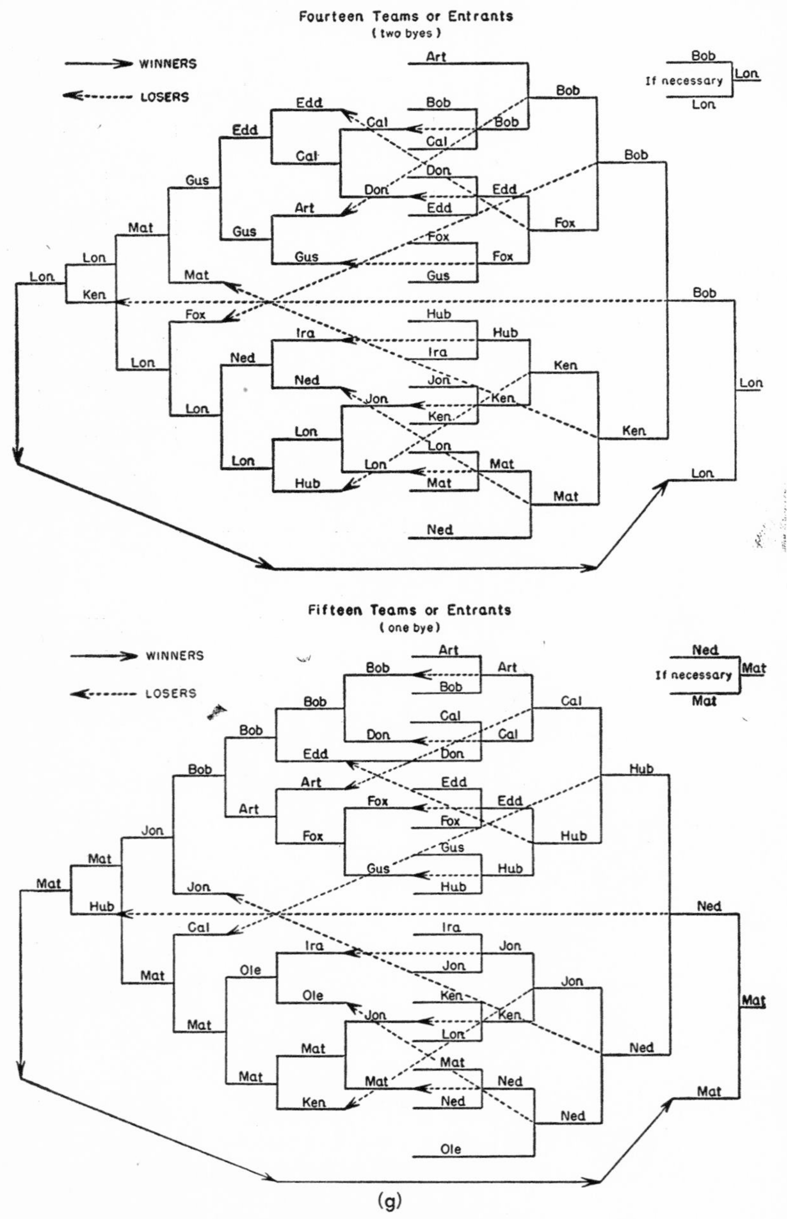

(g)

Figure 62. (Continued.)

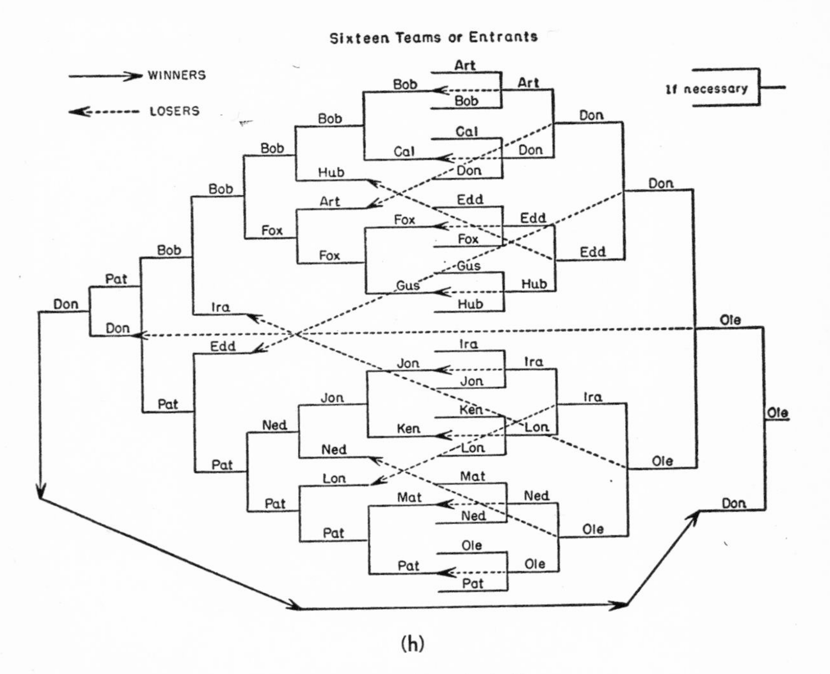

(h)

Figure 62. (Concluded.)

SEEDING PLACEMENT CHART. Where to place seeded players in a tournament is often a problem to directors of tournaments. Though placement was discussed in Chapter 9, Figure 63 solves the problem of placement by presenting the information in condensed form. In this figure the *maximum* number of seeded players for 4, 8, 16, and 32 entries is placed in proper position on the entry brackets for the first round of a tournament. For 4 entries, two players should be seeded; 8 entries, 4 players; 16 entries, 8 players; 32 entries, 16 players. As mentioned before, these are maximum numbers. It is not necessary to seed the maximum number on a particular draw sheet; therefore, with fewer than the maximum number, higher numbers shown on the brackets can be omitted.

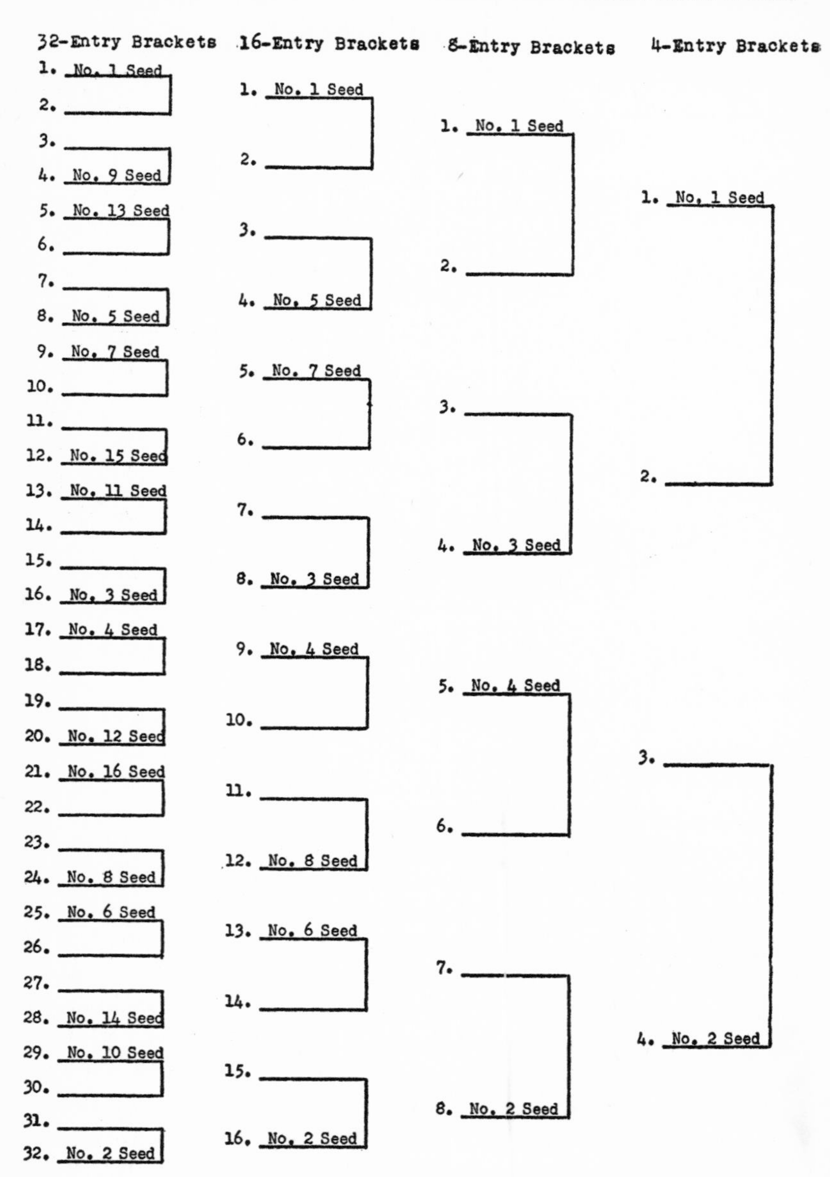

Figure 63. Placement of Maximum Number of Seedings for Four, Eight, Sixteen, and Thirty-Two Entrants.

TABLES OF ROUND ROBIN SCHEDULES. The round robin tables (Figs. 64, a and b) show the schedule for each date or round for 3 through 16 teams or entries. The tables indicate the number of the bowling alley, court, or field and are designed so that team play is distributed as evenly as possible over different fields, courts, or alleys. The numbers which appear for each date are teams scheduled to play on that date. For an uneven number of teams or entries, the number (team) receiving a bye is noted for each round. In drawing up a league schedule and using the information from these tables, all the director has to do is to substitute team names for the numbers.

These round robin tables are excellent time savers and are particularly helpful in organizing "quickie" tournaments such as the "Play 'Til You Win" or Lombard tournaments. This type of competition is usually arranged on the touch football field, softball diamond, basketball court, or bowling alley where numerous students are practicing on a free play basis. Teams are chosen on the spot and shortened games are scheduled for immediate play. The round robin tables facilitate arranging these schedules because it is not necessary to apply the rotation or graph round robin procedures. Team names or numbers are easily substituted for the numbers listed in the tables.

The tables can also be used in conjunction with the tournament calculator in Figure 59. Rather than take the time to compute or count the total number of games necessary to complete a round robin, a quick reference to the calculator will provide this type of information.

The round robin tournament is the most objective method of measuring the ability of competing teams. The greatest disadvantage is the amount of time required to complete it.

Generally, round robin tournaments are not used for more than 16 entries because it takes too much time to complete them. In the case of bowling, however, where there are 16 or more available alleys, and where a tournament can be extended through several months, a round robin tournament of 16 entries is often scheduled.

Teams or Entries	Alleys	Court or Field	1st Date	2nd Date	3rd Date	4th Date	5th Date	6th Date	7th Date	8th Date	9th Date	10th Date	11th Date
3	1 - 2 —	I —	1-2 3Bye	1-3 2Bye	2-3 1Bye	—	—	—	—	—	—	—	—
4	1 - 2 3 - 4	I II	1-2 3-4	1-3 2-4	2-3 1-4	—	—	—	—	—	—	—	—
5	1 - 2 3 - 4 —	I II —	1-2 3-4 5Bye	4-5 2-3 1Bye	1-3 2-5 4Bye	3-5 1-4 2Bye	2-4 1-5 3Bye	—	—	—	—	—	—
6	1 - 2 3 - 4 5 - 6	I II III	1-2 3-4 5-6	4-6 2-5 1-3	3-5 1-4 2-6	2-3 1-6 4-5	1-5 3-6 2-4	—	—	—	—	—	—
7	1 - 2 3 - 4 5 - 6 —	I II III —	3-6 1-5 2-7 4Bye	5-7 2-4 1-3 6Bye	4-5 3-7 2-6 1Bye	3-4 1-2 5-6 7Bye	1-7 4-6 2-5 3Bye	2-3 6-7 1-4 5Bye	1-6 3-5 4-7 2Bye	—	—	—	—
8	1 - 2 3 - 4 5 - 6 7 - 8	I II III IV	1-2 3-4 5-6 7-8	6-8 5-7 2-4 1-3	4-5 1-8 3-7 2-6	3-6 2-7 1-5 4-8	1-7 4-6 3-8 2-5	2-3 5-8 1-4 6-7	4-7 1-6 2-8 3-5	—	—	—	—
9	1 - 2 3 - 4 5 - 6 7 - 8 —	I II III IV —	5-6 3-4 1-2 7-8 9Bye	4-7 6-9 1-8 2-5 3Bye	8-9 1-5 2-6 3-7 4Bye	2-7 4-9 3-8 1-6 5Bye	3-5 6-8 7-9 2-4 1Bye	2-8 1-7 4-5 3-9 6Bye	3-6 5-8 2-9 1-4 7Bye	4-8 6-7 1-3 5-9 2Bye	1-9 2-3 5-7 4-6 8Bye	—	—
10	1 - 2 3 - 4 5 - 6 7 - 8 9 - 10	I II III IV V	1-10 2-9 3-8 4-7 5-6	7-2 6-3 5-4 10-9 8-1	9-8 1-7 6-2 5-3 4-10	4-3 10-8 9-7 6-1 2-5	10-6 7-5 2-1 8-4 9-3	5-9 8-6 7-10 3-2 1-4	3-1 9-4 8-5 7-6 10-2	6-4 5-10 1-9 2-8 3-7	8-7 4-2 10-3 1-5 6-9	—	—
11	1 - 2 3 - 4 5 - 6 7 - 8 9 - 10 —	I II III IV V —	5-6 3-4 9-10 1-2 7-8 11Bye	10-11 8-9 4-5 2-3 6-7 1Bye	3-5 4-6 8-10 7-9 1-11 2Bye	4-7 1-5 3-6 8-11 2-10 9Bye	2-4 9-11 5-7 6-8 1-3 10Bye	1-10 2-7 6-11 4-9 5-8 3Bye	2-8 6-10 1-4 3-11 5-9 7Bye	1-9 3-10 7-11 4-8 2-5 6Bye	4-11 1-8 2-6 7-10 3-9 5Bye	6-9 1-7 3-8 5-10 2-11 4Bye	3-7 5-11 2-9 1-6 4-10 8Bye
12	1 - 2 3 - 4 5 - 6 7 - 8 9 - 10 11 - 12	I II III IV V VI	1-2 3-4 5-6 7-8 9-10 11-12	10-11 8-9 1-12 4-5 6-7 2-3	3-5 2-12 8-10 7-9 1-11 4-6	4-7 1-5 3-6 2-10 9-12 8-11	6-8 10-12 9-11 1-3 2-4 5-7	3-12 4-9 2-7 6-11 5-8 1-10	2-8 6-10 1-4 5-9 3-11 7-12	1-9 7-11 3-10 6-12 2-5 4-8	4-11 2-6 5-12 1-8 7-10 3-9	6-9 1-7 2-11 4-12 3-8 5-10	8-12 5-11 4-10 3-7 1-6 2-9

Figure 64(a). Tables of Round Robin Schedules. Teams or entries, 3-12.

Teams or Entries	Alleys	Court or Field	1st Date	2nd Date	3rd Date	4th Date	5th Date	6th Date	7th Date	8th Date	9th Date	10th Date	11th Date	12th Date	13th Date	14th Date	15th Date
13	1 - 2	I	3-4	8-11	5-10	4-9	6-13	5-8	2-12	1-3	6-7	7-11	5-9	1-13	6-12		
	3 - 4	II	1-2	10-13	7-12	6-11	2-9	3-6	1-7	8-10	5-11	10-12	2-4	3-9	4-8		
	5 - 6	III	5-6	1-12	2-11	8-13	4-11	7-10	8-9	2-6	3-13	3-5	12-13	10-11	1-5	—	—
	7 - 8	IV	7-8	6-9	3-8	1-10	5-12	2-13	3-11	7-9	2-10	4-6	1-11	4-12	7-13		
	9 - 10	V	9-10	4-7	4-13	3-12	1-8	9-12	5-13	11-13	1-9	2-8	6-10	5-7	2-3		
	11 - 12	VI	11-12	2-5	1-6	2-7	3-10	1-4	4-10	4-5	8-12	9-13	3-7	6-8	9-11		
	—	—	13Bye	3Bye	9Bye	5Bye	7Bye	11Bye	6Bye	12Bye	4Bye	1Bye	8Bye	2Bye	10Bye		
14	1 - 2	I	1-2	8-11	5-10	4-9	7-14	3-6	2-12	8-10	4-14	7-11	12-13	3-9	1-5		
	3 - 4	II	3-4	10-13	7-12	6-11	2-9	5-8	6-14	1-3	2-10	1-14	5-9	4-12	7-13		
	5 - 6	III	5-6	1-12	9-14	8-13	4-11	7-10	3-11	7-9	5-11	4-6	8-14	1-13	2-3	—	—
	7 - 8	IV	7-8	3-14	2-11	1-10	6-13	9-12	1-7	4-5	3-13	10-12	2-4	6-8	9-11		
	9 - 10	V	9-10	2-5	4-13	3-12	1-8	11-14	4-10	11-13	6-7	3-5	6-10	2-14	6-12		
	11 - 12	VI	11-12	4-7	1-6	5-14	3-10	2-13	8-9	2-6	8-12	9-13	1-11	5-7	10-14		
	13 - 14	VII	13-14	6-9	3-8	2-7	5-12	1-4	5-13	12-14	1-9	2-8	3-7	10-11	4-8		
15	1 - 2	I	7-8	12-15	2-9	8-14	6-12	1-11	2-8	7-10	4-5	4-9	3-9	3-13	6-10	5-14	13-15
	3 - 4	II	3-4	10-13	1-5	4-15	8-10	7-15	11-15	3-6	12-13	2-7	2-11	8-12	9-11	1-6	9-14
	5 - 6	III	5-6	8-11	3-7	2-13	1-9	6-8	7-14	9-12	10-11	3-5	4-13	1-10	2-14	9-15	1-4
	7 - 8	IV	1-2	6-9	12-14	1-7	3-15	4-10	4-6	11-14	8-9	10-15	5-7	5-11	4-12	11-13	3-8
	9 - 10	V	9-10	4-7	6-13	3-11	4-14	9-13	5-12	5-8	2-3	1-14	6-15	2-15	1-8	2-10	7-12
	11 - 12	VI	11-12	1-3	8-15	5-9	7-11	2-12	1-13	2-4	6-7	8-13	10-14	6-14	5-15	3-12	5-10
	13 - 14	VII	13-14	2-5	4-11	10-12	5-13	3-14	3-10	1-15	14-15	6-11	1-12	7-9	7-13	4-8	2-6
	—	—	15Bye	14Bye	10Bye	6Bye	2Bye	5Bye	9Bye	13Bye	1Bye	12Bye	8Bye	4Bye	3Bye	7Bye	11Bye
16	1 - 2	I	1-5	4-6	13-3	2-14	16-9	15-12	11-8	7-10	12-11	5-15	14-7	8-16	10-1	6-13	9-4
	3 - 4	II	2-6	7-1	14-4	15-3	10-13	9-8	12-5	11-16	1-2	13-7	6-15	4-10	3-12	5-14	16-13
	5 - 6	III	3-7	8-2	15-1	4-16	6-11	5-10	9-14	12-13	5-8	16-6	10-3	2-12	11-4	1-9	7-5
	7 - 8	IV	4-8	3-5	16-2	1-13	12-7	14-11	15-10	6-9	13-15	8-14	9-12	11-1	5-6	7-16	2-3
	9 - 10	V	9-13	14-12	5-11	6-10	8-1	4-7	3-16	2-15	10-9	1-3	11-2	13-5	7-8	12-4	15-14
	11 - 12	VI	10-14	9-15	6-12	7-11	5-2	16-1	4-13	3-8	14-16	12-10	1-4	15-7	2-9	11-3	8-6
	13 - 14	VII	11-15	16-10	7-9	8-12	3-14	13-2	1-6	4-5	6-7	2-4	5-16	9-3	14-13	15-8	10-11
	15 - 16	VIII	12-16	11-13	8-10	5-9	15-4	3-6	2-7	14-1	4-3	9-11	13-8	6-14	16-15	10-2	1-12

Figure 64(b). Tables of Round Robin Schedules. Teams or entries, 13-16.

TEAMS –	1	2	3	4	5	6	7	8	9	10	11	12	13	14	15
1	150	150	150	150	150	150	150	150	150	150	150	150	150	150	150
2		50	100	117	125	130	133	135	137	139	140	141	141	142	143
3			50	83	100	110	116	121	125	128	130	132	133	134	136
4				50	75	90	100	107	112	117	120	123	125	127	129
5					50	70	84	93	100	106	110	114	116	119	121
6						50	67	79	88	94	100	105	108	112	114
7							50	65	75	83	90	95	100	104	107
8								50	63	72	80	86	92	96	100
9									50	61	70	77	84	88	93
10										50	60	68	75	81	86
11											50	59	67	73	79
12												50	59	66	71
13													50	58	64
14														50	57
15															50
16															
17															
18															
19															
20															
21															
22															
23															
24															
25															
26															
27															
28															
29															
30															
31															
32															
33															
34															
35															

Figure 65. Participation-Achieve

PARTICIPATION-ACHIEVEMENT POINT TABLES. Three participation-achievement point tables are shown in Figures 65–67. These should simplify calculations for those who use a participation-achievement point system. Each table is worked out for from one to 35 teams or entrants. Figure 65 shows a major division sport or activity scale, with 50 points the minimum and 150 the maximum. Thus, if a director allocates points to either 16 participants or 16 teams,

19	20	21	22	23	24	25	26	27	28	29	30	31	32	33	34	35
150	150	150	150	150	150	150	150	150	150	150	150	150	150	150	150	150
144	145	145	145	145	146	146	146	146	146	146	147	147	147	147	147	147
139	140	140	140	141	141	142	142	142	142	143	143	144	144	144	144	144
133	135	135	135	136	137	138	138	138	139	139	140	140	141	141	141	141
128	129	130	131	132	133	133	134	134	135	136	136	137	137	138	138	138
122	124	125	126	127	128	129	130	131	131	132	133	134	134	135	135	135
117	119	120	121	123	124	125	126	127	128	129	129	130	131	132	132	132
111	113	115	116	118	120	121	122	123	124	125	126	127	128	128	129	129
106	108	110	112	114	115	117	118	119	120	121	122	124	124	125	126	126
100	103	105	107	109	111	112	114	115	117	118	119	120	121	122	123	123
94	97	100	102	105	107	108	110	112	113	114	115	117	118	119	120	120
89	92	95	98	100	102	104	106	108	109	111	112	114	115	116	117	117
83	87	90	93	95	98	100	102	104	106	107	108	110	111	113	114	115
78	81	85	88	91	93	96	98	100	102	104	105	107	108	109	111	112
72	76	80	84	86	89	92	94	96	98	100	102	104	105	106	108	109
67	71	75	79	82	85	88	90	92	94	96	98	100	102	103	105	106
61	65	70	74	77	80	83	86	88	91	93	95	96	98	100	102	103
56	60	65	69	73	76	79	82	85	87	89	92	93	95	97	98	100
50	55	60	65	68	72	75	78	81	83	86	88	90	92	94	95	97
	50	55	60	64	67	71	74	77	80	82	85	86	89	91	92	94
		50	55	59	63	67	70	73	76	79	81	83	85	87	89	91
			50	55	59	62	66	69	72	75	78	80	82	84	86	88
				50	54	58	62	66	69	71	74	76	79	81	83	85
					50	54	58	62	65	68	71	73	76	78	80	83
						50	54	58	61	64	67	70	72	75	77	80
							50	54	58	61	64	66	69	72	74	77
								50	54	57	60	63	66	68	71	74
									50	54	57	60	63	65	68	71
										50	53	56	59	62	65	68
											50	53	56	59	62	65
												50	53	56	59	62
													50	53	56	59
														50	53	56
															50	53
																50

ble: Major, 50–150.

for example, in a sport tournament, the scale shows that the winner should be awarded 150 points, next highest 143 points, third place 137 points, and so on down the scale, with 50 points for the individual or team in last place. When teams tie for a place in the standings, the number of points allotted to those positions are added and the total is divided by the number of teams tied. Example: Two teams are tied for first place in a 16 team league ($100 + 96 \div 2 =$

TEAMS –	1	2	3	4	5	6	7	8	9	10	11	12	13	14	15
1	100	100	100	100	100	100	100	100	100	100	100	100	100	100	100
2		35	68	78	83	87	89	91	91	93	93	94	95	95	95
3			35	57	67	74	78	82	83	86	87	88	89	90	90
4				35	51	61	67	72	75	78	80	82	84	85	86
5					35	48	56	63	67	71	74	76	79	80	81
6						35	45	53	59	64	67	70	73	75	77
7							35	44	51	57	61	65	68	70	72
8								35	43	49	54	59	62	65	67
9									35	42	48	53	57	60	63
10										35	41	47	51	55	58
11											35	41	46	50	54
12												35	41	45	49
13													35	40	44
14														35	40
15															35
16															
17															
18															
19															
20															
21															
22															
23															
24															
25															
26															
27															
28															
29															
30															
31															
32															
33															
34															
35															

Figure 66. Participation-Achieve

98). Figure 66 shows points scaled from 35 to 100, for participation and achievement in sports allocated to the intermediate division. If there are four teams or individuals in a tournament involving a sport in this category, first place receives 100 points, second place 78 points, third place 57 points, and last place 35 points. This equal distribution of points adds validity to point systems.

18	19	20	21	22	23	24	25	26	27	28	29	30	31	32	33	34	35
100	100	100	100	100	100	100	100	100	100	100	100	100	100	100	100	100	100
96	96	97	97	97	97	97	97	97	97	98	98	98	98	98	98	98	98
92	93	93	94	94	94	94	94	95	95	95	96	96	96	96	96	96	96
88	89	90	90	91	91	91	91	92	92	93	93	94	94	94	94	94	94
85	85	86	67	88	88	88	89	89	90	91	91	91	92	92	92	92	92
81	82	83	84	85	85	86	86	87	87	88	89	89	89	90	90	90	90
77	78	80	81	82	82	83	83	84	85	86	86	87	87	88	88	88	88
73	75	76	77	78	79	80	81	82	82	83	84	85	85	86	86	86	86
69	71	73	74	75	76	77	78	79	80	81	82	82	83	83	84	84	84
66	68	69	71	72	73	74	75	77	77	78	79	80	81	81	82	82	83
62	64	66	67	69	70	72	73	74	75	76	77	78	78	79	80	80	81
58	60	62	64	66	67	69	70	71	72	74	75	75	76	77	78	78	79
54	57	59	61	63	65	66	67	69	70	71	72	73	74	75	76	76	77
50	53	55	58	60	62	63	65	66	67	69	70	71	72	73	74	74	75
47	50	52	54	57	59	61	62	64	65	66	68	69	70	71	72	72	73
43	46	49	51	53	56	58	59	61	63	64	65	66	67	69	70	70	71
39	42	45	48	50	53	55	57	58	60	61	63	64	65	66	68	68	69
35	39	42	44	47	50	52	54	56	58	59	61	62	63	64	65	67	67
	35	38	41	44	47	49	51	53	55	57	58	60	61	62	63	65	66
		35	38	41	44	47	49	51	53	54	56	57	59	60	61	63	64
			35	38	41	44	46	48	50	52	54	55	56	58	59	61	62
				35	38	41	43	46	48	49	51	53	54	56	57	59	60
					35	38	41	43	45	47	49	50	52	54	55	57	58
						35	38	40	43	44	47	48	50	52	53	55	56
							35	38	40	42	44	46	48	49	51	53	54
								35	38	40	42	44	45	47	49	51	52
									35	37	40	41	43	45	47	49	50
										35	37	39	41	43	45	47	49
											35	37	39	41	43	45	47
												35	37	39	41	43	45
													35	37	39	41	43
														35	37	39	41
															35	37	39
																35	37
																	35

Table: Intermediate, 35–100.

The number of teams or entries participating in a particular league determines the size of the point spread between places. In some cases, two whole number intervals are used to eliminate handling decimals or fractions. In the 50-150 participation-achievement point range, the interval for 11 teams is 10, whereas the intervals for 25 teams are 4 and 5. The intervals for 11 teams in the intermediate range (35-

TEAMS –	1	2	3	4	5	6	7	8	9	10	11	12	13	14	15
1	75	75	75	75	75	75	75	75	75	75	75	75	75	75	75
2		25	50	58	62	65	67	68	69	69	70	70	71	71	71
3			25	42	50	55	58	61	63	64	65	66	67	67	68
4				25	38	45	50	54	56	58	60	61	63	63	64
5					25	35	42	46	50	53	55	57	58	60	61
6						25	33	39	44	47	50	52	54	56	57
7							25	32	37	42	45	48	50	52	54
8								25	31	36	40	43	46	48	50
9									25	31	35	39	42	44	46
10										25	30	34	37	40	43
11											25	30	33	37	39
12												25	29	33	36
13													25	29	32
14														25	29
15															25
16															
17															
18															
19															
20															
21															
22															
23															
24															
25															
26															
27															
28															
29															
30															
31															
32															
33															
34															
35															

Figure 67. Participation-Achieven

100) are 6 and 7, and for the same number of teams in the minor range (25-75) the interval is 5.

In Figure 67, the points are scaled from 25 to 75 for participation and achievement in those activities considered minor, in relation to number of players required for a team, tournament method followed, number of games played, and

8	19	20	21	22	23	24	25	26	27	28	29	30	31	32	33	34	35
5	75	75	75	75	75	75	75	75	75	75	75	75	75	75	75	75	75
2	72	72	72	73	73	73	73	73	73	73	73	73	73	73	73	73	74
9	69	70	70	71	71	71	71	71	71	71	71	71	71	72	72	72	72
6	66	67	67	68	68	69	69	69	69	69	69	70	70	70	70	70	71
3	64	64	65	66	66	67	67	67	67	67	68	68	68	68	69	69	69
0	61	62	62	63	64	64	65	65	65	65	66	66	66	67	67	67	68
7	58	59	60	61	61	62	63	63	63	64	64	65	65	65	66	66	66
4	55	57	57	59	59	60	61	61	61	62	62	63	63	64	64	64	65
1	53	54	55	56	57	58	58	59	59	60	61	61	61	62	62	63	63
9	50	51	52	54	55	56	56	57	58	58	59	59	60	60	61	61	62
6	47	49	50	51	52	53	54	55	56	56	57	58	58	59	59	60	60
3	45	46	48	49	50	51	52	53	54	55	55	56	57	57	58	58	59
0	42	43	45	46	48	49	50	51	52	53	54	54	55	56	56	57	57
7	39	41	43	44	45	47	48	49	50	51	52	53	53	54	55	55	56
4	36	38	40	41	43	44	46	47	48	49	50	51	52	52	53	54	54
1	34	36	38	39	41	42	44	45	46	47	48	49	50	51	52	52	53
3	31	33	35	37	39	40	42	43	44	45	46	47	48	49	50	51	51
5	28	30	33	34	36	38	39	41	42	44	45	46	47	48	48	49	50
	25	28	30	32	34	36	37	39	41	42	43	44	45	46	47	48	49
		25	28	29	32	33	35	37	39	40	41	42	43	44	45	46	47
			25	27	29	31	33	35	37	38	39	41	42	43	44	45	46
				25	27	29	31	33	35	36	38	39	40	41	42	43	44
					25	27	29	31	33	35	36	37	39	40	41	42	43
						25	27	29	31	33	34	35	37	38	39	40	41
							25	27	29	31	32	34	35	36	38	39	40
								25	27	29	31	32	34	35	36	37	38
									25	27	29	30	32	33	34	36	37
										25	27	29	30	32	33	34	35
											25	27	29	30	31	33	34
												25	27	28	30	31	32
													25	27	28	30	31
														25	27	28	29
															25	27	23
																25	26
																	25

able: Minor, 25–75.

so on. (See Chapter 10 for an elaboration upon a participation-achievement point system.) Use of these tables eliminates the time-consuming task of making up a point distribution each time a tournament is conducted and makes certain that points are figured and awarded within some consistent pattern.

Bowling individual handicap chart. The bowling individual handicap chart (Fig. 68) can be used for 180, 190, and 200-scratch leagues and for handicaps of 66⅔, 70, 75, and 80 per cent of the difference between the bowler's average and scratch. Scratch is the maximum standard on which each player's handicap is based. The scratch for each league will vary due to the scoring ability of the bowlers but it should be approximately ten pins higher than the highest player average in the league.

With a knowledge of each bowler's average the chart then can be used for calculation. The calculations are then added for the total team handicap for each game. For example, averages for five members of a bowling team in a 75 per cent handicap, 180 scratch league are 140, 145, 160, 164, and 172. The 180 scratch chart indicates that the handicaps are 30, 26, 15, 12, and 6, respectively. Totaling these handicaps gives 89, the total team handicap. This 89 is added to what they actually bowl for each game. Refer to Chapters 7 (bowling and golf sections) and 9 (handicapping section) for additional information on handicaps.

Percentage table. League standings are usually figured on a percentage basis when teams play an equal number of games; the team with the highest percentage of games won is the league winner. To figure and refigure these percentages continually is time consuming. Figure 69 lists percentages for up to 30 games won and serves as a handy reference table. Intramural directors and other personnel in charge of leagues can expand the table beyond 30 games won to include the number of games their leagues play.

To obtain these percentages, the number of games won is divided by the number of games played, with the division carried three places to the right of the decimal point.

$$\text{Example: } \frac{\textit{Games Won} \quad (24)}{\textit{Games Played} \quad (47)} = .511$$

On the table, the percentage figure of .511 is obtained by matching the 24 games won column with the 23 games lost (47 played less 24 won) column.

180 SCRATCH

	Per Cent					Per Cent					Per Cent					Per Cent					Per Cent			
Ave	66⅔	70	75	80	Ave	66⅔	70	75	80	Ave	66⅔	70	75	80	Ave	66⅔	70	75	80	Ave	66⅔	70	75	80
180	—	—	—	—	164	10	11	12	12	148	21	22	24	25	132	32	33	36	38	116	42	44	48	51
179	—	—	—	—	163	11	11	12	13	147	22	23	24	26	131	32	34	36	39	115	43	45	48	52
178	1	1	1	1	162	12	12	13	14	146	22	23	25	27	130	33	35	37	40	114	44	46	49	52
177	2	2	2	2	161	12	13	14	15	145	23	24	26	28	129	34	35	38	40	113	44	46	50	53
176	2	2	3	3	160	13	14	15	16	144	24	25	27	28	128	34	36	39	41	112	45	47	51	54
175	3	3	3	4	159	14	14	15	16	143	24	25	27	29	127	35	37	39	42	111	46	48	51	55
174	4	4	4	4	158	14	15	16	17	142	25	26	28	30	126	36	37	40	43	110	46	49	52	56
173	4	4	5	5	157	15	16	17	18	141	26	27	29	31	125	36	38	41	44	109	47	49	53	56
172	5	5	6	6	156	16	16	18	19	140	26	28	30	32	124	37	39	42	44	108	48	50	54	57
171	6	6	6	7	155	16	17	18	20	139	27	28	30	32	123	38	39	42	45	107	48	51	54	58
170	6	7	7	8	154	17	18	19	20	138	28	29	31	33	122	38	40	43	46	106	49	51	55	59
169	7	7	8	8	153	18	18	20	21	137	28	30	32	34	121	39	41	44	47	105	50	52	56	60
168	8	8	9	9	152	18	19	21	22	136	29	30	33	35	120	40	42	45	48	104	50	53	57	60
167	8	9	9	10	151	19	20	21	23	135	30	31	33	36	119	40	42	45	48	103	51	53	57	61
166	9	9	10	11	150	20	21	22	24	134	30	32	34	36	118	41	43	46	49	102	52	54	58	62
165	10	10	11	12	149	20	21	23	24	133	31	32	35	37	117	42	44	47	50	101	52	55	59	63

190 SCRATCH

	Per Cent					Per Cent					Per Cent					Per Cent					Per Cent			
Ave	66⅔	70	75	80	Ave	66⅔	70	75	80	Ave	66⅔	70	75	80	Ave	66⅔	70	75	80	Ave	66⅔	70	75	80
190	—	—	—	—	172	12	12	13	14	154	24	25	27	28	136	36	37	40	43	118	48	50	54	57
189	—	—	—	—	171	12	13	14	15	153	24	25	27	29	135	36	38	41	44	117	48	51	54	58
188	1	1	1	1	170	13	14	15	16	152	25	26	28	30	134	37	39	42	44	116	49	51	55	59
187	2	2	2	2	169	14	14	15	16	151	26	27	29	31	133	38	39	42	45	115	50	52	56	60
186	2	2	3	3	168	14	15	16	17	150	26	28	30	32	132	38	40	43	46	114	50	53	57	60
185	3	3	3	4	167	15	16	17	18	149	27	28	30	32	131	39	41	44	47	113	51	53	57	61
184	4	4	4	4	166	16	16	18	19	148	28	29	31	33	130	40	42	45	48	112	52	54	58	62
183	4	4	5	5	165	16	17	18	20	147	28	30	32	34	129	40	42	45	48	111	52	55	59	63
182	5	5	6	6	164	17	18	19	20	146	29	30	33	35	128	41	43	46	49	110	53	56	60	64
181	6	6	6	7	163	18	18	20	21	145	30	31	33	36	127	42	44	47	50	109	54	56	60	64
180	6	7	7	8	162	18	19	21	22	144	30	32	34	36	126	42	44	48	51	108	54	57	61	65
179	7	7	8	8	161	19	20	21	23	143	31	32	35	37	125	43	45	48	52	107	55	58	62	66
178	8	8	9	9	160	20	21	22	24	142	32	33	36	38	124	44	46	49	52	106	56	58	63	67
177	8	9	9	10	159	20	21	23	24	141	32	34	36	39	123	44	46	50	53	105	56	59	63	68
176	9	9	10	11	158	21	22	24	25	140	33	35	37	40	122	45	47	51	54	104	57	60	64	68
175	10	10	11	12	157	22	23	24	26	139	34	35	38	40	121	46	48	51	55	103	58	60	65	69
174	10	11	12	12	156	22	23	25	27	138	34	36	39	41	120	46	49	52	56	102	58	61	66	70
173	11	11	12	13	155	23	24	26	28	137	35	37	39	42	119	47	49	53	56	101	59	62	66	71

200 SCRATCH

	Per Cent					Per Cent					Per Cent					Per Cent					Per Cent			
Ave	66⅔	70	75	80	Ave	66⅔	70	75	80	Ave	66⅔	70	75	80	Ave	66⅔	70	75	80	Ave	66⅔	70	75	80
200	—	—	—	—	180	13	14	15	16	160	26	28	30	32	140	40	42	45	48	120	53	56	60	64
199	—	—	—	—	179	14	14	15	16	159	27	28	30	32	139	40	42	45	48	119	54	56	60	64
198	1	1	1	1	178	14	15	16	17	158	28	29	31	33	138	41	43	46	49	118	54	57	61	65
197	2	2	2	2	177	15	16	17	18	157	28	30	32	34	137	42	44	47	50	117	55	58	62	66
196	2	2	3	3	176	16	16	18	19	156	29	30	33	35	136	42	44	48	51	116	56	58	63	67
195	3	3	3	4	175	16	17	18	20	155	30	31	33	36	135	43	45	48	52	115	56	59	63	68
194	4	4	4	4	174	17	18	19	20	154	30	32	34	36	134	44	46	49	52	114	57	60	64	68
193	4	4	5	5	173	18	18	20	21	153	31	32	35	37	133	44	46	50	53	113	58	60	65	69
192	5	5	6	6	172	18	19	21	22	152	32	33	36	38	132	45	47	51	54	112	58	61	66	70
191	6	6	6	7	171	19	20	21	23	151	32	34	36	39	131	46	48	51	55	111	59	62	66	71
190	6	7	7	8	170	20	21	22	24	150	33	35	37	40	130	46	49	52	56	110	60	63	67	72
189	7	7	8	8	169	20	21	23	24	149	34	35	38	40	129	47	49	53	56	109	60	63	68	72
188	8	8	9	9	168	21	22	24	25	148	34	36	39	41	128	48	50	54	57	108	61	64	69	73
187	8	9	9	10	167	22	23	24	26	147	35	37	39	42	127	48	51	54	58	107	62	65	69	74
186	9	9	10	11	166	22	23	25	27	146	36	37	40	43	126	49	51	55	59	106	62	65	70	75
185	10	10	11	12	165	23	24	26	28	145	36	38	41	44	125	50	52	56	60	105	63	66	71	76
184	10	11	12	12	164	24	25	27	28	144	37	39	42	44	124	50	53	57	60	104	64	67	72	76
183	11	11	12	13	163	24	25	27	29	143	38	39	42	45	123	51	53	57	61	103	64	67	72	77
182	12	12	13	14	162	25	26	28	30	142	38	40	43	46	122	52	54	58	62	102	65	68	73	78
181	12	13	14	15	161	26	27	29	31	141	39	41	44	47	121	52	55	59	63	101	66	69	74	79

Figure 68. Bowling Individual Handicap Chart—Single Game: 180, 190, and 200 Scratch. (Courtesy of American Bowling Congress.)

Games Won	1	2	3	4	5	6	7	8	9	10	11	12	13
1	.500	.333	.250	.200	.167	.143	.125	.111	.100	.091	.083	.077	.071
2	.667	.500	.400	.333	.286	.250	.222	.200	.182	.167	.154	.143	.133
3	.750	.600	.500	.429	.375	.333	.300	.273	.250	.231	.214	.200	.188
4	.800	.667	.571	.500	.444	.400	.364	.333	.308	.286	.267	.250	.235
5	.833	.714	.625	.556	.500	.455	.417	.385	.357	.333	.313	.294	.278
6	.857	.750	.667	.600	.545	.500	.462	.429	.400	.375	.353	.333	.316
7	.875	.778	.700	.636	.583	.538	.500	.467	.438	.412	.389	.368	.350
8	.889	.800	.727	.667	.615	.571	.533	.500	.471	.444	.421	.400	.381
9	.900	.818	.750	.692	.643	.600	.563	.529	.500	.474	.450	.429	.409
10	.909	.833	.769	.714	.667	.625	.588	.556	.526	.500	.476	.455	.435
11	.917	.846	.786	.733	.688	.647	.611	.579	.550	.524	.500	.478	.458
12	.923	.857	.800	.750	.706	.667	.632	.600	.571	.545	.522	.500	.480
13	.929	.867	.813	.765	.722	.684	.650	.619	.591	.565	.542	.520	.500
14	.933	.875	.824	.778	.737	.700	.667	.636	.609	.583	.560	.538	.519
15	.938	.882	.833	.789	.750	.714	.682	.652	.625	.600	.577	.556	.536
16	.941	.889	.842	.800	.762	.727	.696	.667	.640	.615	.593	.571	.552
17	.944	.895	.850	.810	.773	.739	.708	.680	.654	.630	.607	.586	.567
18	.947	.900	.857	.818	.783	.750	.720	.692	.667	.643	.621	.600	.581
19	.950	.904	.864	.826	.792	.760	.731	.704	.679	.655	.633	.613	.594
20	.952	.909	.870	.833	.800	.769	.741	.714	.690	.667	.645	.625	.606
21	.955	.913	.875	.840	.808	.778	.750	.724	.700	.677	.656	.636	.618
22	.957	.917	.880	.846	.815	.786	.759	.733	.710	.688	.667	.647	.629
23	.958	.920	.885	.852	.821	.793	.767	.742	.719	.697	.676	.657	.639
24	.960	.923	.889	.857	.828	.800	.774	.750	.727	.706	.686	.667	.649
25	.962	.926	.893	.862	.833	.806	.781	.758	.735	.714	.694	.676	.658
26	.963	.929	.897	.867	.839	.813	.788	.765	.743	.722	.703	.684	.667
27	.964	.931	.900	.871	.844	.818	.794	.771	.750	.730	.711	.692	.675
28	.966	.933	.903	.875	.848	.824	.800	.778	.757	.737	.718	.700	.683
29	.967	.935	.906	.879	.853	.829	.806	.784	.763	.744	.725	.707	.690
30	.968	.938	.909	.882	.857	.833	.811	.789	.769	.750	.732	.714	.698

Figu

The games won are listed vertically along the left margin in Figure 69. Games lost are shown horizontally at the top. To determine a team or individual's won-lost percentage, place your finger or pencil on the number of games won, in the left margin. Then, follow that horizontal line across to the number of games lost, as shown in the group of numbers at the top of table, to obtain the percentage. When teams in a league play an uneven number of games, the non-percentage plan is frequently used. With this procedure, teams are ranked according to won and lost records such as 8–0, 5–2, 4–2, and so on.

	17	18	19	20	21	22	23	24	25	26	27	28	29	30
9	.056	.053												
1	.105	.100												
8	.150	.143	.136	.130	.125	.120	.115	.111	.107	.103	.100			
0	.190	.182	.174	.167	.160	.154	.148	.143	.138	.133	.129	.125	.121	.118
8	.227	.217	.208	.200	.192	.185	.179	.172	.167	.161	.156	.152	.147	.143
3	.261	.250	.240	.231	.222	.214	.207	.200	.194	.188	.182	.176	.171	.167
4	.292	.280	.269	.259	.250	.241	.233	.226	.219	.212	.206	.200	.194	.189
3	.320	.308	.296	.286	.276	.267	.258	.250	.242	.235	.229	.222	.216	.211
0	.346	.333	.321	.310	.300	.290	.281	.273	.265	.257	.250	.243	.237	.231
5	.370	.357	.345	.333	.323	.313	.303	.294	.286	.278	.270	.263	.256	.250
7	.393	.379	.367	.355	.344	.333	.324	.314	.306	.297	.289	.282	.275	.268
9	.414	.400	.387	.375	.364	.353	.343	.333	.324	.316	.308	.300	.293	.286
8	.433	.419	.406	.394	.382	.371	.361	.351	.342	.333	.325	.317	.310	.302
7	.452	.438	.424	.412	.400	.389	.378	.368	.359	.350	.341	.333	.326	.318
4	.469	.455	.441	.429	.417	.405	.395	.385	.375	.366	.357	.349	.341	.333
0	.485	.471	.457	.444	.432	.421	.410	.400	.390	.381	.372	.364	.356	.348
5	.500	.486	.472	.459	.447	.436	.425	.415	.405	.395	.386	.378	.370	.362
9	.514	.500	.486	.474	.462	.450	.439	.429	.419	.409	.400	.391	.383	.375
3	.528	.514	.500	.487	.475	.463	.452	.442	.432	.422	.413	.404	.396	.388
6	.541	.526	.513	.500	.488	.476	.465	.455	.444	.435	.426	.417	.408	.400
8	.553	.538	.525	.512	.500	.488	.477	,467	,457	.447	.438	429	.420	.412
9	.564	.550	.537	.524	.512	.500	.489	.478	.468	.458	.449	.440	.431	.423
0	.575	.561	.548	.535	.523	.511	.500	.489	.479	.469	.460	.451	.442	.434
0	.585	.571	.558	.545	.533	.522	.511	.500	.490	.480	.471	.462	.453	.444
0	.595	.581	.568	.556	.543	.532	.521	.510	.500	.490	.481	.472	.463	.455
9	.605	.591	.578	.565	.553	.542	.531	.520	.510	.500	.491	.481	.473	.464
8	.614	.600	.587	.574	.563	.551	.540	.529	.519	.509	.500	.491	.482	.474
6	.622	.609	.596	.583	.571	.560	.549	.538	.528	.519	.509	.500	.491	.483
4	.630	.617	.604	.592	.580	.569	.558	.547	.537	.527	.518	.509	.500	.492
2	.638	.625	.612	.600	.588	.577	.566	.556	.545	.536	.526	.517	.508	.500

ge Table.

Thus, if Team A has won 10 games and lost 7 games, it has a won-lost percentage of .588. Team B, with a record of 9 games won and 8 games lost, has a percentage of .529. Team A ranks ahead of Team B in this example.

If Team A has won 11 games and lost 7 games, it has a percentage of .611. Team B, with a record of 12 games won and 6 games lost, has a percentage of .667. Team B ranks ahead of Team A in this example. Percentages do not portray true standings when teams play an unequal number of games. Team A with a 2–1 record (.667) may be better than Team B with 5–2 (.714).

SUMMARY

1. The inexperienced intramural director is greatly assisted by ready references to program forms, charts, and tables which serve as a year-to-year working guide.
2. The experienced intramural director and other persons who conduct recreation programs know that convenient forms, charts, and tables speed up program administration.
3. Examples of program forms, charts, and tables are tournament calculators, placement of byes, seeding placement, round-robin schedules, draw sheets for single and double elimination tournaments, participation-achievement point tables, bowling individual handicap charts, and percentage tables.
4. The table of round robin schedules is designed so that team play is distributed as evenly as possible over different fields, courts, or alleys.
5. It is possible to obtain prepared draw sheets from sporting goods companies should the intramural director not wish to make up his own.
6. A detailed explanation of tournament methods and point systems is given in Chapters 9 and 10.

APPENDIX

A. Open House Sports Program

B. Sigma Delta Psi Tests, Requirements, and Scoring Tables

C. Selected References and Rules Sources

A

OPEN HOUSE
SPORTS PROGRAM

SPORTS BUILDING
UNIVERSITY OF MICHIGAN
ANN ARBOR

Wednesday, March 18

Twenty-five Sports Under Way Tonight

ARCHERY .... **Handball Court No. 13**

Exhibition and Match Shooting Under The Direction of Doug Watkins.

BADMINTON .... **Large Gymnasium**

8:30 to 10:00 Exhibition by players of the Detroit Badminton Club. Gerald Burns, Mid-West and State Champion; Constance O'Donovan, State Champion; Miss Peterson, Ohio State Open Champion, Florence Howard, Mrs. Gerald Burns, Mr. and Mrs. Gesamon, Mr. Gould. Mr. Rees Cramer of Detroit Athletic Supply Company will explain some of the finer points of the game.

BASKETBALL .... **Large Gymnasium**

7:00 Residence Hall Championship

PRESCOTT vs MICHIGAN

Brown, Zectner, Myll; Heid, Bodycomb, Schmidt, Telbizoff, Baker — McCormick, Bryan, Avery, Waddles, Ankli, Wiantoles.

Referee, *Hazeltine;* Umpire, *Holman;* Timer, *Nelson;* Scorer, *Bikoff.*

NOTE: Immediately after this game there will be a punching bag exhibition by Robert Haugh.

NOTE: Immediately after this game there will be a demonstration of physical fitness exercises.

8:30 Fraternity Class "A" Championship

DELTA KAPPA EPSILON vs SIGMA PHI EPSILON

O'Hara, Reader, Armstrong, Morris, Troy, Yaap, Furniss — Bartlow, Sears, Zeller, Mikulich, Smith.

Referee, *Nelson;* Umpire, *Bikoff;* Timer, *Sullivan;* Scorer, *Brieske.*

NOTE: Between halves of this game there will be an exhibition of juggling by Mr. A. D. Moore.

NOTE: Immediately after this game there will be a parallel bar exhibition.

9:30 Independent championship.

DIVE BOMBERS vs LUMBERJACKS

Pagel, Robertson, Dean, Harrison, Bare, O'Grady, Davidson, Van Dusen.

Whitaker, Simon, Shanks, Earle, Broman.

Referee, *Sullivan;* Umpire, *Brieske;* Scorer, *Bikoff;* Timer, *Nelson.*

BOXING .... **Large Gymnasium**

Exhibition Bouts, to be alternated with wrestling matches. (See Wrestling).

7:30 Charles Erickson vs Nate Shaffer
8:00 Giles Thielk vs Jack Vaughn
8:30 Don Westfall vs Joe Borgess
9:00 Tom Miller vs Harold Kleinart

Referee and judges: Boxing coach and staff members.

CARBALLO .... **Hand Ball Court No. 3**

7:00 to 10:00 Exhibition matches. Names Posted on Court.

CODEBALL .... **Hand Ball Court No. 5**

7:00 to 10:00 Exhibition matches. Names Posted on Court.

DART BASEBALL .... **Squash Court No. 1**

Team matches by various groups. See Schedule on Court.

DIVING .... **Swimming Pool**

8:45 Members of the Varsity and Freshman squads will give an exhibition of high and low board diving. Martin, Canja, Haughy, Chickering, Holter, Brud, Lary, McDonald.

NOTE: Clown diving by Mack Hayes.

NOTE: Swimming events will come before and after the diving (See Swimming.)

FENCING .... **Auxiliary Gymnasium**

7:30 to 10:00 Exhibition matches by members of the fencing class. Directed by student instructor Ray Chambers.

GOLF .... **Golf Driving Nets**

During the evening, members of the Varsity and Freshman squads will practice in the Golf Driving Nets.

9:00 Discussion of golf techniques in charge of varsity coach and squad members.

GYMNASTICS .... **Large Gymnasium**

8:25 Parallel Bar Exhibition (after Fraternity Basketball Game). Members of the University Exhibition Gymnastic team. Aiken, Burmeister, Buell, Harrelson, Martin, Pease.

HANDBALL .... **Handball Courts**

7:00 to 10:00 Many matches will be played. Names of players will be found on the courts.

JUGGLING .... **Large Gymnasium**

8:45 Exhibition by Mr. A. D. Moore.

LACROSSE .... **Handball Court 11**

7:00 to 10:00 — Demonstration of handling a lacrosse stick and informal game in a handball court. E. Altman, Goldman, Bright.

PADDLEBALL .... **Handball Court 7**

7:00 to 10:00 — Exhibition matches.

PUNCHING BAG .... **Large Gymnasium**

7:40 Exhibition by Mr. Robert Haugh.

SQUASH RACQUETS .... **Squash Courts**

7:00 Individual and team matches.

8:30 All campus championship special individual matches. (See names on squash courts)

9:00 Fraternity Championship .... Courts 2, 4, 6

Pi Lambda Phi vs Phi Delta Theta
Solomon, Franklin, Stern. Faber, Johnson, Scherling.

SWIMMING .... **Swimming Pool**

7:00 Residence Halls. Semifinals of Dual Meets.

CHICAGO vs ALLEN-RUMSEY
WILLIAMS vs WENLEY

7:30 Diving Exhibition.
Varsity and Freshman divers.

8:00 Free style relay race—freshmen, Halliday, Church, Fries, Bricker, Cory, Osborne, Wells, Hamilton, McCarty, Hayes.

8:15 Fraternity Swimming Championships.

9:00 Clown Diving by Mack Hayes.

9:20 Water Polo game. Phi Kappa Psi vs Phi Delta Theta

TABLE TENNIS .... **Large Gymnasium**

7:00	Bill Johnson	vs	Harold King
7:30	Dixon	vs	Chas. Peck
8:00	Wayne Stille	vs	Ted Peck
8:30	Heard	vs	Carl Engle
9:00	Zeta Beta Tau	vs	Phi Kappa Psi

TENNIS .... **Large Gymnasium**

7:00 All Campus final—Faber vs Lewis

7:30 Lawton Hammett vs Jim Porter (Members of Varsity team)
Referee: Varsity coaching staff, assisted by varsity squad members.

NOTE: Immediately following this match Badminton contests will be under way. (See Badminton.)

VOLLEYBALL .... **Large Gymnasium**

7:00	Forestry (Independent Champions) Kennedy, Langenbach, Muzir, Merritt, Ballanca, Michaels, Hauser, Wear.	vs	Winchell House (Residence Halls Champions) Evans, Weintraub, Powers, Fischler, Perham, Coit, Lee.
	Referee: *Bill Caruthers,* Senior I. M. Mgr.		
7:45	Sigma Alpha Mu (Fraternity Champions) Wallace, Pregulman, Schulman, Silver, Fergenson, Krause, Dregulman, Lipnik	vs	Nu Sigma Nu (Pro. Fraternity Champions) Rae, Bittinger, Ryan, Snyder, Carlson, Adams, Montgomery, Beesley.
	Referee: *Bill Caruthers.*		
8:30	Ann Arbor "Y" (State Champions) Cope, Stalker, Shultz, Burnham, Horning, R. Smith, Meyer, Hotzel, Martin.	vs	Detroit Downtown "Y" (Runners-up 1941) Sidloski, Mather, Victor, Goldman, Suder, Warne, Wooster, Gerber, Gobis, Heckert.
	Referee: *V. Nelson.*		

WATER POLO .... **Swimming Pool**

9:00	Phi Kappa Psi (Fraternity Champs) Wendt, Sessions, McCord, Edwards, Roxford, Samper, Bachman, McLogan, Fauver.	vs	Phi Delta Theta (Runners-up) Edison, Atkins, Moore, Gillette, Begle, Trent, Crawford, Emmett, Blodgett.

Officials: Members of varsity swimming staff and squad.

WEIGHT LIFTING .... **Boxing Ring, Large Gymnasium**

8:45 Exhibition by Frank Bright, Robert Beyer, and Stanley Beyer.

WRESTLING .... **Large Gymnasium**

Time	Weight			
7:00	121	Statler—Fletcher	vs	Rozas—Greene
7:15	128	Linton—Allen-Rumsey	vs	Islieb—Adams
7:45	145	Milner—Chicago	vs	Eckber—Fletcher
8:15	155	Gilmore—Prescott	vs	Altese—Prescott
8:45	165	Edwards—Allen-Rumsey	vs	Boucher—Winchell
9:15	175	Earle—Prescott	vs	Myll—Prescott
9:30	Unl.	Williams—Williams	vs	Bryan—Michigan

Referees: Varsity coaching staff and team members.

TONIGHT'S PROGRAM

Sports	25
Contestants	500
Spectators (estimated)	5,000
Officials	100

DIVISIONS OF INTRAMURAL ACTIVITIES

1. Fraternity	2. Independent	3. Faculty	4. Graduate
5. All Campus	6. Residence Halls	7. Informal	8. Remedial
9. Foreign Students	10. Corecreational	11. Extension	12. Instruction

COMING EVENTS

Mar. 19-20 Foul Shooting Contest—All Divisions
Mar. 23 Track Meet—Residence Halls and Independents
Mar. 25 Track Meet—Fraternity
Mar. 26 Swimming Meet—Independents

B

Sigma Delta Psi Tests, Requirements, and Scoring Tables

Sigma Delta Psi is the national honorary athletic fraternity. Many colleges and universities have chapters. To become a member of a chapter, a student must meet certain activity requirements. The tests, requirements, and scoring tables are presented here for the convenience of schools which have chapters or wish to be chartered. Member schools can use the requirements and scoring tables for national and local competition. Schools which are not members can use the requirements for a self-testing program and apply the point tables for local team and individual scoring. Ten students who have the highest total points, as determined by the tables on the basis of individual performances for each test, comprise the team from each member school for national competition. The same pattern can be followed for competition between local intramural organizations, with a possible modification of using less than ten team members.

Individual records indicating the best times, distances, and most points earned can be maintained. Additional information about receiving charters and participating in national competition can be obtained by writing to college and university Intramural Departments.

Sigma Delta Psi is very active as a professional fraternity, and its members hold reunion programs at national and district physical education conventions.

SIGMA DELTA PSI TESTS AND REQUIREMENTS *

TEST NO.		REQUIREMENT
1.	100-yard dash	11⅗ seconds
2.	120-yard low hurdles	16 seconds
3.	Running high jump	Height, weight classification
4.	Running broad jump	17 feet
5.	16-pound shot put	30 feet
6.	20-foot rope climb	12 seconds
	or golf	4 of 5 shots
7.	Baseball throw	250 feet
	or javelin throw	130 feet
8.	Football punt	120 feet
9.	100-yard swim	1 minute, 45 seconds
10.	1-mile run	6 minutes
11.	Front handspring, landing on feet	———
12.	Handstand	10 seconds
	or bowling	160 average for 3 games
13.	Bar vault	Chin high
14.	Good posture	Standard B (H.B.M.)
15.	Scholarship	Eligible for varsity competition

* Reproduced by permission from Sigma Delta Psi.

TEST NO. 2. Five standard low hurdles, placed twenty yards apart, shall be used to a flight. The test to be valid necessitates that all hurdles must remain upright from their bases.

TEST NO. 3. The high jump requirement is based on a graduated scale that considers the height and weight of each individual.

TEST NO. 5. Thirty feet is the requirement for a man of 160 pounds or over, the requirement to be scaled down in accordance with the following proportion for candidates of less weight:

160 pounds is to the candidate's weight as 30 feet is to the requirement.

TEST NO. 6. *Rope Climb.* The candidate shall start from a sitting position on the floor and climb rope without use of legs. Legs may be used in the descent.

Golf. 4 out of 5 shots must land on the fly in a circle (10 ft. radius) from a distance of 75 feet.

TEST NO. 12. *Handstand.* The candidate shall not be compelled to remain stationary during the test, neither shall he be allowed to advance or retreat more than three feet in any direction.

Bowling. The candidate must average 160 for 3 games. Only three games may be bowled in any one day.

TEST NO. 14. The candidate shall be required to pass the B standard of the Harvard Body Mechanics Posture Chart. These charts will be furnished all local chapters. The Director or Committee on Certification should observe the candidate's posture when he is not aware of the fact.

TEST NUMBERS 1, 2, 5, 7, and 8 shall be attempted crosswise or into the wind to be accepted by the Director or Committee on Certification.

The national collegiate rules for the various activities of the tests are the accepted standards.

SIGMA DELTA PSI HIGH JUMP REQUIREMENTS

Candidate	Weight-Class	Jump	Candidate	Weight-Class	Jump
6' 4"	Below 160	5' 4"	5' 9"	Below 150	4' 9"
	160 to 170	5' 3"		150 to 160	4' 8"
	170 to 180	5' 2"		160 to 170	4' 7"
	180 to 190	5' 1"		170 to 180	4' 6"
	190 and over	5' 0"		180 and over	4' 5"
6' 3"	Below 160	5' 3"	5' 8"	Below 140	4' 8"
	160 to 170	5' 2"		140 to 150	4' 7"
	170 to 180	5' 1"		150 to 160	4' 6"
	180 to 190	5' 0"		160 to 170	4' 5"
	190 and over	4' 11"		170 and over	4' 4"
6' 2"	Below 160	5' 2"	5' 7"	Below 140	4' 7"
	160 to 170	5' 1"		140 to 150	4' 6"
	170 to 180	5' 0"		150 to 160	4' 5"
	180 to 190	4' 11"		160 to 170	4' 4"
	190 and over	4' 10"		170 and over	4' 3"
6' 1"	Below 160	5' 1"	5' 6"	Below 140	4' 6"
	160 to 170	5' 0"		140 to 150	4' 5"
	170 to 180	4' 11"		150 to 160	4' 4"
	180 to 190	4' 10"		160 to 170	4' 3"
	190 and over	4' 9"		170 and over	4' 2"
6' 0"	Below 150	5' 0"	5' 5"	Below 140	4' 5"
	150 to 160	4' 11"		140 to 150	4' 4"
	160 to 170	4' 10"		150 to 160	4' 3"
	170 to 180	4' 9"		160 to 170	4' 2"
	180 and over	4' 8"		170 and over	4' 1"
5' 11"	Below 150	4' 11"	5' 4"	Below 130	4' 4"
	150 to 160	4' 10"		130 to 140	4' 3"
	160 to 170	4' 9"		140 to 150	4' 2"
	170 to 180	4' 8"		150 to 160	4' 1"
	180 and over	4' 7"		160 and over	4' 0"
5' 10"	Below 150	4' 10"	5' 3"	Below 130	4' 3"
	150 to 160	4' 9"		130 to 140	4' 2"
	160 to 170	4' 8"		140 to 150	4' 1"
	170 to 180	4' 7"		150 to 160	4' 0"
	180 and over	4' 6"		160 and over	3' 11"

FOOTBALL PUNT

Distance	Points
210'	100*
205'	96.2
200'	92.4
195'	88.6
190'	84.8
185'	81.0
180'	77.2
175'	73.4
170'	69.6
165'	65.8
160'	62.0
155'	58.2
150'	54.4
145'	50.6
140'	46.8
135'	43.0
130'	39.2
125'	35.4
120'	31.6
115'	27.6
110'	23.6
105'	19.6
100'	15.6
95'	11.6
90'	7.6
85'	3.6

120 YARD LOW HURDLES

Time	Points	Time	Points
12.4	100*	15.1	48.7
12.5	98.1	15.2	46.8
12.6	96.2	15.3	44.9
12.7	94.3	15.4	43.0
12.8	92.4	15.5	41.1
12.9	90.5	15.6	39.2
13.0	88.6	15.7	37.3
13.1	86.7	15.8	35.4
13.2	84.8	15.9	33.5
13.3	82.9	16.0	31.6
13.4	81.0	16.1	29.7
13.5	79.1	16.2	27.8
13.6	77.2	16.3	25.9
13.7	75.3	16.4	24.0
13.8	73.4	16.5	22.1
13.9	71.5	16.6	20.2
14.0	69.6	16.7	18.3
14.1	67.7	16.8	16.4
14.2	65.8	16.9	14.5
14.3	63.9	17.0	12.6
14.4	62.0	17.1	10.7
14.5	60.1	17.2	8.8
14.6	58.2	17.3	6.9
14.7	56.3	17.4	5.0
14.8	54.4	17.5	3.1
14.9	52.5	17.6	1.2
15.0	50.6		

RUNNING HIGH JUMP

Height	Points
6' 6"	100*
6' 5"	96.2
6' 4"	92.4
6' 3"	88.6
6' 2"	84.8
6' 1"	81.0
6' 0"	77.2
5'11"	73.4
5'10"	69.6
5' 9"	65.8
5' 8"	62.0
5' 7"	58.2
5' 6"	54.4
5' 5"	50.6
5' 4"	46.8
5' 3"	43.0
5' 2"	39.2
5' 1"	35.4
5' 0"	31.6
4'11"	27.8
4'10"	24.0
4' 9"	20.2
4' 8"	16.4
4' 7"	12.6
4' 6"	8.8
4' 5"	5.0
4' 4"	1.2

BAR VAULT

Ht.	Pts.
7' 0"	100*
6'11"	97.1
6'10"	94.2
6' 9"	91.3
6' 8"	88.4
6' 7"	85.5
6' 6"	82.6
6' 5"	79.7
6' 4"	76.8
6' 3"	73.9
6' 2"	71.0
6' 1"	68.1
6' 0"	65.2
5'11"	62.3
5'10"	59.4
5' 9"	56.5
5' 8"	53.6
5' 7"	50.7
5' 6"	47.8
5' 5"	44.9
5' 4"	42.0
5' 3"	39.1
5' 2"	36.2
5' 1"	33.3
5' 0"	30.4
4'11"	27.4
4'10"	24.4
4' 9"	21.4
4' 8"	18.4
4' 7"	15.4
4' 6"	12.4
4' 5"	9.4
4' 4"	6.4
4' 3"	3.4

100-YARD DASH

Time	Pts.
9.8	100*
9.9	96.2
10.0	92.4
10.1	88.6
10.2	84.8
10.3	81.0
10.4	77.2
10.5	73.4
10.6	69.6
10.7	65.8
10.8	62.0
10.9	58.2
11.0	54.4
11.1	50.6
11.2	46.8
11.3	43.0
11.4	39.2
11.5	35.4
11.6	31.6
11.7	28.6
11.8	25.6
11.9	22.6
12.0	19.6
12.1	16.6
12.2	13.6
12.3	10.6
12.4	7.6
12.5	4.6
12.6	2.6

ONE-MILE RUN

Time	Pts.	Time	Pts.	Time	Pts.	Time	Pts.
4:15	100*	4:49	77.9	5:23	55.8	5:57	33.7
4:16	99.4	4:50	77.3	5:24	55.2	5:58	33.1
4:17	98.7	4:51	76.6	5:25	54.5	5:59	32.4
4:18	98.1	4:52	76.0	5:26	53.9	6:00	31.8
4:19	97.4	4:53	75.3	5:27	53.2	6:01	30.8
4:20	96.8	4:54	74.7	5:28	52.6	6:02	29.8
4:21	96.1	4:55	74.0	5:29	51.9	6:03	28.8
4:22	95.5	4:56	73.4	5:30	51.3	6:04	27.8
4:23	94.8	4:57	72.7	5:31	50.6	6:05	26.8
4:24	94.2	4:58	72.1	5:32	50.0	6:06	25.8
4:25	93.5	4:59	71.4	5:33	49.3	6:07	24.8
4:26	92.9	5:00	70.8	5:34	48.7	6:08	23.8
4:27	92.2	5:01	70.1	5:35	48.0	6:09	22.8
4:28	91.6	5:02	69.5	5:36	47.4	6:10	21.8
4:29	90.9	5:03	68.8	5:37	46.7	6:11	20.8
4:30	90.3	5:04	68.2	5:38	46.1	6:12	19.8
4:31	89.6	5:05	67.5	5:39	45.4	6:13	18.8
4:32	89.0	5:06	66.9	5:40	44.8	6:14	17.8
4:33	88.3	5:07	66.2	5:41	44.1	6:15	16.8
4:34	87.7	5:08	65.6	5:42	43.5	6:16	15.8
4:35	87.0	5:09	64.9	5:43	42.8	6:17	14.8
4:36	86.4	5:10	64.3	5:44	42.2	6:18	13.8
4:37	85.7	5:11	63.6	5:45	41.5	6:19	12.8
4:38	85.1	5:12	63.0	5:46	40.9	6:20	11.8
4:39	84.4	5:13	62.3	5:47	40.2	6:21	10.8
4:40	83.8	5:14	61.7	5:48	39.6	6:22	9.8
4:41	83.1	5:15	61.0	5:49	38.9	6:23	8.8
4:42	82.5	5:16	60.4	5:50	38.3	6:24	7.8
4:43	81.8	5:17	59.7	5:51	37.6	6:25	6.8
4:44	81.2	5:18	59.1	5:52	37.0	6:26	5.8
4:45	80.5	5:19	58.4	5:53	36.3	6:27	4.8
4:46	79.9	5:20	57.8	5:54	35.7	6:28	3.8
4:47	79.2	5:21	57.1	5:55	35.0	6:29	2.8
4:48	78.6	5:22	56.5	5:56	34.4	6:30	1.8

RUNNING BROAD JUMP

Distance	Pts.	Distance	Pts.	Distance	Pts.	Distance	Pts.
25' 0"	100*	22' 3"	76.9	19' 6"	53.8	16' 9"	30.1
24'11"	99.3	22' 2"	76.2	19' 5"	53.1	16' 8"	29.2
24'10"	98.6	22' 1"	75.5	19' 4"	52.4	16' 7"	28.3
24' 9"	97.9	22' 0"	74.8	19' 3"	51.7	16' 6"	27.4
24' 8"	97.2	21'11"	74.1	19' 2"	51.0	16' 5"	26.5
24' 7"	96.5	21'10"	73.4	19' 1"	50.3	16' 4"	25.6
24' 6"	95.8	21' 9"	72.7	19' 0"	49.6	16' 3"	24.7
24'5"	95.1	21' 8"	72.0	18'11"	48.9	16' 2"	23.8
24' 4"	94.4	21' 7"	71.3	18'10"	48.2	16' 1"	22.9
24' 3"	93.7	21' 6"	70.6	18' 9"	47.5	16' 0"	22.0
24' 2"	93.0	21' 5"	69.9	18' 8"	46.8	15'11"	21.1
24' 1"	92.3	21' 4"	69.2	18' 7"	46.1	15'10"	20.2
24' 0"	91.6	21' 3"	68.5	18' 6"	45.4	15' 9"	19.3
23'11"	90.9	21' 2"	67.8	18' 5"	44.7	15' 8"	18.4
23'10"	90.2	21' 1"	67.1	18' 4"	44.0	15' 7"	17.5
23' 9"	89.5	21' 0"	66.4	18' 3"	43.3	15' 6"	16.6
23' 8"	88.8	20'11"	65.7	18' 2"	42.6	15' 5"	15.7
23' 7""	88.1	20'10"	65.0	18' 1"	41.9	15' 4"	14.8
23' 6"	87.4	20' 9"	64.3	18' 0"	41.2	15' 3"	13.9
23' 5"	86.7	20' 8"	63.6	17'11"	40.5	15' 2"	13.0
23' 4"	86.0	20' 7"	62.9	17'10"	39.8	15' 1"	12.1
23' 3"	85.3	20' 6"	62.2	17' 9"	39.1	15' 0"	11.2
23' 2"	84.6	20' 5"	61.5	17' 8"	38.4	14'11"	10.3
23' 1"	83.9	20' 4"	60.8	17' 7"	37.7	14'10"	9.4
23' 0"	83.2	20' 3"	60.1	17' 6"	37.0	14' 9"	8.5
22'11"	82.5	20' 2"	59.4	17' 5"	36.3	14' 8"	7.6
22'10"	81.8	20' 1"	58.7	17' 4"	35.6	14' 7"	6.7
22' 9"	81.1	20' 0"	58.0	17' 3"	34.9	14' 6"	5.8
22' 8"	80.4	19'11"	57.3	17' 2"	34.2	14' 5"	4.9
22' 7"	79.7	19'10"	56.6	17' 1"	33.5	14' 4"	4.0
22' 6"	79.0	19' 9"	55.9	17' 0"	32.8	14' 3"	3.1
22' 5"	78.3	19' 8"	55.2	16'11"	31.9	14' 2"	2.2
22' 4"	77.6	19' 7"	54.5	16'10"	31.0	14' 1"	1.3

JAVELIN THROW

Dist.	Pts.	Dist.	Pts.	Dist.	Pts.
200'	100*	167'	67	134'	34
199'	99	166'	66	133'	33
198'	98	165'	65	132'	32
197'	97	164'	64	131'	31
196'	96	163'	63	130'	30
195'	95	162'	62	129'	29
194'	94	161'	61	128'	28
193'	93	160'	60	127'	27
192'	92	159'	59	126'	26
191'	91	158'	58	125'	25
190'	90	157'	57	124'	24
189'	89	156'	56	123'	23
188'	88	155'	55	122'	22
187'	87	154'	54	121'	21
186'	86	153'	53	120'	20
185'	85	152'	52	119'	19
184'	84	151'	51	118'	18
183'	83	150'	50	117'	17
182'	82	149'	49	116'	16
181'	81	148'	48	115'	15
180'	80	147'	47	114'	14
179'	79	146'	46	113'	13
178'	78	145'	45	112'	12
177'	77	144'	44	111'	11
176'	76	143'	43	110'	10
175'	75	142'	42	109'	9
174'	74	141'	41	108'	8
173'	73	140'	40	107'	7
172'	72	139'	39	106'	6
171'	71	138'	38	105'	5
170'	70	137'	37	104'	4
169'	69	136'	36	103'	3
168'	68	135'	35	102'	2
				101'	1

100 YARD SWIM

Time	Pts.	Time	Pts.	Time	Pts.
:56	100*	1:23	62.2	1:50	26.4
:57	98.6	1:24	60.8	1:51	25.4
:58	97.2	1:25	59.4	1:52	24.4
:59	95.8	1:26	58.0	1:53	23.4
1:00	94.4	1:27	56.6	1:54	22.4
1:01	93.0	1:28	55.2	1:55	21.4
1:02	91.6	1:29	53.8	1:56	20.4
1:03	90.2	1:30	52.4	1:57	19.4
1:04	88.8	1:31	51.0	1:58	18.4
1:05	87.4	1:32	49.6	1:59	17.4
1:06	86.0	1:33	48.2	2:00	16.4
1:07	84.6	1:34	46.8	2:01	15.4
1:08	83.2	1:35	45.4	2:02	14.4
1:09	81.8	1:36	44.0	2:03	13.4
1:10	80.4	1:37	42.6	2:04	12.4
1:11	79.0	1:38	41.2	2:05	11.4
1:12	77.6	1:39	39.8	2:06	10.4
1:13	76.2	1:40	38.4	2:07	9.4
1:14	74.8	1:41	37.0	2:08	8.4
1:15	73.4	1:42	35.6	2:09	7.4
1:16	72.0	1:43	34.2	2:10	6.4
1:17	70.6	1:44	32.8	2:11	5.4
1:18	69.2	1:45	31.4	2:12	4.4
1:19	67.8	1:46	30.4	2:13	3.4
1:20	66.4	1:47	29.4	2:14	2.4
1:21	65.0	1:48	28.4	2:15	1.4
1:22	63.6	1:49	27.4		

20-FOOT ROPE CLIMB

Time	Pts.	Time	Pts.	Time	Pts.
4.0	100*	7.8	67.7	11.6	35.4
4.1	99.2	7.9	66.9	11.7	34.6
4.2	98.3	8.0	66.0	11.8	33.7
4.3	97.5	8.1	65.2	11.9	32.9
4.4	96.6	8.2	64.3	12.0	32.0
4.5	95.8	8.3	63.5	12.1	31
4.6	94.9	8.4	62.6	12.2	30
4.7	94.1	8.5	61.8	12.3	29
4.8	93.2	8.6	60.9	12.4	28
4.9	92.4	8.7	60.1	12.5	27
5.0	91.5	8.8	59.2	12.6	26
5.1	90.7	8.9	58.4	12.7	25
5.2	89.8	9.0	57.5	12.8	24
5.3	89.0	9.1	56.7	12.9	23
5.4	88.1	9.2	55.8	13.0	22
5.5	87.3	9.3	55.0	13.1	21
5.6	86.4	9.4	54.1	13.2	20
5.7	85.6	9.5	53.3	13.3	19
5.8	84.7	9.6	52.4	13.4	18
5.9	83.9	9.7	51.6	13.5	17
6.0	83.0	9.8	50.7	13.6	16
6.1	82.2	9.9	49.9	13.7	15
6.2	81.3	10.0	49.0	13.8	14
6.3	80.5	10.1	48.2	13.9	13
6.4	79.6	10.2	47.3	14.0	12
6.5	78.8	10.3	46.5	14.1	11
6.6	77.9	10.4	45.6	14.2	10
6.7	77.1	10.5	44.8	14.3	9
6.8	76.2	10.6	43.9	14.4	8
6.9	75.4	10.7	43.1	14.5	7
7.0	74.5	10.8	42.2	14.6	6
7.1	73.7	10.9	41.4	14.7	5
7.2	72.8	11.0	40.5	14.8	4
7.3	72.0	11.1	39.7	14.9	3
7.4	71.1	11.2	38.8	15.0	2
7.5	70.3	11.3	38.0	15.1	1
7.6	69.4	11.4	37.1		
7.7	68.6	11.5	36.3		

HAND STAND

Time	Pts.	Time	Pts.	Time	Pts.
60.0	100*	38.0	69.2	16.0	38.4
59.5	99.3	37.5	68.5	15.5	37.7
59.0	98.6	37.0	67.8	15.0	37.0
58.5	97.9	36.5	67.1	14.5	36.3
58.0	97.2	36.0	66.4	14.0	35.6
57.5	96.5	35.5	65.7	13.5	34.9
57.0	95.8	35.0	65.0	13.0	34.2
56.5	95.1	34.5	64.3	12.5	33.5
56.0	94.4	34.0	63.6	12.0	32.8
55.5	93.7	33.5	62.9	11.5	32.1
55.0	93.0	33.0	62.2	11.0	31.4
54.5	92.3	32.5	61.5	10.5	30.7
54.0	91.6	32.0	60.8	10.0	30.0
53.5	90.9	31.5	60.1	9.9	29
53.0	90.2	31.0	59.4	9.8	28
52.5	89.5	30.5	58.7	9.7	27
52.0	88.8	30.0	58.0	9.6	26
51.5	88.1	29.5	57.3	9.5	25
51.0	87.4	29.0	56.6	9.4	24
50.5	86.7	28.5	55.9	9.3	23
50.0	86.0	28.0	55.2	9.2	22
49.5	85.3	27.5	54.5	9.1	21
49.0	84.6	27.0	53.8	9.0	20
48.5	83.9	26.5	53.1	8.9	19
48.0	83.2	26.0	52.4	8.8	18
47.5	82.5	25.5	51.7	8.7	17
47.0	81.8	25.0	51.0	8.6	16
46.5	81.1	24.5	50.3	8.5	15
46.0	80.4	24.0	49.6	8.4	14
45.5	79.7	23.5	48.9	8.3	13
45.0	79.0	23.0	48.2	8.2	12
44.5	78.3	22.5	47.5	8.1	11
44.0	77.6	22.0	46.8	8.0	10
43.5	76.9	21.5	46.1	7.9	9
43.0	76.2	21.0	45.4	7.8	8
42.5	75.5	20.5	44.7	7.7	7
42.0	74.8	20.0	44.0	7.6	6
41.5	74.1	19.5	43.3	7.5	5
41.0	73.4	19.0	42.6	7.4	4
40.5	72.7	18.5	41.9	7.3	3
40.0	72.0	18.0	41.2	7.2	2
39.5	71.3	17.5	40.5	7.1	1
39.0	70.6	17.0	39.8		
38.5	69.9	16.5	39.1		

BASEBALL THROW

Dist.	Pts.	Dist.	Pts.
350'	100*	268	43.3
346'	97.9	265	41.2
343'	95.8	262	39.1
340'	93.7	259	37.0
337'	91.6	256	34.9
334'	89.5	253	32.8
331'	87.4	250	30.7
328'	85.3	247	29.2
325'	83.2	244	27.7
322'	81.1	241	26.2
319'	79.0	238	24.7
316'	76.9	235	23.2
313'	74.8	232	21.7
310'	72.7	229	20.2
307'	70.6	226	18.7
304'	68.5	223	17.2
301'	66.4	220	15.7
298'	64.3	217	14.2
295'	62.2	214	12.7
292'	60.1	211	11.2
289'	58.0	208	9.7
286'	55.9	205	8.2
283'	53.8	202	6.7
280'	51.7	199	5.2
277'	49.6	196	3.7
274'	47.5	193	2.2
271'	45.4	190	1.1

16-LB. SHOT PUT

Dist.	Pts.	Dist.	Pts.
49'	100*	35' 6"	51.4
48' 6"	98.2	35'	49.6
48'	96.4	34' 6"	47.8
47' 6"	94.6	34'	46.0
47'	92.8	33' 6"	44.2
46' 6"	91.0	33'	42.4
46'	89.2	32' 6"	40.6
45' 6"	87.4	32'	38.8
45'	85.6	31' 6"	37.0
44' 6"	83.8	31'	35.2
44'	82.0	30' 6"	33.4
43' 6"	80.2	30'	31.6
43'	78.4	29' 6"	29.6
42' 6"	76.6	29'	27.6
42'	74.8	28' 6"	25.6
41' 6"	73.0	28'	23.6
41'	71.2	27' 6"	21.6
40' 6"	69.4	27'	19.6
40'	67.6	26' 6"	17.6
39' 6"	65.8	26'	15.6
39'	64.0	25' 6"	13.6
38' 6"	62.2	25'	11.6
38'	60.4	24' 6"	9.6
37' 6"	58.6	24'	7.6
37'	56.8	23' 6"	5.6
36' 6"	55.0	23'	3.6
36'	53.2	22' 6"	1.6

BOWLING

3 Game Ave.	Pts.	3 Game Ave.	Pts.	3 Game Ave.	Pts.	3 Game Ave.	Pts.
230	100*	205	75	180	50	155	25
229	99	204	74	179	49	154	24
228	98	203	73	178	48	153	23
227	97	202	72	177	47	152	22
226	96	201	71	176	46	151	21
225	95	200	70	175	45	150	20
224	94	199	69	174	44	149	19
223	93	198	68	173	43	148	18
222	92	197	67	172	42	147	17
221	91	196	66	171	41	146	16
220	90	195	65	170	40	145	15
219	89	194	64	169	39	144	14
218	88	193	63	168	38	143	13
217	87	192	62	167	37	142	12
216	86	191	61	166	36	141	11
215	85	190	60	165	35	140	10
214	84	189	59	164	34	139	9
213	83	188	58	163	33	138	8
212	82	187	57	162	32	137	7
211	81	186	56	161	31	136	6
210	80	185	55	160	30	135	5
209	79	184	54	159	29	134	4
208	78	183	53	158	28	133	3
207	77	182	52	157	27	132	2
206	76	181	51	156	26	131	1

GOLF

Successful Attempts		Maximum Attempts	Points
15	out of	15	100*
14	out of	15	93
13	out of	14	86
12	out of	13	80
11	out of	12	74
10	out of	11	68
9	out of	10	62
8	out of	9	56
7	out of	8	50
6	out of	7	44
5	out of	6	38
4	out of	5	32
3	out of	5	24
2	out of	5	16
1	out of	5	8

C

Selected References and Rules Sources

REFERENCES

AMERICAN ASSOCIATION FOR HEALTH, PHYSICAL EDUCATION, AND RECREATION. *Intramural Sports for College Men and Women. Washington Conference Report.* Washington, D.C.: The Association, 1956. 48 pp.

One hundred and ten delegates from 79 institutions discussed the role of intramurals in the education of college students. Guiding principles are suggested for collegiate intramural programing. Areas include organization and administration, facilities, and types of programs. Criteria appear in checklist form for the evaluation of intramural programs.

BEEMAN, HARRIS F., and HUMPHREY, JAMES H. *Intramural Sports: A Text and Study Guide.* Dubuque, Iowa: Wm. C. Brown Co., 1954. 160 pp.

This book, arranged in 18 units, is designed as a study guide for a professional physical education course in intramural sports. Each unit has an overview of the subject, study questions, and class assignments. Blank sheets are included for class notes and assignments.

BOYDEN, E. DOUGLAS, and BURTON, ROGER G. *Staging Successful Tournaments.* New York:Association Press, 1957. 171 pp.

A practical manual for selecting, planning, conducting, and evaluating tournaments. Contains numerous tournament methods with single and double elimination tournament draw sheets for three through 40 entries. The double elimination tournament draw sheets follow the over–under pattern.

DIVISION FOR GIRLS AND WOMEN'S SPORTS. *Standards in Sports for Girls and Women: Guiding Principles in the Organization and Administration of Sports Programs.* Washington, D.C.: American Association for Health, Physical Education, and Recreation, 1958. 66 pp.

Standards and guiding principles are presented for those who participate in, and those who administer, sports programs for girls and women.

EDUCATIONAL POLICIES COMMISSION. *School Athletics: Problems and Policies.* Washington, D.C.: National Education Association of the United States and the American Association of School Administrators, 1954. 116 pp.

This report, which summarizes a three-year study by the Educational Policies Commission, discusses elementary and secondary school athletics and collegiate athletic policies and practices as they affect elementary and secondary schools. Sections deal with physical education classes, intramurals, and extramurals; interscholastic athletics and school athletic programs. A helpful checklist in the Appendix can be used by school officials to appraise and improve their school's athletic program, including intramural sports.

LEAVITT, NORMA M., AND PRICE, HARTLEY D. *Intramural and Recreational Sports for High School and College.* 2nd ed. New York: The Ronald Press Co., 1958. 327 pp.

This book is a text and reference for those who conduct intramural and other recreation programs in high schools and colleges. It includes desirable practices, policies, and procedures for programs for both men or boys and girls or women. Treats functions of administrative personnel, functions of student organizations; details tournament organization, records point systems, awards; describes the program of activities and the problems in the conduct of the program.

MEANS, LOUIS E. *The Organization and Administration of Intramural Sports.* 2nd ed. St. Louis: The C. V. Mosby Co., 1952. 466 pp.

A comprehensive textbook on intramurals with topics ranging from history, philosophy, and objectives to aids and suggestions for promoting intramural programs. Contains 240 illustrations with many references to existing programs. The bibliography of resource materials is one of the most complete in the intramural field.

SCHEERER, WILLIAM W. *High School Intramural Program.* Minneapolis: Burgess Publishing Co., 1951. 64 pp.

Stresses intramural program practices and problems for small, medium, and large high schools. Considerable attention is given to the adaptability of sports through rule modification and scoring. It also includes several diagrams, forms, and score sheets for high-school intramurals.

OTHER SOURCES

The student of intramurals can locate additional information by checking *magazine* and *book indices* in the school library. The following list suggests possible sources of intramural sports materials:

1. Most textbooks on the *Organization* and/or *Administration* of *Physical Education* or *Athletic Programs* devote a chapter or unit to intramural sports.
2. Numerous intramural articles appear in the professional education journals such as:
   a. *Journal of Health, Physical Education, and Recreation*
   b. *Athletic Journal*
   c. *Scholastic Coach*
   d. *School Activities*
   e. *Physical Educator*
3. Many doctoral and master's theses and special studies on intramural sports are available.

4. Professional association convention proceedings contain intramural reports and surveys:
   a. College Physical Education Association
   b. The American Association for Health, Physical Education, and Recreation
   c. National Intramural Association
   d. Athletic and Recreation Federation of College Women
5. The second edition of Elmer D. Mitchell's *Intramural Sports* (1939) contains many references to older publications now out of print but to be found in many city, school, and departmental libraries.

OFFICIAL RULE BOOKS AND GUIDES

For High Schools

Basketball Rules
Baseball Rules
Football Rules
Six Man Football Rules
Soccer Rules
Track and Field Rules

Write to: National Federation of State High School Athletic Associations, Chicago 3, Illinois.

For Men

AAU Basketball Rules and Guide
AAU Boxing Rules and Guide
AAU Gymnastic Rules and Records
AAU Handball Rules
AAU Swimming, Water Polo, and Diving Rules
AAU Synchronized Swimming Rules
AAU Track and Field Rules and Athletic Almanac
AAU Weight Lifting Rules
AAU Wrestling Rules and Judo
Write to: Amateur Athletic Union of the United States, New York, N. Y.

NCAA Baseball Guide
NCAA Basketball Guide
NCAA Boxing Rules
NCAA Football Guide
NCAA Ice Hockey Guide
NCAA Lacrosse Guide
NCAA Soccer Guide
NCAA Swimming Guide
NCAA Track and Field Guide
NCAA Wrestling Guide
Write to: National Collegiate Athletic Association, New York, N. Y.

For Men and Women

ABC Bowling Guide
American Bowling Congress
Milwaukee, Wisconsin

ABC Badminton Rules
American Badminton Association
Marblehead, Massachusetts
USFSA Figure Skating Rulebook
United States Figure Skating Association
Boston, Mass.
USGA Golf Guide
United States Golf Association
New York, N. Y.
ASA Softball Guide (fast and slow pitch)
Amateur Softball Association
Newark, New Jersey
Official Softball Guide and Rules for Slow Pitching
Umpires' Protective Association
Chicago, Illinois
USSRA Squash Racquets Year Book
United States Squash Racquets Association, Inc.
Buffalo, New York
USLTA Tennis Guide
United States Lawn Tennis Association
New York, N. Y.
Official National Touch Football Rules
Athletic Institute
Chicago, Illinois
USVBA Volleyball Guide
United States Volleyball Association
USVBA Printer, Berne, Indiana

For Women

Aquatics Guide
Archery and Riding Guide
Basketball Guide
Bowling–Fencing–Golf Guide
Field Hockey–Lacrosse Guide
Recreational Games and Sports Guide (Tetherball, Volley Tennis, Deck Tennis, Croquet, Horseshoe Pitching, Skish Bait Casting, Shuffleboard, Paddle Tennis, Lawn Bowling, Table Tennis)
Soccer–Speedball Guide
Softball–Track and Field Guide
Tennis–Badminton Guide
Volleyball Guide
Winter Sports and Outing Activities Guide (Skiing, Skating, Hunting and Riflery, Fishing, and Fly Casting)

Write to: Division for Girls and Women's Sports, American Association for Health, Physical Education, and Recreation, Washington, D.C.

Other Rules Sources

The Athletic Institute, Chicago, Illinois, publishes a comprehensive list of rules sources which can be obtained by request.

Index